Jaguar Books on Lati~ ^ ~~~~~~

Series Editors

WILLIAM H. BEEZLEY, Professor of Histo   ~~ ~~ Arizona
COLIN M. MACLACHLAN, John Christy Barr Distinguished Professor of
History, Tulane University

Volumes Published

John E. Kicza, ed., *The Indian in Latin American History: Resistance,
Resilience, and Acculturation* (1993; rev. ed., 2000).
Cloth ISBN 0-8420-2822-6 Paper ISBN 0-8420-2823-4

Susan E. Place, ed., *Tropical Rainforests: Latin American Nature and
Society in Transition* (1993). Cloth ISBN 0-8420-2423-9
Paper ISBN 0-8420-2427-1

Paul W. Drake, ed., *Money Doctors, Foreign Debts, and Economic
Reforms in Latin America from the 1890s to the Present* (1994).
Cloth ISBN 0-8420-2434-4   Paper ISBN 0-8420-2435-2

John A. Britton, ed., *Molding the Hearts and Minds: Education,
Communications, and Social Change in Latin America* (1994).
Cloth ISBN 0-8420-2489-1   Paper ISBN 0-8420-2490-5

David J. Weber and Jane M. Rausch, eds., *Where Cultures Meet: Frontiers
in Latin American History* (1994). Cloth ISBN 0-8420-2477-8
Paper ISBN 0-8420-2478-6

Gertrude M. Yeager, ed., *Confronting Change, Challenging Tradition:
Women in Latin American History* (1994). Cloth ISBN 0-8420-2479-4
Paper ISBN 0-8420-2480-8

Linda Alexander Rodríguez, ed., *Rank and Privilege: The Military and
Society in Latin America* (1994). Cloth ISBN 0-8420-2432-8
Paper ISBN 0-8420-2433-6

Darién J. Davis, ed., *Slavery and Beyond: The African Impact on Latin
America and the Caribbean* (1995). Cloth ISBN 0-8420-2484-0
Paper ISBN 0-8420-2485-9

Gilbert M. Joseph and Mark D. Szuchman, eds., *I Saw a City Invincible:
Urban Portraits of Latin America* (1996). Cloth ISBN 0-8420-2495-6
Paper ISBN 0-8420-2496-4

Roderic Ai Camp, ed., *Democracy in Latin America: Patterns and Cycles* (1996). Cloth ISBN 0-8420-2512-X   Paper ISBN 0-8420-2513-8

Oscar J. Martínez, ed., *U.S.-Mexico Borderlands: Historical and Contemporary Perspectives* (1996). Cloth ISBN 0-8420-2446-8 Paper ISBN 0-8420-2447-6

William O. Walker III, ed., *Drugs in the Western Hemisphere: An Odyssey of Cultures in Conflict* (1996). Cloth ISBN 0-8420-2422-0 Paper ISBN 0-8420-2426-3

Richard R. Cole, ed., *Communication in Latin America: Journalism, Mass Media, and Society* (1996). Cloth ISBN 0-8420-2558-8 Paper ISBN 0-8420-2559-6

David G. Gutiérrez, ed., *Between Two Worlds: Mexican Immigrants in the United States* (1996). Cloth ISBN 0-8420-2473-5 Paper ISBN 0-8420-2474-3

Lynne Phillips, ed., *The Third Wave of Modernization in Latin America: Cultural Perspectives on Neoliberalism* (1998).
  Cloth ISBN 0-8420-2606-1   Paper ISBN 0-8420-2608-8

Daniel Castro, ed., *Revolution and Revolutionaries: Guerrilla Movements in Latin America* (1999). Cloth ISBN 0-8420-2625-8 Paper ISBN 0-8420-2626-6

Virginia Garrard-Burnett, ed., *On Earth as It Is in Heaven: Religion in Modern Latin America* (2000). Cloth ISBN 0-8420-2584-7 Paper ISBN 0-8420-2585-5

Carlos A. Aguirre and Robert Buffington, eds., *Reconstructing Criminality in Latin America* (2000). Cloth ISBN 0-8420-2620-7 Paper ISBN 0-8420-2621-5

Christon I. Archer, ed., *The Wars of Independence in Spanish America* (2000). Cloth ISBN 0-8420-2468-9   Paper ISBN 0-8420-2469-7

John F. Schwaller, ed., *The Church in Colonial Latin America* (2000).
  Cloth ISBN 0-8420-2703-3   Paper ISBN 0-8420-2704-1

Ingrid E. Fey and Karen Racine, eds., *Strange Pilgrimages: Exile, Travel, and National Identity in Latin America, 1800–1990s* (2000).
  Cloth ISBN 0-8420-2693-2   Paper ISBN 0-8420-2694-0

Strange
Pilgrimages

Strange Pilgrimages

Exile, Travel, and National Identity in Latin America, 1800–1990s

Ingrid E. Fey and Karen Racine
Editors

Jaguar Books on Latin America
Number 22

A Scholarly Resources Inc. Imprint
Wilmington, Delaware

Scholarly Resources Inc.
104 Greenhill Avenue
Wilmington, DE 19805-1897
www.scholarly.com

Library of Congress Cataloging-in-Publication Data

Strange pilgrimages : exile, travel, and national identity in Latin
  America, 1800–1990s / Ingrid E. Fey and Karen Racine.
     p. cm. — (Jaguar books on Latin America ; no. 22)
    Includes bibliographical references.
    ISBN 0-8420-2693-2 (cloth : alk. paper) — ISBN 0-8420-2694-0
(pbk. : alk. paper)
    1. Latin America—Civilization—Foreign influences. 2. Identity
(Psychology)—Latin America. 3. Latin Americans—Europe—
Intellectual life. 4. Latin Americans—United States—Intellectual life.
5. Travelers—Europe—Attitudes. 6. Travelers—United States—
Attitudes. I. Fey, Ingrid Elizabeth, 1968– II. Racine, Karen, 1967–
III. Series.

F1413.S77 2000
980.03—dc21   99-089781

For

E. Bradford Burns (1933–1996),

whose commitment to Latin American cultural history

made this book possible

Acknowledgments

We would like to thank William H. Beezley, Colin MacLachlan, and Anthony McFarlane for their initial encouragement in the conceptual stages of this project. We also express our thanks to Rick Hopper of Scholarly Resources for his guidance and good humor, Linda Pote Musumeci for her editorial assistance, and Lori Underhill and Mike Rabe of Valparaiso University for their technical assistance. As with any collaborative project, this anthology has had a long and circuitous journey to completion, and we would like to express our appreciation to all the contributors for their timely response to our queries and for their patience while the compilation process took place. We hope that this volume will stimulate student interest in issues of travel identity and encourage further research into the underexplored experiences of Latin Americans abroad.

Contents

Introduction: National Identity Formation in an International Context

Ingrid E. Fey and Karen Racine

> We went abroad not to learn the secret of
> others, but to learn the secret of ourselves.
> —José Carlos Mariátegui[1]

History books have taught us that foreigners discovered America. In their pages we read that adventurers traveling the globe in search of riches accidentally stumbled upon a continent previously unknown to them and changed the course of human history. While the notion of "discovery" has rightfully been criticized as Eurocentric, the prolonged and often violent dialogue initiated between foreigners and the people they encountered has continued to draw considerable scholarly attention. Because foreigners have been recognized as incisive commentators on the culture and social relations of the places they visit, travel accounts, such as the narrative of German scientist Alexander von Humboldt, are valuable and authoritative records of Latin American daily life. Yet, the experiences of Europeans and North Americans who have spent time in Latin America are far better known than those of Latin Americans who went abroad and engaged in similar cultural critiques. This anthology aspires to decolonize these voices, to recognize that Latin Americans made their own choices and, far from being the passive recipients of others' ideas and products, considered carefully what they saw abroad and even dared to offer comments to their hosts. By examining the experiences of Latin Americans who have ventured far from home, these "strange pilgrimages," as Gabriel García Márquez has called them, we hope to illuminate the ways in which they were prompted to explore, as Mariátegui so aptly put it, the secrets of themselves.[2]

The chapters in this volume deal with issues raised by Latin Americans' travel and foreign residence in Europe and the United States during the nineteenth and twentieth centuries. The reasons that Latin Americans have chosen to leave their homes, the particular places that have attracted them, and the long-term effects of their time abroad are among the topics explored. Each chapter demonstrates the deceptively simple idea that while living in a foreign environment, an individual becomes more aware of his or her own personal and national identity. Caught between cultures, exiles, travelers, and expatriates find that the values and manners that had guided behavior in their homelands become at best irrelevant and at worst inappropriate in their new countries of residence. To avoid isolation, they must adapt to the new ways and re-create themselves by functioning in a new language, often with a new name and lesser occupation. In short, they must reconsider what it means to be themselves, whether they can remain Mexican, Argentine, or Brazilian in Paris, London, or New York. Foreigners abroad inevitably experience "the creation of identity through the exploration of difference."[3] For this reason, exile communities and travelers provide excellent case studies not only for intellectual and social historians but also for all people concerned with the issue of national identity creation.

While the study of Latin American travelers and exiles is relatively new, the phenomenon of Latin American travel is not. Since the colonial period, Latin Americans of a certain class have managed to keep abreast of international trends and fashions, both in ideas and material possessions, by traveling and residing abroad. Following independence from Spain in the 1820s, economic expansion, improved transportation networks, and an obsession with progress sent a steady stream of upper-class travelers to Europe and the United States, where they sought to learn lessons from those nations that they most associated with modernity. Enrollment in foreign educational institutions almost became standard practice for elite Latin American youths, who flocked to these schools in order to learn the lessons needed to modernize their nations. Residing far from home at an impressionable age, however, taught Latin American students more than just their academic lessons. Travel and foreign residence offered both young and old a chance to step outside themselves, to live a life free of traditional constraints, as well as a rare opportunity to assess their own beliefs and practices by confronting others that are very different.

The phenomenon of Latin American exile also has had a long history. On the eve of Latin America's independence, Europe, and especially England, served as the gathering place for exiles from the Spanish colonies such as Simón Bolívar, who plotted strategies abroad to win national independence. Throughout the nineteenth and twentieth centuries, civil wars and revolutions continued to send Latin Americans into exile. The advent of authoritarian regimes in the mid-to-late twentieth century not only dramatically increased the numbers of exiles but also diversified the residential communities abroad. Whereas exiles of the nineteenth century were primarily political or intellectual elites who had fallen from grace, twentieth-century exiles have included peasants, housewives, students, and labor organizers. As the profile of Latin American exiles has changed, so too have the effects of exile on Latin American identity become more complex.

Strange Pilgrimage's organization closely follows the chronology just described. Part I, "Constructing Nations after Independence and Beyond," explores the ways in which early nineteenth-century travelers and exiles' experiences contributed to the growth of Latin American nationalism in the crucial first years of nationhood. Part II, "Touring Modernity," focuses on the role that travel played in introducing such turn-of-the-century ideologies and cultural practices as feminism, progressivism, and athleticism into Latin America. Part III, "Taking Sides," explores Latin American travelers and exiles' encounters with and participation in political movements such as communism, fascism, and anti-imperialism, which have been pivotal to the history of the twentieth century. Part IV, "The Art of Living and Working Abroad," examines manifestations of Latin American popular culture within the United States. Spanning two centuries and examining diverse people who had different motivations for leaving their homelands, these chapters reflect a central theme which suggests that the creation and re-creation of Latin American identity often took place in an international context.

The study of travel and exile encompasses many academic disciplines, each of which has brought its own methodology and set of motivating questions to the study of dislocated persons.[4] Legal scholars (and government bureaucrats) focus on problem solving—that is, how to provide subsistence for displaced persons while trying to repatriate or resettle them. Anthropologists have found that tribal cultures use banishment as a method of social control to rid the community of elements that have become burdensome. Sociologists focus on groups and patterns and view the outsider as deviant by categorizing motives for leaving and means of departure. Psychologists also deal with the foreigner's motives for leaving home, but prefer to focus on the individual's experience through an analysis of dreams, neuroses, and adjustment problems. Historians write biographies of prominent exiles and are beginning to move into oral histories and studies of entire exile communities.[5]

Perhaps the largest single category within exile and travel studies belongs to literature, literary criticism, and intellectual history.[6] This emphasis is not surprising given the sheer number of literary works produced by persons living outside their native land.[7] Indeed, a recent study included over 550 entries in a dictionary of twentieth-century literary exile,[8] which gives weight to Lloyd Kramer's assertion that "the connection between the exile experience and creative intellectual work is so common that it should be analyzed as a historical pattern rather than a historical accident."[9] Observers agree that language and problems of comprehension are among the exile's central concerns; consequently, intellectuals, as those most immediately defined by language and the need to communicate, obsessively record their experiences and analyze their meaning. This pattern is certainly true of the writers, artists, politicians, and citizens in the chapters that follow. While abroad, these Latin Americans sharpened their powers of observation, honed their expressive skills, and sought forums to make their experiences meaningful for a larger segment of their national communities. In fact, travelers and travel accounts are becoming a major field of study in all disciplines.[10]

Until recently, the sources used for the study of exile, travel, and foreign residence have tended to reflect the nature of those who did the traveling, namely, the educated upper and middle classes, and especially men. Many of the chapters in this anthology reflect that historical pattern and analyze travel accounts or literary works produced by Latin Americans, either during their residence abroad or shortly after their return. Whether it is a poem evoking the natural wonders of Latin America written by Andrés Bello or a saucy samba describing Rio de Janeiro sung by Carmen Miranda, these creative endeavors demonstrate what their authors think about their homelands and national identities while abroad. Other chapters consciously revise the traditional perception and point out a surprising degree of heterogeneity in foreign residential communities through the use of promising but less utilized sources, including archival materials from Latin American embassies and consulates, records from foreign educational institutions patronized by Latin Americans, periodicals printed by Latin Americans living abroad, archives of foreign governmental organizations charged with monitoring the actions of foreign residents, and personal correspondence. Expanding the type and quantity of sources used to examine the experience of exile and travel grounds the intellectual history of travel and exile in its social and historical context. As literary historian William W. Stowe has argued, "writing and travel are *creative* acts. . . . As such, they are also *interpretive* acts, based on particular understandings of their subjects, governed by the interpretive conventions of their practitioners' social and historical situations."[11]

The chapters that follow attempt to incorporate an appreciation for the social and historical situations of their subjects. In other words, while this anthology groups together exiles, travelers, and foreign residents as having parallel experiences in foreign environments, it does not assert that their experiences or situations are identical. Obviously, forced exile is produced by different historical circumstances and requires a different response to the new environment than does temporary residence for educational purposes or travel for leisure and personal edification. The essential elements of exile include forced residence outside a person's native country due to uncontrollable circumstances and a desire and intention of returning home as soon as possible. Clearly this condition is different from that of expatriates, who choose to live abroad and remain free to move back and forth as they wish, or travelers who are simply passing through.[12]

Perhaps the best known and most visible subgroup of Latin Americans abroad are the political exiles who are banished by their government because they hold views and values that conflict with the ruling regime. Recently, political scientist Yosse Shain has adjusted this definition in a discussion of what he calls "the moving frontier of loyalty."[13] According to Shain, the modern political exile justifies his existence by viewing himself as the authentic patriot and the offensive government regime as the traitor. Logically, then, in order to remain loyal to country and culture, the patriot must leave his homeland. Shain's theory departs from previous studies of exile behavior by defining a political exile not by his reasons for leaving the homeland but rather by the activities undertaken once outside it.[14] Literary critic Martin Tucker echoed this view when he observed that the psychic pain of voluntary exile can be just as real as involuntary, "if what follows it is the pattern of exilic behaviour."[15]

Exilic behavior can be characterized as a process of responding to and adapting to a new place of residence while at the same time confronting feelings of separation from the homeland. Both voluntary and involuntary exiles suffer a sense of dislocation and apprehension in their new environment that produces an intensified awareness of personal and collective identity. Paradoxically, while foreigners abroad often suffer pain and loss from homesickness and separation, they also can experience the burst of energy that comes with a renewed sense of purpose. Some foreigners abroad even exhibit a striking hubris, believing that their individual experiences have significance for the greater national community. Vladimir Nabokov, the Russian author of *Lolita* who made a new life and career for himself in the United States, captured the mood perfectly when he spoke of "the gloom and glory of exile."[16] As the chapters that follow confirm, life abroad, especially in exile, is a dramatic, romantic condition in which attention is gained simply by being present and everything seems larger than reality. Living abroad also can be a very lonely existence, full of stress and trials that promise much hardship. In the end, the foreign resident must reach an uneasy truce between the old and the new, the past and the present, There and Here.

The foreigner's psychological experience seems to be the significant factor in his accommodation to a new environment; thus, close attention must be paid to traits that an extended foreign residence tends to produce. A recent study of exile psychology found that all immigrants carry with them "a mixture of anxiety, sadness, pain, and nostalgia on the one side, and expectations and hopes on the other."[17] Studying "the psychopathology of migration," Leon Grinberg and Rebeca Grinberg found that it "is an upheaval which shakes the entire psychic structure"—exiles and emigrés lose all valuable things at once: their language, extended families and friends, culture, customs, climate, and environment, and often their professional standing.[18] As a result, displaced persons frequently suffer mental and physical disturbances deriving from their altered circumstances, which can include weight gain or loss, depression, persecution complexes, money anxiety, loneliness, guilt, and intense pathological nostalgia. Persons leaving home often try to bring as many belongings with them as they can cram into a trunk: photographs, old clothing, memorabilia. For many emigrants, food becomes an obsession; they eat in symbolic, ritual fashion and insist on the same food prepared in the same way as at home.[19] In other words, the physical environment takes on an outsized importance as the foreign residents attempt to order their new world in a comprehensible manner. Climate, geography, flora, and fauna all affect their mental state and may cause intense nostalgia for the sights, sounds, and smells of home.[20] For this reason, many educated persons residing abroad pick up their pens in homage to the natural beauty and splendor of their native lands.

Despite the variety of travel and exile experiences, the process of cultural contact epitomized by the phenomenon of foreign residence is in almost all cases intricately connected to the definition of national identity, an occupation which has dominated international thought since the French Revolution. Nationalism has been called "a doctrine invented in Europe at the beginning of the nineteenth century . . . [which] holds that humanity is naturally divided into nations, that nations are known by certain characteristics which can be ascertained, and that the only legitimate type of government is national self-government."[21] Moreover, important recent studies of nationalism have consistently emphasized the essentially contrived, invented, or imaginary quality of modern nationalism.[22] While noting that "nation-ness is the most universally legitimate value in the political life of our time," Benedict Anderson goes on to observe that "all communities larger than primordial villages of face-to-face contact (and perhaps even these) are imagined."[23] Edmund Morgan, in tracing the origin and development of the idea of popular sovereignty, makes the same case when he writes that "Government requires make-believe. Make believe that the king is divine, make believe that he can do no wrong or make believe that the voice of the people is the voice of God. Make believe that the people have a voice or make believe that the representatives of the people are the people. Make believe that governors are the servants of the people. Make believe that all men are equal or make believe that they are not."[24] As the world became less personal, faster paced, and more complex with technological progress and the expansion of the secular political state, governments and people needed psychological supports to create a sense of legitimacy, belonging, and a shared sense of purpose and pride. This process is not always obvious or conscious, but it is always necessary and most easily achieved when confronting an enemy, an outsider, or Other.[25] This heightened sense of identity, then, should be keenest among travelers, exiles, and foreign residents, for it is while in a foreign context that problems of self-definition through contact with an Other are most acute and pressing.

The following chapters demonstrate that travelers, exiles, and foreign residential communities do indeed provide excellent case studies for these theories of national identity formation because they represent compact linguistic and cultural islands surrounded by a sea of difference. Foreigners abroad must adapt both materially and psychologically to their new circumstances and continually reconsider the values and assumptions with which they have grown up. Just as they have removed themselves geographically from their territory of birth, they must also re-create patterns of behavior to conform more closely to the norms of the host society. The experience of living in a different culture and communicating in a foreign language irrevocably alters an individual's world view and self-identity. For some, it is traumatic; for others, liberating. For all of them, however, the experience is intensely personal.

The study of exiles and travelers underscores the fact that modern national identities are evolving within international, even cosmopolitan contexts. As insights from studies of nationalism and exile overlap, travelers and foreign residential communities reasonably can be seen as vital crucibles of ideological change in their homelands.[26] Such groups , whether expelled by a hostile government or simply attracted to a country out of curiosity, seek to explore their relationship to their own national cultures. In such altered circumstances, surrounded by newness and existing in an inescapably comparative context, the Latin Americans studied in the following selections embarked upon their own strange pilgrimages that may have removed them physically from their nations, but guaranteed that their relationship to their homelands remained the central feature of their lives and work.

Notes

1. José Carlos Mariátegui, *Seven Interpretive Essays on Peruvian Reality*, trans. Marjorie Urquidi (Austin: University of Texas Press, 1971), 284.

2. Colombian novelist Gabriel García Márquez wrote of the often bizarre experience of Latin Americans in Europe in *Strange Pilgrims*, trans. Edith Grossman (New York: Alfred A. Knopf, 1993).

3. Lloyd Kramer, *Threshold of A New World: Intellectuals and the Exile Experience in Paris, 1830–48* (Ithaca: Cornell University Press, 1988), 11.

4. Yosse Shain, *The Frontier of Loyalty: Political Exiles in the Age of the Nation State* (Middletown, CT: Wesleyan University Press, 1989), 7–8.

5. María Christina García, *Havana USA: Cuban Exiles and Cuban Americans in South Florida, 1959–1994* (Los Angeles: University of California Press, 1996); Marc Raeff, *Russia Abroad: A Cultural History of the Russian Emigration, 1919–*

1939 (New York: Oxford University Press, 1990); Shari Benstock, *Women of the Left Bank* (Austin: University of Texas Press, 1986).

6. Paul Ilie, *Literature and Inner Exile: Authoritarian Spain, 1939–1975* (Baltimore: Johns Hopkins University Press, 1980); Michael Ugarte, *Shifting Ground: Spanish Civil War Exile Literature* (Durham, NC: Duke University Press, 1989); Marielena Zelaya Koelker, *Testimonios americanos de los escritores españoles transterrados de 1939* (Madrid: Ediciones Cultura Hispánica, 1985); Terry Eagleton, *Nationalism, Colonialism, and Literature* (Minneapolis: University of Minnesota Press, 1990); Arnold McMillin, *Under Eastern Eyes: The West as Reflected in Recent Russian Emigré Writing* (New York: St. Martin's Press, 1992).

7. "[T]he strongest voices in world fiction today are those of writers in exile, whether they be political exiles like Solzhenitsyn and Gabriel García Márquez or self-exiles like V. S. Naipaul." Charles Michener quoted in Milan Kundera, introduction to *The Book of Laughter and Forgetting* (New York: HarperCollins, 1994). Kundera, a Czech, lived in Parisian exile for thirty years.

8. Martin Tucker, ed., *Literary Exile in the Twentieth Century* (New York: Greenwood Press, 1991).

9. Lloyd S. Kramer, *Threshold*, 229.

10. Mary Louise Pratt, *Imperial Eyes: Travel Writing and Transculturation* (New York: Routledge, 1997); Valene Smith, *Hosts and Guests: The Anthropology of Tourism* (Pittsburgh: University of Pittsburgh Press, 1989); Caren Kaplan, *Questions About Travel: Postmodern Discourses of Displacement* (Durham, NC: Duke University Press, 1996); David Spurr, *The Rhetoric of Empire: Colonial Discourse in Journalism, Travel Writing, and Imperial Administration* (Durham, NC: Duke University Press, 1993).

11. William W. Stowe, *Going Abroad: European Travel in Nineteenth-Century American Culture* (Princeton, NJ: Princeton University Press, 1994), 13.

12. Edward Said, the Palestinian scholar and activist who himself has spent much time and energy in a type of exile, has distinguished among: the refugee, which is a political category created by the twentieth-century nation-state; expatriates, who live abroad voluntarily for their own reasons; emigrés, who may return to their home country; and exiles, who are forced to leave and are cut off from their national community indefinitely. See his many diverse studies, including: *Orientalism* (New York: Random House, 1979) and *Culture and Imperialism* (New York: Vintage, 1994).

13. Shain, *Frontier*, 163.

14. Ibid., 14.

15. Tucker, *Literary Exile*, xv.

16. Vladimir Nabokov, *Speak, Memory* (Harmondsworth, England: Penguin Books, 1969), 214.

17. Leon Grinberg and Rebeca Grinberg, *Psychoanalytic Perspectives on Migration and Exile*, trans. Nancy Festinger (New Haven, CT: Yale University Press, 1989), 9.

18. Ibid., 26.

19. Ibid., 79.

20. Ibid., 79–80.

21. Elie Kedourie, *Nationalism*, revised edition (New York: Frederick Praeger, 1962), 9.

22. Of these the most interesting and important are: Edmund S. Morgan, *Inventing the People* (New York: W. W. Norton & Company, 1988); Linda Colley, *Britons: Forging the Nation, 1707–1837* (New Haven, CT: Yale University Press, 1992); Nicolas Shumway, *Inventing Argentina* (Berkeley: University of California Press, 1991); Roberto González Echevarría, *Myth and Archive: A Theory of*

Latin American Narrative (Cambridge, England: Cambridge University Press, 1990).

23. Benedict Anderson, *Imagined Communities: Reflections on the Origin and Spread of Nationalism* (London: Verso, 1983), 12, 15.

24. Morgan, *Inventing the People*, 13.

25. See two works by Tzvetan Todorov, *On Human Diversity: Nationalism, Racism, and Exoticism in French Thought* (Cambridge, MA: Harvard University Press, 1993) and *The Conquest of America: The Question of the Other* (New York: Harper & Row, 1987).

26. Tucker, introduction to *Literary Exile*, xxiv.

I

Constructing Nations after Independence and Beyond

1

Nature and Mother: Foreign Residence and the Evolution of Andrés Bello's American Identity, London, 1810–1829

Karen Racine

Andrés Bello (1781–1865) was perhaps the most influential figure of nineteenth century Latin American intellectual life. Bello was a Venezuelan who lived in London for twenty years and eventually settled in Chile. Historian Karen Racine links Bello's emerging Americanism to his extended residence abroad, and locates his obsession with key cultural reforms to the two decades he spent observing conditions in England and reminiscing about the land he left behind. While in London, the often-impoverished Bello wrote voluminously about such diverse subjects as education, grammar, orthography, rule of law, cultivation of a patriotic national sentiment, and useful scientific technology. He also was the longest-term permanent resident of an overseas community that, at one time or another, included many notable figures of the Spanish American hemispheric independence movement: Francisco de Miranda, Simón Bolívar, José de San Martín, Bernardo O'Higgins, Fray Servando Teresa de Mier, Lucas Alamán, Bernardino Rivadavia, and José de la Riva Agüero.

This chapter situates Spanish American independence in its international context, and reveals the importance of extended foreign residence upon one of its major intellectual architects. By utilizing insights gleaned from the psychology of exile, Racine finds that one method by which exiles and others can cope with an unfamiliar environment is to imagine themselves to be working productively on behalf of their nation. For Bello, this meant studying British cultural practices that could have applicability for his homeland after independence: Joseph Lancaster's system of mutual education, the jury system, freedom of the press laws, and the patriotic uses of poetry and public symbols. Bello was only the first in a long series of Latin American directing elites who used their time abroad to secure information and observe foreign institutional arrangements in the service of his own country.

> Nature gives us one mother and one mother-
> land. . . . In vain we try to adopt a new country;
> the heart gives itself but once. The hand may
> wave a foreign flag . . . and strangers call you
> fellow-citizen; but what does it matter? The land
> of our birth lives on in the human breast.[1]
>
> —Andrés Bello

Andrés Bello, the father of modern Spanish American jurisprudence, poetry, and education, neatly captured the essence of romantic nationalism in the words quoted above. Essentially subconscious, a relationship with Nature and Mother cannot be unlearned, traded, or renounced—it dwells in the shadows of daily behavior and intensifies with distance from home and family. Outward trappings of citizenship, such as passports, flags, ceremonies, and titles, can be easily assumed but are all the more irrelevant for their very accessibility. What matters is the inner essence, the primal identification with one's roots in home and family that is inextricably linked to the childhood environment and that cannot be cast off, or renounced as readily. Though some may try to pretend otherwise, the land of birth and youth truly remains in the breast; and there is no one for whom this is more true than Andrés Bello.

A remarkable intellect who spent most of his adult life away from his friends, family, and native land, Andrés Bello never lost his sentimental attachment and deep devotion to Venezuela and its people. For two crucial decades Bello lived in London, usually in desperate poverty. During this period of hardship and separation he consolidated his literary and patriotic projects for America. Significantly, Bello reached intellectual maturity in the England of the 1810s and 1820s, which was an aristocratic country of law and order, seeking moderate reform within a constitutional monarchy while facing tremendous changes brought on by the French Revolution, the Napoleonic Wars, and the Industrial Revolution. His confrontation with English politics and society provided Bello with an interesting working model and an alternative to the recently rejected Spanish colonial system. While in London, Bello worked for the utilitarians James Mill and Jeremy Bentham, and their ideas appear not only in his future legal and constitutional drafts but also in his poetry.[2] Through his friendship with influential resident Spanish liberal exile the Reverend Joseph Blanco White, Bello gained access to the upper echelons of the emerging Whig party gathering around Henry, Lord Holland. His proximity to this witty and influential salon society allowed Bello to observe up close the Whigs' attempt to preserve the role of aristocracy and talent as a counterweight to democracy and mediocrity.[3] He worked on translations for the British and Foreign Bible Society and observed the mutual educational experiments of Andrew Bell and Joseph Lancaster. On a more personal level, Bello married twice, suffered the death of his first wife and an infant son, and enjoyed the births of eight of his fifteen surviving children while in London. These two decades were a time of great significance for him, and one which observers consider to be "the most intense interval of his life."[4]

An examination of Bello's intellectual activities while in London reveals not only a growing concern with things American but also his twin obsessions with his return to mother and homeland, and his own potential usefulness to the Spanish American people. In a manner common to exiles, Bello compensated for his loneliness and isolation by throwing himself into the project of raising the cultural level of those he had left behind. He always considered himself to be in transit while in London, and maintained a psychological umbilical cord to Venezuela by imagining himself to be working perpetually and usefully on its behalf.[5] To this end, Bello studied the educational reforms then taking place in England and began to draft his own pilot program for Spanish American education in *Filosofía del entendimiento* (Philosophy of understanding). Bello also conceived the influential *Gramática de la lengua castellana destinada al uso de los americanos* (Grammar of the Castilian language for the use of Americans) and *Principios de la ortología y métrica de la lengua castellana* (Principles of orthology and metrics of the Castilian language)—linguistic projects that recognized the difference between American and European forms of the Spanish language. He wrote epic poems intended to educate Americans about their proud heritage and recent glorious history, and published them in journals conceived as textbooks for the enlightenment of the new republics' citizenry.

Bello's Americanism born of exile is most apparent in his two famous poems, "Alocución a la poesía" (Allocution to poetry) and "La agricultura de la Zona Tórrida" (Agriculture of the Torrid Zone), published in the journals *La Biblioteca Americana* (1823) and *El Repertorio Americano* (1826–27), respectively. In this body of work, jointly known as his *Silvas americanas*, Bello not only extolled the natural beauty of the various American regions but also began to construct a pantheon of national heroes and events for its future civic culture. Furthermore, he established the value of both the pre-Columbian and colonial epochs for the new nations at a time when both had been obscured by the bloody wars of independence. This voice was Bello, the self-appointed moral tutor of the American people, at his most earnest. Viewing the battle from across the Atlantic, Bello did not suffer the usual fate of exiles—that is, a decreased capacity for insight with time and distance,[6] but rather he saw past the immediate divisiveness of the era and began to consider the requirements for a long-term, viable political culture. Quite naturally, Bello looked around him and found in England inspiring examples of a service-oriented aristocracy based on landholding, a dynamic economy springing from industrialization and practical application of scientific advancement, widespread literacy, and the existence of true patriotic spirit and English identity among the people.[7] The new republics needed these very traits, and Bello believed he served the Great Cause of his generation, albeit at a distance, by constructing the "intellectual declaration of independence."[8] There can be no doubt that Andrés Bello became an American while sitting among the books of the British Museum.

Bello's stay in England began in May 1810, shortly after Venezuela's revolutionary junta declared independence from Spain. Foreign Secretary Juan Germán Roscio decided to send a mission to Britain to seek diplomatic recognition, commercial relations, and protection from other powers. He chose as envoys the wealthy and unpredictable Simón Bolívar, the impassioned university administrator Luis López Méndez, and twenty-nine-year-old secretary Andrés Bello, the only one of the group with governmental experience who spoke decent English. The unlikely trio set out for England in June 1810 on a British corvette aptly named *General Wellington* and arrived in Portsmouth in early July after a relatively quick and smooth passage.

The arrival of the envoys from Venezuela was a significant event in London social and political life. Venezuelan expatriate resident Francisco de Miranda, "the Precursor," had been lobbying for British aid to Spanish American independence movements for over two decades, and it seemed that by 1810 his prophesies of a continent ripe for emancipation finally had come true. Miranda was so anxious for the arrival of the three envoys that he could hardly contain himself; he scurried out to Portsmouth to greet their ship so as not to waste a day in making their acquaintance and installed them in London's aristocratic Morin's Hotel.[9] Within days, Miranda arranged a face-to-face meeting between Foreign Secretary Richard Colley Wellesley and the envoys, although he had to settle for the Secretary's grand residence, Apsley House (given by the nation to Wellesley's brother, the Duke of Wellington), as the venue, thus stripping the meeting of any official government sanction. Over the course of the next two months, Wellesley met five times with the Venezuelan delegates and heard their petitions presented in French.[10] Although this first Venezuelan mission did not accomplish much in the practical sense, its real significance is that such high-level meetings occurred at all. The envoys had a private agenda which not only included arms and money but also teachers, machinery, books, and laws.[11]

The so-called Grafton Street Symposium, sixty-three days in the summer of 1810 that Bolívar, López Méndez, and Bello spent with Miranda, initiated a long-term flirtation between the Spanish American independence generation and British culture. During that time, Miranda not only opened his home and considerable library to them, but he also showed the envoys around London and introduced them to important persons including the Duke of Gloucester, the education reformer Joseph Lancaster, and the abolitionist and parliamentarian William Wilberforce.[12] Together they toured the Royal Observatory, Kew's botanical gardens, and the palace at Hampton Court. Noted artist Charles Gill came calling and painted Bolívar's portrait. All of English society appeared to be interested in the exoticism of these "Ambassadors of South America" and, superficially at least, wanted to get to know them.[13]

When Bolívar returned home in September 1810, López Méndez and Bello remained behind in London as the acting Venezuelan mission based at Miranda's Grafton Street house. Since they did not have an operating budget, both men spent their personal fortunes on the needs of the mission and soon languished in absolute indigence.[14] Almost immediately, the loneliness and isolation of his position began to affect Bello. He had no family or close friends in London, no income or steady employment beyond the secretaryship of the ersatz Venezuelan mission, and was unfamiliar with the customs and food. He lived with López Méndez and Miranda's wife and two sons for two years before moving to Somers Town, the poor district occupied by new Catholic immigrants from France, Spain, and Ireland. He was so poor that he lived in constant fear of debtor's prison, and once avoided incarceration solely by the kindness of his tailor, Newport, who allowed Bello to work off the amount he owed by doing chores around the shop.[15] The proud Bello keenly felt the drop in his status.

Throughout his stay in London, money was a constant pressure for Bello and he exhibited a classic psychological condition of exile known as "money hypochondria," the perpetual and persistent fear of homelessness and poverty.[16] His inability to provide enough for himself, and the guilt for abandoning his mother and role as head of the family during such a turbulent time, caused Bello great psychological distress. Recent studies of exile psychology note that those who fall prey to severe homesickness "usually have unresolved problems arising from a conflict relationship with the mother" that actually indicate a morbid dependency on the family unit of origin.[17] Clearly, Bello did share an intense bond with his mother, Ana López, who had been widowed since 1800; and although he lived in complete and utter poverty in London, Bello's petitions to the Venezuelan government repeatedly requested a pension not for himself but for his dear mother's subsistence.[18]

Bello's attachment to his family and familiar surroundings are apparent in a letter he wrote home just one year after his arrival in London:

Dearest Mother,
It is impossible to describe the earnest desire I have to return to the bosom of my family . . . I believe that my return will be soon, and surely not more than six months hence. Meanwhile, with a little bit of patience, beyond these days there must be a better, more relaxing and happier time.

. . . I have not been sick at all since I left Caracas, on the contrary I feel stronger and in better health than ever before.

The head colds I used to suffer have left me entirely. . . . Therefore, I hope that my residence in England will have produced at least the benefit of improvement to my constitution.

Remember me to Florencio, Rosario, Eusebio, Carlos, Josefina and the others; to my uncles and aunts and to all my friends.

I remain your most affectionate son,
Andrés.[19]

This letter reveals several things about the state of Bello's mind produced by his residence abroad: the stubborn belief that his departure for home was imminent, a concern with his health and physical well-being in a strange place, and a desire to be remembered by everyone at home. These are common psychological concerns for persons living in a foreign environment, especially if kept there by forces beyond their control.

Of course, Bello did not go home in six months as he had indicated to his mother. He remained in London for eighteen more years eventually marrying and beginning his family there. Nevertheless, he always viewed his return to Venezuela as imminent and tried to maintain links both to his family and to Spanish American culture. Although he twice married British women, Bello's children all received Spanish names and learned the language of their father. Bello insisted that his sons write to their South American grandmother at least occasionally, and in 1825, Ana López wrote back to her English grandsons whom she called "my beloved Carlos" and "my darling Francisco," pleading for a flower drawn by their own little hands.[20] Bello's devotion to the memory of his mother lasted until the end of his days. In the 1860s in Chile he recalled: "my adored mother, whose memory is never away from me and whom I am not capable of forgetting, neither morning nor night goes by that I do not remember her; whose name is one of the first words that I say when I awake, and one of the last that my lips put to bed."[21] Even when compensation for sentimental hyperbole is granted, Bello's devotion to his mother, the primal symbol of his origin, was morbidly intense and deepened during his residence abroad.

Psychologists note that exiles and others transplanted to a new social environment inevitably must break away from the mother archetype and "fulfill the paternal function by establishing a new context."[22] In other words, Bello, the son and parochial *caraqueño* (person from Caracas), became Bello, the man and greater American by virtue of his extended stay outside his homeland. To achieve this transformation required a new role model, a trustworthy person who could assume responsibility for the emigrant and integrate him into the unfamiliar surroundings. Ethnologists and zoologists call this "imprinting" and note that abandoned persons and even animals latch on to the first friendly face that appears and

emulate its behaviors. So it was with Andrés Bello. Shortly after his arrival in London, Bello entered into a friendship with the Reverend Joseph
Blanco White, who gradually assumed more power within Bello's social
and intellectual orbit.

Blanco White is an interesting figure.[23] He was a Spaniard who voluntarily left his country and spent the rest of his long and idiosyncratic
life trying to turn himself into an Englishman but never quite succeeding.
As editor of the pro-Independence but increasingly moderate London
newspaper *El Español*, Blanco White drew Bello away from the radical
projects of López Méndez and Grafton Street and introduced him to the
more aristocratic reformers of the Holland House circle. After the capture of Miranda and fall of the First Republic in Venezuela in 1812, Bello
moved out of Grafton Street and ceased to participate in the various Ma-
sonic lodges and other projects which swirled about it.[24] He turned instead to serious study at the British Museum and became a regular fixture
at the Library there, seeking its warmth when he could not afford to heat
his own residence.[25]

Thus began Andrés Bello's intellectual quest for the definition of what
it meant to be American and the conscious construction of patriotic civic
cultures for the republics that would emerge after the wars. In retrospect,
it should not be surprising that Bello began his investigations with a study
of the medieval poem of the Cid, which tells the story of a man banished
from his homeland and condemned to live among strangers, a parallel
with himself that Bello could not have overlooked.[26] Of greater practical
importance, however, was Bello's desire to find in the myth-history of the
Cid some proof of a limited monarchy far in Spain's past, which could be
resurrected for the current struggle for constitutionalism.[27] Clearly, the
British example had caught Bello's imagination and, to his credit, he tried
to situate it within the Hispanic context rather than to imitate it blindly.

Despite the exciting intellectual challenges he found there, Bello's
early years in London were so lonely that he even appealed to the Spanish
Embassy for clemency (he had been branded disloyal to the Crown for
participating in the mission of the rebel junta to London) and permission
to return to Venezuela, which had been retaken by royalist forces.[28] The
response was not recorded but, since Bello did not return to Caracas, it is
assumed that permission was not forthcoming. Ferdinand and other Spanish officials may have doubted Bello's sincerity for many reasons. He had
been consorting with some notorious agitators and American rebels in
London, among them the Mexican radical Fray Servando Teresa de Mier
and the turncoat Blanco White.[29] Furthermore, the pro-Independence
Documentos interesantes relativos a Caracas (Interesting official documents relating to Caracas) had appeared in London in 1812, and Bello
was rumored to have written its anonymous prologue.[30] The author
invoked John Locke's work to argue that Spanish Americans had not

received adequate representation in the colonial system and therefore were entitled to assume power to ensure that their own needs would be met.[31] Although the author, which most likely is Bello, clearly came down on the side of independence, the overall tone is one of regret and the desire for future reconciliation. This theme is consistent with Bello's rejection of Spanish political dominance while retaining respect for Spain's cultural achievements.

With his pleas for clemency denied, Bello remained in London. He continued to work at the British Library, undertaking studies of the Spanish language, grammar reform, and the British legal system, and dreamed of the day when he could return home. He kept himself busy and began to adjust to an indefinite stay in England. Through friends in Somers Town, Bello met and married Mary Ann Boyland on May 30, 1814. She was a young Catholic woman of Irish descent who could not speak Spanish but who enjoyed Bello's complete devotion. Together they had three children: Carlos Eusebio Florencio, Francisco José, and Juan Pablo Antonio, who survived just under a year. As a family man, Bello's domestic life took on a measure of contentment but the pressure to earn a living in a foreign country obviously grew more intense.

Manuel Sarratea, then Buenos Aires's representative in London, knew of Bello's dire straits and hired him to do clerical work for the mission. Blanco White also intervened and obtained a small pension for Bello from Lady Holland, and found him work as tutor to the son of former India Undersecretary William Hamilton.[32] When this appointment turned sour, Blanco White again directed Bello to other positions: a secretary transcribing the notoriously bad handwriting of Jeremy Bentham, a collaborator on the translation of Felipe Scío's New Testament for the British and Foreign Bible Society, and a correspondence clerk for the firm of Gordon Murphy & Co.[33] Teaching, translating, and publishing: educated exiles and emigrés commonly hold these types of jobs because they allow the individual to maintain a living tie to their language and culture of origin. When Sarratea offered an opportunity for him to move to Argentina with his young family, Bello chose to remain in London despite his enduring poverty. He not only feared that such a move might mean he would never return home to Venezuela, but also, imperceptibly, he had begun to put down roots and felt more at home in England.

Despite this new bond with England, Bello did not abandon the idea of America or cease to envision a role for himself in its future. In the 1820s, Bello embarked on the next phase of his patriotic project, the publication of his academic studies for the general enlightenment of Americans. In June 1820, at the regular salons held by Colombian envoy Francisco Antonio Zea, he made the acquaintance of Antonio José de Irisarri, a Guatemalan in the service of Chile. Irisarri, the bombastic and haughty scion of an elite Central American family, immediately perceived

Bello's intellectual power and persuaded the Venezuelan to collaborate on a London-based journal, *El Censor Americano* (1820). Shortly after his initial encounter with Bello, Irisarri wrote two enthusiastic letters about his friend. In the first, to his wife, he wrote: "He is a true scholar, by his character and learning, and even in the patience with which he bears his poverty, equal to my own if not greater."[34] To Chile's Secretary of State, Joaquín Echeverría, Irisarri outlined his desire to "cultivate relations with a Mr Andrés Bello, in the confidence of the previously mentioned Zea, and whom I understand is a native of Venezuela. He is a very capable man, of very diverse literature and extensive science, and possesses a seriousness and nobility of character that make him much more worthy."[35]

Bello agreed to join Irisarri and work on *El Censor Americano*. The journal was a short-lived Spanish-language review conceived along the lines of contemporary English magazines, and contained sections devoted to politics, literary criticism, general notices and documents, and a catch-all variety section. This journal was important not for its overall impact, which was negligible, but as the debut effort of London's Spanish American community to join together and create textbooks for the enlightenment of citizens back home rather than propaganda for a British audience.

By the 1820s, the theme of America's salvation and regeneration dominated Bello's thoughts. He had suffered the deaths of his youngest son Juan and beloved wife Mary Ann, who succumbed to tuberculosis in January 1821. These losses, added to Bello's lack of steady income, drove him to despair, and prompted a deep spiritual crisis to which Blanco White alluded in his letter of July 8, 1821: "The firm belief that you have in a kindly God, and in the power of reason to indicate to us what is our duty and in our interest, and to introduce a firm courage in the face of adversity; these are, in my opinion, the most effective resources that you have in your present situation."[36] Bello moved to another house in a vain effort to escape the memory of his dead wife and pleaded with his friend Irisarri to give him meaningful work in the mission of Chile, even flirting with the idea of emigrating there, although he wrote his old friend Pedro Gual that "on the other hand, it is hard for me to renounce the land of my birth, and to have knowledge that sooner or later I would die at the Antarctic pole among the . . . Chileans."[37]

In 1824, Bello married another English woman, Elizabeth Antonia Dunn, and his domestic life settled down once more. He continued to work for the Chilean mission with the understanding that he was always at liberty to cooperate with any of the new American governments should another opportunity arise.[38] He transferred to the Colombian legation after Irisarri's bitter departure from office in 1825 and remained there in frustration until 1829.

While facing these personal trials in London, Bello transformed himself into the interpreter of America. The great psychological need of exiles, and one which often spurs them to great accomplishments, is the desire that "the world shall take notice."[39] This is certainly true of Bello and colored the development of his Americanism while residing in London. Bello's obsession with American identity led him to believe that "it was his duty to explain America, what it was, what it had, what it could achieve, and where it was going."[40] The boy who had been raised to value learning and culture above all else grew up to be the man who would lift up his countrymen, enlighten them with useful knowledge, and instruct them in both their proud heritage and their unlimited economic potential.

Nowhere is Bello's conscious effort to build a patriotic civic culture more apparent than in his *Silvas americanas*, epic poems in which he incorporated American geography, botany, ancient history, and recent experience, into an identity intended to buttress a stable social and political environment. Although he began to incorporate American themes into his poetry even before his arrival in London, this tendency increased in intensity and artistry as the years passed, and culminated in his epic poems "Alocución a la poesía" (1823) and "La agricultura de la Zona Tórrida" (1826–27). Bello intended both epic poems to be part of a larger work entitled "América," although there are significant differences between them in intent, the perception of nature, and the treatment of human society. Nevertheless, the absent poet's obsession with America's past, present, and future remained constant.

In "Alocución," Bello had two goals: to elevate American natural goodness, simplicity, and truth in contrast to European falsity and artifice, and to construct a pantheon of American patriotic heroes and deeds to inspire future generations to greatness. He began by appealing to Poetry to leave Europe "whose time has already passed" and fly to "the world of Columbus," where it would find a home among the flowered plains, the tangled woods, the twisting rivers and a thousand colors.[41] He asked why Poetry, "the wild nymph," would remain in the land of servility and flattery, "that region of light and misery/ where your ambitious/ rival Philosophy" had come to dominate over truth, beauty, and goodness. Instead, Poetry should make its home across the "vast Atlantic" in nurturing, nourishing America. Bello's choice of words reflect his idealized image of America as young, wild, vibrant, fruitful, unspoiled, and innocent. The opening sixty-one lines of "Alocución" set up the contrast between Europe and America, from which Bello goes on to elaborate the tremendous power and productivity of the American continent and the beautiful simplicity of its land and early people. Bello's obsession with American nature should not be too surprising; not only were the Venezuelan plains of his youth an appealing dramatic contrast to the soot and cement of London, but also Nature itself represented a constant element, a greater being that remained unspoiled even as time altered Bello's human relationships in America.

The rest of the expository part of "Alocución" is devoted to the physical environment of the various regions. In these passages, Bello told the reader how:

> Blue banners reverberate
> From Buenos Aires
>
> . . . the valleys
> Of blessed Chile, which enrich
> With golden harvests and smooth fruits
>
> Or the city [Mexico] where the eagle resting
> Upon the nopal, showing the wayward Aztec
> The land of inexhaustible rich veins
> Which almost overfed avaricious Europe[42]

In this land of natural harmony, Bello wrote that "Liberty without laws flourished/ all was peace, contentment and happiness." The remainder of this section is an alphabet of tropical products: sugar, bananas, coffee, cacao, jasmine, cotton, honey, pineapples, all of which indicated the tremendous fertility and variety of the region. This theme, and even some of the wording, was subsequently picked up and expanded in "La agricultura de la Zona Tórrida."

The second section of "Alocución" incorporated the Wars of Independence and outlined their significance for American patriots. Bello expressed horror at the violence and destruction of these conflicts, especially when they degenerated into civil wars, but from his safe distance he was able to see past the blood and divisiveness and begin to throw up heroes. He wrote of "Castelli, who dared" and "Moreno, who with the dignified tone of oppressed people/ outlined their complaints." He remembered the Argentine patriots Balcarce and Belgrano "and the hundreds of others/ who made the native land of glorious riches/ with the spade or with the pen." He entreated:

> Goddess of memory, the hymns are asked of you
> To remember also the empire of Moctezuma,
> Which utterly defeated the opportunism of Iturbide,
> And counts itself among the free peoples.
> Courageous Mexican nation, many
> Wait for your power and your example
> Of liberty; nor is their hope in vain.
> And the bronze colossus will shake off the dust
> Of three centuries from its firm base[43]

Bello memorialized the battles and heroes of Gran Colombia, eulogizing:

> Baraya who also died there, of unsung honour
> Among a thousand other victims, at the hands
> Of your vile servant Morillo

> Baraya died but his example lives.
> Do you think you will drown with blood the fire
> Of liberty in such great souls?[44]

Methodically, Bello scanned the continent and listed the achievements of American patriots including the Mexicans Hidalgo and Morelos, the Colombian Camilo Torres, and the Venezuelans Javier Uztáriz and Juan Germán Roscio. He devoted a whole section to:

> Miranda! whose name also glorifies
> Colombia; constant defender
> Of its rights, of holy laws,
> Of severe loving discipline.
> With reverence I offer to your remains
> This humble tribute.[45]

He ended with the hope that Bolívar, "the Liberator of the Colombian people," would lead America out of its martial struggle and into the glorious future for which it was obviously destined. Although he clearly found heroes on the battlefield, Bello's mature project in "Alocución" is actually a repudiation of the bitter, bloody battles that ravaged America and threatened to divide its people for the foreseeable future.[46] Bello had lived for too long in the orderly, constitutional environment of England and admired its moderation, industriousness, and rule of law.

If the overall ideal of America and Nature in "Alocución" was that of freedom and spontaneity, by 1826 Bello had refocused his thesis, the core of which was already present in his earlier work, to stress the human triumph over Nature and man's ability to harness its power for his own purposes.[47] By 1826, the Wars of Independence for all intents and purposes had been won, Europe had recognized some of the new republics, and the work of rebuilding begged to begin. And, quite naturally for a Creole with landholding aspirations himself, Bello looked to organized agriculture as the best means to prevent social and economic anarchy. He opened "La agricultura de la Zona Tórrida" with the powerful line "Hail, fertile zone!"[48] as though he were addressing true royalty and then followed with a litany of its beneficent gifts: indigo, wine, agave, jasmine, palms, ambrosia, potatoes, corn, bananas, and yucca were merely a few of the products of this "fertile zone." The poem read like a shopping list for all the potential British merchants anxious to trade or invest in the new republics; however, both poems appeared in Spanish-language journals intended for Spanish American readers. Bello intended to instill in Americans a pride in the beauty and fertility of their environment and to offer them practical advice.

La Biblioteca Americana and *El Repertorio Americano* were directed toward an American audience but suffered from the distance to their market; both journals folded after just two issues. By 1827, Bello was ready to return home. London had, in the end, become too expensive and frustrating for him. Perhaps in retaliation for Bello's *Silvas*, which he perceived as a not-too-cleverly disguised criticism of his own leadership, Bolívar demoted his old friend from financial attaché to low-level secretary, a bitter blow which convinced Bello that he could no longer hope for a return to his country.[49] If this situation was not galling enough to a man who had served Venezuela faithfully for seventeen years, Bolívar added insult by going on to reprimand Bello for his seeming inattention to the Liberator's personal financial business in London. Bolívar's actions, coupled with the persistent civil disturbances in northern South America, persuaded Bello that Chile was the most realistic option for a home in America.

Although he had determined to return anywhere in America, Bello always hoped that it would be to Caracas. In 1826 he had written to his boyhood friend Agustín Loynaz: "I want to return to those countries and to spend the rest of my life there, and if it could be Caracas I should be delighted."[50] Even as he prepared for an imminent departure for Chile in December 1828, Bello still hoped for a reconciliation with his native land. He wrote to José María Restrepo, Colombia's Secretary of Foreign Affairs, that "it is probable that I will soon go to Chile; there and everywhere I will take much pleasure in employing myself in the service of [your land]."[51] Bello left London on February 14, 1829, accompanied by his wife Elizabeth and seven children. The third phase of his long and productive life was about to begin.

Carl Jung encapsulated the psychological problem of exile neatly when he wrote that "loneliness does not come from having no people about one, but from being unable to communicate the things that seem important to oneself or from holding certain views which others find inadmissible."[52] Andrés Bello, the towering figure of nineteenth-century Latin American intellectual life, lived as a chrysalis in these conditions for almost twenty years until he burst forth in Chile in 1829 and finally found himself in a position to enact the reforms he previously only had sketched on paper. The manifold accomplishments of his mature career in Chile all began with his studies in London: grammar and orthographic reform, education reform, codification of laws and the writing of Chile's Constitution, the establishment of newspapers and universities, and his forays into poetry, history, and literature. Bello's genuine love for America and things American took on a new meaning during his years of hardship and study in England. While there he associated with other important men from all over America, thereby broadening his familiarity with the continent and the challenges facing it. He also learned from the English; their powerful tradition of legalism and moderate social reforms within an aristocratic society affected Bello deeply.

From the gut-wrenching loneliness of his early years in London and through years of poverty and anonymity, Bello worked on behalf of various Spanish American missions in London, and it was this long residence abroad that was the defining experience of his life. Physically removed from the blood and battle of the Wars of Independence, Bello took on a greater challenge, the liberation of the minds of his fellow Americans. Beginning with his early studies of the Cid, and continuing through the epic poems of the *Silvas americanas*, Bello defined a uniquely Spanish American culture, one that was characterized by freedom in restraint, bountiful nature, heroes past and present, and that offered unlimited potential for its humble inhabitants. This vision, like all his subsequent Chilean efforts, was a realization of the work he had begun in London in the 1810s and 1820s. Remarkable for its prescience and maturity, Bello's Americanism derived its power from the psychological experience of his long-term residence in the England of the early nineteenth century, and its ideological content from the conditions he observed around him during those years.

Notes

1. Andrés Bello qtd. in Rafael Caldera, *Andrés Bello: Philosopher, Poet, Philologist, Educator, Legislator, Statesman* (London: George Allen & Unwin, 1977), 28.

2. There are clear references to the utilitarians' ideas in his 1823 "Alocución a la Poesía." For the long overdue translation of Bello's work into English see Iván Jaksíc, ed., *Selected Writings of Andrés Bello*, trans. Frances M. López-Morillas (New York: Oxford University Press, 1997); and Pedro Lira Urquieta, *Andrés Bello* (México: Fondo de la Cultura Económica, 1948), 94.

3. John Dinwiddy, "Liberal and Benthamite Circles in London, 1810–1829," in *Andrés Bello: The London Years*, ed. John Lynch (Richmond, Surrey, England: The Richmond Publishing Co., 1982): 119–36; Antonio Cussen, *Bello and Bolívar: Poetry and Politics in the Spanish American Revolution* (Cambridge, England: Cambridge University Press, 1992), 89. For the fullest and most recent exposition of the Holland House position, see Leslie G. Mitchell, *Holland House* (London: Duckworth, 1980).

4. Pedro Grases, *Andrés Bello: Primer humanista de América* (Buenos Aires: Ediciones del Tridente, 1946), 68. Arturo Uslar Pietri, in *Andrés Bello, el desterrado* (México: UNAM, 1979), 13 writes that for Bello, London represented "years of intense study and of the definitive formation of his character." Diego Amunátegui Solar in "Semblanza de don Andrés Bello," *Revista Chilena de Historia e Geografía* 73 (#3, Sept.–Dec. 1932): 53 agrees that if Bello had not transcended his national borders, "he never would have composed the works that formed the pedestal of his scientific reputation."

5. Rafael Caldera, *Caracas, London, Santiago de Chile: Three Periods in the Life of Andrés Bello* (Caracas: Republic of Venezuela, Ministry of Foreign Affairs, 1981), 17.

6. Paul Ilie, *Literature and Inner Exile: Authoritarian Spain, 1939–1975* (Baltimore: Johns Hopkins University Press, 1980), 19.

7. For an excellent study of the creation of a national patriotic culture in Britain during this period, see Linda Colley, *Britons: Forging the Nation, 1707–1837* (New Haven: Yale University Press, 1992).

8. The phrase is Pedro Henríquez Ureña's who uses it as a chapter title in *Literary Currents in Hispanic America* (Cambridge, MA: Harvard University Press, 1945).

9. María Teresa Berruezo León, *La lucha de hispanoamérica por su independencia en Inglaterra, 1800–1830* (Madrid: Ediciones de Cultura Hispánica, 1989), 86.

10. José Luis Salcedo-Bastardo, *Crucible of Americanism: Miranda's London House* ([Caracas]: Ediciones Langoven, 1981). The Spanish Embassy in London closely monitored the Venezuelans' activities and sent reports which are held at the Archivo General de las Indias (Seville), Estado 63, N.31 and Estado 87, N.1.

11. Dario Guevara, "Bolívar and Lancaster," *Boletín de la Academia Nacional de la Historia* 51 (Jan.–March 1968): 81.

12. Salcedo-Bastardo, *Crucible*, 19.

13. Berruezo, *Lucha*, 86. In a similar cynical fashion, Uslar Pietri writes that the Caracas deputies merely "were an object of curiosity for this snob society" in *Desterrado*, 10.

14. Pedro Grases, *Tiempo de Bello en Londres y otros ensayos* (Caracas: Biblioteca de Venezolano de Cultura, 1962), 47.

15. Miguel Luis Amunátegui, *Vida de Andrés Bello* (Santiago: Pedro G. Ramírez, 1882), 130.

16. León Grinberg and Rebeca Grinberg, *Psychoanalytic Perspectives on Migration and Exile*, trans. Nancy Festinger (New Haven, CT: Yale University Press, 1989), 94.

17. Ibid., 20.

18. Bello to Juan Germán Roscio (Caracas, June 6, 1810) and a reply from Roscio to Bello (Caracas, June 4, 1811) conceding Ana López a grant of 300 pesos, both reproduced in Pedro Grases, *Algunos temas de Bello* (Caracas: Monte Avila, 1978), 46.

19. Andrés Bello to Ana López (London, October 30, 1811) in Andrés Bello, *Caracas en el epistolario de Bello* (Caracas: La Casa de Bello, 1979), 11.

20. Ana López to Bello's sons Carlos and Francisco (May 15, 1825) in Amunátegui, *Vida*, 4.

21. Andrés Bello in Amunátegui, *Vida*, 4.

22. Grinberg and Grinberg, *Psychoanalytic Perspectives*, 95.

23. Martin Murphy, *Blanco White: Self-Banished Spaniard* (New Haven, CT: Yale University Press, 1989). His own story is told in the heavily censored John Hamilton Thom, ed., *The Life of Joseph Blanco White, written by Himself; with Portions of his Correspondence*, 2 vols. (London: John Chapman, 1845).

24. Cussen, *Bello and Bolívar*, 55.

25. James Mill signed Bello's admission ticket to the Library.

26. The resulting study, *Poema de mi Cid*, did not appear in published form until 1846 as a favor to Queen Isabella in exchange for the return to Chile of a portrait of the conqueror Pedro de Valdivia, Amunátegui, *Vida*, 175. For Bello's connection to Spanish liberal exiles also in London at this time, see Vicente Llorens, *Liberales y románticos: Una emigración española en Inglaterra (1823–34)* (Madrid: Editorial Castilla, 1979).

27. Cussen, *Bello and Bolívar*, 53.

28. Andrés Bello to Count Fernán Núñez (London, June 31 [*sic*], 1813), Real Archivo de Simancas, Estado 8.263.

29. Ernesto Mejía Sánchez, ed., "Don Andrés Bello y el Doctor Mier: Correspondencia," *Anuario de Letras* 10 (1972): 105–32.

30. John Lynch, "Great Britain and Spanish American Independence, 1810–30," in *London Years*, 7–24.

31. Cussen, *Bello and Bolívar*, 38–39.

32. Blanco White to Bello (December 30, 1815) reprinted in Mejía Sánchez, "Bello y Mier," 120. Lady Holland kept meticulous logs of her dinner guests. See British Museum, Add MSS 51950–51954.

33. Amunátegui, *Vida*, 144 wrote that Bello recalled this job with horror, saying that "the Greeks would have done well to include this task among those of Hercules." However, I did not locate any samples of Bello's handwriting among Bentham's papers at the University College, London. See also Bello to Joseph Tarn (Chelsea, January 19, 1818), British and Foreign Bible Society Archives, Home Correspondence (in), Cambridge University Library.

34. Antonio José de Irisarri to his wife (London, October 10, 1820) in Caldera, *Andrés Bello*, 42n; Marquis de Villena to Evaristo Pérez de Castro (London, August 26, 1820), AGI Estado 89, N.45, ff.1–2.

35. Antonio José de Irisarri to Joaquín Echeverría (London, October 10, 1820) reproduced in Guillermo Feliú Cruz, "Bello, Irisarri y Egaña en Londres," in *Andrés Bello y la redacción de los documentos oficiales, internacionales y legislativos de Chile* (Caracas: Biblioteca de los Tribunales del Distrito Federal, Fundación Rojas Astudillo, 1957), 10–11.

36. Blanco White to Bello (Little Gaddesden, Herts, July 8, 1821) in Sergio Fernández Larraín, *Cartas a Bello en Londres* (Caracas: Editorial Andrés Bello, 1968), 105. Bello relied on Blanco White's friendship to see him through this difficult time, and was able to distract himself from his grief by sending Blanco White long assessments of the current states of various regions in America. See, for example, Bello to Blanco White (Austin Friars, June 4, 1821), University of Liverpool, Sydney Jones Library, Blanco White Papers I/45.

37. Andrés Bello to Pedro Gual (London, January 6, 1824) reprinted in Guillermo Guitarte, "Juan García del Río y su *Biblioteca Colombiana* (Lima 1821): Sobre las orígenes de *La Biblioteca Americana* (1823) y *El Repertorio Americano* (1826–7) de Londres," *Nueva Revista de Filología Hispánica* 18 (#1, 1965–66): 128.

38. Grases, *Algunos temas*, 60–61. In this, Bello, of course, had Venezuela in mind.

39. Szabolcs de Vajay, an exile resident in Paris, in Paul Tabori, *The Anatomy of Exile: A Semantic and Historical Study* (London: Harrap, 1972), 27.

40. Caldera, *Andrés Bello*, 4.

41. "Alocución a la poesía" in Andrés Bello, *Obras completas*, prologue by Fernando Paz Castillo (Caracas: Ministerio de Educación, 1952), 1:43–44.

42. [Andrés Bello], "Alocución a la poesía," *Biblioteca Americana*, 2 vols. (1823), 1:5–6.

43. Ibid., 12.

44. [Andrés Bello], "Alocución a la poesía," *Biblioteca Americana*, 2 vols. (1823), 2:3.

45. Ibid., 8.

46. Antonio Cussen in *Bello and Bolívar*, 141 has suggested that "Alocución" be read as a rebuke to Bolívar and that the Liberator himself interpreted it as such, causing hurt feelings and a demotion in Bello's position.

47. Juan Carlos Ghiano, *Análisis de las Silvas Americanas de Bello* (Buenos Aires: Centro Editor de América Latina, 1967), 36–37 calls this Bello's (and by extension, America's) "civilizing mission."

48. "La agricultura de la Zona Tórrida" in Bello, *Obras completas*, 1:66–74.

49. Bello to Bolívar (London, April 21, 1827) reprinted in Amunátegui, *Vida*, 228–29. Bello tried to persuade Bolívar of the illegality of his demotion, and

even complained that he was making so little as it was, that he could barely feed his family.

50. Bello to Loynaz, quoted in Caldera, *Andrés Bello,* 278.

51. Bello to Restrepo ([London], December 2, 1828) reprinted in Raúl Silva Castro, *Don Andrés Bello, 1781–1865* (Santiago: Editorial Andrés Bello, 1965), 29.

52. C. G. Jung, *Memories, Dreams, Reflections*, ed. Aniela Jaffe and trans. Richard and Clare Winston (New York: Vintage, 1965), 356.

2

Extract of a Letter to Señor Don Vicente Azuero, New York, January 19, 1832

Francisco de Paula Santander

Francisco de Paula Santander (1792–1840) is remembered in Colombia as the "Man of Laws" for his steadfast belief in constitutional government and the rule of law. After being sent into exile by Simón Bolívar, Santander spent 1829 to 1832 traveling in Europe and the United States before returning to become the first elected president of the Republic of New Granada. His longtime friend Vicente Azuero (1787–1844) was a lawyer, liberal democrat, and frequent presidential candidate who also spent a year in exile in 1828 for his part in an alleged plot to kill Bolívar. This letter, written while Santander was conducting his tour of the United States, demonstrates his perception of his trip almost as a course in political sociology and as necessary preparation for his eventual assumption of the presidency of the Republic of New Granada. This letter is also interesting in that it presages many of the criticisms that Latin Americans would level at their compatriots who used their time abroad to pick up seemingly frivolous habits that had a debilitating impact upon their nations' economic and moral well-being.

The short time that I have been in this city has permitted me to observe the facility with which simple republican customs become corrupt. Here in this society, there can be found the same aristocracy that there is in absolute monarchies. Here too the aristocracy of birth and wealth predominates, and is contemptuous of those whom they call democrats or jacobins and who do not have large fortunes. Equality exists in the law, yet in the daily social intercourse there is no republicanism. This is attributable to the relationship that these mercantile cities have with Europe, and to the travels that inexperienced young Americans make to Paris and

From *Santander en Europa*, 4 vols. (Bogotá: Fundación Francisco de Paula Santander, 1989), 3:201. Translated by Karen Racine.

London, where they acquire a taste for the habits and manners of a royal court. I infer from this how great is the facility with which they toast those who want us to regenerate in order to make desirable an order of things that feeds pride and aristocracy. He who has predicted a change in this admirable country is not delirious. Luxury is the great corrupter, and here too it is going to be introduced in great strides (I am speaking of the great maritime cities). In Rome, it also began to be introduced first at the tables of virtuous republicans, and therefore perhaps they did not fear that it would be the beginning of the decay and end of such an old republic. We also have the greatest inclination towards luxury, and God free me from temptation of that foreign gold which brings with it sumptuous palaces, coaches, lackeys, great banquets, operas, etc. Liberty would be ruined. It is for this reason that the French cannot form a republic; although they are generally enlightened, their customs cannot coexist with such a system. I predict, therefore, a holy horror from that European love of luxury which corrupts customs and creates an aristocracy. Perhaps some of my compatriots will laugh to hear me speak out against luxury since it is, on the other hand, also a powerful motive to make wealth among the people; well and good if they laugh. I want citizens with republican values and moderate fortunes, although New Granada will never raise itself to the level of England. In these United States, they say that people in the interior are rude, without manners, and almost uncouth; yet all are able to eat, all love their laws, all live contentedly, all are fully aware of their duties to their country, to each other, and to their Creator. In no town in Ohio or Kentucky is there an Italian opera, grand soirées, or luxurious carriages, but there are schools, cheerfulness, charitable societies, roads, canals, and impassive laws. This is what I want for my own country.

3

Brazilians in France, 1822–1872: Doubly Outsiders

Roderick J. Barman

One of the most striking trends to accompany Latin American independence from Spain and Portugal was the growing tendency among elites of the region to regard these former colonial powers as hopelessly backward and retrograde. At the same time, Latin American elites eagerly embraced France as the epitome of modernity and civilization. Indeed, nineteenth-century Latin American elites viewed France as a model for everything from statecraft to fashion, architecture to military matters, literature to social rituals. Naturally, travel to France and especially to Paris accelerated during this period, as Latin Americans made the pilgrimage to witness for themselves the wonders of French culture and society. Historian Roderick Barman examines the flow of Brazilians to France from the time of Brazilian independence in 1822 to the 1870s. He suggests that while a generalized admiration for French culture certainly united Brazilian travelers, particular motivations and needs were also at work. Duress, escape, education, profit, and pleasure all played a role in sending Brazilians of various ages and occupations to France. Similarly, numerous challenges that included separation, culture shock, language, loneliness, and financial deprivation often complicated these Brazilians' time in France.

Barman makes use of Pierre Bourdieu's concept of "cultural capital" to assert that most Brazilians who spent time in France were able to "capitalize" on their European experiences upon their return. For many, a French education and familiarity with French culture translated into real social and economic advancement in their homeland, even helping people of African descent to climb the social hierarchy. Barman argues persuasively that given the importance attached to European experience, few Brazilians spent their time in France languishing in cafés and dance halls. Rather, he depicts the Brazilian presence in France during this period as largely industrious and enterprising. Nevertheless, Barman also finds that it was Brazilians' mastery of French culture that could alienate them from their homeland, making their full reintegration into Brazilian political and social life impossible. While Barman focuses on the Brazilian presence in France, his observations have much relevance for the experiences of other Latin American travelers to the Old World.

"A bony face, a dark skin, a fiery eye, a stiff military bearing are what identify the Brazilian citizen in the middle of the cosmopolitan population of Paris," wrote a contributor to *Les étrangers à Paris* (*The foreigners in Paris*), published in the mid 1840s. "The blood of three different races often mixes in his veins. He himself constitutes a fourth race. If you want to see the character of the Brazilian, you should not visit the residence of the envoy of Dom Pedro II, in the rue Neuve-des-Capuchines. Instead turn your steps towards the Pont-Neuf, enter the passage Dauphin, and there you will find the *Hôtel du Brésil.*"[1]

Of the twenty-four communities of foreigners portrayed in *Les étrangers à Paris*, Brazil was the sole Latin American country to merit inclusion. There is a certain justice to this choice. For many Spanish Americans, Paris was indeed the center of civilization, but Brazilians in particular flocked to France, the very model and exemplar of what they wanted their country to be. The Franco-Brazilian connection predated national independence in 1822 and it endured well into the twentieth century. In the French census of 1891, Brazilian nationals resident in France far outnumbered the citizens of any Spanish American nation.[2] In 1922 the Brazilian government endowed a new chair in the Faculty of Medicine at Paris, evidence of Brazilian medicine's debt to the medical profession in France.

The connection between Brazil and France took many forms and ran in many channels. Educated Brazilians were avid consumers of French culture, particularly books and periodicals, while the small French community in Brazil carried great weight in artistic and literary circles. The most significant channel of influence was certainly the Brazilians who went to France and, by residing there, absorbed its culture and its way of life. Upon their return, they spread that culture and way of life among their countrymen. This chapter examines the group of Brazilians residing in France during the fifty years following independence in 1822. It was during this time especially that Brazil was struggling to form itself as a nation state and when communications with Europe were still slow and uncertain. This text analyzes the reasons why Brazilians went to France, the challenges that they faced, and their experiences there. It concludes by looking at the positions that these travelers held in Brazil following their return home.

The number of Brazilians who went to France in the half century after 1822 is not easy to establish, in part because the reasons for a stay there were so diverse, and in part because the possible destinations within France itself were numerous. Research into a variety of sources suggests that several hundred Brazilians resided in France in the half century after independence. In comparison with the total populations of Brazil and France, respectively nine and thirty-six million in 1872, the group of Brazilians was minuscule in size; however, social and cultural conditions in Brazil magnified its members' importance. Only a small part of the Brazilian population was literate in the nineteenth century, and only a tiny minority possessed the means and the courage to leave their country for a considerable period.

Brazilians who went to France gained, no matter what they actually did there, what Pierre Bourdieu has termed "cultural capital." They acquired cultural and social attributes that allowed them, on returning to Brazil, to exert considerable influence over other groups—power that they used to obtain preferred occupational positions and to legitimate their claims to a greater share of economic resources.[3] Three examples demonstrate this point. Francisco de Sales Torres Homem was the child of a liaison between a Catholic priest and a black street vendor who had been a slave. His exceptional talents soon gained him a reputation as a journalist, but both his physical appearance and his origins kept doors closed to him until he was sent in 1833 (at public expense) to study in France. His sojourn in Paris and acquisition of a law degree acted as the key to his future success.[4] When he died in 1876—suitably in a hotel room in Paris— he was a senator, councilor of state, and had served twice as Minister of Finance. João Manuel Pereira da Silva, a politician who had studied in Paris in the mid-1830s, suffered a crushing defeat in his attempt to be reelected to the Chamber of Deputies in 1856. Thereupon he left for a long visit to France where, in 1858, he placed an article on the Brazilian Empire in the *Revue des Deux Mondes*, the leading scholarly journal in France. This success rehabilitated his prestige and allowed him to resume his political career, which culminated with his selection as senator.[5] Ernesto de Sousa e Oliveira Coutinho was the illegitimate but recognized son of Aureliano de Sousa e Oliveira Coutinho, viscount of Sepetiba, a leading politician. "I arranged to have him educated in France and then he qualified in medicine at Rio de Janeiro," the viscount stated in his will. "I know that, according to the law, he cannot inherit my estate jointly with his siblings who are legitimate offspring and, therefore, I sought to compensate him by educating him in France and providing him with a noble vocation such as medicine with which, if he has good sense, he can enjoy an independent status and make his fortune like so many others in similar circumstances in society."[6]

The attraction of France for Brazilians long antedated the gaining of independence. During the colonial period the principal ties, both psychological and cultural, had been to Portugal, and so it was to the mother country that the Brazilian-born went for education and improvement. Once in Portugal, many were caught by the allure of France, which had exerted its influence over the Portuguese since the early 1500s. By the late eighteenth century, men born in Brazil were studying at French universities. The most celebrated was José Joaquim de Maia Barbalho, a student at Montpellier, who on October 1786 wrote to Thomas Jefferson, then U.S. envoy in Paris, requesting assistance so that Brazil might gain its independence.[7]

Even after Portugal and France went to war in 1808 following the Napoleonic invasion and the Portuguese government's escape to Rio de Janeiro, some Brazilians continued to live in France. One of them was José Antônio Soares de Sousa, who in October 1806 married a French woman. Their first child, a son, was born a year later at 42, rue des Postes in Paris. This child, bearing his father's name, eventually became a leading statesman of the Brazilian Empire, one of the founders of the Conservative party, and a very successful minister of Foreign Affairs.[8] Like other Brazilians, the Soares de Sousa family left France in 1814 when Napoleon I was deposed and the long cycle of wars was over.

The return of peace in Europe encouraged direct exchanges between Brazil and France. The French educational system, created by Napoleon I and retained by the restored Bourbon monarchy, far exceeded the wretched facilities then available in Brazil. The struggle for Independence (1822–1825) and the usurpation of the Portuguese Crown by D. Miguel in 1828 disrupted Brazilian dependence on Portugal. While Great Britain usually treated Brazil with highhandedness, as the commercial treaties imposed in 1810 and 1827 bore witness, France gave far less cause for suspicion.[9] In virtually no time at all, France had replaced the former mother country as the exemplar. "The Frenchman is the beloved child of Brazil's heart, indeed he is," complained a work published in 1857, "the Frenchman in particular enjoys the greatest sympathy."[10]

France drew Brazilians like a magnet, even though, before the coming of the steamship lines in the early 1850s, travel across the Atlantic was not cheap, easy, or certain. Depending upon the winds, the journey on a sailing ship might take six weeks or two and one-half months. "Some hours later I began to vomit," a youth of seventeen described his departure from Rio de Janeiro in 1844. "I found myself obliged to lie down, and prostrate. I remained for 3 days, clothed as I was! I can't describe to you how I felt. On the 4th day I got up feeling well, but without being able to eat meals for two weeks, during which I ate almost nothing, because I had a great difficulty in adjusting to the French food, although in the end I got used to it."[11] Most Brazilians came ashore at Le Havre, a port at the mouth of the Seine River, which conducted the bulk of French trade with Brazil. Far fewer arrived at Brest, Nantes, or Bordeaux, the other Atlantic ports of France. The voyage to Marseilles, which enjoyed a vigorous trade with Brazil, was far enough to discourage Brazilians from making that port their destination.

The travelers to France were overwhelmingly male. In 1825 and 1837 less than 10 percent of the Brazilians listed as being in France were women.[12] Until the final three decades of the century the status of women in Brazil was one of exclusion and seclusion. Females who visited France went as wives, daughters, and mothers. Certainly there were more women present than the diplomatic correspondence records; however, they were not numerous. Most male Brazilians in France were either adolescents or young adults not yet married. Diverse reasons took them to France. Some had to go while others eagerly left Brazil for the land of civilization and pleasure. The causes can be grouped into five categories, embodying increasing degrees of willingness: duress, escape, education, profit, and pleasure. Although some overlap existed between categories, each needs to be considered in turn.

Some Brazilians left their homeland for their country's good. At moments of political crisis in 1822, 1823, and 1842, the Brazilian government deported politicians whom it considered dangerous to the public order. The fact that the place of exile was France and that the exiled received financial support softened the insult and made the banishment tolerable. For instance, in 1823, José Clemente Pereira, who had played an important role in the struggle for independence, told the Brazilian envoy in Paris that he wanted to go back to Brazil but only if the emperor consented.[13] Eventually those deported returned to Brazil, enhanced not only by their status as martyrs but also by their familiarity with France and its culture. At the end of 1842, the Brazilian envoy remarked about the political exiles who had just arrived in Paris: "I am convinced that their first and only concern is to spend in the most agreeable way possible the time they must reside in Europe."[14] The envoy went on to request authorization to grant the men passports to return to Brazil in advance so that, when their exile was revoked, there would be no unnecessary delays.

Some politicians and journalists, facing the government's wrath, found it advisable to withdraw for a time from Brazil. Pedro de Araújo Lima arrived in Paris in July 1824 and remained there (with side trips to the provinces and to Italy) until August 1826, when he returned home to take his seat in the first Chamber of Deputies. Araújo Lima behaved with great discretion while in Paris and went on to serve as regent of Brazil (1837–1840) and three times as prime minister (as the marquis of Olinda). Such good behavior was not the case with José da Natividade Saldanha, who had been an activist in the 1824 uprising in the northeast. From the moment of his arrival in Paris on January 16, 1825, the Parisian police had him under surveillance. His reputation as a radical, his African ancestry, and his contacts with the Brazilian community led to his deportation from France at the start of February.[15] José da Natividade Saldanha was exceptional. In general Brazilians eschewed politics while abroad. When Paris rose in revolt in 1831 against King Charles X, in 1848 against King Louis Philippe, and in 1871 to establish the Commune, Brazilians did not figure among the foreigners supporting the republican and revolutionary cause.

A more subtle form of exile under duress occurred when fathers decided to send their adolescent sons to study in a French *collège* (or high school) or to learn a vocation. In July 1825 the Brazilian envoy listed about thirty-five Brazilians enrolled in high school, but the number was certainly considerably higher.[16] In March 1842 the viscount of Goiana sent his son Aires de Albuquerque Gama, age nine, to be educated in France at the cost of the emperor D. Pedro II.[17] Two years later, a father sending his son to Paris to learn hat manufacturing declared: "Our separation will last for as long as it is necessary for your attaining the goal to which you are destined. All your suffering and work will be rewarded by the profits the future promises you; and if you carry out this task well, you will bless the memory of your father who not without great sacrifice separated himself from you at the age of 17."[18] For ambitious families who stood outside the magic circle of power and influence, sending their sons to France offered the prospects of success and advancement otherwise unavailable in Brazil. Such was the case with Justiniano José da Rocha, a dark mulatto, who was a student at the Collège Henri IV in Paris from 1824 to 1828. He went on to become a leading journalist, publishing newspapers in support of the Conservative party, which rewarded him by arranging his election as a national deputy from Minas Gerais province in 1843, 1850, and 1853.[19]

Another reason for going to France was to escape from a career that had gone sour or a life that had lost its direction. Odorico Mendes played a leading role in the Liberal opposition to D. Pedro I and in the organization of the emperor's dethronement in April 1831. In the mid-1830s, Mendes lost his appetite for politics and, upon retiring from his government post in 1847, withdrew to France where he spent the rest of his days occupying himself with translating Latin classics into Portuguese. In 1876, at the very end of the period under analysis, Francisco de Sales Torres Homem, sick and depressed, abandoned his political career and sailed for France in a vain search for health and happiness. Following the introduction of steamship lines between Brazil and Europe at the start of the 1850s, an innovation which made continued contact with Brazil much more feasible, withdrawal from Brazil and residence in France ceased to be a step of definitive separation. Typical was the case of Aureliano Cândido Tavares Bastos, a member of the Liberal party who had made his reputation as the advocate of structural change. Disillusioned with politics, skeptical that radical reforms could ever be achieved, and suffering in his health, Tavares Bastos moved in April 1874 with his wife and two children to Europe. Settling in Paris, the family adapted with little difficulty to their new life.

Although his letters occasionally expressed a longing for his native land, Tavares Bastos felt entirely at home in Europe and did not greatly protest when the doctors advised that he prolong his stay there.[20]

Education was certainly the principal reason that drew Brazilians to France. At the start of 1825, the British agent at Rio reported that the government intended to send a number of military officers for training in Europe. He remarked that they would probably go to France, "it being the fashion to look to that country for every kind of Education."[21] In the first half of the nineteenth century France possessed the most systematic and inclusive system of schooling in Europe. Secondary and higher education was under the control of a state authority known as L'Université (but which was in no way a university). The system was organized around the acquisition of the *baccalauréat* (successful completion of secondary studies), the *licence* (successful completion of university training), and the *doctorat* (successful completion of a thesis). Most doctorates were in law or medicine; fewer were in science. The key to the system was not attendance in classes but the passing of exams at each level. In addition, there existed a number of specialized technical schools, such as the Ecôles des Arts et Métiers, which offered training in specific vocations. A number of painters and sculptors studied in Paris but many more were attracted to Italy, which was considered in the early nineteenth century to be the center of artistic life and training.[22] The system was well suited to offer education to foreigners who came with specific needs. The quality of education, particularly in medicine and engineering, was very high, probably surpassing the education available throughout the rest of Europe at that time.[23]

The appeal of this system for Brazilians was enormous. Notwithstanding the considerable risks and disadvantages involved, great numbers came to France to study in various subjects and in different regions of the country. While the majority were probably concentrated in Paris, Brazilians can be traced to private high schools in Orléans and Rouen, the Faculty of Law at Toulouse, and the special school of commerce at Marseilles. In October 1829 the Brazilian envoy observed "the advantage which we have already drawn and which can yet flow from the coming to this kingdom of a large portion of the society of the Empire, with the goal of acquiring various types of knowledge, some of which still cannot be fully obtained in our country."[24] A private letter written from Paris in 1837 confirms this assessment of the situation: "Do you want to know, my dear Ângelo, whether I am content with coming to Europe? Oh! My good friend, it's certainly something I will never be able to regret. Would that I had done it a long time ago! And would that I had employed here the 6 years (oh! how I bewail them) that I lost in the uselessness of my [law] studies at Olinda!"[25]

Immediate profit was yet another significant cause for Brazilians to come to France. Brazilian merchants moved to France in order to participate in the transatlantic trade in which Brazilian coffee, cotton, and other primary products were exchanged for French luxury goods and manufactures. These merchants, to be found mainly in Paris and Le Havre, were never considerable in number and they did not form an important or influential part of the Brazilian community. More numerous were the artisans and other skilled workers who crossed the Atlantic in the hope of learning new techniques or otherwise improving their skills in France. In 1839 a painter from Pernambuco took exactly this gamble when he went with his family to Paris, "bringing only small resources which he in a short time exhausted."[26] Already mentioned was Lúcio Antônio Guimarães de Lemos, who ventured to Paris at the age of seventeen to learn the art of making hats. He stayed there for one year, eventually boasting: "I am already making 5 silk hats a day, which is not bad for an apprentice of two months' experience."[27] Artisans wanted to acquire not just technical skills but also familiarity with the French fashions that were faithfully followed by Brazilians with any claim to style.

The final reason why Brazilians came to France was simple pleasure. France, and above all Paris, offered all the comforts of life, the riches of high culture, and the opportunities for self-indulgence. Once experienced, *la douceur de la vie* (the sweetness of life) was hard to resist. José Marcelino Gonçalves, a leading merchant of Rio de Janeiro, moved to Paris around 1820 and never returned to Brazil. Presumably his wealth was sufficient to support life in the French capital. Domiciano de Oliveira Arruda was a *rentier* living on his investments, who died in mid-1849 at no. 18, rue Clichy, Paris.[28] José da Rocha Faria made a considerable fortune supplying the Brazilian forces during the Paraguayan War (1865–1870). At its close, Rocha Faria liquidated his business and settled in Paris, living at no. 80, boulevard Malesherbes, but he took good care to maintain his links with the ruling circles in Brazil, being made successively baron, viscount, and count of Nioac. When D. Pedro II visited Europe in 1876–77, Nioac established a friendship with the emperor that endured until the latter's death in 1891.

In the years before 1870, few Brazilians could afford to settle permanently in France. Much more frequent was the practice of spending a year or so there, at their own or—if they could manage it—at the government's expense. Such was the case with Henrique Veloso de Oliveira, a judge of the Appeals Court at Recife, who "made, from Pernambuco, with the government's consent, a journey through the most cultured countries of Europe." In January 1838 he was at Paris, where he had clearly been residing for some time. In December 1854, after Paulino José Soares de Sousa had completed five successful but exhausting years as Brazil's foreign minister, the new government appointed him on a special mission to negotiate a frontier treaty with France. This mission gave him sixteen months' residence in Paris without too much work or responsibility, since it soon became clear that the French were little interested in concluding a treaty on the frontier between Brazil and French Guiana.[29] Quick visits to Europe became more feasible as time passed and the number of transatlantic steamship lines proliferated. Late in 1868, Cristiano Ottoni, a retired professor of engineering at the Academia de Marinha and a radical Liberal who had just lost his seat as a national deputy, "took a trip to Europe and Egypt, in order to visit the great construction projects, the Suez canal and the Mont Cenis tunnel, and I found myself back here again in January 1869."[30]

While their reasons for travel to France were varied, Brazilians were united in the five challenges that awaited them: separation, cultural shock, language, loneliness, and finances. As has already been stressed, the voyage by sail was long and uncertain. After the early 1850s the steamship cut the length of travel down to one month and above all brought regularity to the journey. Nevertheless, not until the middle of the 1870s did the laying of the South Atlantic cable put Brazil into direct, constant, and almost instantaneous contact with Europe. Prior to that time the Brazilians who went to France were isolated. In 1844 it took three months for Lúcio Antônio Guimarães de Lemos to receive a letter from his father, and so half a year might easily pass before any consultation could occur.[31]

What compounded this isolation from home was the evident cultural shock experienced by those who went to France. Despite the common religion, the two countries differed considerably. The unfamiliar food was a real problem. As one contemporary observer remarked: "generally the Brazilian students who live here in a boarding school or a pension complain about the food, and I think they are right. Having been accustomed to going to the larder for some fruit preserve at any time of the day, here they have to be satisfied with a piece of bread and what passes here for cheese."[32] Lúcio Antônio Guimarães de Lemos asked his father to send him some *doce de goiaba* (guava preserve), for "it does not cost much and it is highly appreciated."[33] Another problem was the cold and dark European winter, which Brazilians found deeply depressing. "The darkness of winter (it is 4 o'clock and I am already using candles), the cold (the thermometer is below zero), the snow which has already started to fall, breed in me a melancholy which I can't dispel," wrote the viscount of Uruguay from Paris early in December 1854.[34] Writing to his parents in January 1863, Antônio da Silva Prado, then studying in Paris, complained that "it rains incessantly, which makes leaving the house unpleasant due to the mud in the streets." A month later he voiced a very different complaint about the weather. "We have had no winter, which hasn't pleased me, because I wanted to see the skating, and there has been insufficient cold to freeze the ponds in the Bois de Boulogne where this recreation takes place."[35]

A third challenge was the necessity to acquire fluent French. Not everyone had the skill of Francisco de Sales Torres Homem. His years in

Paris gave him "a profound knowledge of the French language, which he spoke and wrote admirably," according to the viscount of Taunay, himself bilingual in Portuguese and French.[36] At the other extreme was the viscountess of Uruguay who did not "know a word of French, so that she cannot communicate even with the servants. The worst is that I believe that she will never learn it."[37] Most Brazilians coming to France were not in this predicament, but their command of French was often small or nonexistent. When in the spring of 1825 a government-sponsored group of military officers arrived in Paris in search of training, the Brazilian envoy noted that "they lack the grounding for any of the sciences and even knowledge of the language in which they will be taught."[38]

Brazilians in France generally added loneliness to their difficulties with separation from home, unfamiliar food and climate, and a new language. They were usually young and unmarried. Sometimes two or more brothers came, but often they traveled alone. Paris had all the glamor and all the anonymity of a large city, and Brazilians living there tended to seek out each other's company. The matriculation registers of the Faculty of Medicine at Paris, which include the students' current place of residence, show that the Brazilians studying medicine lived close to each other in groups of twos and threes.[39] In the opinion of Antônio da Silva Prado, who arrived at Paris in January 1863, "in general the Brazilians here are very disunited, to the contrary of what exists with the other nations."[40] However, the writer was a well-financed, well-connected young man, somewhat of a snob, who could afford to pick and choose his acquaintances in the French capital. The advantages that Prado enjoyed did not spare him the sorrows of separation. "It will be quite painful for me to spend this further time away," he wrote to his mother in March 1863 about prolonging his stay in Europe. "It's true that there are many diversions here, but what can make one forget family life, and the pleasures derived from parental love?"[41]

The final and probably most formidable challenge was that of finances. A good proportion of Brazilians in France went there with insufficient resources. In 1826 two brothers in the Collège Royale at Rouen wrote to the Brazilian envoy to explain their desperate situation. They had long wanted to become physicians and their relatives, giving way to their entreaties, sent them off to France, warning the young men that the family's ability to support them there was doubtful. In fact, money from home lasted only for one year and from then on they depended upon advances made by the Le Havre merchant charged with their care. When he cut off funds, they were left without means, turning then to the Brazilian envoy who provided sufficient money for their living expenses and the costs of taking the *baccalauréat*. Thanks to his advocacy, the Brazilian government agreed to fund the two young men's enrollment in the Faculty of Medicine at Paris.[42]

Insufficient means and hard circumstances were a constant theme among Brazilians in France, particularly those who were students. In October 1829 the Brazilian minister recommended that the government not issue passports to prospective students unless they were assured of a sufficient income. However, lack of finances was not always the problem.[43] The supply of funds from Brazil was difficult and uncertain. The usual practice was to arrange for money to be periodically sent (in the form of a bill of exchange) to a merchant in France, called the correspondent, who would then pay the student his *mesada* (monthly allowance). This system was extremely unreliable. The family could fail to supply the funds on time, the bill of exchange could go astray or be dishonored, and the merchant correspondent could default on his obligations or even disappear. Problems of this type recur constantly in the correspondence from the Brazilian envoys in Paris.[44] A typical case was that of Francisco Xavier de Oliveira Pereira, who in 1829 was a second-year law student at Toulouse. His family had stopped sending him a *mesada*, and he was by then 1,635 francs in debt. He turned for relief to the Brazilian envoy at Paris.[45]

The best but by no means infallible way in which to avoid such pitfalls was to secure a stipend from the Brazilian government. Francisco de Sales Torres Homem came in 1832 to Paris ostensibly as a first-class attaché to the Brazilian mission but was excused from performing any diplomatic services so that he could study for a law degree.[46] In the case of another student, the Brazilian legation was ordered to pay him 150 francs per month. The envoy refused to carry out the instructions, since paying out such a sum would have reduced the legation's monthly budget by one half.[47] More common than arrangements of this type was the grant of stipends for study in France by the national or provincial governments. Early in 1825 the imperial government chose a group of well-connected young men, mostly military officers, and sent them to study technical subjects in France. However, the number of these grants was never large, nor did the national or provincial governments provide reliable and long-term support. Grant holders were always at risk of finding their support withdrawn or simply not paid. Early in 1828, a mounting fiscal crisis forced the national government to order the group of young men to break off their studies and to return at once to Brazil.[48] The passage of time did not improve matters. In 1865 a student in Paris wrote to the emperor D. Pedro II, explaining that the province of Bahia had sent him to study architecture. He went on to complain that after two years, the provincial assembly had failed to renew his stipend and so he lacked the funds to complete the final two years of his training.[49]

Given the formidable nature of these challenges, it is not surprising that a number of Brazilians did not stay the course, as the diplomatic dispatches graphically report. Death claimed a few. Some could not resist the manifold pleasures that France and above all Paris offered. Others suffered from a loss of will to continue, physical exhaustion, or lack of funds. The usual outcome was the intervention of the Brazilian envoy, who paid for the individual's return home. But such cases were not common. Most Brazilians were dedicated and hardworking. A report from the prefect of police in Paris from the 1820s observed: "these young men, like the majority of their compatriots, are notable in the Faculty of Medicine for their diligence and their application."[50] Too much depended upon achieving success—their families' expectations and sacrifices, and their personal prospects for future advancement—for the Brazilians in France to yield to the challenges they faced during their time abroad.

The Brazilians' perseverance while in France was not entirely motivated by self-interest. A good number of the young men acquired a sense of mission, as the contents of the review, *Niterói, Revista Brasiliense*, published in Paris in 1836 and 1837, make clear. Proclaiming "our ardent desire to see our country advance on the road of civilization and of progress," the review's editors promised that, after returning to Brazil, they "would continue to sacrifice our studies to the benefit of the country, without expectation of rewards other than the satisfaction of our having contributed to the building of the edifice of our enlightenment."[51] Brazil had to prove itself to be the equal of France, and its citizens residing abroad were battling in that cause. In December 1863, Antônio da Silva Prado, having received three printed collections of poems from home, remarked: "I intend to translate some of them into French in order to show them to some friends, and to have the pleasure of seeing our poets appreciated by strangers, who generally tend to view us as uneducated or savages, reproaches that justice will not support."[52]

For the overwhelming majority of the Brazilians who went to France, the challenges and the sacrifices that they had endured were justified by the benefits they reaped upon their return. Most made successful careers, using the qualifications that they had obtained. The most eminent in terms of public service were Francisco de Sales Torres Homem, viscount of Inhomerim; Carlos Carneiro de Campos, third viscount of Caravelas; and Cândido Batista de Oliveira. Each rose to be a senator and a member of the Council of State, and each served as minister more than once. Others became national deputies and served as provincial presidents. Among those educated in France were several professors at the two law schools, the two medical faculties, and at the Rio Polytechnic School. Their number also included bureaucrats and diplomats. They were poets, painters, and writers. In 1853, of the thirteen *médicos da imperial câmara* (court physicians), seven held degrees from the medical faculties of Paris or Montpellier. Those who pursued less exalted vocations and professions upon their return to Brazil have left scant evidence about their subsequent lives; nevertheless, the fact that the stream of ordinary Brazilians seeking training in France continued to swell during the second half of the nineteenth century suggests that these men also were successful. The number going to France became so great that in December 1880, D. Isabel and the count d'Eu, the heir to the Brazilian throne and her husband, then on a long stay in Europe, played a central role in founding a Brazilian charitable society in Paris. "It can come to be greatly useful for our poor artisans who come here to train and for other Brazilians who don't have the means to return to our country," D. Isabel told her father, D. Pedro II, when making a request for a donation to the fund from her parents.[53]

If most of the Brazilians who had been trained in France did secure success following their return home, a review of the lives of those who made their careers within the ruling circles suggests that the benefits they had gained came at a certain cost. The men trained in France did not dominate the public life of Brazil to the degree that might be anticipated from their superior skills and their copious "cultural capital." In many ways they were and continued to be throughout their lives outsiders in their native land. They had been separated from the bulk of their contemporaries in the crucial years of late adolescence and early adulthood, a period when the networks of friendship and obligation, crucial for subsequent success, were formed. To reach the very top in politics and administration, men had to be true insiders (ideally, graduates of the São Paulo or Recife law faculties), something that the French-educated could never be.[54]

Further, long residence in France made the members of this group distinctive in their outlook, habits, and expectations from those of their contemporaries who had remained in Brazil. In a sense the rewards offered by their native land could not compete with those available in Europe. An excellent example is Antônio Peregrino Maciel Monteiro, who went to France from Pernambuco in May 1823, shortly after his nineteenth birthday. Not until May 1829 did he acquire his doctorate in medicine and he returned home to Pernambuco in August of that year, after an absence of over six years.[55] In 1834 he was elected as a national deputy from Pernambuco and he served from September 1837 to April 1839 as minister of Foreign Affairs. In 1850 he was chosen to be president of the Chamber of Deputies, a position of some influence. Three years later, in September 1853, he used his political connections to secure the post of Brazilian envoy to Lisbon, which he occupied for the rest of his life. Essentially, at the age of forty-nine, he opted out of public life in Brazil and went back to the Europe that had shaped his character and culture. The same held true for two of the three editors of *Niterói, Revista Brasiliense*, young men who in 1837 had vowed that, upon returning to Brazil, they would "sacrifice our studies to the benefit of the country." Francisco de Sales Torres Homem did make his entire career in Brazil, but both Domingos José Gonçalves de Magalhães, viscount of Araguaia, and Manuel de Araújo Pôrto Alegre, baron of Santo Ângelo, did not so persevere.

Gonçalves de Magalhães had a high reputation as a poet and novelist. His service as a government bureaucrat secured him in 1845 a seat in the Chamber of Deputies. However, in 1847, he entered the Brazilian foreign service as envoy in several (mainly European) countries and made only occasional visits to his native land. Pôrto Alegre, a well-regarded painter and writer, held a number of government posts until 1859, when he secured the appointment as consul general in Berlin. He left Brazil never to return.

Ironically, the very qualities that prevented this group of Brazilians from dominating public affairs were precisely those that assured these travelers of their influence on the formation of a national culture. Their familiarity with French culture, their continuing ties with friends in France, and their understanding of the dynamics of European life made them both mentors of their contemporaries, including the emperor, and interpreters to Brazilians of the civilized world that flourished on the other side of the Atlantic. In 1876, D. Pedro II, Brazil's ruler from 1840 to 1889, referred to "my two countries, Brazil and France, the latter the country of my intellect and the former the country of my heart and my birth."[56] Consciously or not, the men who had lived in France provided the model to which cultured Brazilians aspired to conform. By their activities in politics, administration, and culture, the members of this group prevented any questioning of that model or its challenge by a competitor. Indeed, not until the second half of the twentieth century would France be displaced in Brazilian opinion as the ideal society and culture.

Notes

1. Paul Merruau, "Le Brésilien," in Louis Desnoyers et al., *Les étrangers à Paris* (Paris: Charles Warée, n.d.), 361–63. Internal evidence indicates publication after March 1844.

2. There were 866 Brazilians, compared to 366 Argentines, 248 Mexicans, and 190 Chileans; see France, *Dénombrement des étrangers en France (Résultats statistiques du dénombrement de 1891)* (Paris: Imprimerie Nationale, 1893), lxxxvii–lxxxix. Thanks to Dr. Ingrid Fey for this reference.

3. See Pierre Bourdieu, *Distinction: A Social Critique of the Judgement of Taste*, trans. Richard Nice (Cambridge, MA: Harvard University Press, 1984), 53–54, 114–15.

4. Arquivo Histórico do Itamarati (hereafter AHI) Correspondência (hereafter Corr.) 225 - 1 - 4 José Joaquim da Rocha to Bento da Silva Lisboa (future baron of Cairu), n. 18, Paris, August 2, 1833; Raymundo Magalhães Jr., *Três panfletários do segundo reinado* (São Paulo, Brazil: Companhia Editora Nacional, 1956), 3–43; and Alfredo d'E. Taunay, viscount of Taunay, *Reminiscencias*, 2d ed. (São Paulo, Brazil: Companhia Melhoramentos, 1923), 33–80.

5. J. M. Pereira da Silva, "Le Brésil sous l'empereur Dom Pedro II," *Revue des Deux Mondes* 14 (April 1858); and Augusto Vitorino Alves Sacramento Blake, *Diccionario Bibliographico Brazileiro* (Rio de Janeiro: Imprensa Nacional, 1892), 3: 479–85.

6. Fourth paragraph of the will, made on December 31, 1853, quoted in Thalita de Oliveira Casadei, "Testamento do visconde de Sepetiba," *Mensário do Arquivo Nacional* 5, n. 4 (April 1974): 24.

7. See the letters of Maia Barbalho to Thomas Jefferson, Montpellier, October 2 and November 21, 1786, in Julian P. Boyd, ed., *The Papers of Thomas Jefferson* (Princeton, NJ: Princeton University Press, 1954), 10:427 and 546–47.

8. See José Antônio Soares de Sousa, *A vida do visconde do Uruguaí (1807–1866)* (São Paulo, Brazil: Companhia Editora Nacional, 1944), 9–12.

9. On relations between Brazil and Great Britain, see Roderick J. Barman, *Brazil: The Forging of a Nation, 1798–1852* (Stanford, CA: Stanford University Press, 1988), 47–48 and 147–48.

10. Um Brasileiro, *A utilidade dos portugueses no Brasil* (Rio de Janeiro: Typographia Americana, 1857), 65–66.

11. Lúcio Antônio Guimarães de Lemos to José Antônio de Lemos (future baron of Rio Verde), Le Havre, October 5, 1844, transcribed in Roberto Macedo, *O barão de Rio Verde (José Antônio de Lemos), rehabilitação de um esquecido* (Rio de Janeiro: Alba, 1940), 144.

12. Only ten females are included in the list of 137 Brazilians residing in France, drawn up by the Brazilian envoy in July 1825, and none of them has a name, being simply "wife" or "daughter," see AHI Corr. 224 - 4 - 13 "Lista da maior parte dos brasileiros existentes em França em julho 1825," enclosed in Domingos Borges de Barros (future viscount of Pedra Branca) to Luís José de Carvalho e Melo (future viscount of Cachoeira), n. 77, Paris, July 20, 1825. In the list of Brazilians resident in Paris at the end of 1837 and the list of those who had left France during 1837, only 6 out of 146 were female; see the lists in AHI Corr. 225 - 1 - 6.

13. AHI Corr. 224 - 4 - 13 Manuel Rodrigues Gameiro Pessoa (future viscount of Itabaiana) to José Bonifácio de Andrada e Silva, n. 29, Paris, April 14, 1823.

14. AHI Corr. 224 - 4 - 13 José de Araújo Ribeiro to Aureliano de Sousa e Oliveira Coutinho, n. 41, Paris, December 30, 1842.

15. See Alberto Rangel, *Textos e pretextos: Incidentes na chronica brasileira a luz de documentos conservados na Europa* (Tours, France: Typographie Arrault, 1926), 33–35 and 36–38, drawing on the police records conserved in ANP F7 6731–6737.

16. AHI Corr. 224 - 4 - 13 Data taken from "Lista da maior parte dos brasileiros existentes em França em julho 1825," enclosed in Domingos Borges de Barros (future viscount of Pedra Branca) to Luís José de Carvalho e Melo (future viscount of Cachoeira), n. 77, Paris, July 20, 1825.

17. Arquivo do Museu Imperial, Petrópolis, Coleção Pedro d'Orléans e Bragança, Maço 105, Documento 5078 Viscount of Goiana to D. Pedro II, Pernambuco, March 27, 1842.

18. José Antônio de Lemos (future baron of Rio Verde) to Lúcio Antônio Guimarães de Lemos, Rio de Janeiro, July 23, 1844, transcribed in Macedo, *Rio Verde*, 71–72.

19. See Magalhães Jr., *Três panfletários*, 127–59.

20. See the thirty letters written by Tavares Bastos during his voyage to Europe and his stay there in 1874 and 1875 (when he died) transcribed in Aureliano Cândido Tavares Bastos, *Correspondência e catálogo de documentos da coleção da Biblioteca Nacional* (Brasília, Brazil: Senado Federal, 1977).

21. Great Britain, Public Record Office, Foreign Office 13, v. 8 Henry Chamberlain, Consul General, to George Canning, Foreign Secretary, no. 18, Rio de Janeiro, January 31, 1825.

22. AHI Corr. 225 - 4 - 7 Domingos Borges de Barros (future viscount of Pedra Branca) to Luís José de Carvalho e Melo (future viscount of Cachoeira), confidential, n. 17, Paris, June 5, 1825.

23. See Howard Davies Lewis, *The French Education System* (London: Croom Helm, 1985).

24. AHI Corr. 225 - 4 - 7 Marquis of Resende to marquis of Aracatí, confidential, no. 8, Paris, October 1829.

25. João Lins Vieira Cansanção de Sinimbu (future viscount of Sinimbu) to Ângelo Muniz da Silva Ferraz (future baron of Uruguaiana), Paris, March 30, 1837, in *Mensário do Arquivo Nacional* 9, n. 8 (August 1978): 17–19.

26. His name was Joaquim José de Carvalho; see AHI Corr. 225 - 1 - 7 José de Araújo Ribeiro (future viscount of Rio Grande) to Caetano Lopes Gama (future viscount of Maranguape), n. 1, Paris, January 3, 1840.

27. Lúcio Antônio Guimarães de Lemos to José Antônio de Lemos (future baron of Rio Verde), Paris, July 20, 1845, transcribed in Macedo, *Rio Verde*, 153. Lúcio returned to Brazil at the end of 1845, dying on February 2, 1846; see ibid., 56.

28. AHI Corr. 205 - 1 - 11 Death certificate enclosed in José Maria do Amaral to Paulino José Soares de Sousa (future viscount of Uruguay), Paris, no. 8, undated [but June–July 1850].

29. Soares de Sousa, *Uruguai*, 471–566.

30. Cristiano Ottoni, *Autobiographia* (Rio de Janeiro: Typographia Leuzinger, 1908), 174.

31. He had received "some days ago" his father's letter dated August 24; see Lúcio Antônio Guimarães de Lemos to José Antônio de Lemos (future baron of Rio Verde), Paris, December 13, 1844, transcribed in Macedo, *Rio Verde*, 146.

32. Instituto Histórico e Geográfico Brasileiro, Arquivo do Marquês de Olinda, Lata 210, Pasta 26 Copy of Pedro de Araújo Lima (future marquis of Olinda) to Manuel Zeferino dos Santos, Paris, May 31, 1825.

33. Lúcio Antônio Guimarães de Lemos to José Antônio de Lemos (future baron of Rio Verde), Paris, March 17, 1845, transcribed in Macedo, *Rio Verde*, 149.

34. Passage of a letter to José Maria da Silva Paranhos (future viscount of Rio Branco) cited in Soares de Sousa, *Uruguai*, 527–28.

35. Antônio da Silva Prado to D. Veridiana Prado, Paris, January 7 and February 7, 1863, quoted in Hélio Vianna, *Letras imperiais* (Rio de Janeiro: Ministério de Educação, 1961), 71–72.

36. Taunay, *Reminiscencias*, 30. Both of Taunay's parents were immigrants from France, and French was the language spoken at home.

37. Viscount of Uruguay to Paulino José Soares de Sousa Jr., Paris, early May 1855, cited in Soares de Sousa, *Uruguai*, 476.

38. AHI Corr. 224 - 4 - 14 Domingos Borges de Barros (future viscount of Pedra Branca) to Luís José de Carvalho e Melo (future viscount of Cachoeira), n. 72, Paris, July 1, 1825.

39. Based on the addresses given by Brazilian students in the matriculation books of the Faculté de Médecine now held in the Archives Nationales, Paris.

40. Antônio da Silva Prado to D. Veridiana Prado, Paris, January 7 and February 7, 1863, quoted in Vianna, *Letras Imperiais*, 71–72.

41. Same to Same, Paris, January 7 and March 1863, quoted in ibid., 71 and 74.

42. AHI Corr. 224 - 4 - 16 Baron of Pedra Branca to marquis of Inhambupe, n. 203, Paris, August 3, 1826, enclosing an undated letter (in French) from Francisco and Albino Ribeiro da Silva; and 224 - 4 - 18 Baron of Pedra Branca to marquis of Inhambupe, n. 291, Paris, February 2, 1827.

43. AHI Corr. 225 - 1 - 2 Marquis of Resende to marquis of Aracatí, confidential, n. 8, Paris, October 16, 1830.

44. See AHI Corr. 224 - 4 - 13 Joaquim Pinheiro de Campos to Manuel Rodrigues Gameiro Pessoa (future viscount of Itabaiana), Paris, May 20, 1823; 224 - 4 - 13 Domingos Borges de Barros (future viscount of Pedra Branca) to Luís José de Carvalho e Melo (future viscount of Cachoeira), n. 66, Paris, May 9, 1825; 224 - 4 -15 Baron of Pedra Branca to viscount of Paranaguá, n. 115, Paris, January 1, 1826, Same to marquis of Inhambupe, n. 163, Paris, May 21, 1826, Same to Same, n. 176, Paris, May 31, 1826; and 224 - 4 -16 Same to Same, no number, Paris, November 15, 1826.

45. AHI Corr. 225 - 1 - 2 Marquis of Resende to marquis of Aracatí, n. 8, Paris, January 27, 1830.

46. See AHI Corr. 225 - 1 - 4 José Joaquim da Rocha to Bento da Silva Lisboa (future baron of Cairu), n. 18, Paris, August 2, 1833; and 225 - 1 - 5 Luís Moutinho de Lima Alvares e Silva to Manuel Alves Branco (future viscount of Caravelas), n. 26, Paris, July 28, 1836.

47. AHI Corr. 225 - 4 - 8 Sérgio Teixeira de Macedo to Aureliano de Sousa e Oliveira Coutinho, confidential, ns. 8 and 10, Paris, August 29 and October 25, 1834.

48. AHI Corr. 224 - 4 - 19 João Antônio Pereira da Cunha to viscount of Inhambupe, ns. 17 and 19, Paris, April 25, 1828.

49. Arquivo do Museu Imperial, Petrópolis, Coleção Pedro d'Orléans e Bragança, Maço 137, Documento 6703 Francisco de Azevedo Monteiro Caminhoá to D. Pedro II, 106, rue Neuve des Mathurins, Paris, June 18, 1865.

50. Rangel, *Textos e pretextos*, 24, citing an undated report of the prefect of police at Paris.

51. *Niteroy, Revista Brasiliense. Sciencias, Lettras e Artes* (Paris), tomo I, parte II (1837), 262.

52. Antônio da Silva Prado to D. Veridiana Prado, Paris, December 24, 1863, quoted in Vianna, *Letras imperiais*, 82.

53. Arquivo Grão Pará, Petrópolis, XL - 2 D. Isabel to D. Pedro II, 27, rue de la Faisanderie, Paris, December 16, 1880.

54. See Barman, *Brazil*, 219.

55. See Luís Castro Sousa, *O poeta Maciel Monteiro: De médico a embaixador 1804–1868* (Recife: Conselho Municipal de Cultura, 1975), 25.

56. Diary entry for December 18, 1876, transcribed in "Voyage au Haut Nil," *Anuário do Museu Imperial* 8 (1947): 20.

4

"The More I See, the More Surprised I Am": Ramón de la Sagra, Baltimore, and the Concepts of Race and Poverty

Camilla Townsend

Although Cuba remained a colony of the Spanish Empire until 1898, Cuban intellectuals were not isolated from the reformist impulses spreading throughout Latin America during the height of the wars for independence and after. While the majority of the Cuban elite remained committed to slavery and the expansion of sugar production, many educated Cubans considered the growth of such institutions with concern, if not alarm. One of these educated persons was Ramón de la Sagra, a Spaniard who moved to Cuba at a young age to take up a career as a scientist. De la Sagra viewed science as having a vital role in the economic advancement of his adopted homeland. However, for him, economic prosperity was not an end in and of itself but rather a means toward achieving political and social democracy.

Historian Camilla Townsend argues that de la Sagra's conflation of scientific inquiry with economic nationalism and social justice emerged in its most articulate form only after his tour through the eastern seaboard of the United States in the 1840s. He wrote most passionately about Baltimore, a young American city that conjured up images of wealth and dynamism in the minds of Latin Americans who read excerpts from its press in their own newspapers. Like Andrés Bello and many other travelers discussed in this volume, de la Sagra sought useful information that would have a ready application to his homeland's situation. In Baltimore he visited the prison, poorhouse, several factories, and public and private schools. He then summed up his observations while living in Paris, far from his beloved Cuba. Only from such a safe distance was he able to criticize the entrenched economic institutions that he believed to be a hindrance to the national development necessary for the expansion of political and social democracy in Cuba.

As a Spaniard turned Cuban living in Paris, the figure of de la Sagra demonstrates the fluidity of national identity formation within a colonial situation. De la Sagra was in many ways a transnational citizen, both by choice and because he found no real acceptance in either Spain or Cuba. Ironically, de la Sagra's transnational perspective gave him an appreciation for the value of economic nationalism at a time when the majority of Latin American elites were most eager to embrace the internationalism of economic liberalism.

O ne summer Sunday evening in 1835, a gentleman from Cuba strolled through the streets of Baltimore. Ramón de la Sagra had been to the outskirts of town to see the public baths and the city's water supply. It was growing dark by the time he began to make his way back to the home of the doctor he was visiting. A little light escaped from uncurtained windows, and lanterns bobbed here and there in the hands of other people on the move. When de la Sagra reached the white marble tower of the city's new monument to General Washington, he paused. The June air smelled of flowers. There had been a militia display that day and the visiting participants were making camp on the surrounding hillside. A few musicians still played, and the sound carried into the otherwise quiet night. Only a few people talked and laughed as they wended their way home. Stray peach sellers and other peddlers wandered by. The foreigner looked at the people, men and women, black and white, and thought how unfamiliar the scene was to him. "The more I see of this country, the more I admire it, and the more surprised I am," he wrote in his diary that night. He thought of the enslaved people on the plantations of Cuba, and of the peasants he had seen in his youth in Spain. In those places, he thought, at the end of a holiday (military display) like this one, men would be carousing in the streets, wreaking havoc, trying desperately to forget what the morrow would bring. What was the underlying difference? he wondered. It was, he thought, that the people in this new country, with a constitution not yet fifty years old, were allowed their dignity and were not expected to swallow their pain as though it were food.[1]

In the typical vision of the nineteenth-century Latin American traveler abroad, Ramón de la Sagra was awed by the technological progress and high culture that he found in the United States. However, it was not the "bells and whistles" of progress that impressed de la Sagra but rather North Americans' relative social inclusiveness (later he would add that the advantages denied to former slaves were the exception). He believed that the inclusiveness that he witnessed explained the apparent economic prosperity of the young nation.

As a historical figure, Ramón de la Sagra is hard to pin down. He was born in Spain and moved to Cuba when he was twenty-two. He had been treated as an outsider in Havana. At thirty-six he was in the United States on his way to France, where he planned to live and take part in an international community of intellectuals who made their home there. In Paris, he became more Cuban than ever before. Others saw him as the man from the Indies, and he spent the rest of his life writing to and about the island. He was a prodigious scholar who corresponded with Alexander von Humboldt and scientists around the world. De la Sagra has been credited with paralleling the comments of Alexis de Tocqueville and foreshadowing the insights of Karl Marx. This comparison is not to say that he was more acute than either of these intellectuals, but rather that he was a thoughtful and articulate man, steeped in the dialogues of his age, an active element in the world that made the work of Tocqueville and Marx possible. His life of travel and foreign residence suggests the power that such experiences possess to stimulate thought about national development and national identity.[2]

Havana and Cuba

Ramón Dionisio José de la Sagra was born in 1798 in La Coruña, Galicia, the northwestern province of Spain that juts out into the Atlantic Ocean. La Coruña is a port town where a child in the harbor could imagine looking north toward England or west toward the Americas. Ramón's father was a successful merchant who had met his wife while traveling in Saint Augustine, Florida. When Ramón was three, his older brother left for Montevideo, Uruguay, to set up a business, and never came back. After grade school, Ramón attended La Coruña's Nautical School for a year, where all the students studied geography, navigation, physics, and drafting. Then he attended a military boarding school in nearby Santiago de Campostela. When he was eighteen he entered the university there and studied successively pharmaceuticals, math, medicine, and anatomy. Meanwhile, he and a close friend became known for making loud and blunt liberal statements. When the Inquisition threatened to punish him for such thinking, he transferred to the University of Madrid. Throughout this entire period, Ramón daydreamed about the Americas about which he had heard so much during his childhood. Ultimately he knew that he wanted to take his knowledge to the New World.

In 1821, de la Sagra left for Cuba. He went as an assistant to Don Agustín Rodríguez y Fernández, a distant relative who had been awarded the directorship of the new Factoría General del Tabaco, which was intended to render Cuba less dependent on the processing factories in Europe and the United States. De la Sagra had read the work of German traveler and scientist Alexander von Humboldt, including his recent book on Cuba, and so he was familiar with the baron's vision of a "wild and gigantic nature," the discourse of "abundance and innocence" with which he characterized the Americas, and his view of an untamed world

awaiting European knowledge to turn the savannah into fields and the
trees into cabinets.[3] De la Sagra was young, enthusiastic, and full of knowledge. As he crossed the ocean for the first time, he felt the conviction that
he was part of a great project, an ongoing chain of events. He would remember those moments years later in his *Histoire physique, politique et
naturelle de l'Ile de Cuba*: "In tracing the history of the Cuban land, the
imagination turns involuntarily to the discovery of the New World, the
memorable epoch under the Catholic kings when new climates were met
for the first time, new products, even a race of man until then unknown.
There is no point in the [Caribbean] lands or seas . . . that does not call
forth some memory of our first great navigators."[4]

De la Sagra later said that his first trip to Cuba left a deep impression
on him. Within six months, the proposed tobacco factory failed, and he
returned home. But the failure of this first endeavor had not turned him
against moving to Cuba. His understanding of how the world worked in a
practical sense may have changed, but not his hope or his aim of improving it. Moreover, he had spent his months in the Spanish colony forming
close friendships, some of which would last many years. Once back in
Spain, he used the connections provided by those friendships to have himself commissioned as Cuba's Professor of Natural History, in charge of
doing a study of the island. He wanted to use his science and knowledge
to bring the wild grandeur of the New World to its full potential. He spoke
in dramatic terms: "The Island of Cuba, situated under the fortunate skies
of the tropics, the natural vegetation showing all its strength and magnifi-
cence, may be one of the richest possible theaters of scientific investigation. I propose from the moment I arrive to busy myself with the special
charges of the Government . . . both the general project of furthering scientific progress, and the particular aspect of rendering familiar to the
Peninsula [that is, Spain], as far as is possible, all the products of that rich
country."[5] De la Sagra's ideas exemplified his era's faith in the promise of
Western science to bring great changes to distant parts of the globe by
extracting their resources and incorporating them into a network of capitalist trade with Europe. Men like himself would usher in this great new
era by moving between the two worlds. Only later, after his time in the
United States, would de la Sagra's thinking on this subject become more
subtle, as he learned to recognize that science and capitalist development
did not necessarily bring their benefits to everyone.

Back in Spain, de la Sagra once again prepared himself to leave his
country of birth, perhaps forever this time. He did not want to tame the
New World alone. He married Manuela Turnes del Río, whom he had met
while still a student in Santiago, and who had agreed to accompany him
in his new life. When they sailed together in June of 1823, "Manola" was
already pregnant. Once in Havana, de la Sagra threw himself into his new
life. Despite some initial bureaucratic confusion over the granting of his

title and salary, he began teaching classes regularly at the Botanical Garden and took an active role in the Real Sociedad Económica de Amigos del País (Royal Economic Society "Friends of the Nation"). He communicated actively with the *intendente* (governor), who in 1827 named him as the new director of the Botanical Garden and provided the funds for him to start a new scientific journal, *Anales de Ciencias, Agricultura, Comercio y Artes.*[6] His agricultural experiments and records are considered to have been of real theoretical and practical value to Cuba.[7] De la Sagra felt a great energy and commitment and in some ways began to think of himself as Cuban. In the pages of the journal, he began to write about "our Cuba" and "our island."

Despite such apparent personal success, all was not well. The rest of Spanish America was busy proclaiming independence, and, as Spaniards, Ramón and Manuela often felt like outsiders. When their baby son died at eleven months, they were far from their closest connections. No other children were ever born to them. They would later brag that they had never separated from each other during all the years in Cuba. In clinging to each other, they perhaps made it harder to form primary ties with people on the island

De la Sagra was facing feelings that threatened his tranquility. For the first time, he was interacting on a daily basis with enslaved people. The plan of the Botanical Garden indicates that there was a house for the professor on the grounds, as well as houses for the black workers and plots of ground on which they were expected to grow their own food.[8] De la Sagra had to relate with the workers in an immediate sense and could not continue to relegate them in his mind to a theoretical category. Because he had not grown up with slavery, his sudden exposure to its reality caused him to challenge conventional white Cuban wisdom. In calculating Cuba's wealth, for example, he insisted that the usual per capita estimates in fact took account only of the "free class" and not of the "permanent population."[9]

In principle, then, de la Sagra subscribed to the liberal ideal of pro-abolition, but in practice he frequently hurt the slaves. Indeed, he had been raised within the context of Iberian prejudice against dark-skinned Muslims, and in Cuba he socialized in a circle that regarded Africans as having been created by God for the service and pleasure of whites. When he heard of the case of Isabela, an enslaved girl who was purportedly beginning to enter puberty at the age of three, he was fascinated.[10] He commented that in Persia, Arabia, Senegal, and Egypt girls matured as early as eight or nine, but that this case must surely represent a record: "The black race is extraordinarily precocious." He went to see Isabela frequently, measuring, touching, and examining her intimately each time, sometimes bringing medical friends along as well. He was enjoying what he was doing, no matter what the cost to her. The idea that she was a

sexually precocious *negrita*, as he called her, prevented him from seeing
her as a human being, with the same feelings that he had had at her age.
Thus, he was mystified by her evident terror and misery: "In all the time
I visited her I tried in vain to inspire confidence or frankness in her: I
couldn't get out of her mouth one single complete sentence." Yet this same
man published his frustrations that Isabel's owners (and he gave their
names) had never entertained any thoughts as to whether the child's mental development had been as rapid as the physical. What toys did she play
with? What did she like to do by what age? They had not noticed, they
answered. De la Sagra wrote: "Slave children . . . don't resemble other
children in any way. . . . They have barely begun to walk when their parents or their owners give them occupations, chaining their liberty and
reprimanding any individual propensities, thus absolutely preventing the
unfolding of the tumultuous character of a child . . . the development of
faculties and inclinations." Clearly, de la Sagra was unable to recognize
the extent of his own racist inclinations, even as he advocated the improvement of living conditions for the slaves.

De la Sagra may have irritated his friends in the Cuban planter class
with his personal scruples and qualms, but he profoundly angered them
with the pessimistic assessment that he made of the increasingly important sugar complex. In the pages of the journal he admitted that the Cuban economy was currently booming, but he forecast doom because of
the total reliance on certain export crops and the need to import everything "from bread and wine to oil and candles, from shoes to hats, from
the simplest furniture to the most magnificent." He asserted that the crucial questions were whether or not "sugar and coffee would always cover
the cost of all our consumption" and whether "the progress of the popu-
lace is sufficient to give the island's internal commerce all the life, energy, and importance that should characterize it."[11] In 1831 he published
Historia económico-política y estadística de la Isla de Cuba, which generally bemoaned Cuba's dependent position in the international economy.
The great reform that he proposed was to bring white immigrants from
the overpopulated regions of Europe and encourage them to start small
farms. He implied that slavery might then be gradually eliminated.[12] The
Botanical Garden would start the process by making a complete study of
all the viable crops that could do well in a family farm economy, as opposed to a labor-intensive sugar crop, and the results of the study could
be used to attract immigrants.[13]

In the Independence era, Latin American creole elites were caught in
an awkward situation, as Simón Bolívar first pointed out and scholars
have repeated frequently since: they wanted to prove that they were *not*
European in their relations with the Spaniards, and yet they relied upon
being European to retain their privileges in relation to the workers around
them. De la Sagra offended on two fronts: he was a Spaniard telling Cu-

bans how to reconstitute themselves and, more specifically, he was keen on eliminating some of the differences between plantation workers and owners. Some condemned de la Sagra for having criticized the composition of the poems of a well-known Cuban nationalist—which he unwisely did—but the specific form of the criticism that he received indicated that the Cubans' anger stemmed from more than tensions between colony and metropolis. Said his most famous Cuban critic: "He did not respect the confidence that was placed in him, and profited from circumstance to offend respectable people and the generous country he lived in."[14] The man did not speak of de la Sagra's having offended Cubans, but of his having alienated *personas respetables* and *generosos*—that is, the planter class.

In 1828, de la Sagra wrote to a friend, "These people love me less every day, and it is not my fault." A year later he admitted that he wished he had done some things differently: "Maybe I handled it badly."[15] But the damage was done. He no longer felt that he belonged in Spain, and it was too late for him to become fully Cuban. He began to withdraw emotionally. And in 1835, after years of discussion, he and his wife decided to move to Paris, a gathering place for intellectuals and republican-minded exiles from the Americas. They would not go directly, however: they would stop briefly in New York to visit a few scholars and friends. De la Sagra's biographer would later write, "He never suspected the importance that his visit to this new country would have in his life and his plans."[16]

From New York to Washington

The weather was terrible when they docked in New York; nevertheless, de la Sagra felt his spirits rising. The city was exciting. People rushed everywhere and lines of gaily colored coaches stood waiting to take the new arrivals wherever they might wish to go. As night fell on Broadway, the stores lit their gas lamps creating a brilliant effect. "But what pleases me most," De la Sagra wrote in his diary, "is not the pretty view of the city . . . but rather the great commercial activity that I see everywhere, the movement of animated industry, the advancement of the people, their cleanliness, and the general air of well being that all classes seem to have."[17] De la Sagra's conclusions as to universal prosperity were a bit premature, as anyone who had seen the back streets of New York could have told him. Before he left, he was to see great pain and poverty in the United States, but he insisted that he also continued to experience an extraordinary optimism, in that few people were left to sink on their own without access to help.

He and Manuela spent the next six weeks with friends and colleagues in New York and Philadelphia. The time for them to leave for Europe was drawing near, but de la Sagra did not want to go. "I've been thinking," he wrote, "and I've convinced myself that since I have the opportunity to study some of the useful institutions of this country, I shouldn't undervalue it, and that the financial sacrifice that a few more months here would cause me would be small in comparison to what I would learn." He could, he thought, share with people in Spanish realms whatever he might learn about U.S. prisons, penitentiaries, almshouses, shelters, and schools— "all those establishments which are intended to improve the fortunes of those humans who, because of poverty, poor education, or their own vices and lack of will power, fall under the sway, still all too strong, of adversity and calamity." For the first time in years he was almost giddy with excitement, alive "with the delicious sentiments of youthful enthusiasm that have been asleep in me for so long." Before he retired he wrote, "I bless the country that has extended to me this agreeable although unexpected return to myself. . . . Maybe it will even induce me to say good-bye to the study of science!"[18]

Despite his joy, de la Sagra did not find everything in the young United States to his liking. First, their friends insisted that Manuela stay behind in Philadelphia while he went south to see Baltimore and Washington because, they said, the heat and disease of those two cities in summer would surely kill her. So de la Sagra headed south alone, and he recorded a disconcerting sense of loss. Furthermore, the stage drivers were dreadful, traveling with extreme speed, "especially on the downhill slopes, when they leave the bridle unrestrained, which seems to me very dangerous."[19]

De la Sagra had probably prepared himself to be both impressed and repelled by Baltimore, for the city had quite a reputation. At the end of the eighteenth century, it had still been little more than a town. However, during the recent European wars, the city's fortune had been made by its rapid clipper ships, geographically more tucked away and hence less well guarded by Britain than those of Philadelphia. Grain poured out and manufactured goods poured in. The population had more than tripled over the course of a generation. Some of these people did well, but others, especially many newcomers, lived in the alleys of Fell's Point, near the shipyards, and tried to eke out a living by hiring themselves out as day laborers. Like the port of Liverpool in England, the city was known to contemporaries for its great wealth and great poverty.

In less than a week, de la Sagra appeared to be anxious to return to Manuela. The visitor from Cuba saw all the major and some lesser attractions of the city. Since he was interested in commerce and industry, he visited the Exchange, a chemical factory, a tannery, and a brickmaking establishment. His matter-of-fact descriptions indicated that much of the technology was not much different from what he was accustomed to seeing in Spain and Cuba: "Three or four men, a horse grinding the mud, a table, a shed compose the whole, and then the kiln, itself made with unbaked bricks of the factory." His interest in science took him to the museum, a clinic, the hospital, and the medical college. He was most impressed by the nuns who worked in the hospital, least so by the state's method of recompensing the medical professors. The men of science were paid $1,500 per annum for the privilege of working there, it being assumed that they would be able to profit enormously by taking students, selling medicines, etc.[20]

Despite this world's similarities to the worlds that he already knew, de la Sagra's diary entries remained full of energy and an apparent conviction that this country was somehow different. Baltimore was the first place that he reached after he had made his decision in Philadelphia to travel farther. He was ready to be moved. Furthermore, he was without his usual companion and thus more prone to internal soliloquizing and analysis, all the while surrounded by a city that was considered by many to be the subject of interesting speculation. Matters reached a head for him as he surveyed the scene at the base of the Washington Monument. It seems to have been there that he decided that people generally were better off in the United States not because of technology or science, but because the majority were offered the dignity of freedom, decent pay, and the "advantages of their institutions." "How wrong are those in Europe who think that liberty must be associated with disorder, immorality, and irreligion!"[21] When people were not desperate, giving them their freedom did not induce them to behave with desperation. He had already noticed the public schools and the evening classes for working men. The next day he visited the penitentiary and the poorhouse. It was not the architecture or the number of convictions that impressed him, but rather the fact that the inmates in both institutions were taught trades and those in the almshouse were paid for their work. He carefully recorded their wages, noting that unmarried or abandoned mothers could also leave their children in the house during the day for a fee and go out to work in the city if they chose. The children were given their meals and attended school rather than worked.[22]

De la Sagra's impressions were not shared by all visitors to Baltimore. Ironically, the same elements that most moved de la Sagra were those that were most derided by numerous British visitors. "In a country where there is ostensibly no distinctive gradation of classes in the people, one must of necessity sometimes, as on board steamers and canal boats, mix with the *canaille*," said one such traveler.[23] Said another: "The prisoners show to visitors the various articles of manufacture in which they are employed, and explain the steps in the process with as much willingness as ordinary workmen, and without any symptoms of the shame that should be found in such a place."[24] Others disagreed with de la Sagra's assessment of Baltimore. At the same time that the Cuban visitor wandered the city's streets recording his observations, Frederick Douglass was laboring as a caulker in the shipyards, although he was gradually

laying plans for his escape to the North. As a black slave, he knew a quali-
tatively different Baltimore: "Hard brick pavements under my feet . . .
almost raised blisters by their very heat, for it was in the height of summer."[25] He also knew a psychologically different Baltimore. "In childhood, [master Tommy] scarcely considered me inferior to
himself—certainly as good as any other boy with whom he played; but
the time had come when his *friend* must become his *slave*. . . . To him, a
thousand doors were open. Education had made him acquainted with all
the treasures of the world, and liberty had flung open the gates there-
unto."[26] Frederick Douglass knew many in Baltimore who suffered both
materially and psychologically. He knew others like himself whose wages
were taken from them because they were unfree; he knew those who barely
eked out a living because they were using virtually everything they earned
to buy their freedom or that of their loved ones. He knew white children,
too, who were so hungry that they would break the law and teach him to
read in exchange for a bit of bread.

These people were not invisible to de la Sagra. But how could he
explain the presence of poverty in a world that he believed to be so well
designed? Sometimes he blamed the raggedly dressed for their condition,
asserting that they had not taken advantage of the opportunities that he
saw available for them: "Many [of the inmates of the poorhouse] are ro-
bust men, whose vice [of drinking] rather than a lack of work is responsible for bringing them to this asylum."[27] On other occasions he said that
the laws of this new country, although tending in the right direction, did
not go far enough. He refused to travel farther south than Washington,
saying that the preponderance of slaves there would only invite sad comparisons with Cuba, and he complained that even the public schools of
Maryland, although supposedly open, were legally closed to all blacks,
slave and free. He observed that "the Legislature, it seems, has not even
thought about the education of children of color, who are absolutely without schools."[28] Later in life he would make speeches bitterly condemning
the laws in the United States that went further and forbade the education
of slaves and, in some states, of all blacks, connecting this phenomenon
to poverty and a high crime rate among free blacks.[29] De la Sagra was not
always clear in his analysis at this point, but his observations were spur-
ring him to analyze issues in depth that he had only mentioned in passing
while living in Cuba.

De la Sagra kept up his journal throughout his trip, and later exchanged
views with a utopian, Michel Chevalier, a socialist of the Saint Simonian
community whom he met in Washington. At Niagara Falls, he decided to
publish his diary. He worked quickly on the introduction and, within less
than a year of his arrival in Paris, *Cinco meses en los Estados Unidos*
(Five months in the United States) appeared, first in Spanish and then in
French. He insisted that he was not publishing his observations with the

idea that the European nations ought to try to copy the United States; on the contrary, he said, that would not be possible, as they had been steeped for centuries in their own ways and it would be a long and gradual process to extricate the multitude from misery. As far as emulation was concerned, he was thinking of Cuba and also of the South American nations that had recently chosen independence, such as his brother's adopted home of Uruguay. He bluntly explained that the details of his trip might be of "immediate interest to the people of the Americas who speak our own language [Castilian Spanish], and who, in the new regenerative career they propose to pursue, need advice and news from all lovers of humanity."[30]

The Printed Voyage

Ramón de la Sagra would spend most of his remaining years in Paris, largely thinking and writing about Cuba, but exploring other subjects as well. He published over thirty books in Spanish and French, and regularly sent articles to Havana. His greatest achievement was the twelve-volume, beautifully illustrated *Histoire physique, politique et naturelle de l'Ile de Cuba*, in which he overhauled and expanded the *Historia económico-política y estadística de la Isla de Cuba* that he had published in 1831 in Havana. He made the new introduction a treatise on slavery and the future poverty of slave nations, and he thought the topic so important that he later reprinted most of it in *Estudios coloniales con aplicación a la Isla de Cuba* (1845). In the introduction to the *Histoire* he told his readers how he now understood his reasons for being a scholar: "In a word, for the history of a people to be useful to present and future generations, it should include all the parties that constitute the political existence of a modern society, and offer a comparative perspective in relation to those other peoples who share the closest relations or a parallel existence. History written in this way will be not only a faithful representation of the past and present, but also a useful lesson for the future."[31] His outlook had changed while he was in the United States. The introductions to the two "Histories" were profoundly different. He had gone from wanting to offer facts about political economy and agriculture to wanting to analyze the ways in which people thought and felt and the effects that these impressions had upon the political economy. He had altered his understanding of the ramifications of slavery: it was not only a reprehensible practice in a moral sense, but it could also destroy a political economy, even in the presence of science and successful capitalist ventures.

De la Sagra honed his thoughts in the work that he published between his arrival in Paris in 1835 and the first edition of the *Histoire* in 1842. In *Cinco meses* he said that the issue he considered important was "more moral than political." For example, not only were there schools for working people in the United States, but also that the students were treated with respect and had opportunities to work for decent pay. Indeed, what good was it to send a child to school to study the highest moral maxims if he returned each afternoon to misery? Why write criminal codes if young people were practically offered incentives to commit crimes? "Society, like a cruel stepmother, remains silent and indifferent when it sees a young person near the edge of the precipice, and only speaks in a thunderous voice . . . after he has already fallen over the edge."[32] He continued with this theme in a series of lectures that he gave in 1840. He said that Europe faced the "monstrous cancer" of inequality, and that political change would not be enough to cure this disease: the everyday well-being of working people was what mattered. He was not against private property, but he was against privileged access to it. Every human being should have the right to amass wealth, but those who already had succeeded would have to make it possible for others to do so by investing in needed infrastructure and institutions, including schools and also banks that extended credit to the poor. De la Sagra himself temporarily became involved with one such bank.[33]

In the introduction to the *Histoire*, de la Sagra said that he had decided what all this would mean in the case of Cuba: "The social doctrine that I follow is one and indivisible, whether we apply it in industrial Europe with the intent of improving the situation of free men, or whether we make use of it in the Antilles, to relieve the condition of the enslaved."[34] Nevertheless, he said, change was the more urgent where slavery was concerned. Emancipation would have two great results, "one economic, the other moral." In making more than "misery and misfortune" the "prize for the [slaves'] activity"—that is, in allowing them freedom and the right to support themselves well—de la Sagra was convinced that the "interior trade would be augmented" and commerce strengthened. He argued that a country's development was predicated on the existence of a domestic market for goods.

De la Sagra's words can be confusing to the modern reader who is not steeped in his work, for in speaking of the enslaved Africans he makes sudden unexpected attacks on the "vices of their constitutions" even as he advocates emancipation. It is important to read on: he often speaks of white men in this way as well, sparing no one moral condemnation. Indeed, in the *Histoire* he states that the two "castes" are distinguished not by intelligence but only by color, and that in Cuba he has almost never witnessed what he calls "depravity of the heart" among slaves. Sometimes certain actions on the part of slaves were interpreted by whites as a sign of the latter, but were in fact normal reactions to "scorn and injustice" and stemmed from desperation.[35] In Baltimore he had decided that when people were not desperate, they tended to behave more admirably.

Speaking to those readers who, like Cuban planters, were strongly anti-abolitionist, de la Sagra asserted that emancipation was coming eventually. At this point, it was still up to the whites to decide how it would happen. Of course, they could wait until the slaves took matters into their own hands and embarked on a period of bloody civil war. He reminded them of Saint Domingue (Haiti), where the black islanders had launched "the revolution that destroyed the rich culture of that beautiful colony" and wrested their own freedom. As useful food for thought, de la Sagra provided a study of the different ways in which legal emancipation was being conducted by other powers.[36]

In the *Histoire* the thoughts that de la Sagra had articulated in Baltimore showed their impact directly. To attain a peaceful, orderly, and prosperous society, more work had to be done than simply signing some papers to free all slaves. People needed to have confidence in the future. The newly freed needed a means of lifting themselves out of indigence so that they would not lose their faith in the concept of liberty. Without this, he said, they would become bitter and desperate. The daughters would turn to prostitution and the sons would fill the prisons. He had recently observed this phenomenon among many of the free black population of the United States, as they were excluded from the opportunities—like schooling and apprenticeships—available to poor whites.[37]

On the other hand, he said, not all emancipated slaves had become vagabonds. Many had become successful small farmers wherever it was possible. De la Sagra cited such British colonies as Antigua, Guayana, Barbados, and Jamaica where former slaves had been able to buy land and were cultivating it eagerly, and he described the phenomenon of illegal "squatting" in other places. They were resisting plantation labor, as it reminded them of slavery, but they were working hard for themselves. The British plantation lords, desperate for the workers to return to them, were busy attempting to paralyze the blacks' small farms by refusing to rent tracts reasonably, forbidding the cultivation of certain crops, and insisting on permits for travel to and from market. De la Sagra remarked: "What name does this kind of emancipation deserve which has left a man more tightly yoked to his old master by the imperious demands of need, than when he at least received food and clothing in exchange for forced labor?"[38] He sarcastically pointed out that neither former slaves, nor plantation owners, nor abolitionists ended up happy in this scenario.[39]

He made a radical statement when he insisted that successfully chaining the former slaves to the plantations was positive for "exportable production" and indeed for the "metropolis" but distinctly negative for the black family. The interest of the metropolis was not identical to that of the colony's population and hence that of the colony.[40] His suggestion for ameliorating this situation was that Cuba should cut back on the production of sugar and coffee. Production would not have to drop in proportion to every acre excluded from cultivation if newer technology was introduced by the planters. Meanwhile, the landless should be legally

encouraged to work on small farms, preferably by buying land, share crop-
ping if they could not buy, planting tobacco, cotton, and food crops; alter-
natively they might grow silkworms or become miners.[41] The important
elements were that all Afro-Cubans be included in this plan, and that they
should feel that they had control of their own lives.

De la Sagra knew that all of these plans were easier outlined than
implemented. His own quarrels with his peers in Cuba had demonstrated
to him the depth of the planters' resistance, born of the habit of generations. When he was just off the boat from the United States, he had written that white Cubans were absolutely terrified of those whom they had
deprived of rights.[42] He knew it might be many years before decision
makers in Cuba and elsewhere in the Americas were willing to listen to
advice of the kind that he offered. Slavery was in the process of being
abolished in the British Caribbean, and a number of Spanish American
nations would soon follow suit, but the idea of making a means of income
available to former slaves was not a popular one. De la Sagra's was only
one of several economic theories available, and many people did not wish
to broaden the community that shared in opportunity. How some ideas
win and others lose is the crux of the history of political discourse. The
fact that he and those with similar views lost the debate in their own era
does not render their contribution irrelevant. Ideas about equitable distribution remained alive on the island long enough to become part of the
twentieth-century revolution. At the very least their discussion raises the
question of what might have been had Latin Americans chosen another
path of development in the nineteenth century.

Epilogue: Return to Cuba

In Paris, de la Sagra's social world was primarily French, but it was also
Cuban. Although most of the wealthy islanders in the city were transients—
young people there to seek worldly experience, or older people hoping to
prove their sophistication and affluence to those back home—there were
a few who came to live as scholars or to vent their anti-slavery feelings.
These intellectuals were precursors to the American scientific community that would blossom in the French capital toward the end of the century, and a number of them became de la Sagra's friends. The connections
were close enough so that later in life when he returned to Cuba he did
not rent quarters of his own, but rather stayed with the families of various
friends. One such friend was Gertrudis Gómez de Avellaneda, the renowned
Cuban writer of feminist and anti-slavery works. She had moved to Europe at the same time as de la Sagra in 1836; and although she resided
primarily in Spain rather than France, they moved in the same intellectual
circles and came to know each other well.[43]

De la Sagra was in France when the Revolution of 1848 occurred and restored a republican form of government in that country. He was excited at first, seeing hope for change in the midst of anarchy. He gave talks in which he tried to mediate between academics and political agitators, and only gradually became frustrated at how little actually changed for most people as a result of the political unrest.[44] In the late 1850s he experienced what he described as a great crisis in his own life. In some way he lost his wife, Manuela. Either she became incapacitated through a physical or mental illness, or she decided to separate from him. He never said which. He simply stopped referring to her, and after this period he often spoke in his loneliness about the importance of friendship. He made the decision to go home to Cuba to make one last voyage and update his multivolume encyclopedic work. In his view, "the country of my former labors was the only port of salvation in the tempest in which I was caught."[45]

The Cuba of 1859 and 1860 disturbed him deeply. Many of the plantations had introduced the machinery he advocated, but not in order to make room for small farms. In fact, sugar production had expanded. Small farmers were even more squeezed than before, and the slave regime was harsher than ever. He did not give up the old arguments, although they took new forms: he still advocated diversification of the economy, now to include industrialization, and he hoped that the new immigrant Asian workers would be allowed to prosper as more than field hands.[46] Perhaps his friendship with Avellaneda, his growing religious faith, or his loss of Manuela made him more interested in women's issues. Ever since he had been struck by what he saw as the near saintliness of the nuns who worked in the lunatic ward of the Baltimore hospital, he had regarded women as being more spiritual than men. Now he supported the Cuban ladies' schools, charities, and newspapers.

Despite the problems, there was something in that warm green land that still inspired him as it had when he first arrived, barely out of boyhood all those years ago. The land rendered him hopeful. Out on an excursion, he wrote to Avellaneda, who had also returned to Cuba and who had traveled with him briefly: "I would have been glad to have you accompany me on my visits to the three beautiful farms, but I am not so selfish as to have wished you to have been with me on top of the locomotive of the train to Saguas, which I took from the 'Angelita' mill to 'Santa Susana,' comfortably sprawled out and highly entertained atop a pile of wood. Being there, at age 62, satisfied and content, I could only deplore the error of those who think I have become decrepit and spiritless!"[47] Ramón de la Sagra flew down the hills atop the train, looked out at the lush Cuba he loved, and thought of all the places he had been. Swerving around bends in the track, he still believed in the future's possibilities.

Notes

1. Ramón de la Sagra, *Cinco meses en los Estados Unidos* (Paris: P. Renouard, 1836), 115–17.

2. Although he is relatively unknown in the United States, there is a scholarly literature on de la Sagra in Cuba and Spain. Because of the background of the participants, much of the debate has concerned de la Sagra's identity, or degree of alignment with the Old versus the New World. Another related discussion concerns the degree of his radicalism. In Cuba currently, the most common assessment of de la Sagra's politics has him growing ever more conservative with age. See, for example, Ascensión Cambrón Infante, Paul Estrade, and Marie-Claude Lecuyer, eds., introduction to *Ramón de la Sagra y Cuba*, vol. 1 (La Coruña, Spain: Edicios do Castro, 1992). Luis Legaz y Lacambra, "Ramón de la Sagra, sociólogo español," *Revista Internacional de Sociología* 13–14 (1946): 155–82; and the more recent Emilio González López, *Un gran solitario: Don Ramón de la Sagra* (La Coruña, Spain: Caixa Galicia, 1982).

3. Mary Louise Pratt, *Imperial Eyes: Travel Writing and Transculturation* (New York: Routledge, 1992), 120–30.

4. Ramón de la Sagra, *Histoire physique, politique et naturelle de l'Ile de Cuba*, vol. 1 (Paris: Arthur Bertrand, 1842), 1.

5. Ramón de la Sagra to the Sres. de la Junta Directiva del Jardín Botánico, November 28, 1822, cited in Miguel-Angel Puig Samper, "Ramón de la Sagra, Director del Jardín Botánico de la Habana," in *La Sagra y Cuba*, vol. 1, 62.

6. Araceli García Carranza, *Indices analíticos de los anales de Don Ramón de la Sagra* (Havana: Biblioteca Nacional José Martí, 1970), 9–11.

7. See Izaskun Alvarez Cuartero, "La Real Sociedad Económica de Amigos del País de la Habana," and Michele Guicharnaud-Tollis, "Ramón de la Sagra y su contribución a las ciencias en Cuba," in *La Sagra y Cuba*, vol. 1.

8. Puig-Samper, "Director del Jardin," 64.

9. Ramón de la Sagra, *Historia económico-política y estadística de la Isla de Cuba* (Havana: Imprenta de las Viudas de Arazoza y Soler, 1831), 334.

10. De la Sagra, "Ejemplo de pubertad estraordinaria en una niña de la raza negra," *Anales de Ciencias, Agricultura, Comercio y Artes* 2 (August 1827): 51.

11. De la Sagra, "Consideraciones económico-políticas sobre la isla de Cuba," in ibid., 29.

12. Marie-Claude Lecuyer, "La Gran Reforma de Ramón de la Sagra: Utopia y colonialismo," in *La Sagra y Cuba*, vol. 1, 138–39.

13. De la Sagra, "Sobre la Utilidad que resultaría de poseer una historia física, política é industrial de la isla de Cuba," *Anales* 4 (October 1827): 109–10.

14. José Antonio Saco, cited in García Carranza, *Indices analíticos*, 10.

15. Ramón de la Sagra to Tomás Gener, April 13, 1828, and August 5, 1829. Reprinted in *La Sagra y Cuba*, vol. 2, 77–78.

16. González López, *Un gran solitario*, 106.

17. De la Sagra, *Cinco meses*, 1–2.

18. Ibid., 95–97.

19. Ibid., 98 and 129.

20. Ibid., 102, 104, and 107.

21. Ibid., 116.

22. Ibid., 118–28.

23. E. T. Coke, *A Subaltern's Furlough: Descriptive Scenes in Various Parts of the United States, Upper and Lower Canada, New Brunswick, and Nova Scotia* (London: Saunders and Otley, 1833), 69.

24. John M. Duncan, *Travels through Part of the United States and Canada* (New York: W. B. Gilley, 1823), 233.

25. Frederick Douglass, *My Bondage and My Freedom* (New York, 1855), reprinted in *Frederick Douglass: Autobiographies* (New York: The Library of America, 1994), 214.

26. Ibid., 328.

27. De la Sagra, *Cinco meses*, 128.

28. Ibid., 97 and 105.

29. De la Sagra, *Histoire physique*, 61–62.

30. De la Sagra, *Cinco meses*, xxvi.

31. De la Sagra, *Histoire physique*, iii.

32. De la Sagra, *Cinco meses*, xviii–xix.

33. De la Sagra, *Lecciones de economía social dadas en el Ateneo Científico y Literario de Madrid* (Madrid: El Ateneo, 1840), 8–9, 13–19, 38–43, 63; and *Banque du Peuple: Théorie et pratique de cette institution* (Paris: Bureau de la Banque, 1849).

34. De la Sagra, *Histoire physique*, 36.

35. Ibid., 12 and 38–42.

36. Ibid., 27 and 35.

37. Ibid., 37, 67–69 and 78.

38. Ibid., 45–59.

39. Ibid., 84.

40. Ibid., 57–58.

41. Ibid., 106–8. Cuba might use Puerto Rico as a model, he suggested.

42. De la Sagra, "Apuntes destinados a ilustrar la discusión del artículo adicional al proyecto de Constitutión que dice 'Las provincias de Ultramar serán gobernadas por leyes especiales' " (Paris: Maulde et Renou, 1837), reprinted in *La Sagra y Cuba*, vol. 2, 155.

43. Paul Estrade, *La colonia cubana de París, 1895–1898* (Havana: Editorial de Ciencias Sociales, 1984), 5–6. For an excellent new work on Avellaneda which treats her friendship with de la Sagra, see Florinda Alzaga, *La Avellaneda: Intensidad y vanguardia* (Miami: Ediciones Universal, 1997).

44. De la Sagra, *Le Problème de l'organisation du travail* (Paris: Maulde et Renou, 1848). Various versions of this work were published in 1848–49 after the author gave talks before different audiences.

45. Scholars give the date 1867 for Manuela's death, but something dramatic clearly occurred before that. De la Sagra promised that he would "one day reveal . . . the wounds of his misfortune" that made it so difficult for him to "resign himself to wait for the end Providence had ordained," but apparently he never recorded the secret in any surviving documents. See prologue to *Historia física, económico-política, intelectual y moral de la Isla de Cuba: Relación del último viaje del autor* (Paris: Hachette, 1861), 1–4.

46. Lecuyer, "Gran Reforma," 144–46.

47. De la Sagra to Sra. Avellaneda, April 17, 1860. Originally published in the women's newspaper edited by Avellaneda, *El Album cubano de lo bueno y lo bello*, and reprinted in *La Sagra y Cuba*, vol. 2, 278.

5

Intellectuals, Indians, and the Press: The Politicization of Justo Sierra O'Reilly's Journalism and Views on the Maya while in the United States

John F. Chuchiak IV

The Caste War of the Yucatán (1847–1853) is the defining episode of modern Yucatecan history. During that time, approximately 30 to 40 percent of the peninsula's citizenry were killed, the region's productive economic capacity was destroyed, and the previously complacent Yucatecan urban elite finally recognized the tremendous hostility and potential power of the Maya Indians. After shocking and rapid initial territorial losses, the state government managed to win back most of the peninsula by 1853, although the southeastern portion remained in the hands of the Cruzob rebels, under the leadership of their mystical Talking Cross, until 1901.

In this selection, historical anthropologist John Chuchiak traces the intellectual trajectory of Justo Sierra O'Reilly (1814–1861), the most influential journalist-historian of nineteenth-century Yucatán. Chuchiak argues that the dual impact of the Caste War and a year spent in the United States as Yucatecan minister plenipotentiary dramatically altered the way in which Sierra viewed both the Maya Indians and the potential political use of the journalistic form. Before his residence in the United States, Sierra's serial publications were mainly literary and artistic; while there, he quickly had to adapt to a more polemical and political press and brought this new form to the Yucatán. Similarly, as a direct result of his exposure to hardening racial attitudes in the U.S. South, Sierra returned to the Yucatán no longer willing to accept the liberal image of the Maya Indians as docile servants of the white upper classes. Instead, he began to depict them as barbarous savages bent on the destruction of civilization. This chapter provides insight into the little-recognized but vibrant intellectual history of the Yucatán, reveals personal and professional links between that peninsula and the nearby United States, and adds an important facet to the study of the Caste War itself. Furthermore, Sierra's explanation of social conditions in Yucatán as the result of a struggle between

civilization and barbarism after his return from the United States repre-
sents a startling parallel to the experience and ideas of the more famous
Argentine, Domingo F. Sarmiento, who toured North America at the same
time as Sierra's mission.

The most surprising aspect of the Mayá Indians in pre-Caste War Yucatecan histories and travel accounts is their absence. If present at all, they were portrayed as ignorant and submissive natives who lived in harmony under white rule in Yucatán. However, this standard view of the Maya's docility changed during the Caste War due to the concerted efforts of one influential man: Dr. Justo Sierra O'Reilly, journalist, politician, historian, and jurist. Sierra's powerful pen dominated the nineteenth-century Yucatecan press and recast the Yucatecan elite's perception of the Maya from an ignorant yet noble innocent Indian during the early 1840s, to the post-Caste War depiction of a barbarous savage bent on the destruction of civilization. The nature and content of Sierra's journalistic activities changed during his year-long stay in the United States. Before his overseas mission, Sierra held the idealized, liberal image of the Indian and focused his publishing efforts on literary and artistic concerns. While abroad, however, the need to respond to U.S.-style political propaganda campaigns, the pervasive influence of U.S. racial attitudes, and daily news of the Caste War's horrors marked a transition in his view of the Indians. Upon his return from the United States, Sierra's journalistic activities took on a new political purpose, and his reinterpretation of Yucatecan history has influenced subsequent generations to the present day.[1]

During the first half of the decade, Yucatán witnessed the emergence of a distinct intellectual movement, known as the Generation of 1840, the most prominent member of which was Sierra.[2] The previous two decades had seen the rapid rejuvenation of the educational system, which had been in decay since the expulsion of the Jesuits in 1767.[3] In this way, the percentage of literate people in the major urban centers of Mérida, Campeche, and Valladolid increased dramatically. Similarly, the economy of Yucatán experienced the benefits of increased revenues from its export sector, which in turn broadened both the financial support and audience for expanded cultural projects.[4] Young members of the Generation of 1840 began to search in archives and collect valuable documents that they used to write new histories and literary productions of the Yucatán.

Lacking publishing outlets, these brash young intellectuals founded their own presses and newspapers, including the first major literary newspaper in Yucatán, Sierra's *El Museo Yucateco*, which he promised would not contain "one word of politics."[5] Although subsequent historians call this journal the "birth of literature in Yucatán," it survived just two years. Nevertheless, Sierra's work unleashed a demand for literary materials so great that he soon was able to publish a second, longer-lived paper entitled *El Registro Yucateco* (1844–1849), which achieved remarkable circulation figures for its era. In 1846 the newspaper boasted 364 subscribers, some of them purchasing more than one copy each, at a time when the total population of Mérida was still under 30,000.[6] Sierra proclaimed that his newspaper "was a dignified symbol of a society that followed . . . the rapid progress of human understanding." This mission reveals the optimism and progressive spirit that animated Sierra's Generation of 1840. Sierra's journalistic activities during this early period concentrated more on the promotion of high culture in Yucatán than on a realistic analysis of its social and economic conditions.

In the 1840s foreign travelers such as John L. Stephens and Baron von Frederickshall focused the world's attention upon the archaeological ruins of the Mayan cities of Yucatán.[7] Through the work of these foreign adventurers, Yucatecan intellectuals, led by Sierra, became fascinated with their peninsula's long-ignored ruins. A particularly enthusiastic Sierra translated his friend Stephens's travelogue into Spanish in 1848 in order to give his fellow Yucatecans the chance to read this important patriotic work.[8] As an outsider, Stephens understood that the original builders of the cities were not members of some extinct Old World group, but rather the direct ancestors of the "*race* which, changed, miserable, and degraded, still clings around their ruins." However, he noted that Yucatecan intellectuals were more inclined to describe the pre-Columbian inhabitants of these ruined cities as an "ancient race," the trace of which could no longer be seen in the natives of their own day.[9] Sierra explicitly stated in his translation of the travel account that he believed Stephens was mistaken; rather, Sierra pointed out that the Indians he knew "would not have been capable of building these great monuments" due to their profound "ignorance."[10] His tone was not hostile; in his mind, he was simply stating an obvious and daily observed fact.

The early works of the Generation of 1840 most often cast the Maya Indian as a noble savage who was docile, thrifty, frugal, and law abiding. This was the romantic image that the Yucatecan whites had the luxury of believing in during the pre-Caste War years. According to Rousseau, whom they often cited, Nature provided the noble savage with all that he needed for survival with a minimal amount of effort on his part.[11] However, they also characterized the Maya as degenerate, weak, and ignorant. The Yucatecan intellectuals looked on the Indian as a combination of contradictory characteristics. Stephens agreed that the Indian was "a monstrous combination of religion and impiety, of virtues and vices, of sagacity and stupidity, of wealth and misery. . . . Badly educated or, better said, without any education. . . . [The Indian] loves the white man, and avoids his company whenever he can." The image of the humble and docile Indian kissing the hand of the one who punished him is repeated in numerous short stories and miniature novels of the period—for example, Gerónimo Castillo's serial novel *Un pacto y un pleito* (A pact and a lawsuit).[12]

Before the Caste War, and before they had to account to world opinion for that bloody experience, Sierra's generation was content to view the Indians in these paternalistic terms. Although the Maya comprised more than 80 percent of the Yucatán's total population, Sierra and his contemporaries did not consider them worthy of much discussion. In fact, between 1845 and 1849, *El Registro Yucateco* contained only four articles which dealt explicitly with the Indians. Instead, the pages of Sierra's literary journals were dedicated to matters that concerned his urban audience: historiography and philosophy, archaeology, Yucatecan history, the press, education, schools, and the usefulness of the English language in the modern world.

The Generation of 1840's ambivalence toward the Indian ended on July 30, 1847. On that fateful night, several thousand Maya Indians answered the call of revolt and slaughtered three hundred white men, women, and children in the village of Tepich.[13] Some of the very intellectuals who wrote in the columns of these newspapers died at the hands of the Maya, who launched and continued this brutal war of extermination until Porfirio Díaz finally managed to crush the last rebel stronghold in 1901.[14] The Caste War had begun, and nothing in Yucatán would be the same again. Among the smoldering remains of Tepich lay not only the charred remains of its white citizens but also the bourgeois intellectual image of the Maya as docile servants.

The grave situation of the expanding Caste War in Yucatán prompted Governor Santiago Méndez to send Justo Sierra O'Reilly to the United States as his commissioner to ask for the return of the Isla del Carmen, whose port was essential in the commerce of Yucatán; it was the only conduit through which to receive badly needed military aid. The United States had occupied the port since the outbreak of the Mexican-American War, when the U.S. naval fleet under the command of Commodore Matthew Perry had closed its harbors.[15] Assigned a salary of $300 per month, Sierra left Campeche for New Orleans aboard the *Essex* on September 12, 1847, in the company of his secretary, Rafael Carvajal.[16] The port of New Orleans had always been the main point of contact for Yucatecan trade, commerce, and intellectual influence. All news coming from or going to Mexico, especially the nearby Yucatán, flowed through the port of New Orleans, making it the perfect base for his mission abroad.

The U.S. press got wind of Sierra's mission even before his arrival.[17] One Spanish-language newspaper based in New Orleans, *La Patria*, was especially influential in poisoning Sierra's U.S. reception. Located at 137 Chartres Street, the newspaper was owned and edited by two Liberal Spanish immigrants, V. Alemán and Enrique J. Gómez, who had fled Spain in 1816 after the return of absolute monarch Ferdinand VII.[18] From the outset, the editors and writers of *La Patria* did not favor Sierra's mission, a situation fortified by their choice of peninsular correspondents: both Don Juan Bautista Angli in Campeche and the anonymous correspondent from the *Imprenta de Seguí* in Mérida were members of the Barbachanista faction and were therefore Governor Méndez and Sierra's political enemies.

The political climate in the United States during the time of Sierra's mission was one of tension and uncertainty. The ongoing U.S.-Mexican war and the prospect of territorial expansion contributed to even greater polarization in a country already splitting into pro- and anti-slavery camps. Racial tension and awareness were pervasive. *La Patria*, although a Southern newspaper, did not support Sierra's proposed annexation of Yucatán to the United States because its liberal editors feared that a form of slavery existed there. For the editors of *La Patria*, the Indian rebellion in Yucatán clearly had been caused by the whites' oppression of the liberty-loving Indians. Thus, in their opinion, the Yucatecan leaders were not liberals at all, and therefore the editors of *La Patria* could not condone the use of the U.S. military to aid in the suppression of Indians who battled for "self-determination." They looked on the Méndez regime as an illegitimate government and regarded Sierra as an illegitimate commissioner whose mission to achieve annexation did not come from the general consent of the people, but rather from the political machinations of Sierra and his father-in-law, the governor.[19]

Already on unfamiliar territory in the United States, Sierra quickly realized upon his arrival that *La Patria* would be his great enemy, and that its editors were operating according to different journalistic norms than he had been used to in Mérida. In a personal diary written for his wife, on Tuesday, March 7, 1848, Sierra wrote: "I am now finding some very sad truths. While I am placing myself in contact with the men who make and direct politics here, I am more and more alarmed at the fate of Yucatán. And moreover, in augmentation of my mortifications, a damned Spanish newspaper from New Orleans, called *La Patria*, has taken me to task. . . . Politics! Damn politics and moreover damn the miserable and weak way in which some men understand it!"[20] Clearly, Sierra had to respond to the article that had accused him of being illegally commissioned and he promptly launched a retaliatory media campaign on behalf of his commission and the Yucatán government.[21] In this way, immediately upon his arrival in the United States, Sierra's journalism assumed a new, more overtly political purpose, and he wrote that he was busily maintaining "a large correspondence with many newspapers" to defend his cause.[22] It was a new strategy in an unfamiliar environment, which ultimately altered the way he approached journalistic forms and purpose.

The editors of *La Patria* were not his only enemies. U.S. Secretary of State and future president James Buchanan, whom Sierra ultimately blamed for the failure of his mission, leaked secret correspondence to the press in which Sierra begged the United States to send military aid or intervene in Yucatán on behalf of "humanity and civilization."[23] In these missives, Sierra warned that hordes of barbarian Indians were destroying daily the civilization that had taken the whites of Yucatán "300 years to construct."[24] Not only was the orientation of his journalistic activities changing as a result of his time abroad, but Sierra's attitude toward the Maya Indians also was becoming modified by his experiences.

Sierra also found himself under attack by another New Orleans outfit, the *Daily Delta*, a pro-slavery newspaper that attacked not only Sierra but also the entire Spanish "white race" in Yucatán. One particularly inflammatory article on April 21, 1848, contributed to the politicization of Sierra's journalism as it ridiculed his tactics and argument as "effeminate" and weak. In this harsh manner, the editors of the *Delta* represented Southern white racist attitudes when they failed to see a difference between the Maya Indians and the Yucatecan elite. Instead, these North American commentators suggested that perhaps it was the "degenerate white race" of Yucatán that was really at fault in the Caste War: "it strikes us as the very height of impudence in Mr. Justo Sierra, after admitting the irresistible superiority of the so-called savages . . . to ask the United States to interfere on behalf of a miserable, cowardly minority, who because they are an imperceptible shade lighter than the vast majority, think they are entitled to the aid of all civilized nations. . . . It is the common device of the degenerate Spanish race of the Mexican States, to style the enemies who prove too strong for them, savages, barbarians."[25] Sierra had run up against Southern U.S. attitudes of the day, which perceived the world in racial terms yet failed to perceive the distinction between European-descended Yucatecans and Maya Indians that was so clear to Sierra at home. To the editors of the *Daily Delta* the two categories meant more or less the same thing. In the United States, Sierra was simply a Mexican.

As for the newspapers that were on his side, Sierra could only count on the moderate Washington-based paper, the *National Era*, and a few other lesser Midwestern papers whose editors continued to provide Sierra with a forum to publish his views. They took up Sierra's evolving argument that the Caste War was essentially a war between "civilization and barbarism." Similar to the world view of Domingo F. Sarmiento, who blamed the rural gauchos for Argentina's backwardness, Sierra viewed the struggles of Yucatán as a battle between civilization (the Yucatecan elite) and barbarism (the rebellious Maya). For this expedient reason, a few U.S. editors championed Sierra's vision of Indian barbarity, likely with their eyes on the expanding U.S. frontier, and agreed that it was the "wild Indians who for centuries strove to expel or exterminate the whites in Yucatán."[26] Clearly, his time in a United States embroiled in racial politics changed the nature and content of Sierra's journalism and his view of the Yucatecan Maya fighting the Caste War at home.

The editors of the anti-Sierra *La Patria* directly caused the final defeat of the Yucatán Bill that Sierra had managed to get presented in Congress. On May 14, 1848, the eve of the congressional vote on the Yucatán Bill, *La Patria* accused Sierra of lying in his correspondence to Secretary of State Buchanan. *La Patria* also accused the Yucatecan whites of breaking the peace treaty of Tzucacab that had been signed only a few weeks before with the Indian caudillo Jacinto Pat.[27] Persuasive speeches by Southern senators such as John Calhoun of South Carolina blamed the white population of Yucatán "for having brought ruin upon themselves, by the policy of elevating to their own level, in terms of political rights, an inferior race."[28] Sierra realized that this hostile onslaught signaled the failure of his mission. Even the Northern papers began to publish the reports from *La Patria*. The *Baltimore Sun*, a paper that had permitted Sierra to submit his letters, now supported the "noble spirit of Jacinto Pat."[29] Sierra lamented in his diary on May 28, 1848:

> I have had a terrible day filled with anger and desperation. The Spanish newspaper from New Orleans has assassinated us. The calumnious material that they published against the whites of Yucatán saying that they had treacherously violated the peace accord celebrated with the Indians, has spread throughout the entire country and it has excited the most hateful sentiments against us. What brutal and savage slander! I have been enclosed in my room, reading and writing: writing articles that no journalist wants to publish, because they all look at us with distrust. What a sad role I am playing in these moments![30]

Sierra continued to describe La Patria as a shameful newspaper that brazenly asked its readers, "Who are worse, the Indians or the whites?" Sierra bristled at this rhetorical question that only added "insult to injury" for those Yucatecan elites struggling to stave off the bloody Maya hordes back at home.[31]

Throughout his long political battle in the U.S. press, the Caste War had hindered communications, and no letters from his government reached Sierra for many months. Ironically, then, Sierra too was forced to rely on reports from the hated *La Patria*. Sierra considered his isolation and lack of correspondence a terrible ordeal. To make matters worse, he was lonely. His secretary, Carvajal, had grown too ill to aid him in his duties or provide much of a personal link with his life back home. Thus, as news of massacres continued to pour in from the Yucatán, Sierra grew increasingly bitter. Faced with the rigid attitudes of Southern racism and the negative opinion of both the Indians and Mexicans in general in the U.S. press, Sierra's own view of the Indians changed. From May 1848 onward, he took his pen in hand and counterattacked those whom he came to see as his true enemies, and by extension the enemies of humanity and civilization: the Maya Indians.

The attacks of the New Orleans papers *La Patria* and the *Delta* disturbed Sierra's sensibilities greatly and evoked strong reactions. His struggles with these papers had a lasting effect on him, his journalism, and his view of the Maya Indians. He accused their editors of being "ferocious beasts like the savages of our unfortunate country who assassinate women and children. I prefer a thousand times over the frank and virulent hatred of other journalists, than this cruel and brutal deception undertaken by the *Delta* of New Orleans, for such ignoble motives."[32] This vitriol spilled over to his work and, especially after news arrived of the Indians' murder of his own brother, Sierra's hatred for the Indians grew. In one of the more desperate entries in his travel diary, Sierra lamented: "What a sad fate our unfortunate country suffers. . . . What a sad fate it would be for us all if that hateful and damned infernally savage race comes to dictate the law there!"[33]

Sierra's disillusionment and politicization while in the United States led him to renounce his earlier paternalistic ideas of the educability of the Indians. He wrote:

> I have always had pity for the poor Indians, my conscience has always suffered for their condition, and more than one time I have made efforts to better their situation, so that they were relieved of burdens that appeared to me to be very onerous. But, what savages! Infamous brutes that bathe themselves in blood, in fire, and destruction. I want nothing more today than the disappearance of that damned race, and that it never again will appear among us. What we have done to civilize that race has only been converted into our own destruction, and it is certainly very sensible and very cruel to have to repent now for actions that once appeared good to us. Barbarians! I damn them today for their savage ferocity, and for their frantic hatred and for their ignoble desires for extermination.[34]

He later wrote that the Anglo-Saxon mode of colonization, which pushed the Indians away and exterminated them, was the best means of creating a liberal and peaceful society. With this new mentality, Sierra undertook a monumental reinterpretation of Yucatán's colonial history in order to prove that the Maya were not docile innocents, but rather "brutal, scheming, and warlike savages, whose goal was nothing less than the destruction of civilization." Three themes became Sierra's obsession: the Indians' savage ferocity, their fanatic hatred of the whites, and their desire for the extermination of civilization. Sierra returned home from the United States a changed man, one with a new mission in life. He spent the rest of his days combing through the annals of Yucatecan colonial history to locate the origins of the Indians' hatred of the white race, and to absolve his generation of any guilt in causing the recent devastation in his beloved homeland.

Upon his return from the United States until his death in 1861, Sierra published a total of eight newspapers, all of which exhibited a much stronger political and polemical edge than his pre-mission endeavors. More-over, Sierra's subsequent work created both support and opposition, and thereby politicized the Generation of 1840. A comparison of his two peri-ods of journalism reveals the extreme politicization that Sierra's publish-ing activities underwent after his trip to the United States. The rapid decline of his literary newspapers and a sharp increase in political newspapers after his one-year stay clearly indicate the dramatic impact of his trip on his intellectual orientation.

If Sierra had learned one thing in the United States, it was that the issue of race was a major factor in shaping that country's image of the Yucatecan elite. In the eyes of the U.S. press, Yucatecans were merely a little lighter than the Indians. Motivated by these attacks, Sierra dedi-cated himself to answering the criticism he had received in the United States, especially from Senator Calhoun and others, who viewed the lib-eral Yucatecans' extension of certain political rights to the Indians as their most serious mistake. In order to launch his re-interpretation of history and the defense of liberalism in Yucatán, Sierra established *El Fénix* (The phoenix), an appropriate name for this influential paper that he planned to use to create a new Yucatán out of the ashes left behind by the Caste War.

Sierra needed to explain to the world that urban Yucatecans were not the same as Maya Indians. He realized that he could not convince the U.S. press, or anyone else, that the urban Yucatecans were pure whites, so he attempted to create an image of the Indians' inferiority that was not based entirely on racial classifications. Sierra decided to show that the Yucatecan whites were superior because they were members of civilized society. In order to make the contrast clear, Sierra was faced with the task of show-ing to the world the savage state of the Indians of Yucatán. Through close to a hundred articles and editorials in *El Fénix*, Sierra was able to justify his position historically and describe the Indian as a barbaric savage. In a series of articles collectively titled *Consideraciones sobre el orígen, causas y tendencias de la sublevación de los indígenas, sus probables resultados y su posible remedio* (Considerations on the origin, causes, and tenden-cies of the subjugation of the Indians, their probable results, and their possible remedy), Sierra re-examined the colonial history of Yucatán in order to discover the reasons for the Caste War. He concluded that the repressive Spanish colonial system of labor and tribute, the Indians' in-nate hatred of the white race, and the barbaric Maya religion were direct causes. He also condemned the early Independence-era liberals for being "too naively idealistic," a flaw that had led to the liberation of the Indians without first "civilizing them enough to enjoy the privilege and exercise of liberty." In Sierra's argument, the nature of the Indians made it impos-sible for them to be educated, for they had nothing but scorn for the white race and civilization in general, as the many colonial rebellions and the recent Caste War had proven. Moreover, the Indians still practiced their religion and idolatry, which, in his opinion, was "partly the cause of their barbarity and brutish nature." Nevertheless, Sierra did not condemn all Indians uniformly. Since he was not basing his ideas of Indian inferiority on purely racial categories, Sierra could make an exception for those Xiu Indians who had always lived among the whites and had become civilized through the "Catholic religion and education."[35]

This radical change in the perception of the Indian in the Yucatecan press is vividly illustrated in a comparison of two images in Sierra's own newspapers. Figure 1 shows the ideal of the noble savage portrayed in Sierra's earlier literary newspapers; the second image (Figure 2) clearly reveals the post-mission and post-Caste War "barbarization" of the Indians by portraying their savage destruction of the village of Tepich. The startling differences between the two images is illustrative of the change in attitudes that Sierra underwent after his difficult trip to the United States.

Through his reinterpretation of colonial Yucatecan history, Sierra attempted to vindicate his generation's treatment of the Indians as harmless, docile servants. In his paper *El Fénix*, he warned the Yucatecans that they had made a mistake, not in giving the Indians rights but in giving rights too early to a group who were neither civilized nor educated

Prior to the Caste War, Yucatecan whites depicted the region's native people as harmless, obedient children. From *El Registro Yucateco* (Mérida: Imprenta de Castillo y Compañia, 1846), facing p. 425. *Courtesy of the Latin American Library, Tulane University*

enough to know how to employ them. In his journalistic activities from 1848 to 1856, Sierra re-conceptualized the Yucatecan elite's view of the Indian, at the same time barbarizing the natives and absolving his generation of the guilt of having caused the Caste War through their lack of attention to Indian matters. By refuting the arguments of the U.S. press, Sierra argued that it was not his generation that oppressed the Indians to the point of rebellion. Rather, it was the Indians who harbored an inherent hatred of the white race that only manifested itself when previous generations "used them in their factious political battles." In this case, he claimed that the "barbarity of the Indians, forced upon them by 300 years of colonialism," had caused the rebellion. Thus, the Caste War was not the Yucatecans' fault, but rather a result of a corrupt Spanish colonial past. Sierra's newspapers defended the extermination of the Indians and, in many instances, demanded it.[36]

Caste War violence against whites prompted a new vision of the Maya natives as menacing and barbarian. From *Enciclopedia Yucatanense, Conmemorativa del IV Centenario de Mérida y Valladolid (Yucatán)* (Mérida: Edición Oficial del Gobierno de Yucatán, 1947), 3:256. *Courtesy of the Latin American Library, Tulane University*

Faced with the disintegration of order under the onslaught of the "barbarous hordes," the Yucatecan elite and Sierra, their chief spokesman and historian, searched desperately for the causes of the Caste War and for ways to quell the rebellion that threatened to overwhelm them. While failing in its declared ambitions, Sierra's trip to the United States in 1847–48 had the effect of politicizing his journalism and producing a reformulation of Yucatecans' image of the Indian. Sierra's subsequent emphasis on order, and his censure of the earlier Liberals' foolish gift of political equality to the ignorant Indians, makes him a member of the pre-positivist group of Mexican intellectuals who were the predecessors of men such as Sierra's son Justo Sierra Méndez, and Ignacio Altamirano, who (perhaps heeding Sierra's advice) attempted to educate the Indians while keeping order until the proper time came to raise them to equality in terms of civil liberties. In this way, Sierra served as an intellectual bridge between the early Liberal ideas of the Independence period (such as those of Lorenzo Zavala) and the later pessimistic ideas of Spencerian racism and Mexican Positivism that attempted to educate the Indians in order to integrate them into the society. Sierra's generation, in his opinion, had to reestablish order from the chaos unleashed by the early Liberals' premature grant of liberty to an ignorant and oppressed group of savages who were not educated enough nor civilized enough to have earned it. Maintaining order would be the first step in the future integration of the Indians into the national economy and the civil ("civilized") state of Yucatán. However, neither Sierra nor his own aging generation of intellectuals lived to see the fruition of their project; rather, they passed the challenge on to their children, including Sierra's own son, the famous positivist Justo Sierra Méndez, who was born, like the phoenix, out of the ashes of the Caste War era.

Notes

1. See Allen Wells, "Forgotten Chapters of Yucatán's Past: Nineteenth Century Politics in Historiographical Perspective," *Mexican Studies* 12, no. 2 (Summer 1996): 195–229; Gilbert M. Joseph, "From Caste War to Class War: The Historiography of Modern Yucatán, c.1750–1940," *Hispanic American Historical Review* 65, no. 1 (1985): 111–34; Jeffrey T. Brannon and Gilbert M. Joseph, eds., *Land, Labor, and Capital in Modern Yucatán* (Tuscaloosa: University of Alabama Press, 1991).

2. Gabriel Ferrer de Mendiola, "Justo Sierra O'Reilly: Literato, jurista, político, historiador," in *Enciclopedia Yucatanense* (Mérida: Edición Oficial del Gobierno de Yucatán, 1946), 7:207; Julio Jiménez, "Justo Sierra O'Reilly: Federalista," in Julio N. Jimenez, Fernando Vales Tenreiro, Augustin Rebolledo Quintero, and Carlos Barrera Jure, *Segunda certamen de biografias de Yucatecos ilustres: Dr. Justo Sierra O'Reilly* (Mérida: Ediciones de la Universidad de Yucatán, 1977), 12; Leopoldo Peniche Vallado, *Promotores e historiadores de la rebelión maya de 1847 en Yucatán* (Mérida: Fondo Editorial de Yucatán, 1980).

3. Gabriel Ferrer de Mendiola, "La educación pública y privada en Yucatán, Siglo XIX," in *Enciclopedia Yucatanense* (Mérida: Edición Oficial del Gobierno de Yucatán, 1944), 4:100–101.

4. Gilbert Joseph, *Rediscovering the Past at Mexico's Periphery: Essays on the History of Modern Yucatán* (Tuscaloosa: University of Alabama Press, 1986); Allen Wells, *Yucatán's Gilded Age: Haciendas, Henequen, and International Harvester* (Albuquerque: University of New Mexico Press, 1985); Jorge González Durán, *La rebelión de los mayas y el Quintana Roo chiclero* (Mérida: Talleres Gráficas, 1974); Moisés González Navarro, *Raza y tierra: La guerra de castas y el henequén* (México: El Colegio de México, 1979).

5. Carlos Menéndez, *La evolución de la prensa en la Península de Yucatán a través de los últimos cien años* (Mérida: Talleres de la Compañia Tipográfica Yucateca, S.A., 1931), 7–10; Antonio Canto López, "Historia de la imprenta y del periodismo en Yucatán," *Enciclopedia Yucatanense* (Mérida, 1947), 5:5–51, 64; Justo Sierra Méndez, *Obras completas del Maestro Justo Sierra* (México: UNAM, 1949), 5:18.

6. For population figures and other social indicators in Yucatán, see Carlos Escoffie, *Mérida viejo, 1831–1931* (Mérida: n.p., 1932), 2–4.

7. See Sierra O'Reilly's article and the letter from Frederickshall in *El Museo Yucateco* (1841), 1:178–82.

8. See John L. Stephens, *Incidentes del viaje en Yucatán*, trans. Justo Sierra O'Reilly (Mérida: Imprenta de Castillo y Compañía, 1848).

9. John L. Stephens, *Incidents of Travel in Yucatan* (New York: Dover Publications, 1963), 1:168.

10. See Sierra's edition of Stephens, 111n., and articles in *El Registro Yucateco* such as Juan José Hernández, "El Indio Yucateco" (1846), Gerónimo Castillo, "El Indio Yucateco" (1845), "Costumbres de las Indias de Yucatán" (1846), and Vicente Calero, "Tutulxiu y Cocom" (1846).

11. *El Registro Yucateco* (1846), 3:425. The text includes a citation from Jean-Jacques Rousseau.

12. See *El Registro Yucateco* (1846), 4:250; ibid., 1:291–93 passim.

13. Antonio Betancourt Pérez, "La insurrección Maya de 1847," in *Yucatán, Textos de su historia* (Mérida: Gobierno del Estado de Yucatán, 1988), 2:56–121.

14. The Caste War of Yucatán did not end until 1901. See Nelson Reed, *The Caste War of Yucatan* (Stanford: Stanford University Press, 1964); José Esquivel Pren, "La guerra de castas transforma el pensamiento Yucateco," *Historia de la literatura en Yucatán* (Mérida: Ediciones de la Universidad de Yucatán, 1975); Serapio Baqueiro, *Ensayo histórico sobre las revoluciones de Yucatán desde el año 1840 hasta 1864*, 2 vols. (Mérida: Imprenta de Manuel Heredía Argüelles, 1879); Ramón Berzunza Pinto, *Guerra social en Yucatán* (Mérida: Ediciones del Gobierno de Yucatán, 1981).

15. Perry was considered an expert eyewitness on the Caste War and wrote many letters, some in favor of Sierra and others in which he insulted the Yucatecos for their "cowardice in the face of the Indians." See Appendix to Carlos R. Menéndez, *La celebre misión del Doctor Justo Sierra O'Reilly a los Estados Unidos de Norteamérica en 1847 y 1848* (Mérida: Talleres de la Compañia Tipográfica Yucateca, 1945), 257–95.

16. For the family connections, see Justo Sierra Méndez, *Obras*, 11–17. For more information on the political situation in Yucatán at the time, see Serapio Baqueiro, *Estudio biográfico del excellente Sr. D. Miguel Barbachano y Tarrazo antiguo gobernante de la peninsula yucateca* (Mérida: Tipográfia de Gil Canto, 1896), 16–40; "Los comisionados de Yucatán," *La Patria* (February 23, 1848), Historic New Orleans Collection (hereafter HNOC).

17. "Letter from Yucatan," *New York Tribune* (October 5, 1847); Justo Sierra O'Reilly, *Diario de nuestro viaje a los Estados Unidos (La pretendida anexión de Yucatán)* (México: José Porrúa e Hijos, 1938), 53.

18. See front page, *La Patria* (May 7, 1848), HNOC.

19. In the article entitled "Opiniones de Yucatán," *La Patria* (April 5, 1848), basing their information on a "Pro-Barbachanista paper" (*La Unión* of Mérida) reported that the majority of the Yucatecans were against his offer of the Yucatán to the United States. They reported the opinions of the majority of the Yucatecos, which included statements such as "we are going to remain enslaved."

20. Justo Sierra O'Reilly, *Diario*, 68.

21. "Los comisionados de Yucatán," *La Patria* (February 23, 1848), HNOC.

22. Justo Sierra O'Reilly, *Diario*, 85.

23. "When the editor of the New York *Herald*, whose editor seems to be the personal secretary of Mr. Buchanan, having charge of all of his state papers, publishes a letter from Mr. Justo Sierra *urging our government to interfere on behalf of the white inhabitants against the Indians.*" In "Yucatan," *New Orleans Daily Delta* (April 21, 1848), HNOC.

24. See *Carta de Justo Sierra, Nombrado comisionado de Yucatán, a James Buchanan, Secretario de Estado de los Estados Unidos* (April 3, 1848), printed in Carlos Menéndez, *La misión*, 26–29.

25. "Yucatan," *Daily Delta* (April 21, 1848), HNOC. Sierra bitterly commented on the cynicism of this paper's editors who, he claimed, had offered to change their position for a certain sum of money. Sierra, *Diario*, 72.

26. "Yucatan and Communications from M. Justo Sierra to the Senate," *New Era* (May 4, 1848).

27. "El porvenir de Yucatán," *La Patria* (May 14, 1848), HNOC.

28. "Yucatan and a Letter from Justo Sierra," *New Era*, [Washington, DC] (April 20, 1848). For other views of Calhoun, see Menéndez, *La misión*, 53.

29. "Correspondence of the Baltimore Sun on Yucatan," in *Richmond Enquirer* (May 16, 1848).

30. Justo Sierra O'Reilly, *Diario*, 96.

31. Ibid., 94.

32. Ibid., 82.

33. Entry for April 10, 1848, Sierra, *Diario*, 74.

34. Ibid., 75.

35. Sierra, *Los indios de Yucatán*, 1:22–23.

36. On the front page of the first issue of *El Fénix*, Sierra's paper demanded "Death to the savages!" Moreover, only months after returning from the United States he wrote that "the indigenous race . . . must be vigorously subdued and even removed from the country . . . their ferocious instincts, exposed in those dark hours, must be repressed with a strong hand. Humanity and civilization so demand it." See "Guerra de Bárbaros," *El Fénix*, no. 4 (November 15, 1848).

II

Touring Modernity

6

The Lure of Paris

Rubén Darío

*Rubén Darío (Nicaragua, 1867–1916) was a poet and journalist. He is
credited with having initiated the first truly Spanish American literary
movement, Modernismo, which formed part of a general reaction against
Latin America's Hispanic cultural heritage. Modernistas such as Darío
aspired to create new modes of expression that were freed from classical
Spanish poetic forms and drew upon a variety of avant-garde French poetic styles to revitalize their own work. For them, Paris represented both
an escape from the provincialism of Latin America and an ideal toward
which Latin American artists were to aspire. Frequently, however, the actual city did not measure up to the Paris of their imaginations. Poverty,
culture shock, indifference to their talents, and dissolute life-styles all
tarnished the hopes and dreams that had lured Latin American writers to
Paris in the first place.*

*Darío traveled to Paris first in 1892, and the ambivalence that he felt
toward his adopted city dominates this short article, which appeared in
the Argentine newspaper* La Nación. *Written toward the end of his life,
when he suffered from the effects of alcoholism and depression, the article points to the perils of pursuing one's desire for a Paris life-style. At
the same time, it elaborates on the wonders to be found in the French
capital if the visitor was extremely wealthy. Ironically, Darío's use of
French words and his references to famous members of Paris society reveal his rather arrogant mastery of French ways; however, the cynicism
that pervades the article belies his own feelings of rejection by that same
society. Indeed, for all of Darío's apparent love of Paris, the city never
really embraced him in return.*

As I was conversing with friends and old colleagues about my upcoming return to Europe, a young man, whom they had just introduced
to me, approached me. He had a tranquil appearance, but his face and

From Rubén Darío, "El deseo de París," *La Nación*, October 6, 1912. Translated by Ingrid E. Fey.

slightly disheveled hair revealed a sense of purpose and a desire for ad-
ventures. He took me aside, and said:

"Since you have lived for so much time over there, could you give me
some information? . . . For some time, I have had the desire to abandon
this place of merchants, and I have resolved to go to Paris. . . ."

"Oh, Paris!" I replied enthusiastically. "You are going to Paris at such
a lovely age! . . . How happy you must be! . . . Are you rich? Yes, no doubt.
. . . Your wealthy father and mother will fill your wallet. . . . At such an
age of illusions and enthusiasms! You are going to Paris. . . . You will go
aboard [the oceanliner] preparing, with a wonderful crossing, your entry
into the City of Light, the capital of love and pleasure. . . . And you will
arrive bursting with illusions and pesos, that is to say, with francs, to take
possession of happiness, at least for a while. . . . You will stay in the
Hotel Majestic . . . unless you prefer the Ritz or another of the luxurious
and bustling *caravansérails* of that glorious city. . . . You will go to the
races, naturally . . . you will take your cocktails in the bar of the Chatham,
unless you prefer [the bar] in the Carlton. . . . How much you are going to
enjoy yourself! . . . Past midnight, after the theater or the music hall, *chez
Maxim's*—I don't recommend it much; it's a little *démodé* [out of fash-
ion]—*you will go to the Café de Paris, or to the Abbaye de Thélème, which
are more elegant. Champagne, lots of champagne! When you tire of the
hotel, you will surely rent a garçonnière, a garçonnière worthy of someone like you.*[1] . . . Ah, my dear young man, youth! . . . Whoever you are!
It won't be strange for you to have your little scandal or duel, yes, it is
possible. . . . You will spend Carnival in Nice; you will go to Biarritz; . . .
You will have fun; you will thank God for having made you the son of a
father of great fortune! . . ."

The young man interrupted me:

"It's not what you think; permit me; you are quite mistaken. . . . I am
not rich, nor is my family rich. . . . I dedicate myself to writing; and here
I am drowning, I don't find wind for my wings, I can't give impulse to my
inspiration, to my desires for glory. . . . A few friends and colleagues
listen to me, read my prose, applaud my verses. . . . In the newspapers, as
you know, they don't want to know anything of poetry. . . . And they prefer [to print] what comes from abroad. . . . Thus, I want to go to Paris. I
have seen that others have gone: and you yourself, haven't you lived in
Paris for many years without being a man of fortune? And that famous
Central American writer, from Guatemala [Enrique Gómez Carrillo]. . . .
And others, whose names we both know. . . ."

A little stupefied, I began to strangle his illusions:

"But, my esteemed young man, do you know what you are saying?
Do you understand what you are saying? To go to Paris, without any sup-
port, without money, without a base. . . . Do you know any French? . . .
No? . . . Well, it's a thousand times worse to go to Paris in these condi-

tions. . . . For what? You will have to undergo horrible privations. . . . You will wander past third-class hotels behind people who speak Spanish in order to obtain work one day out of thirty, something to prevent death by starvation, being what here they call *pechador* and in Spain *sablista* [a sponger].[2] . . . To struggle in Paris, in order to live in Paris with literature. . . . But this is a dream among dreams! . . . Without knowing French as you know your own language! . . . The cases that you have cited are the exceptions. . . . And the Central American from Guatemala has relied heavily upon his special talent, his name, and a devil of a lot of work . . . for Spain, for other American republics. . . . And he and I have also been diplomats and consuls. . . . And that terrible Puerto Rican [Luis Bonafoux]. . . . If you knew the strife, the difficulty of daily work, the incessant squeezing of one's wits and all with great fame. . . .

"What have you imagined Paris to be like? If you could see the immigrants in Paris who speak Spanish and who wander hither and thither looking for some occupation. . . . If you knew the talented young and old writers who have to type or work on commission for a printer or in bookstores in order to lunch and dine for one franc twenty-five. . . . Don't let the price fool you! . . . In a short time your stomach will be in tatters and you will die poisoned and devoured by microbes. . . . Yes, my dear young man, this is Paris without money. . . . And to find a small position with a business in which Spanish is spoken, a position that would be unacceptable to you in any other situation, you will have to really pound the pavement. . . . And you will have to withstand inquisitive stares and impatient, cold, even vicious gestures. . . . And you will have to go to the Latin Quarter to bother poor students who are your compatriots, or artists who are on scholarships, or even the artists without scholarships, those who live off something.[3] . . . Later, your poor clothing will begin to wear out, if it hasn't already become worn out, and you will have to replace it because if you don't, the concierges will be given orders to tell you when you appear: '*Monsieur est sorti!*' And to replace your worn-out clothing, how are you going to do it? . . .

"You will tell me that your dreams of being an artist will enable you to overcome everything, that you will go to the museums. You will breathe in the environment, and in this environment, along with the contemplation of this light and enchanting wonder that characterizes all things Parisian, you will be able to resist all of the bitter moments and threatening miseries. . . . But this will be worse, my dear young man! . . . Because you will be tantalized, because you will have water, or better said, champagne and kisses within reach of your lips and you won't be able to drink. . . . And you will be, therefore, the most wretched man on earth. You will get together with young men who are so much like you that they could be your brothers . . . and who, in your small rooms, will help you to have a little hope and who will applaud your nocturnal creations, if you even have the energy to write by this point. . . . Beyond this, among your no-madic acquaintances you run the risk of moving in the company of petty thieves, swindlers, and men capable of just about anything. . . . Since you won't have any sure means of eating or finding a place to sleep, you will become a burden, a mosquito, a flea, living off those working people whom you go to visit. . . . Don't go to see Bonafoux, because for such cases he has in his house in Bois Colombe a pair of ferocious dogs. . . . Don't go to see Gómez Carrillo, because *il en a soupé* from so many, and the advice that he often gives is suicide. . . . Yes, my dear young man, this smiling writer will advise you to kill yourself, and he'll even offer the use of one of his swords. . . . As for me, I beg you not to visit me.

"And nevertheless, don't, don't become too sad, or angry either. . . . I could very well be mistaken. . . . You tell me that you have done much writing—several volumes of poetry, some plays, a number of short nov-els, a growing number of short stories. . . . Ignore me if you discern a lack of hope in my words and unselfish advice. . . . Judge that I surely am, in spite of my good fame, perhaps an envious, mean man . . . one of those hoary folk who supports the old and who doesn't want to give a chance to young people, who carry with them the future. . . . Perhaps you imagine that, out of egotism, a few men and I have made it in Paris, and we don't want anyone else to come and compete with us. . . . Ah, my dear young man, if you could only see in the depth of my soul the sincerity of all that I have told you, how much you would thank me! . . . But I see that you are resolved, isn't that so? . . . And after all, nothing can be certain in this world. . . . Who knows but that in what I refer you to I have made the greatest of errors! . . . Who knows if you are a genius, a colossal genius, to whom is destined a complete triumph, to reign over Paris. . . . Who knows? Possibly in a short time, after you arrive, sooner or later, I will see you in an automobile in the Bois [de Boulogne], in the company of Mona Delza or any one of the other really darling courtesan actresses of Paris. . . . And with a substantial deposit in the Banco Español del Rio de la Plata, or in the Crédit Lyonnais. . . . You have Paris on the brain and you want to conquer Paris. . . . Maybe you are right. . . . Go, possibly I could have been mistaken in my judgments and experience. . . . Go, my dear young man, go! . . . *Audentes fortuna juvat*. . . . And after all, you have two resources of last resort. . . . Go to your consul so that he can repatri-ate you . . . or throw yourself into the Seine!"

Notes

1. A *garçonnière* is a small apartment rented by a young man for his private use, often for romantic liaisons with women.

2. Darío alludes to the practice that cash-strapped Latin Americans in Paris took up to earn a little money—that is, they would hire themselves out as tour guides and personal assistants to their compatriots who were visiting the city.

3. As Latin American governments became more established, they increasingly provided funds for the study of art and music in Europe. Usually, however, the "scholarships" were quite meager and were months in arrears. "Latin Quarter" refers to the area on the Left Bank of the Seine where the Université de Paris (Sorbonne) is located; the relatively low cost of rents in this area helped it to become home to many students and artists.

7

Frou-Frous or Feminists? Turn-of-the-Century Paris and the Latin American Woman

Ingrid E. Fey

Paris has often been regarded as the most feminine of cities, a city famous for its cuisine, romance, and fashion, with an inexplicable aura of drama and mystique. Nevertheless, by focusing on the experiences of students, journalists, artists, writers, and diplomats, most of the scholarship that has explored the Latin American presence in Paris has tended to emphasize that of males rather than females. Roderick Barman, for instance, notes that "the travelers to France were overwhelmingly male" (Chapter 3).

As historian Ingrid Fey demonstrates, this situation changed dramatically by the last third of the nineteenth century. By that time, a thriving Latin American community numbering in the thousands had established itself in Paris. Fey's study demonstrates that women comprised a very substantial segment of the Latin American population in turn-of-the-century Paris. In so doing, she revises the standard image of the Latin American in Europe as a young gentleman traveler pursuing experience and education. Exposure to Parisian intellectual trends, political movements, and social mores often pressed Latin American women to question the limitations placed upon women in their homelands. However, as Fey suggests, the taste of freedom enjoyed by Latin American women in Europe did not necessarily translate into an outright rejection of their national heritage; rather, these women often became convinced that the modernity and progress that their nations struggled to achieve could only be attained through a reevaluation of the role of women in society.

In his 1903 novel *Los transplantados*, Chilean writer Alberto Blest Gana parodied the trials and tribulations of the Latin American colony in Paris at the turn of the century.[1] In this tale, Paris exercises a bewitching yet debilitating effect upon its American pilgrims. Latin American men lose health and fortune to the world of prostitutes in the *demi-monde*.

Latin American women either surrender themselves to the frivolity and commodity fetishism of the city or pursue their personal agendas, unbound by the traditional constraints of family, propriety, and patriotic duty. These superficial "frou-frous" and proto-"feminists" reject their national heritage and familial responsibilities in their obsessive efforts to penetrate the upper echelons of Parisian society.[2] In Blest Gana's novel, travel and foreign residence result in Latin Americans' loss of national identity—such experiences are ultimately subversive to the national project, and women are not left out of this subversive experience.

Through their rejection of family and nation, these frou-frous and feminists are a much greater threat to Latin American identity than the heroine of Blest Gana's novel, who commits suicide rather than consummate a forced marriage to a European nobleman. Because of her dramatic act, the heroine remains loyal to her family by going through with the arranged marriage. She also stays true to her Latin American sweetheart by not sexually consummating the marriage. Symbolically, she adheres to her society's expectations of ideal womanhood. By contrast, the frou-frous and feminists who populate the novel threaten Latin American culture and society with extinction by rejecting their nations' idealized models of modest, obedient daughters, faithful wives, and patriotic mothers.

While making for good melodrama, these fictionalized depictions of Latin American women in Paris as frou-frous or feminists simplify the ways in which many of these female travelers viewed Paris. They also reduce in complexity the ways in which their Parisian experiences impacted their sense of national identity.[3] While women's travel in Europe—and to Paris especially—could test their commitment to their nations' traditions, it did not necessarily press them to wholeheartedly reject their national identities. Usually, Latin American women, like their male counterparts, tried to selectively integrate new trends into their national heritage. Therefore, Parisian experience could simultaneously strengthen and weaken Latin American women's commitment to the traditions and customs of their homelands.

Just as for North American women travelers, the challenge for Latin American women living in or visiting Paris at the turn of the century became how to reconcile a European-style taste for freedom with the traditional patriarchal customs and mores of their homelands.[4] Indeed, the excitement, opportunity, and threat of Paris lay in the fact that as both a mythical and real city, it provided Latin American women with a more liberating foil to their own societies. Broadly speaking, the French capital was more liberal than the cities of Latin America in three overlapping ways: spatially, culturally, and intellectually. First, Latin American women enjoyed the spatial freedom that Paris offered. They appreciated the openness of the boulevards and the myriad places in which "respectable" women could congregate. Second, they tended to equate Parisian culture with a "modern" culture, which stood in contrast to their traditional ones. By taking part in the latest trends—whether in moral values, novels, music, or fashion—they implicitly critiqued their own societies' traditions and mores. Third, Latin American elite women valued Parisian intellectual circles' tendency to treat them as autonomous individuals with opinions that were important. Despite continued legal restrictions on women in France and widespread condemnation of the "New Woman," Latin American women viewed Paris as being less inhibiting in many ways than their own nations.[5]

Not Just Gentlemen Travelers: Latin American Women in the City of Light

Men's travel accounts and more recent scholarship on the Latin American presence in Paris have both tended to overlook the great numbers of Latin American women in the city. Contemporary travel accounts, poetry, and novels by men often emphasized the "mythic Paris" that revolved around the sexual pleasures to be found there. Latin American men tended to equate Paris with the free release of their male instincts without incurring responsibilities. One Mexican traveler, for example, explained that upon entering Paris for the first time, he felt like a man embarking upon his honeymoon, a sentiment that revealed his clear understanding of the city as a site of sexual initiation and gratification.[6] Recent scholarly studies of the Latin American presence in Paris have further highlighted its masculine nature by focusing upon the careers of diplomats, writers, political activists, and painters.[7]

Coexisting with the Latin American male presence in Paris was a sizable female population. According to the French census of 1891, there were 2,354 Latin American females living in France as compared to 2,474 males. More specific figures from the French police reveal that adult women made up approximately 25 percent of the Latin American colony in Paris, with adult men and children under eighteen comprising 40 percent and 36 percent, respectively.[8] A wide range of other sources from the period also affirm that considerable numbers of women traveled to the city, sometimes passing through, often staying for long periods of time, or returning to Paris frequently.[9] Clearly, by the late nineteenth century, the Latin American presence in Paris was primarily a familial one that encompassed men, women, and children; the city was not just a stop for young rakes on their grand tour of Europe.

Like the Latin American male population, the female population was extremely heterogeneous. The most economically and socially humble women were those who came to Paris as servants with either Latin American or French families. Women making up a middle- and upper-middle-class group included nuns in French convents, writers, students of music, art, and the sciences, and wives of struggling writers, painters, doctors, political activists, and journalists. At the top rung were women who benefited from investments in real estate, commerce, and mines in Latin America and Europe. Cutting across class distinctions were differences in nationality, education, occupation, and acculturation to French society. The vast differences that existed between Latin American women in Paris can be appreciated by citing the divergent experiences of two women who spent most of their lives in the French capital. One woman at the top of the socioeconomic hierarchy was the Argentine Mercedes Balcarce de Gutiérrez Estrada. Born in Paris, Balcarce was the granddaughter of famed Independence fighter General José de San Martín, daughter of an Argentine diplomat, and wife of a wealthy Mexican diplomat. For much of the turn-of-the-century period, her mansion on the edge of Paris was the center of an active social whirl of Latin Americans and Europeans alike. During the First World War (1914–1917), her stately home became a hospital, ministering to the needs of the French army.[10] At the other extreme was the Mexican Juana Nava, who came to France as a servant in the 1830s; by the 1890s, Juana Nava was old, infirm, alone, and living off the charity of other Mexicans in the city.[11]

Women's activities in Paris were also diverse. While servants and middle-class women spent much of their time caring for their employers or families, wealthy women were able to devote their energies and resources to other activities. Rich or socially prominent Latin American women frequently served as important guardians of national customs and interests in Paris. A number of women held salons in which compatriots gathered for refreshment, entertainment, and company. At social gatherings in their homes traditional Latin American foods occasionally appeared alongside lavish French buffets. *Smart*, a magazine produced by a young Brazilian woman in Paris on the eve of World War I, described the cliquish nature of the Brazilian colony. In general, the journal depicts a society that was relatively self-reliant and self-absorbed. Its members were almost completely Brazilian, generally from São Paulo, and of the economic and social elite.[12] Latin American women also participated in charity work, helping struggling compatriots to eke out an existence or to find a means of returning to their homelands. During the late nineteenth century, for example, a Mexican nun living in a Parisian convent worked with the Mexican consulate to care for a string of indigent Mexican women in France. In 1905 two Brazilian women organized a concert to benefit a sick artist.[13] In spite of their activities on behalf of their compatriots, elite Latin American women also turned their attentions to the attractions of Paris. Significantly, it was this involvement in social, cultural, and intellectual activities that could force them to reevaluate the traditions of their homelands.

"Beyond the Garden Walls": The Spatial Freedom of Paris

For all of Latin America's infatuation with "progress" in the nineteenth and early twentieth centuries, the status of women in the region continued to lag behind that of women in two of Latin America's industrialized models of modernity, namely, the United States and Great Britain. Michael Johns has noted that the tenacity of traditional attitudes toward female behavior was, paradoxically, one of the most striking features of Buenos Aires— arguably the most "modern" of Latin American cities in the early twentieth century. There, in the Argentine capital, elite women were rarely left alone with men outside of the family, even in their own homes, to which they were confined for much of the time. With a few exceptions, the streets and cafés of Buenos Aires were the domain of men; women who ventured forth were often subjected to catcalls and leering looks.[14] Given such a restrictive environment, it is easy to comprehend why, for Latin American women at the turn of the century, the relative spatial freedom of Paris was one of the most appealing features of the city. Paris, with its boulevards, museums, department stores, cafés, hotels, tearooms, ice skating rinks, and other centers of sociability, provided numerous locations in which respectable ladies could pass the time and meet new people, free from the protective gaze of their menfolk.

At the beginning of her anonymous 1889 guidebook written for Latin American women traveling to Paris, an Argentine woman signalled the relative freedom allowed women as one of the most striking differences between Paris and her homeland. Above all, women were free to walk the streets of the city, even in bad weather. Such a female presence, the author explained, gave the city a certain animation. Women also were able to travel alone and unaccompanied. In response to the understandably incredulous reader, the author affirmed that "nothing is easier here than [traveling alone], which is so difficult in Buenos Aires."[15]

A novel by the Argentine Felisa de Onrubia published forty years after the above-mentioned guidebook reveals a continuity in this vision of Paris as a place of spatial liberation, but goes further to link that physical freedom with sexual and spiritual freedom. Most likely this shift in emphasis reflected the increased awareness of feminist ideologies both in Europe and in Latin America.[16] In the novel, Marieta, a recent widow, views her trip to Paris as an opportunity to let flower her personal identity. Living in the city, following her whims, flirting mercilessly with men, Marieta feels as though she has escaped out of one self to become at last more liberated personally and sexually. She urges her prudish companion, Dionisia, to take advantage of all that Paris has to offer. When Dionisia finally asks an acquaintance to visit her at their hotel, Marieta clucks, "Who cares nowadays about how one establishes relationships? What's important is that it be convenient. What's more, *hotels are neutral places, and receiving a visit in them doesn't compromise us in the same way that opening the doors of our homes might*" (emphasis added). For her part, the more conservative Dionisia questions the profundity of such freedom, and throughout the novel she insinuates that Paris's more open social mores are superficial and insincere rather than truly liberating. However, Paris does offer more freedoms than her homeland where, she explains, "[women's] liberty is that of a child in a garden. Nevertheless, she is prohibited from going beyond the garden walls."[17]

From the lists of Latin American travelers to Paris it seems clear that women acted upon a recognition of this relative freedom of movement. Although women rarely traveled completely alone, they often did so without male accompaniment. Registration rolls from the Mexican consulate in Paris document the arrival of many such women. Frequently, they were married, single, or widowed property owners traveling only with other female relatives or domestic servants. There were also individual and small groups of female teachers who went to Paris, perhaps to work for a Mexican family or to study French educational systems. A few Parisian hotels even made their popularity among single Latin American women travelers a primary selling point in their advertising.[18]

Diverse reasons impelled these women to venture off to Europe alone or in groups comprised entirely of other women. Undoubtedly, many women traveled alone because their husbands were not interested in visiting Europe or had to remain behind to oversee the family's business interests.[19] Europe also offered a safe and respectable place for widowed or separated women to live as they pleased, free from their societies' intense glare but not completely isolated since so many of their compatriots were in Europe at any given time. The Argentine widow Elvira Aldao spent many years traveling on the Continent with her sister, niece, and nephew. Both her sister and niece were estranged from their husbands, and, according to their descendants, they stayed in Europe even as World War I raged on in order to keep the boy free from the influence of his father, who was a known thief.[20] For many years, the Argentine writer Eduarda Mansilla lived in various places in France near her daughter, who had married a French nobleman. Meanwhile, Mansilla's husband served as the Argentine minister to England. In the early 1880s, Eduarda Mansilla installed herself in an apartment in the chic section of the Parisian Right Bank while her husband assumed a post as Argentine minister to the Austro-Hungarian empire in Vienna. The couple's son cited health reasons for his mother's stay in Paris, but from other sources it is apparent that the couple was probably separated, a state of affairs that would not have been easy to maintain in Buenos Aires, with its close-knit and gossipy elite society.[21] Although the lives of a few women are not necessarily representative of all Latin American women traveling and living alone in

Europe, their experiences do suggest that European travel provided a means by which those elite women desiring separation from their husbands could live relatively free of both patriarchal control and intense social scrutiny. Most women in such situations led their independent lives somewhat quietly; however, some women took the freedoms of European life—especially Parisian life—to heart, and attempted to find ways to introduce the different values that they admired abroad into their personal lives and homelands.

The Shock of the New: Paris and the Modern Latin American Woman

As the quintessential model of modernity for Latin American elites at the turn of the century, Paris also provided a model of modern values and attitudes regarding acceptable female behavior. Participating in Parisian culture could acquaint women with behavioral patterns not yet accepted by their own societies. The tensions that such newly acquired attitudes and values produced within Latin American society were clearly evident in Blest Gana's novel; likewise, these tensions emerged in both the lives and writings of Latin American women themselves.

Parisian society enabled women to both reaffirm and challenge Latin America's expectations for them. Indeed, many Latin American women continued their normal range of social activities while in the city. For example, Isabel Pesado, the wife of a wealthy Mexican businessman, was well known for her religiosity during her long residence in Paris. Both she and her husband, Sebastián de Mier, maintained regular contacts with a group of Mexican nuns in the Parisian convent of the Sisters of Mercy. Isabel was known for living a fairly quiet life, hosting few receptions, and making an annual Good Friday pilgrimage to honor the Virgen de los Dolores at a church on the Avenue Hoche. Following the death of her husband, Isabel retreated into seclusion, earning from the Pope the title of Duchess de Mier for her piety and generous donations to the Church.[22] At the other extreme were women such as Veridiana Prado, the matriarch of the prestigious and wealthy Prado family of São Paulo, Brazil. According to Darrell Levi, Veridiana found the atmosphere of Paris to be quite liberating and empowering. In fact, Levi argues, it was Veridiana's exposure to European culture that pushed her to leave an unsatisfactory marriage and build her own home in São Paulo where she held an important salon—a far cry from the Catholic ideal of womanhood.[23]

The life and work of Venezuelan novelist Teresa de la Parra provides further insight into the ways in which a Latin American woman's Parisian experience could challenge a number of fundamental facets of her homeland's social morality. Her first novel, published in the early 1920s before de la Parra had visited Paris, revealed Latin American women's expectations of the city and the ways in which their conceptions of Paris contrasted with their feelings about their own societies. In the novel, which in English is entitled *Iphigenia (The diary of a young lady who wrote because she was bored)*, an idealized Paris represents liberation from the traditional social obligations of a repressively patriarchal Venezuelan society. Clearly taking aim at many of her nation's most cherished social values regarding women, de la Parra's novel created a scandal when it was first published in a Caracas newspaper.

Iphigenia's protagonist is María Eugenia, a young girl who passes through Paris on her way home to Venezuela from a Spanish convent school. In Paris she squanders the last of her father's inheritance on gowns and other luxuries in an effort to shock her family in Caracas. The following excerpt describes María Eugenia's mental transformation as it took place in the lobby of a Parisian hotel: "I said to myself that with twenty thousand francs and a little ingenuity it was possible to do a lot. Then I thought that I might well leave my whole family in Caracas *épaté* with my Parisian elegance. I finally deduced that in order to do so it was indispensable to wear more form-fitting dresses and to cut my hair *á la garçonne*, just like a certain lady who at that moment stood out in the group in front of me because of her very lovely figure."[24] For María Eugenia, being Parisian meant being different from Venezuelan society and, by extension, opposed to it in certain ways. She would, as bohemians aspired to do, *épater* (shock) the Caracas bourgeoisie by assuming the airs and appearance of a Parisienne. Significantly, upon María Eugenia's return to Venezuela, her aunt shudders to think of women's freedoms in Paris and blurts out: "It impresses me as one huge house of corruption let loose on the streets. An honorable woman with any self-respect can't walk alone in Paris, because you see horrors! Horrors!"[25]

As the rest of the novel makes clear, María Eugenia's physical and mental transformation in Paris produced a complex intellectual change that leads the heroine to resist—at least temporarily—the social constriction of Venezuelan society. As María Eugenia spends days and weeks in the boredom that Caracas's patriarchal society imposes upon her, she fantasizes about her time abroad. In this context, Paris represents travel, freedom of movement, and sophistication. The city provides an environment in which Latin American women can create a new image or persona for themselves without having to kowtow to societal expectations that circumscribed a woman's life within the four walls of a city home. Her one chance for "freedom"—elopement with a dashing bohemian intellectual from Caracas—likewise involves Paris, as her suitor specficially invokes it as the site for their love's ultimate consummation. "Think . . . think!" he implores. "Like all lovers hungry for voluptuous pleasures, we will weave our first nest under some eave in the shadow of a tree, in that *Parisian* springtime, always rosy and blooming with flowers."[26] [emphasis added]

In the real life of Teresa de la Parra, participation in Parisian culture also offered opportunities to imagine and realize an independent vision of her self and career. French literary historian Paulette Patout has argued that it was through the reading of French novels in translation that the young de la Parra gained much of her writing style and interest in becoming a writer in her own right. In 1923, after publishing *Iphigenia* in a Caracas newspaper, de la Parra was able to travel alone to Paris, where she quickly became involved in Latin American literary circles. In 1924, de la Parra earned international acclaim when her novel won the French publisher Casa Editora Ibero-Americana's annual prize of ten thousand francs. Soon afterward, the novel was twice translated into French. Moreover, while in Paris she purportedly embarked upon a love affair with the Ecuadorian writer and diplomat Gonzalo Zaldumbide, a relationship that never resulted in marriage.[27] Although gaining notoriety as an author within Caracas, de la Parra's connections to the French literary scene were important as an early catalyst to her literary career and as a means of reaching an international reading public and all of the financial and intellectual rewards that such exposure could confer. Thus, in both the life and literature of Teresa de la Parra, Paris figured as an important environment in which to test the limits of her Latin American values and as a powerful foil for exposing the limitations placed on women by the patriarchal society from which she came.

"Permitted to Think, Feel, and Say So Freely": The Intellectual Freedoms of Paris

As de la Parra's life suggests, for a small group of elite Latin American women, time in Paris offered freedom and opportunities to develop an intellectual persona. With its numerous newspapers, reading rooms, lectures, universities, art schools, and scholarly societies and congresses, Paris offered both male and female intellectuals opportunities not always available in their own countries, which were just beginning to develop academic infrastructures. These centers of intellectual exchange often were more receptive to women than were comparable organizations in Latin America.

The Peruvian Aurora Cáceres (1872–1958) was one woman who made the most of her experiences in Europe to develop an intellectual persona. She was the daughter of a former president of Peru and spent many years abroad while her father fulfilled obligations as an ambassador. While in Paris in the early years of the twentieth century, she attended classes at the Sorbonne and began her career as a writer.[28] In addition to contributing articles to journals and newspapers in Peru and Europe, she published several books and established a Pan-Latin organization of writers in Paris, which brought together some of the most renowned writers from the so-called Latin nations of Europe and America. She also gave lectures in the city and attended various international congresses.

In 1909 both French and Latin American writers feted Cáceres in honor of her book *Mujeres de ayer y de hoy* (Women of yesterday and today), which described female achievements across history. In this book, Cáceres registered her impressions of turn-of-the-century feminism in Latin America and Europe with the intent of revealing how the difficulties of modern life had forced women into more active roles as workers and political activists. In addition, as a book written in Spanish, it clearly targeted a Spanish and Latin American audience and aimed to prove the merit of women's political, artistic, and literary accomplishments across time in order to promote their involvement in these spheres in the present.

The book's longest section deals with French feminism and reveals how Cáceres's experiences in Paris shaped her general philosophy about the role of women in modern society. Like such Paris-based North American women writers as Gertrude Stein and Edith Wharton, Cáceres found that France provided a particularly stimulating intellectual environment that was open to women's endeavors, particularly literary ones.[29] She observed that in Paris, "daily we see appear the new books by women in the shop windows of bookstores, masterfully written, without being unworthy in the least alongside more notable authors." Cáceres developed personal relationships with various important French women writers, and these writers were inspiring as role models and mentors. In contrast to the stereotype that depicted French women as being "frou-frous," Cáceres found that the most interesting women in Paris balanced beauty and elegance with intelligence and spirituality. She believed that her friend, Jeanne Catulle Mendes, was a fine example of the modern woman: "in addition to her renown as a poet, she also is said to be one of the most fashionable, elegant women [in Paris]."[30]

Cáceres found in the French feminist community an open and respectful place in which women could air their opinions about a variety of issues affecting the conditions of women in that country. Although information remains sketchy, it appears that Cáceres had regular social contact with numerous French feminists and attended their meetings.[31] Moreover, in her book, when describing the Congrès Féministe of Paris of 1908, Cáceres marveled at the subdued nature of the men in the audience and their deference toward female participants. She explained that "we find the men less arrogant than in masculine congresses; maybe we are mistaken, but it appears that they have a timid aspect . . . in contrast, the female speakers have a resolute attitude, grave and dignified; nothing shocks, nothing provokes criticism or ridicule."[32] In this situation, men and women actually functioned equally in the discussions at hand.

The notion that men and women needed to be equal partners in both material and intellectual work was a vital element in French feminism that assumed primary importance in Aurora Cáceres's thinking and behavior.[33] The belief also led directly to her marriage in Paris to, and her separation from, the Guatemalan writer Enrique Gómez Carrillo. Cáceres's memoirs, which cover the year of their courtship and marriage (1906–07), revealed the different ways in which Latin American men and women could respond to the Parisian environment. They depicted a woman torn between her intellectual abilities and literary aspirations on the one hand and her social, familial, and religious obligations on the other. Although initially troubled by Gómez Carrillo's reputation as a bohemian with a rather unrespectable life-style, Cáceres believed that his unconventionality would produce the kind of collaborative marriage that she so desperately desired. In her diary she noted that "no one has understood better how to treat me like a writer and not like a society woman, because if there is something that I love in life it is the literary profession, in which one is permitted to think, feel, and say so freely."[34] In addition, Gómez Carrillo sent Aurora books by French writers and addressed her as his "intellectual sister" in his letters. In days when Latin American men wrote often of women's deficiencies in education and creativity, this was a striking gesture on Gómez Carrillo's part. A future with him appeared to have numerous benefits: "Enrique offers me a dazzling future: traveling all over the world, writing about the marvels that I am going to know while being with him."[35]

However, after their marriage, the very unconventionality that had first drawn Aurora to Enrique eventually led to their separation. For her, "bohemian Paris" did not offer the respectability and stability that she craved and it proved to be all too traditional in its treatment of women. In the end, Enrique above all sought a martyr to his own work rather than the truly equal intellectual and spiritual companion that Aurora's experiences in Paris had led her to aspire to be. Enrique explicitly expressed his need for a rather traditional wife in a letter written to Aurora as the marriage was crumbling: "I am accustomed to pampering, flattery, and adulation. . . . Bohemia is not made for women like you, friends of consideration, Christian on the outside and thirsty for attention."[36] Far from desiring the "intellectual sister" who could "think, feel, and say so freely," Enrique at bottom required what every good Latin American patriarch desired: a stay-at-home wife devoted to his every need, regardless of his behavior.

Conclusion

In spite of Blest Gana's exaggerated depictions of Latin American women in Paris, it is clear that their presence was much more varied and complex than he described it to be. They were not all fabulously wealthy social climbers, and many women were able to achieve the balance between their national identities and Parisian influences that Blest Gana appeared to advocate in his novel. Nevertheless, Latin American women's connections to Paris—whether within the city as travelers or viewing it from afar as idealistic fans—did stimulate them to question their own societies' expectations. The physical openness of Paris made the city an attractive place for unaccompanied women and allowed them opportunities to mingle with diverse groups of people in ways not always possible within Latin America. Although difficult to document, such spatial freedom also could facilitate sexual liberation. Latin Americans' equation of French culture with modern culture often led Latin American women to question traditional customs and values as being antithetical to the progress that their nations sought to achieve—a progress that was very much equated with Parisian models.

Finally, Paris's intellectual infrastructure and relative receptivity to women's contributions in that realm, in addition to its lively feminist movement, made the city particularly supportive for Latin American women intellectuals. In Paris there were opportunities to study, publish, and meet other intellectuals who, according to Latin American women themselves, were often more open and respectful of women's accomplishments and aspirations than Latin American men. All of these overlapping freedoms contrasted with Latin America's lack of such opportunities, and the evident contrasts were part of what moved women to ponder ways in which to incorporate greater opportunities within a Latin American context. Rather than being a purely subversive experience, Latin American women's travel and foreign residency in Paris—and in Europe in general—encouraged them to reform their nations' attitudes toward women in order to facilitate the march of progress and modernity in the region.

Notes

1. Alberto Blest Gana, *Los transplantados*, 2 vols. (Paris: Garnier Hermanos, [1903]).
2. "Frou-frou" is a term that became popular in nineteenth-century France to describe women whose primary preoccupation was the cultivation of their beauty and appearance. Often associated with the *demi-monde*, or the world of prostitutes, this type of woman lived to fulfill the sexual needs of men.
3. I do not specifically analyze women's involvement in Parisian feminist organizations; instead, I look at more general reactions to and actions within the French capital. Somewhat by necessity, my analysis deals mainly with upper-class, educated, "white" women; however, as the essay makes clear, these were by no means the only Latin American women residing in Paris at the turn of the century. Ingrid E. Fey, "The First Tango in Paris: Latin Americans in Turn of the Century France, 1880–1920" (Ph.D. diss., University of California at Los Angeles, 1996); Jeffrey Needell, *A Tropical Belle Epoque* (Cambridge, England: Cambridge University Press, 1987); Mauricio Tenorio Trillo, *Mexico at the World's Fairs: Crafting a Modern Nation* (Berkeley: University of California Press, 1996).
4. Shari Benstock, *Women of the Left Bank: Paris, 1900 to 1940* (Austin: University of Texas Press, 1988), 10.

5. Ironically, although many North American and Latin American women found Paris to be a liberating environment, France lagged behind the United States and England in the struggle for women's rights. The French legal system, which was based on the Napoleonic Code, severely limited women's rights. Under its laws, all women were considered to be permanent minors. Furthermore, specific statutes required that women obey their husbands. Essentially, French women had hardly any legalized control over their public or personal lives.

6. Felipe Teixidor, *Viajeros mexicanos (Siglos XIX y XX)* (Mexico: Ediciones Letras de México, 1939), 133. Needell has observed that for Brazilian men, involvement with Parisian women was often used as an opportunity to convey to others a sense of their wealth, sophistication, and modernity. Needell, *Tropical Belle Epoque*, 161.

7. See, for example, Paul Estrade, *La colonia cubana de Paris, 1895–1898. El combate patriótico de Betances y la solidaridad de los revolucionarios franceses* (Havana: Editorial de Ciencias Sociales, 1984); Ramón Favela, *Diego Rivera: The Cubist Years, 1913–1917* (Phoenix: The Phoenix Art Museum, 1984); Marc Cheymol, *Miguel Angel Asturias dans le Paris des années folles* (Grenoble, France: Presses Universitaires de Grenoble, 1987).

8. Although the overall ratio of Latin American males to females was nearly equal, when age is taken into account, the ratio becomes significantly less so. Many females in France appear to have been children under eighteen accompanying their families. However, these general figures do not include the many hundreds, if not thousands, of Latin Americans who passed through Paris as travelers in any given year, among whom women figured prominently. France, *Dénombrement des étrangers en France (Résultats statistiques du dénombrement de 1891)* (Paris: Imprimerie Nationale, 1893), xxxviii–xxxix, lxxxvii–lxxxix.

9. These sources include newspapers and magazines published in France and Latin America at the turn of the century, memoirs and diaries, novels, registration rolls from the Mexican consulate in Paris, and correspondence in the Mexican legation from the Archivo Genaro Estrada in Mexico City.

10. Béatrice Ferrari, "La colonie argentine de Paris et la guerre," *Paris Buenos Aires* 15 (1919): 2–6.

11. Archivo Genaro Estrada (Mexico City), Leg. 17, Exp. 4; Leg. 21, Exp. 4; Leg. 42, Exp. 1.

12. See *Smart. Petite Revue Mensuelle*, 1911–12. This magazine was published by Caroline Penteado. Contributors were from her circle of friends and included both French and Brazilian teenagers and young adults.

13. "Echos de partout," *Le Brésil*, March 5, 1905, 3. The event's performers included Guillermo White, a Cuban violinist who had served as a tutor to Dom Pedro II's children. The son of a French father and Cuban slave, White was one of the few visibly black Latin Americans to achieve prominence in Paris during this time.

14. Michael Johns, "The Antinomies of Ruling Class Culture: The Buenos Aires Elite, 1880–1910," *Journal of Historical Sociology* 6:1 (March 1993): 85–88.

15. Una Argentina, *Vida de París* (Buenos Aires: Félix Lajouane, 1889), 5–8.

16. By the 1920s, a range of feminist issues had made their way into the political landscape of Latin America. For an account of the rise of feminism in the Southern Cone, see Asunción Lavrin, *Women, Feminism, and Social Change in Argentina, Chile, and Uruguay, 1890–1940* (Lincoln: University of Nebraska Press, 1995).

17. Felisa de Onrubia, *Pasa una mujer* (Buenos Aires: Talleres Gráficos Argentinos L. J. Rosso, 1931), 46–47, 72, 182.

18. *L'Argentine* 1 (July 1, 1908), 8.

19. According to their descendants, such was the case with Susana Torres de Castex and her daughter, Susanita Castex y Torres de Apellániz. Interview by the author with José de Apellániz and Susana Apellániz de Ibarbia (Buenos Aires, June 28, 1996).

20. Interview by the author with Celina María Aldao and Angeles Moreno del Campo de Miguens (Buenos Aires, July 4, 1996).

21. When Agustín Arroyo went to replace García as minister in Vienna in 1890 (García had died a couple of years earlier), Arroyo found the legation in disorder. Making matters worse, the longtime separation between Manuel and Eduarda— who by then was living in Vienna—had become public knowledge in Viennese diplomatic circles. Agustín Arroyo to José E. Uriburu (Vienna, October 27, 1890), Instituto Bibliográfico "Zinny" (Buenos Aires), Caja CUR-10; Daniel García Mansilla, *Visto, oido y recordado: Apuntes de un diplomático argentino (Primeros venticinco anos)* (Buenos Aires: Editorial Kraft, 1950), 1:172.

22. Teixidor, *Viajeros mexicanos*, 64, 71; "Apuntes," *Europa y América*, October 5, 1894, 3.

23. Darrell E. Levi, *The Prados of São Paulo, Brazil: An Elite Family and Social Change, 1840–1930* (Athens: University of Georgia Press, 1987), 62–66.

24. Teresa de la Parra, *Iphigenia (The diary of a young lady who wrote because she was bored)*, trans. Bertie Acker (Austin: University of Texas Press, 1993), 14.

25. Ibid., 32.

26. Ibid., 325.

27. Paulette Patout, "Teresa de la Parra, París, y *Las memorias de Mama Blanca,"* in *Las memorias de Mama Blanca, Edición crítica* (Spain: Colección Archivos, 1988), 153–55, 164.

28. Alberto Tauro, *Enciclopedia ilustrado del Perú* (Lima: Peisa, 1987).

29. These and other women writers from the United States are described in Benstock, *Women of the Left Bank.*

30. Z. Aurora Cáceres, *Mujeres de ayer y de hoy* (Paris: Garnier Hermanos, [1909]), 217, 226. This belief directly contradicted the standard popular stereotype of the French feminist as being homely and overly aggressive. Jean Rabaut, *Féministes à la belle époque* (Paris: Editions France-Empire, 1985).

31. In an undated card from Aurora Cáceres to Argentine writer Manuel Ugarte, she invited him to have tea at her home. She promised that Ugarte would be able to meet some of the French feminists (no names are mentioned) to whom she had told so much about him. Archivo General de la Nación (Argentina), Sala VII, Leg. 2215.

32. Cáceres, *Mujeres de ayer y de hoy*, 298–99.

33. Ibid., 215.

34. Z. Aurora Cáceres, *Mi vida con Enrique Gómez Carrillo* (Paris: Garnier Hermanos, 1909), 30.

35. Ibid., 62–63.

36. Ibid., 227–28.

8

The Impact of Imported Sports on the Popular Culture of Nineteenth- and Early Twentieth-Century Mexico and Central America

Richard V. McGehee

In recent years the number of Latino athletes in the United States has increased dramatically, particularly in the most "American" of sports, baseball. Dominicans, for example, now form the largest segment of foreign players in the U.S. major leagues. In this selection, sports historian and professor of kinesiology Richard McGehee links the history of travel and sports in Latin America. He discusses the role of foreigners in bringing these sports to the region and the less commonly studied experience of sports participation as a facet of Spanish American youths' foreign residence. When these young people returned home, they brought back not only educational skills learned abroad but also their new favorite forms of recreation.

Along with these imported games came new values and skill requirements, including recreational teamwork, national (and international) communication, the co-ordination of competitions, and media publicity. McGehee shows that these travel- and sports-related activities both reflected and contributed to modern national identity formation throughout Latin America. Furthermore, the importation of foreign words necessary to express elements of the games that had no counterpart in the Spanish language heightened awareness of language and national identity, occasionally touching off xenophobic reactions. McGehee argues that the importation of foreign sports, their local development under the influence of a multitude of international guises, and the Latin Americans' eventual entry into world-class competitions as representatives of their own nations all indicate the interconnectedness of travel, sports, and national identity in the twentieth century.

For much of Latin America's modern history, sports have not been "national" in the sense of having teams represent nation-states at international competitions. Supporters' allegiance was to their town, school, or region, and the general public was little concerned with, or even interested in, sports on a broader national level. This situation began to change in the late nineteenth and early twentieth centuries, when the diffusion of modern organized sports paralleled the development of the national political state. It was at that time that sports popular during the colonial period, such as horse racing, cockfighting, and bullfighting, began to lose their monopoly on the public's attention. Soccer, baseball, football, fencing, bicycling, and other foreign sports started to make their appearance at the end of the nineteenth century as a result of Latin America's incorporation into the global economy.

While foreigners in Latin America certainly played a central role in promoting these new sports, Latin Americans also were key actors in this process. Typically, elite Latin American youths frequently studied in Europe and the United States where they participated in school and club sports. While abroad, they not only learned the rules of these new team sports but also absorbed the games' larger culture, which stressed competition, teamwork, and physical strength. These values contrasted with those of traditional sports inherited from the Spanish colonial era, which rewarded artistry, cunning, and technical skill. Returning to their own countries, these young men, and occasionally young women, brought back both athletic equipment and an enthusiasm for this modern type of sports participation. Once home, they initiated their friends and acquaintances into these new cultural forms. In this way, for Latin Americans, sports became a vital link between the authentic nation at home and communities abroad. They also offered a way to preserve cultural and social connections while in foreign residence and provided an event around which to organize. In the modern age, sports, travel, and national identity were increasingly linked.

**Foreigners and Nationals Initiate and
Promote Modern Sports in Latin America**

Knowledge of and enthusiasm for new and foreign sporting activities developed in Latin America as the result of two forces: the presence of foreigners in the region and the promotional activities of Latin American travelers who became aficionados of different sports while living abroad. Foreign businessmen and their wives were frequently the agents who introduced their own preferred sport to the Latin American countries in which they resided. For this obvious reason, residents in the major cities, port towns, and plantation areas were the first to be exposed to the new games. Some foreigners restricted their activities to their own expatriate groups, but many of them also made significant efforts to popularize their sport among the citizenry of their host countries. Foreign military personnel also facilitated the introduction of certain sports into Latin America. Soccer-playing British seamen and baseball-playing American sailors and marines organized exhibitions of their sports and competitions for local teams when they visited Latin American ports. Additionally, recreational activities of U.S. military personnel stationed in Nicaragua, the Dominican Republic, Cuba, Puerto Rico, and the Canal Zone of Panama brought attention to the sports they played, especially baseball. Of course, the warmth of the reception given to these military men and their games varied with the current international political climate, a factor that points to another important function of sports participation—as a bellwether of inter-American relations.

High society in Porfirian Mexico during the 1890s enthusiastically adopted the sports being played in the United States and Europe, and continued to dominate the country's sporting activity through the 1920s.[1] Participation in sports of foreign origin, which typically required expensive equipment and the luxury of leisure time, was a visible indicator of a certain economic status and cosmopolitan life-style. Spanish national champion jai alai players were brought to Mexico in 1895 to inaugurate one of the earliest frontons in Mexico City. The Spanish Basque ball game, *pelota vasca*, which was played with hands, paddles, and racquets, caught on among the wealthy who could afford to build their own courts or belong to clubs that had custom-built facilities. The first soccer club in Mexico was established by British miners in Pachuca in 1900, and other Britons introduced the sport in Orizaba, Mexico City, and other locations soon afterwards. This sport was dominated by foreigners until 1912, after which time an increasing majority of the players were Mexicans. Boys attending the Colegio Williams de Tacubaya and the Escuela Nacional Preparatoria in Mexico City were introduced to soccer and a variety of other imported sports in the 1910s and 1920s.[2]

Baseball was yet another sport introduced by foreign residents in Latin America. In Mexico, American expatriates actively promoted their national pastime during the early 1900s, even persuading the world champion Chicago White Sox to visit Mexico City in the spring of 1907 to play an exhibition game. Around the same time, Cubans, whose island was under U.S. military occupation at the time, introduced baseball to the Yucatán. With this kind of international promotion, baseball had become the "king of sports" in Mexico. By 1926, as many as seventy or eighty amateur games were being reported in the capital city each Sunday, and a few professional ball clubs already existed there and in Veracruz as well.

The private association that did most to spread modern sports activity among Mexicans was the Young Men's Christian Association (YMCA). Some Mexicans, such as Enrique Aguirre from Mexico City and Oscar

Castillón from Monterrey, had attended the YMCA college in Springfield, Massachusetts, and returned home to become enthusiastic YMCA physical directors. The "Y" was an important promoter of basketball, swimming, track and field, volleyball, and other sports activities in the country, and used these sports to propagate a platform stressing hard work, family, Christian morality, charity, and virtuous living. In this way, sports' link to a larger social context, one affected by residence abroad, becomes apparent. With the belief that sports promoted physical health and spiritual well-being, Mexico City's branch of the international YMCA sponsored a track and field competition in 1915, leading to the establishment the next year of the Interscholastic Track and Field Meet, which became an annual event. The "Y" organized the first all-Mexico basketball league in 1912 and initiated the first national championship in 1919. Similarly, volleyball was introduced as a YMCA activity in Mexico City and Monterrey in 1917, and its popularity spread rapidly. By 1921 volleyball league play was being held in several metropolitan areas and had permeated the more elite Mexican schools. In 1921 volleyball was included in the program of activities of the Interscholastic Athletic Federation, and in 1927 the first school championships were held with the participation of seventeen male and four female teams.

Some boxing activity existed in Mexico in earlier years but its popularity greatly increased in the 1920s with the visits of such foreigners as Jack Johnson, Jack Dempsey, Sam Langford, and Luis Angel Firpo.[3] Several Mexican boxers trained with Johnson during his year-long residence in Mexico City during 1919–20. Dempsey was especially popular in Mexico, as evidenced by a crowd of 5–10,000 fans who mobbed him when he arrived at Mexico City's railroad station in 1925. By 1928, Mexican boxers were represented in their country's Olympic delegation, and one of Mexico's first two Olympic medals was won by the flyweight Francisco Cabañas in 1932.

In Guatemala, the link between foreign travel and the introduction of new sports was particularly evident. Guatemalan boys who attended school in England and Belgium brought soccer with them when they returned home and founded the first soccer club, the Guatemala Foot-Ball Club, in 1902.[4] Among the pioneers of Guatemalan soccer who learned the sport in Europe between 1895 and 1902 were Eusebio Murga, Delfino Sánchez Latour, and Carlos and Jorge Aguirre Matheu, who attended St. George's College in Weybridge, England; Francisco Sánchez Latour, the English Naval Cadets Academy; Luis Pedro Aguirre, Rafael Rodezno, and Lorenzo Foncea, Crystal Palace Engineers School of London; Rafael Aparicio, Brighton College; and Jorge Romaña, Gustavo Novella, Raúl Angulo, Brussels' Collège de Melle.[5] In fact, the first uniforms of the Guatemala Foot-Ball Club were identical to those of England's St. George's College.

Arturo Aguirre Matheu, younger brother of Carlos and Jorge, learned to play soccer in Guatemala from his returning siblings and went on to become both a founding member of the Hércules Club and captain of its soccer team in 1910. When the Hércules Club shifted its emphasis to baseball in 1910, Arturo also took up this foreign sport until his own eventual departure for a European education in 1912. In France he studied at Versailles' Jules-Ferry school before enrolling in the School of Public Works Engineering in Paris. While residing abroad, Arturo Matheu played soccer with the Jeunesse Sportive de Colombes, the Club de Melun, and was captain of his university team, which took the championship title for two consecutive years. In 1918, Matheu played for the Sport Athletic-Bordeau Etudiant Club, which was runner-up in the championship of southwestern France. The high point of his competitive international athletic career came shortly before Matheu's return to Guatemala in 1919, when he proudly competed in the Paris Olympics, "the first time the emblem of Guatemala was seen in an Olympic stadium."[6] Matheu, like countless other athletes before and after him, became even more aware of his Guatemalan identity by representing his people abroad, gloriously dressed in his nation's colors, and displaying its best accomplishments to a worldwide audience.

Guatemalans who attended school in the United States introduced baseball to their compatriots upon their return home. Both soccer and baseball, as well as cycling, basketball, tennis, track and field, and other sports, rapidly became established in Guatemala City and, to a lesser extent, in Quezaltenango.[7] The names of many of the clubs and teams in the early years of Central American sports reflect their foreign inspiration. Between 1906 and 1931, Guatemalan soccer teams bore the names Michigan, Ohio, Oakland, Berkeley, Racing, Portland, Halifax, United, Standard, Texas, España, and Allies. Baseball clubs were called Chicago, New York, Manchester, Chile, Denver, Japón, Colombia, Tíber, Filadelfia, Países Bajos (Low Countries), Cleveland, Washington, and Boston. Occasionally, American sailors from ships docked at Puerto Barrios traveled to Guatemala City to watch and play baseball games, which sparked rivalries between the North American sportsmen and their Guatemalan opponents. National pride in Guatemalan soccer reached a new high in 1920, when the Hércules Club defeated the team of the British ship *Cambrian*, the first loss for the *Cambrian* in more than a year. In Guatemala as elsewhere, sports acted as a barometer of international rivalry and developed alongside the growth of foreign economic and political influence in Mexico and Central America.

Nicaraguan youths' foreign residence also helped to introduce baseball to that country.[8] After the expulsion of the Jesuit order from Nicaragua in 1881, young David Arellano and his two brothers were sent abroad by their father to attend Jesuit schools, first in Costa Rica and then at St. John's College, a high school linked to Fordham University in New York City. From 1880 to 1891, Arellano pitched for the school's baseball team, including an exciting exhibition game against the professional New York Giants. It was a heady brush with stardom for the patriotic young Nicaraguan who, upon returning home to a hero's welcome in Granada, persuaded his brothers to join him in founding a baseball team so that he could continue to play the American game. Later that same year, the phenomenon had caught on; the Recreation Society of Managua, a recently established club presided over by former national president Adán Cárdenas, organized a baseball team, which entered into competition with the Arellanos brothers, thus extending the long-standing political and social rivalry between Managua and Granada into the realm of sports. All of the first baseball players in Granada and Managua were members of politically conservative elite families, but after the arrival of Liberal General José Santos Zelaya to the presidency in 1893, baseball's socioeconomic base became more diverse, reflecting the growing power of middle sectors in the region's urban areas.[9]

In 1903 another Nicaraguan alumnus of New York's St. John's College, Juan Deshón, introduced the American national sport to his hometown of Chinandega while visiting there on his school vacation. Deshón returned to the United States to pitch for Cornell University and reportedly received offers to play for the New York Giants and Yankees, a story he proudly retold to anyone willing to listen. Like Arellano, success and recognition abroad meant a great deal to Latin American youths, as a sort of sure-fire way to ride to a position of power, or at least prestige, once they returned home to their own countries. Once back in Nicaragua, Deshón organized the Titán Club in Chinandega and mystified batters with his curve ball for a few years until others learned how to throw it.[10] In 1904 two baseball teams were organized in Masaya, and in 1905 in Managua, American Consul Carter Donaldson helped organize the Boer Club, the most famous Nicaraguan team over the years.[11]

The link between foreign residence and baseball's popularity in Nicaragua was strong in the early twentieth century; nevertheless, its popularity was also bolstered by the presence of the U.S. troops in that country. U.S. Marines stationed in Managua (1912–1933) fielded baseball teams and supplied officials for Nicaraguan baseball, boxing, and basketball competitions, just as they did supervisors for ballots and elections. Visiting crews from U.S. and British warships docked at the port of Corinto on the Pacific coast competed against the resident U.S. forces as well as Nicaraguan teams. In the era when Augusto César Sandino's guerrilla forces in the Las Segovias mountains were staging strikes against the U.S. occupation forces, Nicaragua's baseball players took a similar satisfaction in defeating U.S. and British teams on the playing field. During a seemingly hopeless match between Chinandega's local team, Titán, over the boys from the U.S.S. *Galveston*, the Nicaraguan team was down 15–9 when they took their last at-bats. Yet, as the newspaper reported the next day, "Titán seems defeated; but the nine Nicaraguan boys, as if in a war between races, exalted by their Nicaraguan pride, as though inflamed by powerful Indian blood, entered the bottom of the ninth with an enthusiasm spurred on by the screams of the crowd." After two Nicaraguan scores, *Galveston* changed pitchers. "Titán can't adjust to the new pitches and makes two outs. Hope dies in the thousands of spectators. But suddenly the batters regroup and attack furiously. The new pitcher watches his balls hit all over the field by the formidable Nicaraguan batters. A double by García ties it up 15–15. The spectators go crazy with emotion. With García on second, Cano hits a clean triple that gives the game to Titán."[12] The American pastime, the glorious game learned by Nicaraguans while in the United States, had become a metaphor for emerging Nicaraguan national pride. The Titáns had beaten the Yankees at their own game.

When a youthful Anastasio Somoza, the future U.S.-handpicked leader of the Nicaraguan National Guards and eventually president of the country, returned to León, Nicaragua, after his studies in the United States, he too promoted sports learned while away at school, notably boxing and baseball. In power during the 1940s and 1950s, Somoza operated his own baseball team, Cinco Estrellas (Five Stars). Baseball became inseparable from the image of Nicaraguan culture; before the revolutionary Sandinista decade of the 1980s, professional teams competed at a high level, attracting players from Cuba, the United States, and other countries. With the rise of the professional game in the 1930s–1950s, baseball players from Cuba, Nicaragua, the Dominican Republic, Mexico, and other Latin American countries had many opportunities to travel overseas as individuals and touring teams, which indicates the growing importance of sports in the modern world and the desire to use sports to represent one's nation positively on the world stage. To field a competitive international team proved that a nation had made it, metaphorically speaking, into the "big leagues."

Young men returning from studies overseas also introduced soccer to Costa Rica, and foreign residents in the country were active participants and promoters of the sport. Teams playing in the first formal competitions in 1898 were referred to as "Foreigners" vs. "Costa Ricans," but the game soon came to be dominated by native sons and caught on in all the principal cities. The Catholic Church became a supporter of soccer as early as 1904, and, by 1907, priests were not only founding soccer clubs but also offering church plazas as practice grounds.[13] Furthermore, church fund-raising activities, called *turnos*, as well as the annual year-end civic celebrations, started to feature soccer games and other sports activities as a way to make money for social causes. Business opportunities quickly followed the introduction of modern team sports in Central America. Costa Rican baseball had originated in precisely those regions most associated with foreign economic development, along the Caribbean coast dominated by Americans, Europeans, and West Indians near Limón. The sport was especially popular with black residents, who fielded at least three ball clubs during the 1920s.[14]

Baseball also spread throughout the Caribbean islands. In the 1860s and 1870s young Cubans such as Nemesio Guillot and Esteban Bellán studied in the United States and learned to play baseball. Guillot brought the sport back to Cuba in 1866 and shortly thereafter helped establish Cuba's first professional teams, the Habana Baseball Club (1872) and the Matanzas Club (1873). Significantly, almost all players on these teams had attended schools and colleges in the United States. Bellán had played college baseball at Fordham University and then joined the professional leagues to play for the Troy Haymakers and the New York Mutuals (1873). He helped arrange the first professional game in Cuba, between Havana and Matanzas, in 1874. When the Almendares Club was formed in 1878, the three clubs organized themselves into Cuba's first professional league.[15]

Soon baseball's popularity spread throughout Cuba, and Sunday afternoon games were being played in nearly every town. More than two hundred teams were founded between the late 1870s and early 1890s. Major league teams from the United States began to visit the island; the Philadelphia Athletics played a series of exhibition games against Cuban professionals in 1886. Cubans who emigrated to the United States played baseball, especially in Key West and Tampa, Florida, which were already havens to large numbers of Cuban exiles and immigrants. Among the other elements of Cuban culture that were flourishing in Key West in the 1890s, there were four baseball teams (Cuba, Fe, Habana, and Esperanza). Ybor City (Tampa) had its first Cuban baseball team in 1887 and soon there were two more.[16] The popularity of baseball and competitive successes of Cubans and Cuban national teams grew throughout the twentieth century, one of the many high points being construction of Havana's Cerro Stadium in 1946. While many opportunities in Cuban sports before 1959 were largely limited to a small and relatively wealthy elite, baseball (and boxing) was available to all, and allowed players to earn a living as professionals. From Cuba, the game diffused to other Spanish-speaking islands in the U.S. orbit, including Puerto Rico and the Dominican Republic.[17]

Americans and West Indians brought baseball to Panama in the 1880s, but by the 1890s many teams had at least two or three Panamanians. The first Panamanian players are described as being from the highest levels of society. Around 1894 the Panama Athletic Club had evolved into an exclusively Panamanian team and was reported to be the best in the country. Perhaps the first team outside of Panama City was organized among United Fruit Company employees in Bocas del Toro (1906). The presence of foreign workers and American military personnel in the Canal Zone additionally promoted baseball in the early years of the twentieth century, but within the Canal Zone play was segregated into Colored Leagues and others for white North Americans. The first visit of a professional baseball team to Panama came in 1912, when the Class A New Orleans Pelicans played five games in the Canal Zone.[18]

Sports, Journalism, and the Importation of Language

Just as sports themselves were imported, so the language used in the games was also heavily laced with English terminology and words derived from English. It was probably easier at first to use English expressions than to invent new ones, especially because many of the players had spent time in English-language schools abroad; but, as the games began to acclimatize to their new lands, more Spanish terms crept in, making the sports themselves seem less foreign. The Hispanization of sports terms increased with each decade of the twentieth century, along with the rising tide of cultural nationalism throughout Latin America. There was some usage of English words, including: baseball, inning, field, out, pitcher, sportsman, match, score, ring, and round to express new sports terms. However, Spanish terms were used if a corresponding concept was available. Some such translations included *batazo limpio* (hit), *partida* (game), *pugilista* (boxer), *juez* (umpire), and *cesto* (basket). A new jargon that combined elements of both languages into "Spanglish" also sprang up to assist new players, fans, and journalists in expressing new athletic forms; these could be literal Spanish translations of English terms, combinations of English and Spanish words, or phonetic Spanish spellings of the English original; examples include: *carrera* (a run in baseball), *esportivo/deportivo* (sporting), *aut* (out), *champeón* (champion), *embasado* (a player on base), *doble ply* (double play), *jit limpio* (clean hit), and *off-said* (off-side).[19] There was an identifiable trend away from the heavier use of English in the first twenty years of the twentieth century, through a transition period in the 1920s, toward the greater adoption of Spanish terms and invention of new words, such as *béisbol* and *fútbol*, in the 1930s. However, English and Spanglish persist to the present in Latin American sports and its literature. For example, Nicaraguan writer Sergio Ramírez used the terms "pitcher," "strike," "inning," "infield hit," and "out" in his stories; Mexican novelist Vicente Leñero coined the verb *chutar*, meaning to take a shot on goal in soccer.[20] Language, one of the primary indicators of national identity, changed with the introduction of imported sports to the region.

These terms also diffused throughout society and began to be used metaphorically with reference to non-sports activities. One notable editorial in a Managua daily newspaper predicting the imminent fall of a political family named Tijerino sprinkled baseball imagery and language

throughout, telling readers that "in the political game, the Tijerinos, having struck everybody out (*dejado a todos en el guante*) to ensure their
victory, sent up a high ball (*fly*) that should have given them a home run
(*home rum*), but a fielder (*filder*) snagged the fly (*fly*) in the instant that
the runner arrived at home (*home*)—the runner was called 'out,' representing in this case the Tijerinos."[21] Another news item, referring to students who had failed their exams in the School of Medicine and Pharmacy,
said they had been *noqueados* (knocked out).[22]

While notices of sports activity were almost non-existent in newspapers before 1900, by the 1920s they were common. Most newspapers had
no separate sports pages, but games or matches were often considered
important enough to be reported on page one. Responding to increasing
market demand, Mexico City newspapers, such as *El Universal*, *El Demócrata*, and *Excélsior*, began to devote an entire section to sports at least
one day each week. Most games, including bullfights in Mexico, were
held on Sundays, allowing the Monday or Tuesday editions to report the
results. As newspapers began to receive notice of world news through
wire services, they provided game results and other sports information
from the United States and Europe, knowing that their upper-class reading public would be familiar with these places and interested in maintaining a nostalgic link with cities in which they had lived. Through this source
of information, as well as radio and films, Latin Americans became familiar with foreign sports heroes as varied as Jack Dempsey, Babe Ruth,
Tex Rickard, and Suzanne Lenglen.

U.S. and other foreign sporting news was reported in many Mexican
and Central American newspapers in the 1920s. Foreign cables brought
game and fight results, league standings, contract negotiations, and other
news, including reports of American football, which sometimes was confused with soccer. Box scores of U.S. major league baseball games were
carried by the principal Mexico City papers and occasionally appeared in
Central American papers. The link between journalism, the emerging national sports culture, and a profit-oriented capitalist economy is clear.
Advertisements for foreign and national products appeared in Latin American newspapers, often featuring foreign athletic heroes trading on their
popularity abroad. Charles Atlas promoted his body-building course, translating his slogan, "I myself was once a 97-pound weakling" for a Spanish-speaking audience [*Yo mismo fui un alfeñique de 44 kilos*].[23] Similarly,
Jess Willard explained how an iron supplement aided his boxing triumphs,
and Jack Dempsey posed with a variety of cars, an L. C. Smith type-
writer, and Buen Tono cigarettes. After beating Jack Dempsey, Gene
Tunney expressed his preference for Dos Equis beer. Movies starring
Dempsey were shown in Mexico, and fight movies showcasing several
boxers were projected in Mexico and Central America. Dempsey's popularity was so great that Mexican newspapers interviewed him in the United

States, and round by round commentary during his bouts with Gene Tunney in 1926 and 1927 was sent to radio receivers controlled by the principal newspapers in Mexico City. These postings were placed in movie theaters, on screens atop downtown buildings, and on blackboards in the newspaper offices. *El Universal* and *Excélsior* competed to see which could deliver the most rapid and complete fight coverage. Mass media, journalism, and sports combined to fortify an expanding market economy in the major cities of Central America, capitalizing both on the cosmopolitan tastes acquired by the elite during travels and foreign residence abroad and on the increasing popular interest in these originally foreign athletic events.

Sports culture also spawned publications specifically devoted to the games and their players. The Athletic Club of Guatemala began publishing a bimonthly journal entitled *El Sport* in 1899. This was probably the first sports-related periodical in all of Central America, representing a significant investment for a club that only had around twenty members at that time. Many of its articles publicized the results of sporting events in Europe, or special interests of its proprietors; one prominent advertisement promoted a book by the club's director, fencing master Pietro Lanzilli, called *Código del honor para América Latina* (*Honor code for Latin America*), which was described as "333 pages; an extremely useful item for judges, lawyers, surgeons, military men and everyone who finds himself involved in an affair of honor." For the elites, sports and sports publications not only provided community among themselves and with their European counterparts but also a vehicle by which foreign values might be transferred. In the 1890s the magazine, *La Ilustración Guatemalteca*, featured society news and literary articles and also occasional mention of socially prominent Guatemalans' cycling activities. *Nicaragua Informativa*, a magazine established in Managua in 1917, included sports items and photographs (baseball, soccer, tennis, basketball, boxing) during its first years, but by 1925 it carried few mentions of sports and afterwards became strictly a literary journal. Managua also briefly had a small sports magazine called *El Field*, a promotion of "Tex Rickard" Ramírez. Significantly, both the magazine and the Central American sports figure were explicitly conjuring up imported images in their names, indicating the vital link between things foreign and the emergence of sports culture in this region.

In San José, Costa Rica, the magazine *Deportes* (Sports) was founded in 1924. It not only covered local activities (in San José, Alajuela, Heredia, Cartago, Puntarenas, and Limón) but also sporting news from the United States and Europe, instructional articles on technique and health, editorials promoting Costa Rican sports and physical education, and a serialized story translated from English: "Mac the Pitcher." Occasionally, foreign photographs were misinterpreted (perhaps in jest), as on the October 22,

1924, cover, which featured six U.S. bathing beauties—described as being the female basketball champions of the United States. The caption opines that "any male team would gladly let themselves be vanquished by such angelic *basket-ballistas*." An American football punter in classic pose (no helmet, kicking foot above head, support foot off ground) was said to be a soccer goalie heroically defending his goal; here, the caption implored local players to learn such a spectacular move.

Traveling Athletes: International Sports, Nationalism, and Politics

The athletes of Guatemala, El Salvador, Honduras, and Costa Rica competed in Guatemala City in a multisport festival in 1921. This event was held to celebrate the centennial of independence for the region and probably also reflected the political disposition of Guatemala's government in favor of Central American Union.[24] This first Olympic-type festival was supposed to be continued in two years in San Salvador, but the Salvadorans kept postponing it, and finally Costa Rica hosted the next edition in San José, in the last days of 1924 and first of 1925. Ultimately, however, only a group of Canal Zone athletes and a baseball team from Nicaragua participated in San José's games. Nevertheless, there are a few indications that by this time some connotation of "national" was occasionally becoming explicitly associated with sports. The San José magazine, *Deportes*, conducted a contest among its readership to select players in each position for the Costa Rican "national" soccer team.[25] The winners would be those respondents whose own ballots most closely matched the official selection. Unfortunately, no foreign teams entered the soccer competition of the 1924–25 "Olympics," and the only game played was a contest between two Costa Rican clubs for the national championship.

Guatemala and El Salvador continued sports connections in the 1920s, with the Salvadorans competing in tennis in Guatemala in 1920 and the two countries playing a home-and-home basketball series in 1926. Boxers were particularly mobile in the Central American region. Nicaraguan boxers experienced considerable success in El Salvador and Guatemala in the 1920s. Guatemala's first excursion out of the country for soccer play came in 1923 with a visit to Mexico City. The visitors won both games held at the Club Real España, and a trophy donated by President Alvaro Obregón was presented to them by the Secretary of Public Education, José Vasconcelos. A third game was canceled because of revolutionary activity threatening the capital, and the Guatemalans left Mexico City the night of the second game, traveling by train to the U.S. border and New Orleans, where part of the team took the first boat back home. This circuitous route was necessary because rebels were occupying Veracruz and the railway to the south was cut. Some of the Guatemalans stayed a few days longer in New Orleans and played two games with a local team composed of Britons, Hispanics, and Hispanic Americans.[26]

A group of Mexican athletes traveled to Guatemala City in 1923 for soccer, basketball, and tennis matches, which were probably Mexico's first international competitions in these sports. The same year, a basketball team from the Mexico City YMCA played a series of games in Texas, Louisiana, and Cuba. The Mexican soccer team América played three games in Cuba in 1926, and Cuba's Fortuna soccer club played in Costa Rica in 1925 and 1926. In the 1920s, Costa Rican soccer teams played in Nicaragua, Guatemala, and Jamaica, and the Ticos hosted soccer teams from Cuba, Peru, Ecuador, Colombia, and Jamaica as well as a baseball team from Panama. Also during the 1920s, Cuban baseball teams visited Mexico and Panama.

In 1924, Mexico's first Olympic representation competed in Paris. The Mexican government was reluctant to support the team, but travel funds were raised through activities sponsored by the two principal Mexico City dailies, *Excélsior* and especially, *El Universal*. To help their fundraising efforts, Mexico's athletes were portrayed as ambassadors for the nation, whose presence in Paris would show the world the progress of Mexican culture. Two pistol shooters, two tennis players, and fifteen track and field athletes participated in the preliminary rounds but were unable to advance to the finals. However, it was proudly reported that the sight of sophisticated Mexican athletes strolling the streets of Paris, speaking French and English, and "not wearing feathers and rattles" was an eye-opener for observers.[27]

Latin Americans have been involved in the modern Olympic Games since their beginnings. Argentinean José Benjamín Zubiaur was a member of the first International Olympic Committee in 1894, and Chile was represented by a single track athlete, Luis Subercaseaux, in the first Olympics in Athens in 1896. A Haitian (shooting) and two Cubans (fencing) participated in the Paris Olympics in 1900. Cuban fencer Ramón Fonst won an Olympic gold medal (and a silver) in 1900, and he and teammates won several medals at the 1904 Olympics in St. Louis. Fonst lived in Paris for many years and developed his Olympic-caliber fencing skills there. There was no further Latin American participation in the Games until 1912, but in the 1920s several more countries became involved and still more in 1936 and later years. Uruguay won the Olympic soccer competition in Paris in 1924 and in Amsterdam in 1928, with Argentina taking the silver medal in 1928. Olympic participation and success became a rallying point and motive for feelings of nationalism. This sentiment is increasingly the case in more recent years, as Latin American countries have become part of the global village and as sports have become more important. While Cuba, Brazil, and Argentina are especially prominent in international sports, all Latin American countries participate at the regional level. The Central American, Central American and Caribbean, Pan American, South American, and Bolivarian Games offer Olympic-type multisport competition, and other regional championships are contested in individual sports. These regional festivals offer many more opportunities for athletes to travel, and for developing national and regional solidarity, than do the larger events, which are restricted to the world's sporting elites.[28] At all levels of competition, however, participation in international events was and is viewed by Latin Americans as a means of demonstrating national pride and progress before a global audience. Athletes, like movie stars and artists, must assume the role of unofficial ambassadors abroad.

Conclusion

Foreign residence among young Latin Americans during the latter part of the nineteenth century and the early twentieth century, which was mainly for the purpose of secondary school and university study in Europe and the United States, provided a vital opportunity for them to learn the modern sports that had developed in those areas. Upon returning to their countries, they became active promoters, by organizing teams and by teaching techniques and rules to friends who had not traveled overseas. Mexican and other Latin American graduates of the YMCA college in Springfield, Massachusetts, shared their new knowledge and enthusiasm with YMCA members throughout the region. Foreigners resident in Latin America and foreign military troops stationed there also were important promoters of modern sports, organizing clubs and teams not only among themselves but also in the general communities. Although the imported sports were nearly exclusively the property of social elites from the earliest period until well into the 1920s, many games did eventually draw participants from most levels of society. Reporting of foreign sporting personalities and events in Latin American newspapers and magazines brought sports to the attention of local people. Foreign-language (mainly English) terminology was not only associated with the imported sports but also affected culture in the form of metaphors employed in everyday language.

The new activities supplemented and, to some extent, supplanted traditional recreations. At first, only club loyalties were involved for fans, but competition on a geographically wider basis gradually led to identification with teams from different cities and then finally, with the advent of international competition, to nationalistic feelings associated with the activities of national selections. There was a vital link between foreign travel and the introduction of modern sports in Mexico and Central America, most typically in the form of a residential school experience on the part of upper-class males. These boys would study abroad, participate in varsity sports, and then return home anxious to replicate their favorite new pastimes among their fellow citizens. In this way, other features of modern culture followed: entertainment as profit-making venture; the creation of a celebrity culture, including product endorsements; the expansion of modern mass media; and national entries into international competitions as an exercise in patriotism.

Notes

1. For developments in Mexico in the 1890s and early 1920s, see William Beezley, *Judas at the Jockey Club* (Lincoln: University of Nebraska Press, 1987); and Richard V. McGehee, "Sports and Recreational Activities in Guatemala and Mexico, Late 1800s to 1926," *Studies in Latin American Popular Culture* 13 (1994): 7–32. One of the earliest European sports introduced in Mexico in the nineteenth century was cricket, which was being played there by Englishmen as early as 1827.

2. Sports at the National Preparatory School included: boxing, gymnastics, wrestling, hiking, basketball, baseball, volleyball, fencing, and American football. Several of the school's students traveled to Paris as members of Mexico's first Olympic representation in 1926.

3. See Richard V. McGehee, "The Dandy and the Mauler in Mexico: Johnson, Dempsey et al., and the Mexico City Press, 1919–1927," *Journal of Sport History* 23 (1996): 20–33. The Argentinean Luis Firpo was a great hero to the Mexicans, who hoped he would become the first Latin American world heavyweight champion. Firpo's fame was widespread in Middle America; in the 1920s a Nicaraguan named his champion fighting cock "Firpo," and a Salvadoran soccer club that still exists also bears the boxer's name.

4. The Guatemala Lawn Tennis Club, founded in 1916, also still exists. Compare Leif Yttergren, "Stockholm and the Rise of Modern Sports, 1860–1898," *International Journal of the History of Sport* 13, no. 3 (1996): 404–8.

5. J. A. Guzmán, ed., *Guatemala deportiva: Historia del fútbol nacional en sus bodas de oro* (Guatemala: Tipografía Nacional, 1953), 6.

6. Ibid., 51–52.

7. See Richard V. McGehee, "The Rise of Modern Sport in Guatemala and the First Central American Games," *International Journal of the History of Sport* 9, no. 1 (1992): 132–40.

8. Jorge Eduardo Arellano, *El Doctor David Arellano (1872–1928)* (Managua: Edición del Autor, 1993), 16.

9. Arellano, *David Arellano*, 16–18; Carlos J. García S., *Reseña de cien años de béisbol en Nicaragua* (Managua: [n.p.], 1991), 3–6; *Nicaragua Informativa* 18 (June 1918): 9–10. In addition to the prominent families represented by Managua's and Granada's first baseball players, John May was captain of the Managua team and John Campbell played for Granada. David Arellano was Nicaragua's diplomatic representative in Washington, DC, in 1910 and Nicaraguan Minister of Public Instruction during 1918 and 1919.

10. Arellano, *David Arellano*, 18; García S., *Reseña*, 6.

11. García S., *Reseña*, 6; *La Prensa Literaria* (Managua), June 17, 1905.

12. *El Comercio* (Managua), March 10, 1922.

13. Chester Urbina Gaitán, "La Iglesia Católica y el origen del fútbol en Costa Rica (1904–1921)," paper presented at 43rd Annual Conference of the South Eastern Council on Latin American Studies, San José, Costa Rica, February 28, 1997 (based on Urbina's bachelor's thesis: Chester Urbina Gaitán, "El fútbol en

San José, Memoria de proyecto de graduación para optar al grado de Licenciado en Historia," Universidad de Costa Rica, San José, 1994).

14. See Richard V. McGehee, "Sport a la Tica and the Absence of Costa Rica in the 'Central American Olympics' of 1926," paper presented at 25th Annual Convention of the North American Society for Sport History, Springfield College, MA, May 26, 1997; and Francisco Enríquez Solano, "El turno: Un espacio de diversión en Costa Rica (1835/1930)," paper presented at the Tercer Congreso Centroamericano de Historia, San José, CR, July 16, 1996.

15. See Louis A. Pérez, Jr., "Between Baseball and Bullfighting: The Quest for Nationality in Cuba, 1868–1898," *The Journal of American History* 81, no. 2 (1994): 493–517; and Richard V. McGehee, "Baseball, Latin American," in *Encyclopedia of World Sport*, ed. David Levinson and Karen Christensen (Santa Barbara, CA: ABC-CLIO, 1996), 84–90.

16. Pérez, "Between Baseball," 499.

17. See Thomas E. Van Hyning, *Puerto Rico's Winter League: A History of Major League Baseball's Launching Pad* (Jefferson, NC: McFarland, 1995); Rob Ruck, *The Tropic of Baseball: Baseball in the Dominican Republic* (Westport, CT: Meckler, 1991); and Alan M. Klein, *Sugarball: The American Game, the Dominican Dream* (New Haven: Yale University Press, 1991).

18. See Ramón G. Pérez Medina, *Historia del baseball panameño* (Panama: Dutigrafia, 1992). In 1921 a team from Limón, Costa Rica, traveled to Bocas del Toro for two games (*La Tribuna* [San José, CR], October 1, 1921).

19. Additional examples from sports language in Nicaraguan newspapers, 1916–1923, include the following: *deportar* (to play); *clubs*; *sior stop* (shortstop); *pitchar* (to pitch); *batería* (batters); *arrancamontes* (hard grounders); *capote* (kaput, shutout); *mandar un peón a la base* (to walk a batter); *faul balls* (foul balls); *línea* (line drive); *sacrificio*; *robada de home*; *cuadro y campo* (infield and outfield); *foot-ballistas*; *center-forwars*; *shoot*; *dirbleo* (dribbling). Also see Joseph L. Arbena, "Sports Language, Cultural Imperialism, and the Anti-Imperialist Critique in Latin America," *Studies in Latin American Popular Culture* 14 (1995): 129–41.

20. Sergio Ramírez Mercado, "Juego perfecto," in his collection *Clave de sol* (México, D.F.: Sol y Arena, 1992); Vicente Leñero, *El evangelio de Lucas Gavilán* (Barcelona: Editorial Seix Barral, 1979), 136.

21. *El Comercio*, January 4, 1925. The expressions in parentheses are those used in the original text. *Dejado en el guante* literally translates as "left in the glove"; in the early years of Nicaraguan baseball, it meant striking out a batter.

22. *El Correo* (Granada, Nicaragua), February 18, 1925.

23. The words are a translation of the familiar North American slogan, "I myself was once a 97-pound weakling." A young Nicaraguan in Sergio Ramírez's story, "Charles Atlas también muere," not only obtains the master's bodybuilding course, but he also becomes virtually another Atlas himself and manages to travel to New York City to meet his idol—with disastrous consequences. See translation: "Charles Atlas Also Dies," *Aethlon* 10, no. 2 (1993): 1–11.

24. On the general topic of nationalism and sports, see Joseph L. Arbena, "Nationalism and Sport in Latin America, 1850–1990: The Paradox of Promoting and Performing 'European' Sports," *International Journal of the History of Sport* 12, no. 2 (1995): 220–38, and "The Diffusion of Modern European Sport in Latin America: A Case Study of Cultural Imperialism?" *South Eastern Latin Americanist* 33, no. 4 (March 1990): 1–8.

25. *Deportes* (October 1, 1924): 2.

26. Guzmán, *Guatemala deportiva*, 92–94.

27. *El Demócrata* (Mexico City), July 20, 1924.

28. See Wolf Krämer-Mandeau, "Latin America and the Olympic Games: A 'Blank Spot' in Sports History," *Studies in Latin American Popular Culture* 14 (1995): 143–69; Richard V. McGehee, "Latin America and the Caribbean in the Modern Olympic Movement," *Journal of the International Council for Health, Physical Education, Recreation, Sport, and Dance* 32 (1996): 13–15.

9

(En)Gendering Cultural Formations: The Crossings of Amanda Labarca between Chile and the United States

Sandra M. Boschetto-Sandoval

Amanda Labarca (Chile, 1886–1975) was a well-known educator, feminist, cultural critic, and historian. She is also considered to have been one of the founders of socialist feminism in Latin America. Literary historian Sandra Boschetto-Sandoval writes of the ways in which a lifetime of international travel contributed to Labarca's gendered approach to national identity formation. She focuses most closely upon Labarca's time at Columbia University in the years just preceding World War I, which she considers to have been the formative intellectual and social experience of Labarca's later philosophy.

Boschetto-Sandoval reveals the full emotional and intellectual impact of Labarca's stay in New York City through her analysis of Labarca's semiautobiographical novel, En tierras extrañas *(In strange lands). She asserts that Labarca's experiences reaffirm the notion that responses to travel and foreign residence are gendered. When comparing practices of an unknown land with one's homeland, it is not surprising that different roles and expectations for men and women are among the first things to impress the foreign traveler. Labarca's involvement with progressive education also underscores the notion that embracing foreign ideologies did not always lead Latin American intellectuals away from questions of nationalism and, in fact, often had the reverse effect. Indeed, Labarca's political formation and adherence to feminism clearly evolved within an international context, foreshadowing the important role that other foreign ideologies then emerging in Europe would play in Latin American political and cultural circles in the 1920s and onward.*

Cultural identity—particularly the issue of how to make sense of the relations among Europe, the United States, and Latin America—is a central theme in nineteenth- and twentieth-century Latin American social thought. However, the discourse of Latin American cultural identity has continued to reproduce, for the most part, a male view of what it would mean to liberate the region from social oppression. There is a great need to break out of this pattern of cultural interpretation, which "assigns the value 'cultural identity' to a discourse produced almost exclusively by men, while 'gender identity' becomes the specialized province of women's theorizing."[1] These very issues of the relations between cultural identity and self-knowledge, cultural identity and nationalism, and cultural identity and liberation from underdevelopment already were concerns of many reform-minded female intellectuals in the nineteenth century. These women's life work was characterized by a "tension between the search for change within the domestic political arena and the transnationalist view that seeks ethical, moral, and substantive support beyond the boundaries of the imagined national community."[2] This essay explores the gendered critique of cultural practices and nationalist ideology in the work of Amanda Labarca Hubertson (1886–1975), who is acknowledged as not only a founder of socialist feminism in Latin America but also as one of the region's most progressive educators.

As a renowned Chilean educator, feminist, and cultural critic, Amanda Labarca has been characterized by several contemporaries as a positivist, a scientific humanist, and an educational integralist. Scientific humanism is an ideological school born of the Enlightenment which expressed faith in reason and considered culture and civilization as a process and a development. Educational integralism called for the physical, mental, moral, and spiritual enhancement of the student as well as for the development of a sense of social responsibility. In its entirety, educational integralism sought to bring the individual into harmonious relations with his physical and social environment, and to inspire him to contribute to the material, moral, and spiritual welfare of society.

To these concepts, Amanda Labarca brought a concern for the role of women in history. Committed as she was to the idea that women constitute the basis of universal progress, Labarca saw the issue of women's rights as both a political and a moral mandate. Most of her arguments for women's equality focused on the status of women in the workplace and were again cast in terms of cultural evolution and social progressivism through education. In her books she traced the slow development of the emancipation of women, their importance to racial survival, and the need for their full, free, and equal participation in the life of the community and nation. For Labarca, there could be neither real progress nor true democracy without women's cooperation. The freedom and equality of women and the employment of their full latent capacities promised to create a superior world order and to save civilization from devastating wars and continual crises.[3]

During the mid-nineteenth century, nation building, autonomy, and self-identity were essential preoccupations of the creole elites in South

America. Chile by this time had become a worldwide banking center, boasting the first major railroad in South America. The opening of the University of Chile to women students in 1877 ushered in a new era of progress in educational opportunity and in the cultural life of Chile. Labarca herself noted that the period between 1880 and 1890 was marked "both by a new secular spirit in, and a rapid expansion of, women's secondary and technical education."[4]

In 1906, Amanda Labarca began her professional career in education and her welfare work for the emancipation of Chilean women. Chile had embarked upon a new wave of proletarian social unrest, and the eagerness of the emerging middle class to participate in the political direction of the nation through the recently created Democratic and Radical parties meant that the pressure for ideological transformation and social change was increasing. Nationalism and feminism also became firmly entrenched in Spanish America and were the subjects of widespread public discussion during this time. In the early decades of the twentieth century the expansion of female education in Chile meshed with the corresponding nation-building project and its associated drive to modernize and to develop an educated citizenry. This context provides the basis for Labarca's discourse on cultural identity, nationalism, and feminism.

Amanda Labarca's forebears were farmers who lived in the village of Huacarhue, about seventy-five miles south of Santiago. Her father, Onofre Pinto (1861–1914), was a successful merchant in the capital city who was stern in character, well read, and inclined toward a more liberal attitude toward religious faith and practice than was common at that time. She undertook her higher academic studies at Santiago College, an establishment that was maintained by members of a Methodist mission with headquarters in New York. There, among foreigners, she found "generous, idealistic, and liberal teachers."[5] In her own assessment of early North American influences on Chilean pedagogical science, Labarca cites Domingo Faustino Sarmiento, the Argentine politician, writer, and educator who had fled to Chile during the dictatorship of Juan Manuel de Rosas in Argentina (1840–1852). In 1845, Sarmiento traveled to the United States to study the North American system of education. These travels, including Sarmiento's personal contact with educator Horace Mann, produced two influential books, *La educación común* (Universal education) and *De la educación popular* (About popular education), which stressed the importance of common primary education.[6] Beginning in 1904, when Carlos Fernández Peña founded the Chilean National Education Association, Chilean administrators and educators directed all national scholarship recipients to the United States. In this way, Labarca and her husband, Guillermo Labarca, were able to travel together in 1911 to New York and Columbia University, which "attracted them with its powerful magnet of grand professors."[7]

Between 1911 and 1952, Amanda Labarca undertook a total of ten trips to the United States, first as a student and subsequently as an educator, lecturer, Chilean representative to the first General Assembly of the United Nations (1946), and chief of the United Nations Commission on the Status of Women (1948–49). When she first arrived at Columbia in 1911, American education was in a state of transition and experimentation. Whereas in European countries the aim was to discover new methods for better imparting the traditional culture, in the United States energy was focused on the need to adapt culture and liberal education to modern demands and conditions. John Dewey, fresh from his experimental work at the University of Chicago, had by that time done more to spread the ideals of the New Education than any other living educator. With a background in social psychology, Dewey pointed enthusiastically to the need for initiative, originality, and resourcefulness in the new pedagogy, deeming these qualities essential to the life of a free society.[8] People educated in this way are inevitably agents of constructive social change, and the schools that educate them are thereby intimately bound to the larger cause of reform.[9] Labarca understood that this new strategy could aid in the "practical realization of a system that would lead to the strengthening of a real democracy [in Chile]" along with the growth of public solidarity and true civic action toward the betterment of her own Chilean society.[10] As she herself recognized, "I owe to American pragmatism, to William James, to John Dewey quite a few of my ideas, as well as pedagogical and social tendencies, as can be verified by my works."[11]

In a 1955 article—more memoir than journalistic essay—Labarca recalled, in a mixture of reverence and affection, her classroom encounters with John Dewey at Columbia University, where she took courses in comparative literature, philosophy, and the contemporary European theories and practices of education:

> Attracted by his fame, his students numbered in the hundreds. Tall, thin, lacking in gracefulness, his gestures carefully measured, his large bifocals never resting perfectly horizontal on his nose, he would come to class as if almost in a trance. He would spread his papers out on his desk and begin to lecture, slowly, with phrases that seemed to unravel his thoughts as if he had just then begun to approach the problem under discussion. His words seemed to size up the slippery idea; he would advance cautiously; that one was not exactly what translated the truth; he would backtrack and start over; his countenance would suddenly take on a new luster; there finally was the precise answer![12]

She remembered the students feeling that they were privileged witnesses to his thought processes. Admiring the audacity and depth of his concepts, the students were also attracted to his supreme simplicity. She marveled that "when we approached him at the end of our day, he would listen to us with reverence, as if the student and not the teacher at that moment constituted the hope of the world."[13] It was under Dewey's guidance and tutelage that Labarca admitted to developing the traits of "stubborn patience" and honest hard work and humility, "learned not in books but in daily interactions with peers and professors."[14]

The 1955 essay, published three years after Dewey's death, is also a testimony to Labarca's experience as a foreign traveler visiting the United States for the first time. The opening lines of the essay evoke the mixture of apprehension and admiration that Carlos Solar, a fictional character in the autobiographical novel *En tierras extrañas* (In foreign lands) (1915), later experiences: "A girl of only twenty years, I had just disembarked in New York for the first time. The English I had learned was hesitant and scant. But no one was surprised at my accent when I went to register for classes. I was just one among tens of thousands of students that summer. We would sit in our classrooms, irrespective of color and dress, light-skinned and dark, blacks and whites, yellow and copper colored, some with their hair to the wind, others with it gathered in turban or fez."[15] Amazed exhilaration at North American racial heterogeneity is evident in her description of student life at Columbia, where she not only experienced love, friendship, and camaraderie but also perceived a healthy work ethic and an individual perseverance to better one's lot regardless of race, class, or social standing. "The young mulatto girl always loaded down with books, not wishing to draw attention to herself, wasn't she the same one we had applauded frantically at the last concert? Tom, our philosophy classmate, wasn't he the one who had waited on us at the restaurant? And Juanita, the cleverest young woman who helped us decipher our notes, wasn't she the one who cleaned our dormitory rooms?"[16] These personal impressions of hard-working students leading multifaceted lives, combined with the academic study of Dewey's pragmatic philosophy, influenced Labarca throughout her adult life.

While in the United States (1910–1912), Labarca took advantage of the summer vacation period to visit Middlebury, Vermont, where her husband had previously been a student. Together they spent two months living in a community on Deer Isle, Maine. Of this latter experience she wrote: "It was during this period that I really lived with the people and deepened my admiration and affection for them. . . . The islanders, descendants of Revolutionary War veterans, had kept the Puritan faith and customs intact. It was hard to brand such people as materialists. . . . By contrast the people of Deer Isle and, in large measure all North Americans, seemed to us as simple, as free from complications as a sheet of paper on which all sorts of things are printed, some abhorrent, others intelligent and beautiful, but no longer mysterious, once the language in which they are written is understood."[17] Her academic studies at Columbia did not distract Labarca from her ardent preoccupation with human beings and their social problems. "I used to rob time," she later wrote, "from seminars, to attend meetings, read pamphlets, and talk with leaders and people of the vanguard. For it seemed to me that the educational task was intertwined with the very warp and woof of the social fabric, and that the academic disciplines could not be understood apart from humanity's quest for change and fulfillment."[18]

These early trips and experiences abroad provided material for two books, *Actividades femeninas en los Estados Unidos* (Women's activities in the United States) and *En tierras extrañas*, both written in 1914. The first, *Actividades femeninas*, was a series of lectures delivered at the University of Chile under the auspices of the National Education Association. The lectures traced the development of the education of women in the United States, their changing legal status, their successes in obtaining economic and spiritual freedom, and, especially, their participation in the community through service clubs. The underlying philosophy of these movements and activities as expressed by Ellen Key, Jane Addams, Ida Tarbell, and others was discussed. "All these lectures are given," Labarca explained, "with the hope that they might be an example for the incorporation of Chilean women into the life of the Chilean community and nation."[19] In 1914 she wrote, "I am not a militant feminist, nor am I a suffragist, for above all I am a Chilean, and in Chile today the vote for women is out of order." This perspective coincided with the widespread reluctance of South American feminists to support suffrage until well into the 1930s, since the majority believed that most women had not yet attained a sufficient level of education to fully utilize the privilege. However, Labarca revised this opinion after a second trip to the United States in 1918. In 1957 she explained her changed attitude in this way: "I confess that when I arrived in the United States for the first time, I was far from the convinced feminist that I have been ever since. It was the example of the North Americans that impelled me to drive and struggle until I obtained more civil and political rights for my feminine compatriots."[20] Labarca's altered conception of feminism was due, in no small measure, to her period of foreign residence in the United States.[21]

In July of 1918 the Chilean government commissioned Labarca to make a study of educational systems in the United States. Through visits to schools in California, Louisiana, Illinois, Iowa, Wisconsin, Missouri, Ohio, and New York, she was able to make a thorough investigation of the development of educational theory and practice. Her report appeared in 1919 as a book entitled *La escuela secundaria en los Estados Unidos* (Secondary education in the United States), which she hoped might aid educational reforms in Chile.[22] Her exposure to the progressive educational movement in the United States also resulted in the creation of Chile's first experimental high school, the Liceo Experimental Manuel de Salas, later known as the Institute of Educational Research of the Faculty of

Philosophy and Education of the University of Chile. The Liceo was considered to be the best institution of its kind in Latin America.[23]

When Amanda Labarca published *Nuevas orientaciones de la ensenãnza* (New trends for education) in 1927, she had recently returned from another prolonged visit abroad. In keeping with Dewey's educational outlook, Labarca called for a school that would send into society people who were able to understand it, to live intelligently as part of it, and to change it to suit their visions of the better life. And just as Dewey had viewed democracy as the crux of the earlier movement, so Labarca saw the triumph of self-expression in education as the key to a creative revolution for Chile. The romanticism of Rousseau, the scientific humanism of the Enlightenment, the evolutionary theories of Darwin, Spencer, and Bergson, and psychological approaches to education all coalesced in the new ideology and methodology of the New Schools or Active Schools, as Dewey-inspired educational institutions were called. Nevertheless, a theory that seemed to harmonize the school with the larger social environment and that cast the school as a lever of reform inevitably faced a twofold difficulty: first, in determining which social goals to serve in the school; and, second, in deciding whether or not to embark on an ever broader program of political reform outside the school. Labarca struggled with their resolution for most of her professional career. The new philosophies and practices clashed with several older tensions in Chile such as that between Church and State, hierarchical and democratic society, and the will of the elite to prolong a monoculture in the face of an emerging middle class and a pluralistic society. These controversial issues underlay the so-called Difficult Years and the crisis of the period of reforms and counterreforms of 1925–1931. Given these antecedents, Labarca's biographer, Catherine Manny Paul, notes that "it was something of a daring adventure for Labarca to offer these guideposts for an effective educational system aimed at the enhancement of the individual in search of an integral education, and the coming of age of a nation."[24]

In 1935, Amanda Labarca, together with the president of the University of Chile, Juvenal Hernández, and other distinguished professors visited Los Angeles, San Francisco, Chicago, and New York. This trip resulted in the *escuelas de temporada*, or seasonal schools, and began frequent faculty and student exchanges between the North American educational centers and the University of Chile, which later became known as the University of the Americas. While in the United States, Labarca was also able to report on Depression-era programs for rural development then being carried out by the extension departments of private and state universities and by the U.S. Department of Agriculture. This information was later used to complete her 1936 book, *Mejoramiento de la vida campesina* (Improvement of the life of the peasant).

Amanda Labarca, c. 1930. She championed education and women's rights throughout her long career. *Courtesy of Rosita Enríquez*

In 1939 she was hired to teach a course on social problems in Latin America at the summer session of the University of California at Berkeley, and visited schools in Chicago and Berea, Kentucky, where she gave a series of lectures.[25] In 1939, Labarca was also president of the executive committee of the Chilean National Commission of Intellectual Cooperation. This committee organized the First American Conference of the National Commissions of Intellectual Cooperation in close connection with the League of Nations and the Institute of International Education in New York and Geneva. In 1946 she was appointed as a delegate to the United Nations General Assembly and was designated chief of the United Nations Commission on the Status of Women for 1948–49. She organized the meeting of the International Commission of Women, which met at Beirut, Lebanon, in 1949. In these positions she had occasion to work with Eleanor Roosevelt.

In 1957, Amanda Labarca wrote an essay entitled "Toward a Better Understanding," which summarized the impressions that she had made during her many visits to the United States during the years 1911–1952. She was impressed by the egalitarianism of a social democracy, yet disconcerted by the tendency toward megalomania and uniformity, the shocking discrimination against blacks, the predominance of big business in politics and in U.S. foreign policy, and the utter ignorance about Latin America on the part of the masses. Labarca stressed how much the educational system she encountered had impressed her as an instrument necessary for "building a true patriotism," one that would "educate for harmony" without solidifying differences and inhibiting original initiative.[26] However, she tempered her admiration with caution, noting that "an aspect of North American communication media that we often discussed at the United Nations is the tendency toward uniformity. In so incessantly repeating certain slogans, in so constantly insisting that certain procedures are necessary, that given lines of international policy are the only ones compatible with progress, that those who deviate from traditional beliefs are renegades or Communists, the North Americans are in effect solidifying differences and inhibiting original initiative: they are little by little transforming the individual into a number, collective society into a mass of robots." This robotization that Amanda Labarca foresaw as the threat of "super-nationalism" could be countered only by what she termed *eros pedagógico*, or an "education to hemispheric harmony," whereby nations would see themselves as interdependent members of a "family of nations."[27] In her ideal vision, "small countries would recover more international strength and an economic significance that today they barely glimpse. In preparing for that future, the school plays an essential role: that of inculcating a humanism that at once embraces family, neighborhood, region, country, continent, and world."[28] Therefore, for Labarca, national consciousness and unity were profoundly connected to the construction of a "world culture" in which the enhancement of the individual and, in turn, with the larger self as represented by family, local community, nation, and intercultural and world societies was necessary.[29]

Amanda Labarca's feminist-educational-intercultural ideology is best reflected in her little-known novel, *En tierras extrañas*, written in 1914 and published the subsequent year. In the text, Carlos Solar Donoso travels from Chile to the United States on the recommendation of his father, a wealthy landowner and mining entrepreneur, in order to "accomplish something useful." The opening arrival scene is tempered with both distrust and doubt, as New York Harbor and the Statue of Liberty seem not so much to *acoger* (embrace) the beleaguered traveler as to *desafiar* (challenge) him.[30] Carlos is greeted by several nurturing natives, one of whom, his father's North American friend, encourages him to "ennoble his life and serve his country" by undertaking a program of interdisciplinary study at Columbia University. The well-intentioned man advises Carlos to "take courses in metallurgy, but do not forget those pertinent to the organization of communities, those of industrial organizational administration, and, above all, those pertaining to social and political economy."[31] His pragmatic education is emotionally balanced when he encounters Eve Wright, a social worker whom he befriends and later romances. As bearer of a utopic ideal for Carlos, Eve serves as his spiritual catalyst, the integrator who will restore his "orderly harmony."[32] Because nationalist patriarchal rhetoric calls for the sacrifice of passion to patriotic idealism, or perhaps because Eve reminds Carlos of his mother, she is soon killed, murdered by hoodlums hired by a textile magnate, whom Eve had threatened with exposure for breaking child labor laws. Carlos returns to Chile at the conclusion of the novel saddened but transformed, and with his new patriotic ideal intact. He returns believing that "from pain a new soul would grow, prepared to undertake any struggle, any sacrifice, in order that in some small part of the world the Ideal might blossom."[33]

En tierras extrañas may be read on several levels: as Labarca's first experiment in autobiographical fiction, as a testament to Dewey's pragmatic and progressive pedagogy and its relevance to Chilean democratic nationalistic goals of progress and development, and as an intercultural reflection for broader international understanding.[34] *En tierras extrañas* also coincides with Doris Sommer's assessment that sense and sensibility, productivity and passion were conjoined to direct the national effort toward a "future ideal . . . a realizable utopia. . . . This America aspired to a modernity metonymized from the other, Northern, America."[35] Nevertheless, while flirting with eroticism and nationalism, Labarca's text also deviates from the usual construct of nineteenth-century Latin American novels that sought to consolidate the legitimacy of an emerging nationalist rhetoric through romance. This difference is seen not only in the obvious failure of the marriage and/or miscegenation between Chilean Carlos and North American Eve, but also in the failure of the very project of romance and passion itself. As one critic noted in his review, the novel is not so much about sensibilities as it is about ideas or aspirations, one of which was the incorporation of women's previously excluded voices into the nation-building project.[36] Perhaps for this reason Labarca has her fictional protagonist, Carlos Solar, remark: "We are currently experiencing a period of acute crisis [in Chile], in which it will perhaps become necessary to reconstruct on new foundations the government of the entire republic, but already there are those who are building with tenacity and faith the groundwork of a grandiose future."[37] Amanda Labarca inserted herself fictionally and as a male protagonist into the discourse of the nation-building project, and thereby identified herself with those who were building the future of Chile. Thus, the motif of reconstruction that runs throughout Labarca's conception of national subject formation is far from the traditional view of nationhood, as reflected in patriotic/patriarchal novels organized around a purely erotic rhetoric.

More than simply a guide or nurturing native, the North American suffragette Eve, whom Labarca curiously identified as having ancestral connections to Chile, speaks for the female author and all Latin American women who were clamoring for participation in the socio-national agenda. Yet as a single, female orphan, Eve also represents the many women threatened with both physical and spiritual "deterritorialization" as they chose to abandon traditional male protection (fathers, brothers, or husbands) in search of their own role outside traditional patriarchal institutions. Indeed, Eve is eliminated precisely, as the newspaper headlines revealed, when she exits out into the street to accomplish her daily rounds.[38] Having observed the ways in which women in the United States moved around with relatively more public freedom than they did in Chile, Labarca appears to have used this experience to illustrate the fate that would befall women in her own country who step outside of their traditional roles.

The friendship that Carlos establishes with Eve may also be viewed as a potent site for reframing relations of contact between men and women (and metonymically between nations or cultures), that is, relations based not on possession and mastery but on mutual respect and affection.

Labarca philosophized on this ideal relationship between men and women in several of her writings, believing it to be the means by which Chileans could achieve a true perspective on reality.[39] As he recognizes the impact of his friendship with a woman, Carlos remarks on the social conditioning that had prevented a similar blossoming on his own soil: "He would never have imagined himself as the companion, the friend of any woman; he had never guessed that he would speak of his dreams with [a woman] who could understand them. And suddenly, the whims of fate had brought him to discover his new awareness before the bright eyes of his foreign friend."[40] Indeed, Carlos owes to Eve his initiation into a world based not simply on material gain but on faith and altruistic sacrifice, a world seen through women's eyes. To Carlos's ambitious rhetoric of the capitalist vanguard, circumscribed by the "conqueror's pattern of loving and leaving,"[41] Eve offers a feminine counter-knowledge, a form of patriotism based on social motherhood. Opposed to what she perceives as militaristic nationalism displayed on parade, Eve inspires Carlos to move toward a "patriotism of creative force."

This gendered view of creative patriotism articulates a major tenet of pragmatic philosophy: the radical rejection of the passive spectator in the attainment of knowledge and views of truth. The active creative agent, through his or her encounter with others and other meanings, helps structure the objects of knowledge and cannot be separated from the world in which such objects emerge. Therefore, Labarca suggests that diversity of experiences made possible by a course of action such as travel should be promoted whenever and wherever possible. In contrast with objectivist conquest/discovery rhetoric, whose authority is monologic and self-contained, Labarca's creatively patriotic text is resolutely dialogical or diacultural, seeking out rather than defying "strange" knowledge.[42] Carlos becomes the learner, initiated into love and knowledge by the "strange" Other. With his idealism intact, Carlos's circular expedition ends at the beginning: on board the *Magdalena*, which will take him out of the public and the new (male) space and back to the familiar and the enclosed (feminine) space. Thus, filtered through a feminine perspective of restored continuity, of feminization of (male) culture, and in what could be called an act of anticonquest, the text presents a gendered and social rather than national allegory. Ambiguously or ironically, the ending of Labarca's novel not only points to the unwritten demise of certain women (as postulated by Eve's own death) but also idealizes the feminized hero as an aggressive, interactive seeker of knowledge who, regardless of gender, is the one called to fashion the new republic.

In her gendered critique of the discourse of national consolidation, Labarca toys with the metaphor of "travel" and of "traveling through" various ports of call. Therefore, rather than calling for tradition and single-voicedness, she calls for dynamic dialogue and growth through change.

The metaphor of "travel" is not only thematic but also structural. Labarca wrote a novel that bridged autobiography with social analysis, personal history with journalism, and politics with romance. She viewed growth in a similar way as inherently moral; just as extended travel could lead to an expansion of perspective, so could its richness of experience. "Meteor-like visits engender only superficial impressions," Labarca would later note. "To see is not to understand. The stronger the personality of the observer, the less likely it will be influenced by exotic novelty. What one sees is the multiform product of an historical past, of a way of life, of a philosophy of existence, of a different appreciation of values. In a rapid gaze, one captures only the appearances. If one ignores the hidden contexts, one can easily arrive at completely erroneous conclusions."[43] Like Dewey, Labarca believed that existence is by its nature filled not just with the stable but also with the precarious, not just with the enduring but also with the novel, not just with conformity but also with diversity, and it is this dynamic that provides the materials for ongoing understanding.

Like Carlos in a "strange land," Labarca's identity as a Chilean and South American was forged and developed during her many travels to the United States and Europe. One of the most persistent charges she faced as she tried to forge a new consciousness of her nation's social reality was the accusation of being an *europeizante*, or someone who uses Western European constructs as models for local development and progress. Labarca's *europeismo* is easily misunderstood precisely because of the generally strong dependence on Europe and North America characteristic of South American intellectuals. She has left behind a number of statements saying that there was no salvation for Latin America apart from Europe, and even favored large-scale European immigration. Nevertheless, she also recognized that "it was necessary to know who we are and what we want as far as nationhood is concerned. We cannot copy other systems, because our past, our customs, our ideals, and our needs are different. We have absorbed such attitudes in the works of the great North American educators, Dewey above all. This lesson of independence, of autonomous responsibility has developed in Chile thanks to the combined influences of North American pedagogical science, and of the persevering efforts, work, and research of our own Chilean educators who study in North American universities."[44]

It was natural that as Latin American intellectuals sought to create decolonized values and hegemonies after Independence, they selected and adapted other foreign perspectives. This "cultural adultery" may explain the ambivalence inherent in Labarca's creative patriotism.[45] On the one hand, Labarca affirmed difference and nonindustrial and feminocentric values; on the other, she reaffirmed patriarchal privilege. The inclusive national utopia envisioned at the conclusion of *En tierras extrañas*, for example, rings hollow, inasmuch as men (even if feminized) are still called to realize the ideal, while women are called merely to transmit it to their posterity. Although Labarca's perspective in 1914 certainly cannot be described as "feminotopic"—an idealized world of female autonomy, empowerment, and pleasure—her ambivalent encounter with North America does project a newly unveiled landscape that seeks to separate mastery from domination, knowledge from control, even while it consistently asserts its own kind of mastery and its own kind of power in a world that is both certain and uncertain. The cultural identity of a people, the sum of their creative legacy, is equally part of a creative process and is always in a state of evolution or transformation.

Knowledge results not only from a traveler's experiences and interactions but also from powers of observation and sensibility. Richard Hofstadter has observed that the Progressive mind was typically a journalistic mind, and that its characteristic contribution was that of a socially responsible reporter-reformer.[46] Just as Dewey was perceived as "sensitive to the movement of things about him,"[47] so too the dialectic between Labarca as observer and Labarca as reformer is apparent everywhere. In all her writings she enthusiastically and consistently points to the concern with initiative, originality, and resourcefulness, deeming these qualities central to the life of a free society. Virtue is taught not by imposing values but by cultivating fair-mindedness, objectivity, imagination, openness to new experiences, and the courage to change one's mind in the light of further experience. Like Dewey, Labarca was not a revolutionary but a reformer. She similarly was skeptical of panaceas and grand solutions for eliminating evils and injustices in society. She also firmly believed that a realistic scientific knowledge of existing conditions and a cultivation of women's, as well as men's, imaginations could ameliorate the human condition.

Like her own self-invention, Amanda Labarca's construction of national and cultural identity remained fluid and changeable, like that of the traveler-pedagogue whose claims, beliefs, and theories can be useful and reliable but whose obsolescence can always be imagined, whose provisional grounds are useful springboards for future investigation but whose usefulness derives in part from their very fluidity and changeability. Thus, in sharp contrast to a philosophical tradition where the certain and stable are regarded as ontologically superior and epistemologically more valuable, Labarca as socially responsible reporter-reformer set forth the belief that chance, difference, and anomaly—values garnered through foreign contacts and deposited in many and diverse writings—are as important cultural components to self/national definition as are stability, certainty, and normalcy, the orderly emblems of more traditional nation-building projects.

Notes

1. Ofelia Schutte, *Cultural Identity and Social Liberation in Latin American Thought* (Albany, NY: SUNY Press, 1993), 15.

2. Francesca Miller, *Latin American Women and the Search for Social Justice* (Hanover, NH: University Press of New England, 1991), xiv.

3. Amanda Labarca, *¿Adónde va la mujer?* (Santiago: Imprenta Letras, 1934), 21, 224, 227, 237. Unless otherwise referenced, all translations from the works of Amanda Labarca Hubertson are my own.

4. Amanda Labarca, "Women and Education in Chile," *Women and Education* series, vol. 5 (Paris: UNESCO, 1953), 27.

5. Amanda Labarca, "From Chile," in *As Others See Us: The United States Through Foreign Eyes*, trans. M. Joseph Franz (Princeton, NJ: Princeton University Press, 1959), 310.

6. Amanda Labarca, "Influencias norteamericanas en la educación chilena," in *La nueva democracia* (New York: Committee on Cooperation in Latin America, 1961), 78.

7. Ibid., 79.

8. Edward Slosson, *The American Spirit in Education* (New Haven: Yale University Press, 1921), 267.

9. John Dewey and Evelyn Dewey, *Schools of To-Morrow* (New York: Dutton, 1915), 294.

10. Labarca, "Influencias norteamericanas en la educación chilena," 79.

11. Amanda Labarca, as quoted in Jaque D. Juvenal Hernández, *Discurso de recepción (7 de Diciembre de 1970) Instituto de Chile* (Santiago de Chile: Editorial Andrés Bello, 1970), 22.

12. Amanda Labarca, "Allá en Columbia, cuando John Dewey," in *La nueva democracia*, 33.

13. Ibid., 33.

14. Ibid., 35.

15. Ibid., 33. Her novel *En tierras extrañas* contains references to her encounters with U.S. racism, anti-Semitism, and gender bias while a student at Columbia. Carlos expresses shocked embarrassment, for example, when students approved of the lynching of "Negroes" and Jews because they are "stupid; they aren't good for anything but evil." Ibid., 40.

16. Ibid., 34.

17. Amanda Labarca, "Hacia un entendimiento mejor" (Toward a better understanding), unpublished manuscript, quoted in Catherine Manny Paul, *Amanda Labarca H.: Educator to the Women in Chile (The Work and Writings of Amanda Labarca H. in the Field of Education in Chile)* (Cuernavaca, Mexico: Centro Intercultural de Documentación, 1968), 2/9.

18. Labarca, *¿Adónde va la mujer?*, 5–6.

19. Amanda Labarca, *Actividades femeninas en los Estados Unidos* (Santiago: Imprenta Universitaria, 1914), 173–75.

20. Labarca, "From Chile," 316.

21. Paul, *Amanda Labarca H.*, 2/12.

22. Amanda Labarca, *La escuela secundaria en los Estados Unidos* (Santiago: Imprenta Universo, 1919), 13.

23. Labarca, "Influencias norteamericanas en la educación chilena," 80.

24. Paul, *Amanda Labarca H.*, 3/7–3/8.

25. *Berkeley Daily Gazette*, July 19, 1939.

26. Labarca, "From Chile," 318.

27. Ibid., 321–24.

28. Amanda Labarca, *Bases para una política educacional* (Buenos Aires: Editorial Losada, 1944), 204.

29. The intent here is to treat the two phenomena—utopia and ideology—within a single conceptual framework. As Paul Ricoeur writes in *Lectures on Ideology and Utopia* (New York: Columbia University Press, 1986), 1, "the organizing hypothesis is that the very conjunction of these two opposite sides or complementary functions [utopia and ideology] typifies what could be called social and cultural imagination." Karl Mannheim also confronts the intersection of "ideological and utopian distortions" in his book *Ideology and Utopia* (San Diego: Harcourt Brace Jovanovich, 1985); and Terry Eagleton, in his definition of ideology, cites "identity thinking" and "socially necessary illusion" as essential components in *Ideology: An Introduction* (London: Verso, 1991), 2.

30. Amanda Labarca, *En tierras extrañas* (Santiago: Imprenta Universitaria, 1915), 14.

31. Ibid., 26.

32. Ibid., 20. While the name Eve Wright obviously is laden with all kinds of implications and connotations, Labarca may have assigned the young social worker that name with more political than symbolic intent. Eve is, after all, the first woman to open Carlos/Adam's eyes to a new social reality—a remaking of existing social conditions. The lesson he learns with her death is that the problem is to build not a perfect but a better society. Thus, she awakens him—literally thrusting him out of the paradise of romance and into reality—to the need to harmonize individual needs with those of the larger social environment.

33. Ibid., 329.

34. Paul, *Amanda Labarca H.*, 6/8.

35. Doris Sommer, *Foundational Fictions: The National Romances of Latin America* (Berkeley: University of California Press, 1991), 14.

36. Manuel Parra, "En tierras extrañas," *Las Últimas Noticias* (July 15, 1916), 3.

37. Labarca, *En tierras extrañas*, 78–79.

38. Ibid., 291.

39. Amanda Labarca, *Actividades femeninas en Chile* (Santiago: Imprenta La Ilustracíon, 1914), 7, writes that "the friendship between a man and a woman and the exchange of ideas between them is perhaps the only means of acquiring . . . thought that is not marked by unilateralism. The interpretations of the world that each gender forges for him/herself complement each other to include distinct phases of the prism of truth."

40. Labarca, *En tierras extrañas*, 91.

41. Mary Louise Pratt, *Imperial Eyes: Writing and Transculturation* (London: Routledge, 1992), 319.

42. I have borrowed the term "diacultural" from my student, Saralinda Blanning, who, in her master's thesis, "From a Multicultural Perspective to Diacultural Perspectives: Reconceptualizing Multicultural Pedagogy" (Michigan Technological University, 1994), uses it to emphasize the roles of perspective and interaction when dealing with multiple cultures.

43. Labarca, "Influencias norteamericanas en la educación chilena," 81.

44. Ibid.

45. The term is Mary Louise Pratt's as discussed in her essay "Criticism in the Contact Zone," *Critical Theory, Cultural Politics, and Latin American Narrative*, ed. Steven Bell, Albert May, and Leonard Orr (Notre Dame, IN: University of Notre Dame Press, 1993), 83–102.

46. Richard Hofstadter, *The Age of Reform* (New York: Alfred A. Knopf, 1955), 185.

47. Lawrence A. Cremin, "John Dewey and the Progressive Education Movement, 1915–1952," in *Dewey on Education: Appraisals*, ed. Reginald D. Archambault (New York: Random House, 1966), 11.

III

Taking Sides

10

Latin Americans in Paris in the 1920s: The Anti-Imperialist Struggle of the General Association of Latin American Students, 1925–1933

Arturo Taracena Arriola

Although fought primarily in Europe, World War I had many significant implications for Latin America and greatly impressed a generation of its intellectuals who were coming of age during this period. The war temporarily crippled many Latin American economies as German U-boat activity made transatlantic shipping nearly impossible. In the realm of international politics, the war brought unwelcome attention to Latin American governments that were uneasy about taking sides in the conflict. Domestically, populations divided between those supporting the Allies and those supporting the Axis powers. At the war's conclusion, the United States clearly had emerged as the world's strongest economic, political, and military power, aggravating Latin Americans' long-standing distrust of the "Colossus of the North." At the same time, the success of the 1917 Bolshevik Revolution in Russia presented an inspiring example of national recovery and reorganization that stood in direct ideological opposition to the capitalism and colonialism viewed by many to be at the roots of World War I.

Guatemalan historian Arturo Taracena examines a group of Latin American university students and journalists caught up in the vortex of postwar ideological battles while living in Paris during the late 1920s. Drawn to the French capital from many countries for a variety of reasons (some as exiles, others as students or writers), these young people quickly recognized their shared concerns and interests as they sought out the

Abridged and translated from "La Asociación General de Estudiantes Latinoamericanos de París (1925–1933)," *Anuario de Estudios Centroamericanos* (Universidad de Costa Rica) 15, no. 2 (1989): 60–80. Translated by Kent Dickson. Reprinted by permission of the *Anuario de Estudios Centroamericanos* and Arturo Taracena Arriola.

companionship of other Latin Americans in the city. Anxiety over U.S. imperialism in the region quickly emerged as one of the most salient issues to unite the Latin American youth in Paris.

To evoke the presence of Latin American intellectuals in Paris during the 1920s, especially those gathered under the AGELA (Asociación General de Estudiantes Latinoamericanos/General Association of Latin American Students), means not only rescuing a part of Latin America's political and cultural history from oblivion but also recalling a historical fact that has marked the region's reality throughout the twentieth century: North America has intervened in the internal affairs of every country on the continent. AGELA was founded under postwar conditions that conspired to cause dozens of Latin Americans of the bourgeoisie and middle class to cross the Atlantic to establish themselves in Paris, London, Madrid, and Berlin. Some were sent by their parents to pursue higher education, others were attracted by the political and intellectual climate which had produced the Allied triumph and the Bolshevik Revolution, and still others had been forced into a European exile. While their reasons were varied, a group of young Latin Americans representing the generation born between 1885 and 1906 came together in the French capital. Searching for knowledge, their time in France made them conscious of America and of the ills that it suffered. The prevailing cultural, political, and ideological atmosphere—especially the solidarity and ebullience of postwar France —made them privileged persons. Because of this unique environment, what began as a student initiative rapidly became an anti-imperialist movement which turned the defense of Augusto César Sandino's struggle in Nicaragua into a search for continental dignity.

Latin American solidarity in the face of military and economic occupation came about in great part due to the efforts of writers and students in foreign residence. The "great anti-imperialist protest of Latin America" was held in Paris at the Salle des Sociétés Savantes on June 29, 1925, under the presidency of the famed Spanish philosophers Miguel de Unamuno and José Ortega y Gasset. Among the Latin American orators who participated, the Uruguayan Carlos Quijano pointed out the importance of anti-Monroism (meaning opposition to the Monroe Doctrine) and anti-Americanism for Latin America. The Argentine José Ingenieros took a similar stance, denouncing the trickery of the United States in introducing the Regional Inter-American Pact—which had not yet been ratified by any Latin American government—into the Treaty of Versailles. The Peruvian Víctor Raúl Haya de la Torre spoke of the necessity of building a new *latinoamericanidad* (Latin American identity) that would be both anti-imperialist and non-Marxist. Finally, the Guatemalan Miguel Angel Asturias emphasized that the problem of imperialism demanded a solution originating from the American sub-continent.[1] Latin Americans from throughout the continent met and began to discuss issues that concerned them all.

Although the exact date of AGELA's founding remains unknown, it occurred sometime in late October 1925. An article by Armando Maribona published in the Guatemalan newspaper *El Imparcial* on November 21 of that year reported that the idea for creating the solidarity organization originated with a group of Latin Americans in Paris. The group was comprised of Maribona himself, who, in addition to being a correspondent for the Cuban journal *Diario de la Marina,* was already a well-known caricaturist; the Costa Ricans Padilla Castro and Mario Lujan, a medical student; the Argentine Rolando Martel, a painter of anarchist opinions who wrote for *Diario de la Marina*; Miguel Angel Asturias, already a lawyer and correspondent for *El Imparcial* of Guatemala; the Peruvian José Félix Cárdenas Castro, a painter; the Cuban Antonio Battorno, also a painter; the Nicaraguan Diego Manuel Sequeira, a law student; and the young Venezuelan architect Aurelio Fortoul. Despite differing national origins, Paris had drawn them all; and, once there, they observed the example of French students and workers and began to unite around their common causes.

Maribona recounted the difficulties the students had in getting the organization off the ground, such as lacking means and facing the ill-will of the Parisian authorities. Helped by advice from Professor Ernest Martineche, they ultimately succeeded. They were soon joined by Quijano, already an attorney and correspondent for Montevideo's *El País*. AGELA's initial objectives included: a) the abolition of nationality within the group; b) a co-operative organizational structure; c) leadership through a governing board (there would be no elected president); d) a system of proportional representation by country in the elections for the governing board; and e) pro-Latin American propaganda as one of the organization's chief tasks.[2] Despite these rather confused initial goals, and the heterogeneous nature of its members, AGELA rapidly became organized under the strong leadership of Quijano. On November 15 a governing junta was elected, and Quijano won the post of General Secretary.

On the 30th of the same month, with the purpose of obtaining nonprofit status for the organization, Quijano delivered (as stipulated in the French law of July 1, 1901) a letter to the Paris Prefecture of Police stating the names and addresses of the student board members, the location of AGELA's headquarters, number 55, Quai de la Tournelle, and a copy of its by-laws. The by-laws contained twenty-nine articles which had as their goals: a) the defense and protection of the economic and moral interests, as well as the cultural development, of the Latin American students; b) pro-Latin America propaganda; c) the possible creation of similar institutions across Europe; and d) the establishment of relations with all other student institutions in the world, especially those in America. AGELA was registered definitively with the Prefecture of Police on December 11, and its notice of approval appeared in the *Journal Officiel* on January 8, 1926.[3]

Integral to the founding and the political functioning of AGELA was a confirmation of the "pertinence of a new generation, arising in a culminating historical moment and for that reason called to play a decisive role in the future."[4] This postwar Latin American generation witnessed a series of unprecedented historical occurrences, such as the Bolshevik Revolution, Latin American university reform, the consolidation of North American hegemony in the capitalist world—especially in Latin America—the crisis of liberal democracy in Europe, and the rise of fascism. Latin America's viability lay in its unity. The poem "Nosotros" (We), which Asturias read at an AGELA banquet in 1925, is a testimony to this attitude:

>Like an ardent bronze alert
>Let the shout of young America sound;
>"No more sad and servile peoples;
>Enough of slave traders and clowns."
>
>We must cease being the blind accomplices
>Of tyrants and perverse Judases.
>Erase the absurd boundaries,
>The Andes are not twenty, but one!
>
>We do not want the illusory America
>With a foreign soul and beggar's brain;
>Let the genius of a new world shine
>In the pampas, the jungle, and the mountains.
>
>Functionaries without pay or master
>Of the audacious fabric of the future,
>We will knit a red shroud
>For the enslaved, grotesque America.
>
>With vigorous rebellious hammers
>We will shape the new America
>In the living forge of the people,
>Yes, we!, we, WE![5]

With equal force, Quijano expressed the same idea in his article, "La Asociación General de Estudiantes Latinoamericanos en París. Su obra y su programa" (AGELA: Its work and its program), published in *El País* of Montevideo:

>If we do not want to perish, we must apply ourselves to study, to study, and to study—against stupid demagoguery, against charlatanism, against ignorance, against narrow regionalism, a product of precisely that willful ignorance that comes from staying inside one's own country. The men who meet and work in AGELA, animated by one ardent desire, tomorrow will no doubt exercise . . . directive action in America. They will scatter throughout our continent and will bring forth from their

current labors not only knowledge of other peoples and other problems essentially the same as ours, but also general ideas for action. That is why they are "learning" now, their thoughts constantly fixed on their homeland, determined that the continent shall not "perish."[6]

These "men who meet and work in AGELA" intended to create a proud new future for Latin America, and crafted their continental project together while in foreign residence in France.

Two days before the association was legalized formally, on January 6, 1926, in the Salle des Sociétés Savantes on the Rue Danton, AGELA organized an event in which famed Mexican philosopher José Vasconcelos participated. Three hundred people attended and the speakers included Vasconcelos, Alberto Zérega Fombona, Alcides Argüedas, Luis López de Mena, and Carlos Quijano. Quijano contented himself with holding up France and its democracy as examples for Latin America, while Vasconcelos called for Latin American unity in standing up to the United States, defended the republican idea, and censured Mexican President Plutarco Elías Calles without naming him. Ambassadors Alfonso Reyes (Mexico), Gonzalo Zaldumbide (Ecuador), and Manuel Peralta (Costa Rica) were present, and the guest of honor was the famous Peruvian writer Ventura García Calderón, meaning the association had attracted the attention and implicit support of important governmental figures.[7]

During the remainder of 1926, AGELA's principal activity appears to have been to organize dinners of public recognition in which cultural and political matters mingled with bohemian ones. Writing for the July 15 issue of *Diario de la Marina*, Rolando Martel reviewed a June dinner concert in honor of the Cuban musician Diego Bonilla: "in the café-restaurant La Rotonde, a common meeting place of cosmopolitan bohemians, we met for a friendly, unofficial dinner—Cubans and Argentines, Dominicans and Costa Ricans, Spaniards and Mexicans, and that excellent friend of Spain and Ibero-America, Charles Lesca."[8] The unpublished photograph that accompanies these lines from AGELA's celebration on September 15, 1926, the day of Central American independence, demonstrates the pan-Latin American participation in this organization's activities (Figure 4).[9]

For his part, in *El Imparcial*, Miguel Angel Asturias filed an account of the dinner organized in honor of the Spanish sculptor Mate Hernández in which one hundred and twenty Latin Americans participated. Asturias recorded that:

> After the poets finished, it was the politicians' turn. The discussion revolved around an interesting subject: the need for the youth of America to act in their respective countries—no longer content as before with a formulaic opposition that never produces concrete results, or with an indifference that aids and abets the crimes which the old guard politicians daily commit against their unhappy nations. It is fine that our

Banquets and other celebrations cemented ties among Latin Americans living in 1920s Paris. *Courtesy of Jorge Luis Arriola*

youth dedicate themselves to journalism, to influencing through the power of the word, but this can't be their only role. For their works to be truly transcendent and effective they must govern. Governing, that's the job that belongs to today's youth. And it is not possible to govern while shirking responsibilities, but rather by facing up to reality. To govern, one must go into government, and to go into government one must let go of some of his prejudices in exchange for the great good which it is possible to do from there.[10]

With these lines Asturias anticipated what would happen to a large part of AGELA's members upon their return to America. France was serving as their school for political action. However, things did not always go as planned, as the young, enthusiastic intellectuals ended up being absorbed into the old political machinery, abandoning the social ideas that had so excited them while in Europe. Among the few who managed to sustain these ideals after returning to America were Quijano, Juan Isidro Jiménes Grullón, and Jorge Luis Arriola.

AGELA obtained practical aid from the director of the Maison des Grands Journaux Ibéro-Américains (Office of Important Ibero-American Newspapers). Alejandro Sux made the facilities of this organization available, which allowed AGELA to set up an information office for Latin American students arriving in Paris.[11] Similarly, sporting activities were encouraged—particularly football, which, Arriola recalled, the members of AGELA played regularly on the soccer fields of Croix de Berny. The Argentines, Uruguayans, and Peruvians stood out. According to the Peruvian Felipe Cossío del Pomar, the fields were next door to the Porte d'Orléans. The same author, however, claimed that the matches were organized by the APRA cell (Alianza Popular Revolucionaria Americana/ Popular Revolutionary Alliance of America), which had become active slightly after the founding of AGELA, and operated within a rhetoric of the necessity of physical culture, which leads one to believe that the group was influenced by fascist governing styles.[12] The reality was somewhat different: the first Uruguayan triumph in Olympic soccer, won in 1924 in a Colombes stadium, transcended mere sports and gave Latin Americans a rallying point in opposition to Europe. Arriola remembers even today how the football team of Latin American students from the Sorbonne defeated its French counterpart and how this was cause for collective satisfaction (Figure 5).[13]

Soccer teams boosted morale among Latin American students in Paris and promoted positive images of the region abroad. *Courtesy of Jorge Luis Arriola*

AGELA's public activities were marked from the beginning by the anti-imperialist sentiment already embraced by its principal intellectual mentors: Ugarte, Ingenieros, Vasconcelos, and by its General Secretary, Quijano. On the occasion of the "Great anti-imperialist rally of Latin America" held on June 29, 1925, Quijano had sketched the following ideas: "the current conflict between Mexico and the United States is not simply another episode in the battle between Yankee imperialism and Latin America. . . . It is also an episode in the fight between two distinct economic visions. To fight by Mexico's side is to fight for the revolution against capitalism, and this delineates our position at all points."[14] And yet it was not until 1927 that this anti-imperialist activity took shape. On January 13, in the Salle des Horticulteurs on the Rue Grenelle, the United Front of Workers and Intellectuals of Latin America, the public name of the APRA cell in Paris, called a Latin American rally to support Nicaragua, in protest against North American intervention in that country.[15] Although the meeting reflected APRA's advocacy of a third way between capitalism and communism, AGELA openly supported the event. Moreover, to prove the popularity of this cause, AGELA member Miguel Angel Asturias and Nicaraguan journalist Eduardo Avilés Ramírez requested a statement of support from French intellectual Romain Rolland, who, in a letter dated from Villeneuve on January 11, proclaimed himself in solidarity with the protest. The Spaniard Miguel de Unamuno did the same.[16] APRA tradition further holds that the orators on this occasion included APRA founder Víctor Raúl Haya de la Torre, Chilean poet Vicente Huidobro, Sian Ting, a member of the Chinese Nationalist Kuomintang, and representatives of Nicaragua, Haiti, and the Dominican Republic. Speeches focused on aspects of Monroism and the U.S. Marines' presence in Central America and the Caribbean.[17]

The fight to defend Nicaraguan sovereignty would become the axis of AGELA's activism. On January 21, 1927, in the Salle des Ingénieurs Civils, the Secretary General, Carlos Quijano, gave a lecture about Nicaragua and U.S. imperialism. He based his speech on the economic and political information that Debayle Sacasa had collected for his doctoral thesis in law for the School of Political Sciences of Paris. The lecture kicked off a bitter debate between Quijano and the North American journalist Paul Scott Mower, director of the European edition of the *Chicago Daily News*, who, according to the Uruguayan, took up the issue with him one week later in the Salle de la Societé de Géographie, under the patronage of the magazine *Renaissance Latine*.[18] Quijano published an expanded form of his lecture one year later under the title *Nicaragua: Ensayo sobre el imperialismo de los Estados Unidos* (Nicaragua: An essay on U.S. imperialism).

At the beginning of February, AGELA organized a rally to protest the arrival in Paris of Emiliano Chamorro, ex-dictator of Nicaragua, who, after renouncing the presidency on October 30, 1926, disembarked in the French capital as the new ambassador. The protesters booed Chamorro upon his arrival in the Montparnasse station, a scene that Asturias recorded in the pages of *El Imparcial*:

> Emiliano Chamorro's arrival occasioned the gathering of a hundred or so Latin American students: . . . Central Americans, Mexicans, Cubans, Argentines, Uruguayans, Peruvians, Venezuelans. The youth of America awaited the traitor at the station gates, without uneasiness, firm in their resolve to punish him upon his arriving in Paris. The clocks struck seven in the evening. Among a group of passengers came Don Emiliano, a bit

wary—perhaps he had heard the news that we were waiting to "welcome" him— and as he emerged from the gate a great number of tomatoes and rotten eggs rained down upon him accompanied by shouts of "Traitor!"[19]

On another front, AGELA launched a campaign of sending protest telegrams to President Coolidge and the Nicaraguan government expressing —in the words of the *Revue de l'Amérique Latine*—"the true sentiments of the youth of Latin America."[20] Then, on February 3, 1927, the student association joined the popular protests put together by French trade unions and political organizations in support of life and liberty for the militant North American anarchists Nicola Sacco and Bartolomeo Vanzetti.[21] For the Latin Americans, Paris was a school in activist solidarity.

The gradual radicalization of AGELA's activities began to create an ideological chasm between the students and the circle of intellectuals and diplomats of the older generation resident in Paris. In the pages of the *Revue de l'Amérique Latine*, Lesca and Francisco García Calderón lamented that for its meetings AGELA "should call almost exclusively on speakers known as agitators of the extreme left."[22] In a "Manifesto to the Latin American Students of Paris"—directed to AGELA—Manuel Ugarte wrote with indignation:

> Let us not accept, then, differences between liberals and conservatives, and let us come together against the doomsayers, against the presidents anointed by the White House, against every form that the miserable egotism of petty strongmen takes in our republics. The only one of them who deserves our enthusiastic loyalty is General Sandino, because he and his heroic guerrillas represent the popular reaction of our America against the treasonous oligarchies, and the resistance of our whole populace to Anglo-Saxon imperialism. The farce of the Nicaraguan elections lays bare the inevitable downfall of those who, faced with a choice between their own interests and those of their country, chose their own. The future will see the disapproval that they deserve descend upon them. This same future will also see the altruistic figure of Sandino lifted up.[23]

Ugarte had been named an honorary member of AGELA in January 1928 and, in a letter answering him in the name of the association, Quijano commented: "Thank you for your beautiful message, which we read and which made us laugh in our meeting. I suppose you have been informed of its success. Guesde said that *Le Temps*, the bourgeoisie incarnate in a newspaper, reported it."[24]

AGELA's radicalism did not end there. Later, amplifying the scope of its criticism with the backing of the Liga de los Derechos del Hombre (League of the Rights of Man), AGELA organized on May 4, 1928, a demonstration in support of the Venezuelan students incarcerated by order of General Juan Vicente Gómez. Under the leadership of Víctor Bosch, the Venezuelan students Fabela and Escalón declared that three hundred of their colleagues lay in prison in that country because of anti-dictatorial activities, and that they were being threatened with execution.[25] According to Norberto Galasso, Ugarte received a telegram from AGELA saying that the Venezuelan government was "preparing to execute students— Association urges you send cable demanding pardon." The Argentine politician did so immediately, calling world-wide attention to the matter and keeping Gómez from carrying out his plans.[26] Finally, on November 13 of that year, AGELA organized a meeting to protest the incarceration of Cuban students by Gerardo Machado's dictatorship. Joining this demonstration was the recently created ANERC (Asociación de Nuevos Emigrados Revolucionarios de Cuba/New Revolutionary Cuban Immigrants' Association), which had been founded in August by fifteen Cuban students exiled in France. Their spokesman was José Felipe Chelala Aguilera, one-time secretary to the director of the University of Havana and co-founder of the Cuban Communist Party. In addition, the student association distributed around Paris a flyer, "Against the Tyranny of Machado."[27]

In *El Desastre*, former Mexican Minister of Education and Culture José Vasconcelos revealed that as early as 1926, an ideological confrontation between communists, fascists, and Apristas was taking shape in the heart of AGELA:

> The subject which would later divide the Student Association, almost putting an end to it, became a hot topic: Bolshevism and its American application. . . . To publicize the discussion, a debate was organized. Representatives of all sectors of opinion would speak. For example, the Venezuelan Zérega Fombona represented the tendency that was scientificist, hierarchical, almost fascist, after the manner of [Charles] Maurras. A regressive rightism that goes along picking up the human cast-offs of discredited dynasties has always irritated me. The extremists who deify Stalin, the ex-seminarian, irritate me to an equal degree.[28]

If the ideal of hemispheric solidarity was easily agreed upon, it proved far more difficult for the youths to agree on a strategy when Paris offered exposure to many competing theories of revolution and politics.

AGELA emerged at the same time as the APRA cell in Paris, toward the end of 1925. More precisely, the latter came into existence by taking advantage of AGELA's founding, which was very warmly welcomed among the Latin American students residing in Paris.[29] Among the Peruvians making up the cell were José Félix Cárdenas Castro, Felipe Cossío del Pomar, Eudocio Ravines, César Vallejo, Edgardo Rozas, and Rafael and Alfredo González Willis. For his part, Haya de la Torre had met Carlos Quijano in Buenos Aires when he and the group Ariel had organized a reception for the Peruvian in 1922.[30] When the Aprista project stopped being simply a political initiative of the Peruvians and aspired to organize all Latin Americans living in Paris, it must have entered into conflict with

AGELA, especially if AGELA's leaders sympathized partially with the communist current, as in Quijano's case, or were full-fledged communists, as with Fortoul, who was a militant in the French Communist Party, or anarco-unionists, as in the case of Rolando Martel.[31]

Another example of the way in which Haya de la Torre used AGELA's labors to his own advantage can be found in the organization of the rally in support of Nicaragua held on the Rue Grenelle, January 12, 1927. Romain Rolland had sent his message of support to the APRA committee of Paris, since it was this group that had taken the initiative to organize the rally.[32] However, it was the Guatemalan Asturias and the Nicaraguan Avilés Ramírez who had contacted the French author, raising the question of whether they did so as members of APRA or as part of the support that AGELA lent to the rally.[33] The success of the rally for Nicaragua contrasted markedly with the mediocre turnout of the later official inauguration of APRA's Center of Anti-Imperialist Studies held on January 20 of that year.[34] What is certain is that each time Haya de la Torre passed through Paris, the APRA cell managed to exercise a certain political sway over the Latin American community in the French capital, momentarily frustrating the efforts of the communists to organize it. That same year, from an optimistic vantage point across the Atlantic ocean, the Aprista leader wrote that "APRA is becoming the most powerful anti-imperialist organization in America." [35]

There can be no doubt that the ideological confrontation that occurred during the Anti-Imperialist Congress of Brussels between Haya de la Torre and Ravines, on the one hand, and Quijano, supported by the cream of Latin American communist leaders of the moment, on the other, only deepened AGELA's internal contradictions. Quijano would have been closer to the Apristas' position since he had felt the impact of the Russian Revolution only indirectly and gave more importance to the crisis in European democracy. He was also known to have stated that faced with "the capitalist economy, [he] opposed to it [a] socialist economy, without implying, for a moment, either submission to a particular sect or the transplanting to America of the methods that belong to Europe."[36] Haya de la Torre's disappointment was great. Not even Deambrosis Martins, Jiménes Grullón, or Debayle Sacasa, despite their committed anti-imperialism and resistance to a strategy of class conflict, allied themselves with the Apristas to counteract the "predominant communist affiliation" of the Latin American delegates. From that moment forward, the idea of a Third Way, a so-called Chinese path, began to lose ground among the Latin Americans resident in Europe. Haya de la Torre's rival Mariátegui's call to form a Socialist Party in Peru gave the idea its coup de grâce. As has already been stated, the Parisian cell of APRA was torn apart by internal crisis in 1929. By that time, César Vallejo had already broken ranks and joined the communists.

Besides a competition for membership and an ideological battle with
APRA, a number of problems emerged to dampen enthusiasm for AGELA
by 1929. Asturias's disenchantment with the organization was already per-
ceptible. He pointed out in his journalistic writings that the students had
abandoned their ideals and fixed their gaze on professional success. Likewise, he denounced the "satellites" and "minor societies" that orbited about
the university association, in a clear allusion to the growing influence of
the communists.[37] Then too, AGELA's cohesiveness was not due solely to
anti-dictatorial and anti-imperialist sentiments; it owed much to the students' need to establish cultural and personal links that would allow them
to successfully negotiate the foreign environment. True, many of the participants ended up discovering America in Europe, in the words of
Mariátegui, but the majority maintained their political ambiguity because
of the social class from which they had come. AGELA's activities were
also hindered because of its hazy relationship with Latin American diplomatic circles, which represented the very dictatorships that AGELA was
denouncing. Finally, the elitism of the group's Latin American mentors
meant dependence on the Parisian intellectual establishment.

Political disenchantment with AGELA was perhaps strongest among
the group's older mentors within the Parisian Latin American community.
Alcides Argüedas, José Arzú, Gonzalo Zaldumbide, Alberto Zérega Fombona, and the García Calderón brothers were diplomatic representatives
of their respective countries, and certainly did not share the more radical
political positions of the youths Quijano, Cárdenas Castro, or Martel.
While Martel was known for his extremism, a politically militant anarco-
unionism which he shared with his countryman Luis de Filippo,[38] Zérega
Fombona represented the fascist strain which followed Maurras, leader of
the ultra right-wing organization Action Française. The same year that Quijano published an essay about U.S. intervention in Nicaragua, Francisco
García Calderón wrote in *El Tiempo* of Bogotá that "to be brutally honest
we must confess that the United States intervenes (in Latin America) where
it finds permanent discord, the alternating extremes of anarchy and dictatorship. Even in the American Mediterranean—in the Antilles, in Central
America—it respects the established democracies, El Salvador, Costa
Rica."[39] As in any foreign residential community, such as the Latin Americans in Paris, the heightened political awareness, coupled with the fluid
nature of its membership, meant that tensions and conflicts inevitably arose.

By May 28, 1930, the student organization found itself in a full-blown
internal crisis.[40] That year it was only able to organize one public event: a
ceremony commemorating the centennial of Simón Bolívar's death, which
consisted of installing a plaque at number 2A, Rue Vivienne (presently
annexed to the National Library). The political situations of both Latin
America and France, strongly affected by the world-wide recession, had
changed. On a personal level, protest activities began to give way to pro-

fessional ones and the diplomatic or political careers of the recently gradu-ated young Latin Americans.

AGELA's old guard began returning to the New World in 1928 and had all gone by 1933. One of the first to leave was Carlos Quijano, who joined the recently formed Uruguayan Pro-Nicaragua Concentration, made up primarily of university students, and led a protest movement in Uru-guay against "the armed occupation of Nicaragua by the United States."[41] Quijano's return to America was followed by many Latin Americans linked to AGELA. Maribona moved back to Cuba in 1930 to practice his profes-sion after having worked as a caricaturist for the French newspapers *Le Figaro* and *L'Intransigent* and having lived briefly in Madrid. Cossío del Pomar, who one year earlier had been the secretary of the Association of Foreign Artists of Paris, went back to Peru in 1931 in order to share the APRA experience with his countrymen. Fortoul likewise returned to his country in 1931, sometime in the month of January, to found the Venezu-elan Communist Party. He was captured by Gómez's police on May 29 of that year, and spent several years in prison. Early in the 1930s he went home to the Dominican Republic, and in July 1934 he was apprehended on Rafael Trujillo's orders. After spending more than a year in prison he went into exile in Cuba, where he continued fighting against the Trujillo dictatorship.[42] Martel's case is dramatic. He remained in France as the secretary of the Argentine Consul in Cherbourg, Eduardo Murga. Both men later moved to Havana, where Murga was transferred. Maribona main-tained that Murga did not know his secretary's real name until after Martel's death. For many years, according to the Cuban painter, the ex-founder of AGELA had professed "rightist ideas and sentiments."[43]

Of the Central Americans, Asturias remained in Paris until 1933, but, beginning in 1930, he was increasingly removed from university political circles, dedicating himself to his journalism for *El Imparcial* and to the manuscript of his novel, *El Señor Presidente*. Arriola had returned to Gua-temala in 1930, where the Ubico dictatorship overshadowed him until 1944, when he became prominent as a leader of the October Revolution that ushered in the reformist governments of Juan José Arévalo and later Jacobo Arbenz. Debayle Sacasa went back to Nicaragua in 1928 and took the position of civil judge in the city of León. In 1933 he was named the Minister of Government by President Juan Bautista Sacasa, his uncle, who was overthrown by Anastasio Somoza in 1934. The death of Nicaraguan guerrilla leader Sandino fell between the two events. The Costa Rican Padilla Castro was named consul of his country in Bristol in 1927, and, two years later, was transferred to London. He returned to his homeland in 1932. Finally, the Salvadoran Toño Salazar traveled to New York in 1930, going from there to Montevideo where he took up residence.

Asturias has left the best description of AGELA's collapse in an ar-ticle which appeared in *El Imparcial* of Guatemala in October of 1930:

"our revolutionary shout found an echo in America because we demanded of America's youth a concrete vision of what is American. The much-mourned Mariátegui cried from his sick-bed in Peru for the new genera-tions to reckon with reality, to think only of how to face our problems head on, not to dally with fictitious creations, daughters more of the imagi-nation than of reality. And the American hours that we live are hours of moral bankruptcy."[44] Three years later Asturias would pay dearly for this bankruptcy, which he denounced. The anti-imperialist battle was moving from Central America to Cuba, and French solidarity went with it.

Notes

1. Armando Maribona, "La gran manifestación anti-imperialista latinoamericana celebrada en París," *El Imparcial*, Guatemala, September 26, 1925.

2. Armando Maribona, "La Asociación de Estudiantes Latinoamericanos," *El Imparcial*, Guatemala, November 21, 1925.

3. *Journal Officiel de la République Française, Lois et Décrets*, LVIII Année, No. 6, Paris, January 8, 1926, 383.

4. Gerardo Caetano and José Pedro Rilla, *El joven Quijano (1900–1933): Izquierda nacional y conciencia crítica* (Colección Temas del Siglo XX, 38. Ediciones de la Banda Oriental, Montevideo, 1986), 43–44.

5. Miguel Angel Asturias, "Nosotros," *El Imparcial*, Guatemala, October 11, 1930.

6. Carlos Quijano, "La Asociación General de Estudiantes Latinoamericanos en París. Su obra y su programa," *El País*, Montevideo, May 4, 1927, cited by Caetano y Rilla, *El joven Quijano*, 43.

7. Archives Nationales de Paris, *Ministère de l'Intérieur, F1 13435 Pays Étran-gers. Surveillance de leurs ressortissants résidents en France. Amérique Latine (1914–1933). Généralités*. Report of the Prefecture of Police, dated January 1, 1926.

8. Rolando Martel, "Envío de Lutecia. Concierto y almuerzo. Diego Bonilla héroe del arco." *Diario de la Marina*, Havana, June 15, 1926.

9. Jorge Luis Arriola—to whom I owe various pieces of information presented here—preserved the photograph.

10. Miguel Angel Asturias, "Comida de Estudiantes," *El Imparcial*, Guatemala, November 29, 1926.

11. Marc Cheymol, *Miguel Angel Asturias et la France: Un séjour décisif, Paris, 1924–1933* (Thèse de Doctorat d'Etat, Paris IV, 1982), 320.

12. Felipe Cossío del Pomar, *Victor Raúl: Biografía de Haya de la Torre*, Part I (México: Editorial Cultura, 1961), 272–74.

13. Jorge Luis Arriola, verbal report to the author; Caetano y Rilla, *El joven Quijano*, 41.

14. Carlos Quijano, "¿Existe un imperialismo yanqui?" *El País*, Montevideo, August 12, 1925, and August 13, 1925, cited by Caetano and Rilla, *El joven Quijano*, 51–52.

15. Archives Nationales de Paris, *Ministère de l'Intérieur, F7 13435 Pays Étrangers. Surveillance de leurs ressortissants résidents en France. Amérique Latine (1914–1933). Nicaragua*. Report of the Prefecture of Police, dated Janu-ary 14, 1927.

16. Cheymol, *Miguel Angel Asturias et la France*, 337–39; *Amauta*, No. 6, Lima, February 1927, reproduced Rolland's letter. See also: Luis Alberto Sánchez,

Apuntes para una biografía del APRA. I. Los primeros pasos 1923–1931 (Lima: Mosca Azul Editores, 1978), 45.

17. Cossío del Pomar, *Victor Raúl*, 274–75; Víctor Raúl Haya de la Torre, *Obras completas*, Vol. 1, 142–47.

18. Carlos Quijano, *Nicaragua. Un pueblo, una revolución. Ensayo sobre el imperialismo de los Estados Unidos* (México: Editorial Pueblo Nuevo, 1978), 3–11.

19. Miguel Angel Asturias, "La llegada del traidor," *El Imparcial*, Guatemala, February 12, 1927.

20. *Revue de l'Amérique Latine*, Year 6, Volume XII, No. 62, Paris, February 1, 1927, 3.

21. Jorge Luis Arriola, as told to the author.

22. *Revue de l'Amérique Latine*, Year 6, Volume XII, No. 64, Paris, April 1, 1927.

23. *Amauta*, No. 16, Lima, July 1928, 34.

24. Letter from Carlos Quijano to Manuel Ugarte, January 19, 1928, Archivo General de la Nación, Buenos Aires, cited by Norberto Galasso, *Manuel Ugarte. II. De la liberación nacional al socialismo* (Buenos Aires: Colección Los Americanos, EUDEBA, 1973), 149.

25. Archives Nationales de Paris, *Ministère de l'Intérieur, F713088. Ligue de Droits de l'Homme (1916–1932)*. Report of the Prefecture of Police, dated May 4, 1928.

26. Telegram signed by Carlos D'Ascoli to Manuel Ugarte, Archivo General de la Nación, Buenos Aires, cited by Norberto Galasso, *Manuel Ugarte*, 154.

27. Archives Nationales de Paris, *Ministère de l'Intérieur, F7 13435. Pays Étrangers. Surveillance de leurs ressortissants résidents en France. Amérique Latine (1914–1933). Cuba.* Confidential report no. 2078 from the Minister of the Interior to the Minister of Exterior Relations, dated March 1, 1929.

28. José Vasconcelos, *El Desastre*, 4th ed. (México: Ediciones Botas, 1934), 641.

29. Cossío del Pomar, *Víctor Raúl*, 267; Eugenio Chang Rodríguez, *La literatura política de González Prada, Mariátegui y Haya de la Torre* (México: Colección Stadium 18, Ediciones de Andrea, 1957); Percy Murillo Garaycochea, *Historia del APRA, 1919–1945* (Lima: Imprenta Editora Atlántica, 1976).

30. Cossío del Pomar, *Víctor Raúl*, 267. Edgardo Rozas died in an apartment on the Rue Sèvres, Paris, July 30, 1928

31. Armando Maribona, *El arte y el amor en Montparnasse. Documental novelado. París 1923–1930*, Testimonial prologue by Miguel Santiago Valencia (México: Ediciones Andrés Botas, 1950), 98 and 396–97; Fernando Key Sánchez, *Fundación del Partido Comunista de Venezuela* (Caracas: Fondo Editorial 'Carlos Aponte', 1984), 12–13 and 17.

32. *Amauta*, No. 6, Lima, February 1927, 4; Eudocio Ravines, "La actual etapa del capitalismo," *Amauta*, No. 10, Lima, December 1927, 56–58.

33. Cheymol, *Miguel Angel Asturías et la France*, 337–39.

34. Víctor Raúl Haya de la Torre, "¿Qué persigue el Centro de Estudios Anti-Imperialistas del APRA en París?," *Obras completas*, Vol. 1, 142–43.

35. Víctor Raúl Haya de la Torre, "El sentido de la lucha anti-imperialista," *Amauta*, No. 8, Lima, April 1927, 39–40.

36. Caetano and Rilla, *El joven Quijano*, 48–52; Carlos Quijano, "¿Existe un imperialismo yanqui?" *El País*, Montevideo, August 12, 1925, and August 13, 1925.

37. Miguel Angel Asturias, "Ojo nuevo," *El Imparcial*, Guatemala, August 24, 1929.

38. Maribona, *El arte y el amor en Montparnasse*, 98 and 396.

39. Francisco García Calderón, "Nuevo aspecto del Panamericanismo," *Repertorio Americano*, Vol. XVII, No. 13, San José de Costa Rica, September 22, 1928, 177–78. This article was taken from Bogotá's *El Tiempo*.

40. Préfecture de Police de Paris, *Bureau des Associations Loi du 1er. Juillet 1901. Dossier: Association Générale des Etudiants Latino-Américains*. No. AM 32 142.

41. Cayetano and Rilla, *El joven Quijano*, 60–61.

42. Juan Isidro Jiménes Grullón, *Una Gestapo en América*, 4th ed., Prologue by Raúl Poa (Havana: Editorial Lex, 1948).

43. Maribona, *El arte y el amor en Montparnasse*, 396.

44. Miguel Angel Asturias, "Revolución universitaria y horas americanas," *El Imparcial,* Guatemala, October 13, 1930.

11

Encounter of Two Revolutions: Mexican Radical Elites in Communist Russia during the 1920s

Daniela Spenser

The Mexican Revolution that began in 1910 was the first of the great twentieth-century social and political revolutions. Unlike later Latin American upheavals of the twentieth century, foreign ideologies—especially those of the Marxist persuasion—played little role in instigating the revolution. Nevertheless, by the 1920s, much of Mexico's intellectual leadership found itself irresistibly attracted to the Bolshevik Revolution as it unfolded in the Soviet Union. Muralists Diego Rivera and David Alfaro Siqueiros are perhaps the best-known Mexicans to have taken up the cause of the Soviet Union; however, admiration for the Soviet regime was widespread in Mexico, even if firsthand knowledge of what was actually taking place in the Soviet Union was quite rare.

Latin Americans were quick to travel to those countries that they believed offered insight into the best means to modernize their lands. Many Mexicans made their way to Soviet Russia. Historian Daniela Spenser, who has done much research on the triangular relations between Mexico, the USSR, and the United States during the twentieth century, focuses upon the experiences of a few Mexican revolutionaries who spent time in the Soviet Union during the 1920s. She argues that disillusionment characterized their reactions to the Soviet revolutionary experiment. As a result, these Mexican revolutionaries lost their fascination with socialism and in turn helped to moderate the aims of Mexico's revolution. Real-life experience in Soviet Russia did not radicalize Mexicans; instead, it made them quite hesitant to apply Soviet tactics to the Mexican situation. This chapter contributes to the current revision of the revolution's legacy in Mexico that stresses certain continuities between the pre- and post-revolutionary eras. Here, then, the relative conservatism of Mexico's revolutionary elite is explained as being in part the result of Mexican activists' travel and foreign residence in Communist Russia.

We would gain a great deal, human justice would
gain a great deal, if all people of our America
and all the nations in old Europe understood that
the cause of the Mexican Revolution, like the
cause of unredeemed Russia, is and represents
the cause of humanity, the supreme interest of
all the oppressed.

—Emiliano Zapata, 1918

I don't know what Socialism is, but I am a
Bolshevik, like all patriotic Mexicans. The Yankees do not like the Bolsheviks; they are our
enemies; therefore, the Bolsheviks must be our
friends, and we must be their friends. We are all
Bolsheviks.

—*Jefe militar* in Aguascalientes, 1919

P rior to the Bolshevik Revolution, Russia was a blank spot on the mental map of most Mexicans. Mexico's memory of the Spanish viceroys'
fear during the eighteenth century of the prospect of Russian settlements
on America's Pacific coast had long faded. The anxiety of the Independence movement's leaders concerning the tsar's military support of Spain
in its dispute with the colonies was also long forgotten. Fortunately for
Russia, Tsar Alexander II's ideological kinship with the Emperor
Maximilian, who sat on the Mexican throne from 1864 to 1867, did not
go as far as Russia's diplomatic recognition of Maximilian's illegitimate
rule. Thus, despite Russia's imperialist record, it left no traces in the Mexican historical memory.[1] Nevertheless, relations between the two nations
proceeded very slowly. It was not until 1891, during the government of
Porfirio Díaz, that Russia and Mexico established diplomatic relations.
In 1909 the two nations signed a trade treaty that never got off the ground.
Before the Bolshevik Revolution, Russia and Mexico had not been able
to establish any long-standing political, economic, or cultural links.
    This situation changed dramatically in the wake of the October Revo-
lution of 1917. The Bolshevik victory fired the imaginations of many
Mexican workers, peasants, artists, intellectuals, and politicians, all of
whom quickly identified themselves with Soviet Russia. They found most
inspiring the Bolshevik leaders' promises to redeem not only inhabitants
of the Russian empire but also the downtrodden of the entire world. This
pledge made some people in Mexico believe that the revolutionary tide
surging in Russia would in due time engulf Mexico itself. In their thinking, such a revolutionary wave also might remove the obstacles that were
then preventing enforcement of the revolutionary laws embodied in
Mexico's 1917 Constitution, namely, foreign and national interest groups.

Mexico, like Russia, lay on the periphery of the world capitalist system. But unlike Russia—which in one bold historical sweep rid itself of the political, social, and economic shackles imposed upon it by the combination of foreign capital, feudal landholdings, foreign-held factories, and subservience to the imperialist powers—Mexico's opposition to the revolution's constitutional reforms remained unyielding. Opposition to radical change in Mexico was spearheaded by national and foreign land, mine, oil, and factory owners, who in turn rallied the support of the Mexican military and several foreign governments to their cause. True, the elimination of foreign enterprises from Mexican soil had never been in the Mexican Revolution's program. Rather, Mexico's revolutionaries sought to curtail the foreigners' legal power while at the same time making sure to harness and unify foreign capital and the existing national productive forces behind a program of national reconstruction and modernization.

Despite revolutionary calls for unity, domestic resistance to these reforms resulted in unending class warfare, in both the countryside and the cities. U.S. governmental and private opposition to the reforms hindered Mexico's development. Stimulated by the example of the Bolshevik Revolution, the Mexican radical elite in power proposed to assume tactics similar to those used by the Bolsheviks: the expropriation of land without indemnization, collective agriculture, economic self-sufficiency, mass education, and an active policy of anti-imperialism. Some observers believed that an alliance with Soviet Russia would facilitate the implementation of such programs and strengthen Mexico in a world hostile to revolutions.

For many Mexicans enthralled by the example of Russian communism, there appeared to be no better way to learn about the country than to visit it. Throughout the 1920s a number of Mexico's intellectuals working for the state visited the country of their dreams in order to learn from its experience with revolutionary politics.[2] However, upon arrival in communist Russia, these Mexican travelers were often forced to recognize that, in action, their idealized visions of communism were often far from reflecting reality. Largely hidden from the outside world, the Soviet experiment underwent a transformation from 1917 to 1929, during which time the party launched a radical overhaul of the entire economic and social landscape through a program of massive industrialization and agricultural collectivization. During their visits to the Soviet Union, the Mexican radicals learned of the social and political costs of that process. As a result, by the end of the 1920s, the Bolshevik Revolution had shifted from being a mirror of the Mexican Revolution toward constituting a reverse image of Mexico's economy and polity. What had originally seemed an inspiration to Mexico's radicals, on closer scrutiny and through direct exposure to Soviet reality, became a path to avoid. Ironically, the Bolshevik

Revolution's evolution influenced the course of the Mexican Revolution by contributing to the latter's conservatism. Mexican travelers' experiences in Russia played an important role in this reevaluation of the Communist revolution.

Mexico's Radical Political Elite

The Mexican Revolution changed the class origin of the individuals in government from an upper to a middle level. As a result, a new feature of the administrations of the 1920s was the involvement of a radical intellectual—as opposed to social or economic—elite in positions of political importance. Disunited and often confused, this intellectual elite hoped to give the revolution a program and ideology, in order to renovate, develop, educate, and redeem Mexican society and invigorate the state.

On the whole, the radical political elite believed that Mexico's government should serve the people. Critical of the country's past administrations, which they viewed as agents of political aggression and economic privilege, the radical elite believed that it was the state's duty to ameliorate the social inequalities created by the capitalist economic system.[3] While growing up, these intellectuals read works by the Russian anarchist Pyotr Kropotkin, the French anarchist thinker Pierre Proudhon, and their Mexican counterpart Ricardo Flores Magón. As adults, they pored over the writings of Marx, Lenin, and the Russian Marxist ideologue Nikolai Bukharin. Hence, the ideas that this group of radical intellectuals espoused were an amalgam of Mexican liberalism, Christian and agrarian socialism, and some Marxism.[4]

Having politically come of age during the epic phase of the Mexican Revolution (1910–1917), the intellectuals who identified themselves with the revolution and with the state were ready and eager to work for their country. In their late twenties and early thirties during the 1920s, this radical elite was well aware of the difficulties encountered in carrying out the reforms called for by the Constitution of 1917. Emiliano Zapata's intellectual heirs took his agrarian reform project to the government and worked to implement it from above. Another stream of intellectuals, in origin beholden to Francisco I. Madero's democratic ideas and later recruited by the "First Chief" of the revolution, Venustiano Carranza, similarly believed that the state should be the agency to bring about the reforms that no revolutionary faction had managed to enforce during the civil war.[5] Hoping to radicalize or influence the government to initiate land distribution and redeem the underclass from ignorance, poverty, and a lack of resources, the radical political elite intended to work within the state, rarely outside it, and only occasionally in opposition to it. This elite adhered to a vaguely defined socialism, yet its main concern was with how Mexico's traditions of radicalism and liberalism could intersect with the socialisms of European origins—whether it was utopian socialism or Bolshevism—to construct an authentically Mexican progressive program and practice.[6]

From a distance, and often without a thorough understanding of Soviet events, many radical administrative and intellectual cadres of the Mexican Revolution (some of whom would actually visit the USSR) looked toward the Bolshevik Revolution for inspiration. They were far from adopting the entire Bolshevik blueprint but were ready to borrow useful ideas to energize the Mexican Revolution. José Vasconcelos spoke openly about his admiration for Anatolii Lunacharsky's mass education program in Soviet Russia that served him as a model after which to pattern his own educational policies for Mexico. As minister of education in the early 1920s, Vasconcelos spread the gospel of mass education throughout the Mexican countryside by disseminating long-established political texts and those of socialist thinkers. The able economist and sociologist Rafael Nieto, whom historian Jesús Silva Herzog called "an indecisive Marxist," did not think that the Mexican Revolution could be legislated when so few people at the top had everything and the majority at the bottom had so little. Despite Nieto's criticism of the revolution, he served the Carranza administration (1917–1920) as undersecretary of treasury and public credit, and held high-level positions in successive governments. Silva Herzog occupied numerous posts in the Ministry of Finance during the 1920s, hoping to improve from within the government of which he was highly critical. In 1928, Silva Herzog's curiosity to learn about ways and means to industrialize a backward country impelled him to request from President Emilio Portes Gil the post of envoy to Moscow to study the Bolshevik Revolution at close range. Manuel Gómez Morín was a consultant to the Soviet embassy advising the Russians on matters concerning bilateral trade at the same time that he worked in Mexico's state bank.[7] Ramón P. de Negri, who was one of the most ardent Mexican admirers of the Bolshevik Revolution, served in the foreign service as well as in numerous other positions in government during the 1920s. Juan de Dios Bojórquez, who held similar posts, also longed to visit the Soviet Union throughout the 1920s.[8] Yet another fan of the Soviets was the agricultural engineer Marte R. Gómez, who worked diligently in different capacities to speed up agrarian reform in the Mexican countryside, even when the state backed away from the program of land distribution in the latter half of the 1920s.

In private (but only in private lest they alarm certain foreign powers and political moderates and conservatives), these administrators held the view that Mexico's revolutionary government should expropriate land from its owners, Mexican and foreign alike, and transfer the means of production from hacendados and foreign entrepreneurs to land-hungry peasants. Marte Gómez believed that the Constitution of 1917, which sanctioned private property, prevented the government from being anticapitalist. But like the rest, Gómez came to make a virtue out of the existing legal system and pushed it as far as it would stretch. In 1930, when he found that he could not carry out the agrarian reform single-handedly, he resigned as minister of agriculture. Gómez left Mexico and crisscrossed Europe (on a government stipend) until a more propitious time came to renew the agrarian reform. Some dreamers among the intellectuals—de Negri among them—hoped that the "world revolution" would engulf Mexico and sweep away the economic and political structures that the state was unable or unwilling to eliminate by itself. There were also revolutionary firebrands in public service such as the congressional deputy Rafael Ramos Pedrueza and the Communist senator Luis Monzón. These characters were a thorn in the government's side but their supposed danger to the government's stability was grossly exaggerated by the press. Except for Luis Monzón, whose ideas blurred with those of the international communist movement formulated by the Comintern, none of the others joined the Communist Party, although some were fellow travelers. Nevertheless, it was this radical elite that prompted the government to establish diplomatic relations with the Soviet Union and cultivated personal relations with the Russian envoys in Mexico and Soviet intellectuals in Moscow.[9]

The First Encounter with the Bolsheviks

The Soviet myth—as distinct from Soviet reality—acted upon the people who believed in it on both rational and irrational levels. Following the human atrocities and economic calamities caused by the First World War, it seemed reasonable to favorably compare the state of affairs in Russia with that of the Western world. Knowledge of what was happening in Soviet Russia was fragmentary and it assumed the character of legend: the "people" held power on one sixth of the Earth; private ownership, the greed for power, and social distinctions had been abolished. According to the legend, in the Soviet Union there were no longer distinctions between rich and poor or masters and servants.[10]

In early 1919, Lenin sent his trusted comrade Mikhail Borodin to the New World to deliver support to the Soviet Trade Delegation in Washington and to seek Mexican recognition of the Soviet regime. While in Mexico, the Soviet envoy met with politicians and labor leaders and confirmed the legend in person. Even though President Carranza brushed aside suggestions that he initiate official relations with the Bolsheviks, his interior minister did not pass up the opportunity to meet discreetly with Borodin. Moreover, when Ramón P. de Negri, the Mexican Consul General in New York and ardent supporter of the Bolshevik Revolution, was approached by two Soviet officials requesting permission for a Soviet trade mission to Mexico, he wrote enthusiastically: "I feel that it is of great importance to our government to study the tendencies of Soviet Russia's Administration because of the sympathy that it has displayed toward us, and because the government of the United States, despite its intransigence toward that regime, seems to be now repentant, willing to send special agents to Russia to study the present state of affairs."[11]

De Negri could not have known that U.S. government advisor William C. Bullitt's special mission to Soviet Russia in February 1919 was not to seek reconciliation with the Bolshevik Revolution but rather to make peace with its leaders in exchange for Russia's payment of its foreign debt. Nor could he have known that the situation in Russia was not what he and other supporters of that revolution had believed. Instead of a popular democracy, the Bolsheviks were building a proletarian dictatorship that first exhorted the masses to take control over their lives and to exercise their creative initiative, only to later employ, out of "necessity," dictatorial power over them. The party conceived of the gradual "withering away" of the state as society reappropriated its functions but, like any other ruling class, eventually transformed itself into a strong state as its central principle of power.[12]

The Mexicans had no idea that in March 1921, Lenin had introduced the party's New Economic Policy (NEP) as a direct consequence of the human suffering of the early radicalism in Soviet Russia. They were ignorant of the devastating results of the Soviet government's abolition of an economy based on money exchange and its coercion of the peasants into giving up their harvests to feed the hungry urban population and soldiers fighting domestic and foreign counterrevolutionary forces during the civil war and the foreign intervention of 1918–1920. The NEP's restoration of the previously abolished trade relations; the market economy, national currency, and private property; and the Soviet government's adoption of a more gradual process toward economic reconstruction and the improvement of the people's lot were generally compared favorably in Mexico to the country's own revolutionary reforms.[13]

Alvaro Obregón, Carranza's successor in the presidency, became interested in the new Soviet experiment from the point of view of workers' organization of production and state management. In mid-1921, Obregón sent a delegation to Russia consisting of two workers, both members of the state-backed labor organization, the Confederación Regional Obrera Mexicana (CROM), and one of his close allies in government. This delegation was entrusted not only with learning about Soviet Russia but also with turning the trip into a propaganda tour on behalf of the Mexican Revolution and its laws. The visitors' trip to Soviet Russia disappointed on both scores. In Moscow the apparatchiks from the Communist International lectured the Mexican labor leaders on the virtues of communism and on the drawbacks of their friendship with the anti-Communist, U.S.-based American Federation of Labor.[14] The trip greatly disillusioned

Obregón's political crony, the radical engineer and leftist deputy Luis León. He had been expecting prosperity; instead, he saw poverty so daunting that even his careful guide and interpreter could not hide it from him. Indeed, the trip failed to portray Soviet Russia as the workers' paradise. León was further dismayed by how isolated and ostracized Soviet Russia was in relation to the Western world. After having left the country, he found himself barred from entering Austria and Italy soley because his passport bore a Soviet visa. However, upon León's return to Mexico, President Obregón personally restrained him from telling a curious press the details of his journey so as to prevent the conservatives in government and society from gloating with cynical joy at Russia's troubles. In the end, León could not escape from the journalists, and his declarations, which were mildly critical of the present state of affairs and expressed hopes for the future, pleased no one. The Right did not hear what it wanted to have confirmed, namely, that the Bolshevik government was tottering, while the radical wing in the government and Mexico's socialists and Communists accused the deputy of having fabricated his impressions, asserting that he had never gone farther than Leningrad.[15] At that moment, in 1921, the radical elite was not ready to confront even a slightly critical position about the Soviet Union that could erode the myth of a Communist workers' paradise.

The Second Encounter with Soviet Reality

News coming from the Soviet Union following the introduction of the NEP appeared to assure the superiority of socialism over capitalism at least as the NEP was observed on the periphery of the capitalist system. Mexican newspapers reported political peace and a modicum of economic recovery in the Soviet Union. During 1925 and a part of 1926, small-scale entrepreneurs obtained a reduction on their tax burden, which had a revitalizing impact on other private traders, called Nepmen. The flow of goods and credits from the state to the private sector increased as did the number of private traders and the value of their sales. Sympathetic observers attributed this growth in trade figures to the "new trade practice." However, a twenty percent increase in public expenditure over the previous year and a reduction of agricultural taxes meant that either an economic miracle had truly taken place or that the numbers had been fabricated, since no European country had ever achieved a similar balance of payments, even with the help of foreign capital. Figures demonstrating the steady progress made by Soviet industrialization, in terms of an expansion of output, employment, productivity, and profitability, impressed the Mexican economists and architects of the state.[16]

Yet this dizzying economic success only masked a number of profound problems within the Soviet Union. Political maneuvering inside the party, confined to upper echelons of the political society, was hidden from the public eye. A good deal of the factional struggle reflected ongoing debates about the continuation of the NEP. Most Bolsheviks considered the NEP a temporary expedient before a genuine socialist reconstruction of the economy and society could be undertaken. In the eyes of many, the NEP fostered a new capitalist class, which, they feared, would constitute a counterweight to the party's own influence over the society. Stalin was increasingly unwilling to remain within the bounds of the NEP, recognizing the limits that it imposed upon state action. Moreover, in late 1927 and early 1928 there was an unexpected shortfall in grain procurements. Official agencies increased the price of grain at the expense of industrial crop production and the pace of industrialization. These new difficulties set in motion the Stalinist revolution.[17] From 1929 onward, the state forcibly collectivized the countryside, dispossessed both rich and poor peasants of their land, and rationed food so that grain could be transferred to the cities and exported in exchange for the capital goods necessary to speed up the breakneck pace of industrialization.

This radicalized environment was the scenario in 1929 when several of the Mexican intellectuals, who had promoted Soviet-Mexican friendship and clamored for the adoption of some of the Soviet economic and political principles, visited the Soviet Union. For each of them, the trip was an eye-opening experience. One by one, each man lost the illusion that the Soviets had something to teach the Mexicans. The first to arrive in Moscow in February 1929 was Jesús Silva Herzog, who secured a diplomatic post in order to study the Bolshevik Revolution.[18] The first three months of his diplomatic career were exciting. He met such famed Soviet personalities as Commissar of Culture Lunacharsky, party ideologue Nikolai Bukharin, and Comintern president Grigorii Zinoviev. He also dined with the poet Vladimir Mayakovsky. Silva Herzog was eager to open the embassy to visitors to exchange ideas and experiences, and he expected that the doors of Soviet institutions would likewise be opened to him. To his chagrin, few people came to the Mexican embassy, and only the International Agrarian Institute extended an invitation to him, in this case to give three lectures on Mexico. The press commented upon Silva Herzog's first lecture but ignored the other two. He later learned that the institute's director had been reprimanded for having allowed a representative of a "petty-bourgeois" nation to speak in a Communist institution. He was also shocked to discover that the Mexican painter Xavier Guerrero, who was studying in Lenin's school for cadres, had been discouraged from maintaining any contact with him. Thus, Silva Herzog's social contacts were limited to the circle of foreign diplomats in Moscow, whom he found to be unbearably boring.

Silva Herzog kept himself alive intellectually with his study of Russian and Soviet economics and the few trips that he was able to make outside of Moscow. He gleaned from statistical figures that the workers' living conditions and salaries were higher than those of their Mexican counterparts. He also found the Soviet educational system to be outstanding. Initially, too, he justified the existence of the political police (Gosudarstvennoe Politicheskoe Upravlenie, or GPU), which he considered necessary for the consolidation and defense of the Soviet government. Further reading of the official Soviet handouts greatly impressed Silva Herzog with the social role of the army. Two years of military service aimed to shape a soldier into a Communist, who would then return to his village as a "civilizing agent." Silva Herzog was so moved that he boasted to the Mexican government that "it would be convenient for a well-prepared and honest Mexican military to come here to study these things. [T]he experiment carried out in Russia is one of the most important episodes in history. Upon its success or failure the immediate future of all nations depends. One has to be blind or stupid to deny the social, economic, and political transcendence of what is happening here."[19] He hoped that Mexico could adapt aspects of consumption and production cooperatives, military and educational institutions, and methods to spread culture among the masses. In general, Silva Herzog greatly admired the Soviets' bold move to industrialize outside of the capitalist system, "thus trying to modify the development of the world's economic history."[20]

If Silva Herzog's social life was limited before July 1929, he was totally ostracized by Soviet institutions following the Mexican government's assassination of two peasant leaders in the state of Durango. In March 1929 one part of the Mexican army disobeyed the high command and took up arms against the legitimate government. The Mexican Communist Party took advantage of the chaotic situation and advised the armed peasants who had supported the government to rise up in insurrection against it. The section of the army that remained loyal to the government rounded up and shot the peasant ringleaders, Guadalupe Rodríguez and Salvador Gómez. Soon thereafter, articles attacking the Mexican government for its action appeared daily in the Soviet press. Silva Herzog found the articles offensive. Making matters even worse, the Comintern had issued a manifesto to the Mexican, Latin American, and world proletariat, urging it to stage street protests against the Mexican government. Subsequently, Silva Herzog reported interception of his mail and such extensive spying on the embassy that he found it necessary to send a messenger to Berlin every time that he needed to send a dispatch to Mexico.[21]

At the same time, Eduardo Villaseñor and Juan de Dios Bojórquez, close friends of Silva Herzog and themselves government officials eager to come into contact with the Soviet Union, visited Silva Herzog in Moscow. The ambassador could not hide from them his disappointment with the ways in which the Soviets mistreated Mexico. Reflecting upon his position in the Soviet Union, the significance of Mexican-Soviet relations, and the two revolutions, Silva Herzog, like so many Mexicans, once believed that the Soviet Union sympathized with Mexico's efforts to improve the economic and political conditions of the proletariat and was in agreement with Mexico's progressive ideology. He once was convinced that the two countries had common interests and believed that Mexico's "disinterested and generous gesture" to recognize the Soviet Union in spite of tense relations between Mexico and the United States would have inspired respect in the Soviet Union. But, as a result of his time in Moscow, he realized that such beliefs were not true. Mexico had made a mistake, "an error which we should have recognized a long time ago." The countries that were best received in the Soviet Union were either neighbors or those that had substantial trade with it; Mexico was in neither category. Moreover, in spite of the fact that the Comintern had attacked Mexico's Communists for being lukewarm and opportunist, they continued to receive orders and material help from the Comintern. In fact, the Mexican Communists' anti-government campaign received its inspiration from Moscow.[22]

By December 1929, after ten months in Moscow, Silva Herzog had become depressed by his experiences there and he conveyed his disappointment to his Mexican visitors. The Soviet Union, governed by the Communist Party, had turned the dictatorship of the proletariat into the dictatorship first of the Central Committee, and, in the final analysis, of Stalin. Some things had been accomplished to benefit the Russian people, "but more has been said about it than realized. The books of propaganda that we read in Mexico with pathetic good faith exaggerate one hundred percent."[23] Nevertheless, Silva Herzog elaborated at length upon the early fruits yielded by the First Five-Year Plan. He was impressed by the methods employed to increase production, but also observed with concern the rising cult of Lenin and the draconian punishments meted out to workers and managers for petty corruption. Popular discontent was kept in check by the feared political police. In foreign policy, the Soviet Union maintained economic and political relations with governments that it deplored and fought against through the Comintern. This policy, which seemed irrational to foreign admirers of the revolution, was politically and intellectually logical and convenient for the Russians, who considered that in the long run Soviet success meant capitalist ruin, while capitalist success spelled Soviet ruin.

Eventually, Silva Herzog questioned the very necessity of maintaining relations between Mexico and the Soviet Union. The Soviet embassy in Mexico City had attained its goal of becoming an active center of Communist propaganda. By contrast, the Mexican embassy's role in Moscow remained dull and precarious. The embassy was unable to do any good owing to the hostile environment and Soviet obstruction of its activities. In Moscow, the Mexican ambassador was a passive observer of events:

the Soviet government prevented its people from learning about other cultures and denied the validity of different roads toward the improvement of the lives of the majority. Silva Herzog observed that Mexico and the Soviet Union had failed to develop any nexus, due to the lack of racial, historical, or linguistic common ground: "I believe, frankly, that deep down they sneer at our noble and somewhat romantic attitude to have in Moscow a costly mission even though we have no material interests to defend."[24]

There was not then, nor would there be in the future, any common economic interest between the two countries. Russia would export what it could, which was not much, and buy little in return. While Soviet companies could work freely in Mexico, Mexican companies could not do the same in the Soviet Union because of the state monopoly on foreign trade. The ideology of the Russian Revolution was different from that of Mexico: the abolition of private property and internationalism contrasted greatly with the Mexican ideology of private property, nationalism, and democracy. The Mexican Revolution built upon an inherited culture, while the Russian Revolution strove to create a new one. Silva Herzog concluded that similarities between the two revolutions were false, explicable only by Mexican ignorance of Soviet reality. In his view, the Mexican mission in Moscow was superfluous.[25]

When in 1929, Eduardo Villaseñor, a trade attaché in London, visited Silva Herzog in Moscow, he still cherished the hope that the Bolshevik Revolution could rectify the course of its Mexican counterpart by expanding beyond Soviet national boundaries. On his return from Moscow, he wrote to Marte Gómez about his trip: "Extremely interesting! Above all, because of the prejudices I abandoned along the way."[26] His disappointment derived from his realization that "the world revolution," which he had expected to bring down the barriers to socialist revolution in Mexico, was no longer on the Bolshevik agenda. Moreover, Mexican subordination to Soviet-style politics was unacceptable. There was little left to do, Villaseñor mused, but to find an accommodation with the Mexican style of politics:

> We cannot be Communists subservient to Moscow, or agents of New York or Washington, or *slow-motion* socialists like the English. [H]istoric, geographic, even climatic conditions force us to be different. Let us be Marx's disciples, but not dirty agents of Moscow.
> The solution can be found only by a new generation of Socialists, neither Communist, nor English, but Mexican . . . within a political party of the type that can exist in Mexico and not only within our imagination. . . . [W]e have no other remedy than to pluck up our courage and drink that dirty water of our politics, and, if we want to, clean it up a little bit and improve it. Good-bye, dreams of world Revolution, today more distant than ever! Good-bye, hope that the natural process of the world will resolve our problems! We cannot but rely on ourselves.[27]

Marte Gómez himself lost his sympathy for the Soviet Union, although in his case, disillusionment emerged primarily in response to the First Five-Year Plan's policy of forced collectivization. His whole life had been bound up with agrarian questions in Mexico; the agrarian reform's fortunes were effectively his own. When at the end of 1929 the Mexican government declared that the agrarian reform was over in México, Gómez lost his job. Thanks to a monthly government pension, he spent two years traveling in Europe, waiting for Mexico's anti-*agrarista* spell to pass. Gómez knew from his own experience that the government had itself slowed down or prevented land distribution to landless peasants in order to safeguard other interests.[28] Having been in Europe since May 1930, Marte Gómez applied for a Soviet visa but was denied entry to the Soviet Union. Observing the Soviet drive toward collectivization from afar, he was disturbed to see that peasants who wanted to own a piece of land had been forced to give it up. Then, as throughout his life, Gómez would remember a phrase attributed to Lenin: "Peasants have the right to err; we have no right to contradict their aspirations."[29] What Gómez had in mind was Lenin's warning to the Bolsheviks not to alienate the peasantry, recognizing their "petty-bourgeois" limitations and appreciating the stresses and strains associated with the forced food procurement during the civil war. But Stalin was at the helm of the party and history was in the process of being rewritten, even Lenin's history.

Although the disappointment and disillusionment that characterized these Mexican travelers' impressions of Soviet communism had stemmed from their firsthand experiences with the USSR, their changed attitudes were not unique. Indeed, throughout 1929 there was a different perspective toward the Soviet Union on the part of both the Mexican radical elite and mainstream politicians and newspapers. Soviet press attacks on Mexico and the Mexican Communists' new-found opposition to the government had a demoralizing effect on the radical elite and prompted Mexican opponents of communism to highlight the dark side of the Bolshevik Revolution.

Conclusion

The same radical elite that had been instrumental in establishing diplomatic and friendly relations with the Soviet Union in the early 1920s advocated their rupture in 1929. True, the Bolshevik Revolution had energized the radical governing elite's ideas, but in the long run it had provided few lessons and little practical guidance for applying its utopian vision to Mexico. As more and more information about the Soviet Union reached the outside world, and as visitors to the Soviet Union learned themselves, the reality was harsher than what they had envisioned. By comparison, the Mexican Revolution seemed the best and only option for the redemption of the underprivileged and for the economic reconstruction of the entire country.

In addition, U.S. anti-Bolshevism served not only as negative publicity but also as a political weapon against Mexico throughout the decade. For example, anti-Bolshevism played a significant role in restraining Mexican radical statesmen from implementing strong measures against property holders. Yet U.S. interference in Mexico's internal affairs has to be measured against the evolution of the Bolshevik Revolution itself. In this light, it is doubtful whether Mexico, in the U.S. sphere of influence, could have successfully adapted any of the Soviet methods of organizing its own national economy and society.[30] The radical elite and press debated the question intermittently during the 1920s. By the end of the decade the issue was finally settled by the changes effected in the Soviet Union. The radical turn in Soviet internal policy away from the NEP toward its liquidation, and in foreign policy from containment to confrontation with the Western world, which manifested itself as interference in the internal affairs of Mexico, were among the factors that most alienated Mexico's radical elite.

Mexico's rupture of relations with the Soviet Union in 1930 was an unforeseen result of ten years of its experience of revolutionary politics while being a neighbor of the United States and a potential ally of the Soviet Union. The initial legendary success of the Bolshevik revolutionary state in empowering workers and peasants in the face of foreign adversaries had provided the Mexican radical elite with the hope that a similar achievement was possible in Mexico. However, the Bolshevik Revolution gradually lost its authority among the radical elite in Mexico because the Soviet state had failed to fulfill that hope in the only country that appeared to have abolished all the obstacles to its full realization. For a number of influential radical elites, their time in Soviet Russia proved critical to communism's fall from grace. In time, the disillusionment that characterized the experiences of Mexican travelers to the Soviet Union gradually eroded the revolutionary élan of an entire generation of Mexican revolutionary elites.

Notes

1. Russell H. Bartley, *Imperial Russia and the Struggle for Latin American Independence, 1808–1828* (Austin: University of Texas Press, 1978), 3–13 and 142; Héctor Cárdenas, *Las relaciones mexicano-soviéticas* (Mexico: Secretaría de Relaciones Exteriores, 1974), 22–38; Stephen Clissold, "Soviet Relations with Latin America between the Wars," in J. Gregory Oswald and Anthony J. Strover, eds., *The Soviet Union and Latin America* (New York: Praeger, 1970), 15–23.

2. See also William Richardson, " 'To the World of the Future': Mexican Visitors to the USSR, 1920–1940," *The Carl Beck Studies*, no. 1002 (January 1993).

3. Sheldon Liss, *Marxist Thought in Latin America* (Berkeley: University of California Press, 1984), 209.

4. James W. Wilkie and Edna Monzón de Wilkie, *México visto en el siglo XX: Entrevistas de historia oral* (Mexico: Instituto Mexicano de Investigaciones Económicas, 1969), 608–34; Jesús Silva Herzog, *Trayectoria ideológica de la Revolución Mexicana, 1910–1917 y otros ensayos* (Mexico: SEP/SETENTAS, 1973).

5. Robert E. Quirk, *The Mexican Revolution, 1914–1915* (New York: W. W. Norton, 1960), 10.

6. Barry Carr, *Marxism and Communism in Twentieth-Century Mexico* (Lincoln and London: University of Nebraska Press, 1992), 4.

7. Wilkie and Wilkie, *México*, 169; Silva Herzog, *Trayectoria ideológica de la Revolución Mexicana*, 327.

8. The adoption of the name Soviet Union took place in 1924.

9. In 1924, Mexico was the first country in the hemisphere to establish diplomatic relations with the Soviet Union. See Daniela Spenser, *El triángulo imposible: México, Rusia Soviética y Estados Unidos en los años veinte* (Mexico: Casa Chata, 1997).

10. Arthur Koestler, *Arrow in the Blue* (New York: Stein and Day, 1969), 327.

11. Ramón P. de Negri to Hilario Medina, New York, 11 February 1920, Archivo de la Secretaría de Relaciones Exteriores (hereafter ASRE), exp. 17-17-336.

12. Lewis H. Siegelbaum, *Soviet State and Society between Revolutions, 1918–1929* (Cambridge, England: Cambridge University Press, 1992), 10–12.

13. "El Noveno Congreso de los Soviets aprobó la Nueva Política Económica anunciada por Lenin," *Excélsior*, 27 December 1921.

14. Comité Ejecutivo de la Sindical Roja Internacional to the CROM, Moscow, 27 October 1921, Russian Center for Preservation and Study of Documents of Contemporary History, fond 534, register 7, file 224.

15. Luis León, *Crónica del poder en los recuerdos de un político en el México revolucionario* (Mexico: Fondo de Cultura Económica, 1987), 143–44.

16. "El Gobierno Ruso se aparta de sus principios para dar mayor libertad al campesino," 9 January 1925; "Las finanzas soviéticas" by Luis Lara Pardo, 11 March 1925; "La Tercera Internacional está por desaparecer," 26 March 1925, *Excélsior*.

17. Siegelbaum, *Soviet State and Society*, 188.

18. Jesús Silva Herzog, *Una vida en la vida de México* (Mexico: Siglo XXI/SEP, 1986), 110–11.

19. "Informe confidencial," Jesús Silva Herzog to Undersecretary of Foreign Relations, Moscow, 6 May 1929, ASRE, 39-8-14.

20. "Informe económico confidencial," Silva Herzog to Undersecretary of Foreign Relations, Moscow, 4 July 1929, ASRE, 39-8-14.

21. Spenser, *El triángulo imposible*, chap. 8.

22. "Informe político confidencial," Jesús Silva Herzog to Ministry of Foreign Relations, Moscow, 4 July 1929, ASRE, 14-25-2.

23. "Informe," Silva Herzog to Undersecretary of Foreign Relations, Moscow, 3 December 1929, ASRE, 39-8-14.

24. Silva Herzog to SRE, Moscow, 4 December 1929, ASRE, 14-25-2.

25. Silva Herzog, *Una vida*, 117.

26. Ibid., 116.

27. Villaseñor to Marte Gómez, London, 16 December 1929, Marte R. Gómez, *Vida política contemporánea: Cartas de Marte R. Gómez* (Mexico: Fondo de Cultura Económica, 1978), 249–50; Wilkie and Wilkie, *México*, 654.

28. Gómez to Emilio Gutiérrez, 26 February 1930, Gómez, *Vida política*, 262; Wilkie and Wilkie, *México*, 91.

29. Cited in Wilkie and Wilkie, *México*, 98 and 104–7; Gómez to Calles, Paris, 13 November 1930, Gómez, *Vida política*, 308.

30. U.S.-Mexican relations in the era of the "Red scare" is developed in Daniela Spenser, "Uso y abuso de la ideología en las relaciones entre Estados Unidos y México durante los años veinte," *Secuencia*, no. 34 (January–April 1996): 31–62.

12

Mexicans, Migrants, and Indigenous Peoples: The Work of Manuel Gamio in the United States, 1925–1927

Arthur Schmidt

Manuel Gamio (1883–1960) was Mexico's first professionally trained archaeologist and a pioneer in the emerging field of applied anthropology. A student and close friend of famed anthropologist Franz Boas, Gamio received both his master's degree in 1911 and his doctorate in 1921 from Columbia University, and throughout his life acted as an intermediary between the academic and political communities in Mexico and the United States. Historian Arthur Schmidt reconsiders Gamio's legacy by focusing on a well-known but relatively unstudied facet of his career: his time in exile (1925–1928). Most of this period was spent in the United States, where Gamio lectured at the University of Chicago and undertook an unprecedented survey of Mexican migrants in the United States under the sponsorship of the Social Science Research Council. Gamio's own condition of exile seems to have colored his choice of subjects for investigation, for, by studying the lives and experiences of Mexican migrants, most of whom were indigenous workers, Gamio sought to understand their connection to the homeland that they and he had left behind.

There are clear indications that Gamio's thought broadened and matured as a result of his experience in the United States. He became more deeply involved with the issues of contemporary society and relatively less involved with archaeology than he had been previously. Contact with U.S. scholars such as Robert Redfield proved crucial to his command of the methodologies of applied anthropology. Furthermore, in Mexico, Gamio had called for uplifting the Indian through an incorporation of indigenous folkways into a more enlightened national culture. During his extended residence in the United States, Gamio began to view the "bitter humiliations" that Mexican migrants suffered as ultimately beneficial. He argued that U.S. society was a "gigantic university" that nurtured a heightened Mexican national consciousness while instilling in the migrants modern behavioral traits that he found useful for his nation's economic, social, and cultural progress.

Manuel Gamio gained considerable renown during his lifetime as an enterprising social scientist and, since his death in 1960, has been lauded as "the first properly trained archaeologist to emerge from Mexico," "the first applied anthropologist," and "the first professional Mexican anthropologist."[1] Trained by the German-born U.S. anthropologist Franz Boas, Gamio combined his own form of intellectual nationalism with the cultural relativism of his mentor. Gamio, like so many other Mexican thinkers who gained prominence at the time of the Revolution, sought to rescue his country from "backwardness."[2] He strove to redeem Mexico's indigenous peoples while simultaneously promoting the fusion of races, languages, and cultural traits that he considered necessary for the formation of the "coherent and defined nationality" that his nation lacked.[3] His most famous work, *Forjando patria*, laid out the basic ideas of *indigenismo* that would shape Mexican government policy toward indigenous peoples for most of this century.[4]

Less well-known than Gamio's life-long *indigenismo* is his work on Mexican immigration in the United States in 1926–27, which was an effort that enjoyed the support of the Social Science Research Council and led to the publication of "the first important book-length study of the social impacts of Mexican immigration."[5] Unlike his *indigenista* scholarship, this project had few reverberations, and despite the critical praise he received from reviewers at the time, "Gamio remained a voice in the wilderness" in both Mexican and U.S. immigration debates. In Mexico, "his moderate, researched, and reasoned arguments" ran counter to the prevailing climate of hostility toward emigration. In the United States, his published study appeared precisely at the moment of widespread deportation of Mexicans that characterized the early years of the Great Depression.[6] Gamio's pioneering work in the United States still remains "a comprehensive analysis of the Mexican immigration experience" of the late 1920s and a model for researchers in both countries.[7] Nevertheless, treatments of Gamio's life and thought continue to give it scant attention. A recent book on Gamio by his granddaughter devotes less than ten pages to his experience in the United States, while two other reexaminations of his life have ignored this part of his scholarship entirely.[8]

The opportunity to work abroad came at a crucial moment when circumstances in Mexico denied Gamio the means to carry out the applied anthropological studies so important to the development of his professional identity as an internationally known social scientist. From the time he completed his major study of the ruins at Teotihuacán in 1922 until his appointment as director of the Instituto Indigenista Interamericano in 1942 (a position he kept for the rest of his life), only the directorship of the immigration study offered Gamio the institutional support necessary to put his wide-ranging research ideas into practice.[9] His work on Mexican immigration reinforced his intellectual shift from archaeology to applied anthropology.[10] Gamio was the only Mexican scholar during this time to study both indigenous peoples and migrants to the United States. He appreciated the extent to which neither group belonged within the structure of post-revolutionary Mexico's national order. This research project did not produce a wholesale change in the structure of his thought, but it did oblige him to reformulate many of his previously held concepts and diversified his thinking about what it meant to be Mexican. Like the migrants he studied, he suffered the experience of being unable to make a living in his own country while being denied full acceptance in the United States.

Born in 1883 to a family of relatively comfortable circumstances in Mexico City, Gamio spent two years as a young adult on his father's *finca* (rural estate) in the state of Veracruz, where he gained a personal awareness of rural Mexico and its indigenous peoples. Subsequently he became a student of archaeology and history as well as a part-time instructor at the Museo Nacional. His work gained the attention of Zelia Nuttall, a U.S. expatriate amateur archaeologist who helped to arrange for Gamio to study at Columbia University in New York, under Franz Boas.[11] Columbia awarded him an M.A. in 1911, after which he returned home to publish *Forjando patria* in 1916 and headed the Dirección de Antropología for seven years. Gamio's leadership of the reconstruction of Teotihuacán earned him a Ph.D. from Columbia in 1921 and solidified his position as an important figure in American continental archaeology and anthropology.[12] Nearly three decades later, in 1948, the university recognized his lifetime accomplishments with an honorary degree. Gamio's personal contacts in the United States not only enhanced his own reputation but also broadened professional opportunities for researchers in both countries. Throughout the early 1920s, he facilitated the work of major U.S. anthropologists and archaeologists in Mexico, both intellectually and politically, by providing introductions and assistance wherever possible.

Mexico's new president Plutarco Elías Calles appointed Gamio to the post of Undersecretary of Education in December 1924. Gamio felt obliged to take the position; however, as a social scientist first and foremost, he expressed serious misgivings over the budget cutbacks that had curtailed scientific research in Mexico. "In effect, as you suppose," he wrote to his former teacher Boas, "I have not been able to 'defend myself' against having to accept the post of Subsecretario de Educación Pública." Boas sympathized with Gamio: "I cannot help regretting that you can no longer give your whole energy to anthropological problems. Anyway you know that my best wishes are with you."[13] As he had anticipated, Gamio soon found himself frustrated by conditions in the Ministry of Eduation that prevented him from carrying out his program of indigenous education. He publicly denounced the corruption tolerated by his immediate superior, Secretary of Education José M. Puig Casauranc. President Calles, however, sided with Puig and forced Gamio from the government in June. Less than a month later, Gamio informed Boas of his intention to leave Mexico. "My plans are to head soon to the United States," he wrote. "Once I am there I will figure out what line of conduct would be convenient to adopt in terms of my activities."[14]

The mid-1920s constituted a propitious time for Gamio to journey northward. The idealized figure of the Native American was a prominent symbol of the intense cultural interchange between Mexico and the United States. Such U.S. intellectuals as Carlton Beals, Anita Brenner, John Dewey, Frank Tannenbaum, and Edward Weston were fascinated by the efforts of Mexican politicians and *indigenista* intellectuals to "redeem" their country's indigenous population through agrarian reform, education, the promotion of craft industries, and other measures.[15] The newly emerging field of anthropology created strong ties between U.S. and Mexican scholars. When Gamio traveled to the United States in mid-1925, his previous academic connections served him well, providing U.S. institutional patronage for his talents at a time when both politics and finances constricted his professional opportunities at home.[16] Shortly after arriving in the United States, Gamio headed for Guatemala to conduct a short-term archaeological and ethnographic study commissioned by the American Archaeological Society. The following year, he joined former Secretary of Education José Vasconcelos for a series of lectures on "Mexican civilization" at the University of Chicago under the sponsorship of the Norman Wait Harris Memorial Foundation.[17] Gamio's major academic coup was landing a contract with the Social Science Research Council (SSRC) in late 1925 to direct a study of Mexican immigration to the United States.

The SSRC was formed with extensive underwriting from the Rockefeller family in 1923–24; its stated mission was to promote scientific research into major social questions, including migration.[18] The flow of Mexicans across the border had already become a controversial public issue. Perhaps 1.5 million Mexicans entered the United States between 1890 and 1929 due to the employment demands of U.S. agriculture, mining, and railroads, the labor shortages of World War I, and the turmoil of the Mexican Revolution.[19] Gamio stepped into this new context with alacrity, gaining the confidence of the SSRC's Committee on Scientific Aspects of Human Migration and securing its funding endorsement. In December 1925 the SSRC accepted Gamio's recommendation and awarded Robert Redfield $3,000 for "a study of Mexican Peasant Communities." At the same meeting, the Council granted Gamio himself $16,000 for his proposed "Preliminary Survey of the Antecedents and Conditions of the Mexican Population in the United States, and the Formation of a Program for a Definite and Scientific Study of the Problem."[20] Over the next four years, upon the recommendation of overseers Fay-Cooper Cole of the University of Chicago and Roland B. Dixon of Harvard, the SSRC continued to finance Gamio's study until its completion. In total, the Council spent about $20,000, roughly two-thirds of which went to Gamio in salary and travel expenses for himself and for an assistant journeying with him.[21]

Gamio's strange pilgrimage to the United States extended his lifelong desire to use scientific knowledge to promote a strong, unified Mexican citizenry. Rather than a detour forced upon him by political exile, Gamio's contract with the SSRC was a new means to an old end. Gamio saw both Mexico's indigenous peoples and its emigrants as marginalized elements whose incorporation into society was essential for the construction of his country's identity. In his view, the character of Mexico's history, economy, and social relations had left most Mexicans in conditions of "utter wretchedness and . . . [in a] defective hybrid culture" that required amalgamation into a modern, national mestizo culture.[22] As an applied anthropologist, Gamio regarded scientific research as the essential prerequisite to change the conditions that trapped indigenous peoples in "backwardness" and forced migrants to leave their homeland in search of earnings in the United States.

In Gamio's vision for Mexico's national development, immigration research possessed two important attributes. First, just as with research on indigenous peoples, migration studies required large-scale comprehensive projects, the same method of *investigación integral* that he had long advocated as an *indigenista*.[23] "The fundamental causes of Mexican immigration to the United States are, as we have indicated, economic," he wrote to the SSRC in 1927, "but the phenomena developed therefrom are of multiple nature: racial, cultural, social, etc. Therefore, in order to come to a scientifically satisfactory conclusion upon this problem, it is necessary to investigate both its antecedents and its actual development in all these aspects, besides the economic."[24] Second, migration studies offered a means to examine not only immigration but also indigenous issues. "This migratory movement," he wrote in the conclusion to *Mexican Immigration*, "affords an opportunity to make scientific studies on the frontiers of both countries on hundreds of thousands of individuals derived from many different Indian and mestizo groups. This could be done there far more cheaply and easily than could be done in the regions of their provenance, in view of the time and expense that would be required to go to these different points of origin. . . . An anthropological bureau could be established at one of the ports of entry, for instance, Ciudad Juárez, El Paso. This bureau would function during the period of the year in which the entry or departure of Mexican labor is the greatest."[25]

The expansiveness of Gamio's thought ultimately set the Mexican anthropologist and the newly born SSRC on divergent paths, the former advocating a long-term commitment to migration research, the latter pulling back. The proposal approved by the SSRC in December 1925 envisioned a six-month investigation in each nation that would then lead to "a program for an exhaustive study of the problem . . . in which individuals, institutions, and even governments of other Latin-American countries may find an opportunity to collaborate."[26] Gamio evidently hoped that U.S. philanthropic institutions would fund his interests in comprehensive social research in Mexico for years to come.[27] As his work on Mexican immigration unfolded, he articulated the need for regional studies in Mexico similar to the ambitious ones for indigenous areas that he had advocated in the Teotihuacán study in 1922. In August 1927 he offered the SSRC a $12,200 proposed budget for a "Study of background and causes of the emigration from the regions of Jalisco, Michocan [*sic*] and Guanajuato to the United States" to be carried out in 1928. The following month, his preliminary research report to an SSRC conference in Hanover, New Hampshire, strongly advocated further research.[28]

The SSRC saw the issue differently. Despite the continued support of Professors Cole and Dixon for Gamio, others within the SSRC distrusted his proposals, especially as Gamio's travels and financial pressures caused delays in preparing the 1926–27 study for publication. The Mexican government agreed in November 1927 to share the financial costs for Gamio's further research to the tune of $500 per month, but it ceased payments in June of the following year. The assassination of General Alvaro Obregón in 1928 dealt a further hard blow to Gamio, who believed that the President-elect had offered "enthusiastic assistance for the integral study of immigration and emigration through a project of thorough sociological and anthropological research."[29] Although U.S. Ambassador to Mexico Dwight W. Morrow donated funds to the costs of Gamio's work and promised to look for further foundation support, the SSRC remained reluctant. In his August-September 1930 report, SSRC President Edwin B. Wilson alleged that Gamio's study was "always a source of perplexity throughout its progress and not a finished product in which . . . the Council has any reason for pride." Nevertheless, in a question that would have been dear to Gamio and to later generations of U.S. social scientists, Wilson asked, "What, if anything, does the Council propose to do about the development of social research in the great laboratory of social change across the Rio Grande?" Wilson recommended that the SSRC use caution with non-U.S. scholars and stay away from "general descriptive surveys of this sort in which the problem was obviously never sharply focused." Under the editorship of Robert Redfield, Gamio's research was finally published in 1930–31 after the SSRC paid a $2,200 subsidy to the University of Chicago Press in exchange for a twenty-five percent royalty return.[30]

Gamio's experience in the United States ultimately proved disappointing for his ambitious research agenda. "Although in beginning the work we anticipated its deficiencies," he wrote in the introduction to *Mexican Immigration*, "we nevertheless found them, on completing the task, even greater than we had imagined."[31] The institutional world of U.S. social science philanthropy in which he had placed high hopes no longer bore any interest in his large-scale schemes. By 1928 the pressures of making a living once again took him away from full-time engagement in indigenous or migration research. Although he continued to advocate comprehensive projects for the study of indigenous peoples and the reincorporation of returned migrants, Gamio found no means to fund them.[32] He suffered a prolonged period during which the lack of money obliged him to accept jobs "that did not always coincide with his professional interests" until he was appointed director of the Instituto Indigenista Interamericano in 1942.[33]

Despite the disappointments, Gamio's work on Mexican immigration to the United States constituted an important social analysis that transcended many of the prevailing conventions of his time. It was no easy feat for a Mexican scholar to gain acceptance for a major research project *within* the United States, as the dismissive comments about foreign scholars from SSRC president Wilson suggest. A pioneering effort of the scope that Gamio undertook could not be faultless. Gamio was aware that the seventy-six interviews contained in *The Mexican Immigrant* did not really constitute a scientific survey even as they formed the basis for many of his loose generalizations about migrant behavior in *Mexican Immigration*. Gamio called them "subjective observation" and noted that "the value of autobiographies is generally slight and relative."[34] Nevertheless, these interviews exercised an impact on Gamio, leading him beyond the framework of his *indigenista* writings and enabling him to identify lower-strata elements of Mexican society as instruments of constructive change.

In Mexico, Gamio's liberal nationalism and his scientific training often placed him in a contradictory position with regard to those whom he studied. While he exhibited obvious sympathy for indigenous cultures, the purpose of his research was to provide the basis upon which others could act to change those cultures. Mexican indigenous peoples were not the creators of *indigenismo*—they were its objects. As the late Guillermo Bonfil Batalla has noted, "Analyzing indigenista efforts from 1916 to the end of the 1970s, one can confirm the constancy of Gamio's strategy. An integral plan of action was postulated, which would simultaneously attack all the aspects of the 'indigenous problem.' These included economic development, education, health, political organization, ideology, and so on. This multiple effort was to be based on scientific research, which would reveal deficiencies, problems, and possibilities so that the necessary 'cultural change' could be carried out with the least possible conflict."[35]

The factual evidence of Mexican migration obliged Gamio to transcend this *indigenista* intellectual formulation. While he interpreted indigenous groups as imprisoned within their cultural legacy, he defined Mexican immigrants as an instrument of change. For Gamio, the experience of immigration created the cultural transformation that indigenous peoples could experience only through paternalistic government programs. "It is not enough to provide the Indian with modern machinery," he told his 1926 audiences in Chicago. Without "an effective substitution of the instruments and institutions of modern civilization, or . . . a fusion of the modern and the primitive, . . . industrial instruments will have no cultural dynamic influence."[36] Gamio argued that changes in the material possessions of immigrants were indicators of "cultural dynamic influence." Migrants held the potential capacity to change Mexico, to equip their country to incorporate rather than to expel them. Gamio compiled an inventory of the possessions taken back to Mexico by 2,104 returnees and found himself profoundly impressed by the "new needs [that] have been created during their stay in the United States." A profound change in psychology had taken place, he believed, not just a change in material culture: "Although the immigrant often undergoes suffering and injustice and meets many difficulties, he undoubtedly benefits economically by the change. He learns the discipline of modern labor. He specializes. He becomes familiar with industrial and agricultural machinery. He learns about scientific intensive agriculture. He observes and learns about the transformation of raw material into industrial products. He becomes a laborer of the modern type, much more efficient than before. Could all the immigrants return to Mexico, they would do much to make of it a great industrial and agricultural country."[37]

Through modernization the Mexican emigrant to the United States became the prototype of the new national citizen for Gamio. Mexico's conditions might have originally marginalized migrants in a fashion analogous to its indigenous peoples, but their immigration experience converted them into the agents of national modernization, not its objects. U.S. society, in Gamio's view, was the "university" in which the habits of progress were learned. Migrants returned home as the protagonists of Mexican history. "Mixed civilization," the cultural context for most migrants in Gamio's view, occupied a position for him similar to that of mestizo culture in his *indigenista* writings—the national goal toward which a progressive Mexico should head. Gamio considered repatriates "who had seen firsthand the favorable conditions under which the American laborer lives" as a fundamental cause of the upheavals of the Mexican Revolution. Along with railroads, modern communications, the spread of popular education, and rapid industrial or agricultural development, "the return of hundreds of thousands of immigrants from the United States who brought new ideas and tendencies" constituted a source of fundamental change.[38] Gamio documented the economic impact of migration through his original, pioneering use of the records of postal money orders that Mexican immigrants sent home to family members. Economically, he argued, "emigration acts as a real safety-valve for men out of work. Moreover, the immigrants constantly send from the United States to Mexico . . . comparatively large sums of money."[39]

The study of Mexican immigration did not wipe away Gamio's scientific paternalism entirely, however. He retained his existing patterns of thought and failed to develop a more structural analysis of class and ethnicity.[40] Gamio contended, for example, that a "fairly large proportion" of Mexican immigrants carried the traits of "ancient aboriginal civilization" and came from indigenous and mestizo social groups "still in relatively inferior stages of development." Immigrants manifested, he wrote, the legacies of a "more primitive environment," a "folk culture" based upon "unquestioned convention and on the intervention of the supernatural, an attitude traditional from remote times and little changed by contact with modern civilization."[41]

Gamio distrusted the random influence of Mexicans returning from the United States, both because of the unpredictable character of their impact and the inability of "the small town or rural backward culture which they left" to absorb them constructively. While he recognized that poor organization and insufficient government support had doomed efforts to form agricultural colonies of returnees. Gamio continued to argue that a carefully planned effort at colonization projects could develop strategic nuclei for the education and uplifting of rural Mexico.[42]

Gamio's study challenged many of his country's opinions about migrants to the United States and about their relationship to Mexican national identity. Influential patriotic circles in Mexico found it difficult to accept the reality that revolutionary Mexico could not provide a livelihood for those who sought work in the United States. Even more painful to confront, however, was the notion that emigration could be beneficial both to the migrants themselves and to Mexico as a whole. In addition, Gamio offended Catholics by arguing that experience in the United States weakened religious fanaticism among these migrants and that exposure to Protestantism was largely harmless and potentially even constructive.[43] Mexico's intellectual climate in the 1920s offered hostile ground for the reception of Gamio's findings. In fact, neither of Gamio's two volumes was published in Mexico until 1969, when the National University issued *The Mexican Immigrant* with an introduction by Gamio's former intellectual opponent, Gilberto Loyo.[44] Gamio's work ran against the prevailing opinion of many observers that departure to work in the United States constituted a betrayal of Mexico. He even argued that residence north of the border enhanced the sense of national identity among Mexicans, particularly among those with darker skins and lower social status who would be less likely to gain acceptance in U.S. society than their lighter-skinned compatriots. Gamio contended that "many inhabitants of rural districts in Mexico have little notion of their nationality or their country. They know their town and the region in which it is situated, and this is a 'little country' for them. It is a notable fact that people of this type, when they become immigrants in the United States, learn immediately what their mother-country means, and they always think of it and speak of it with love."[45] Here, one can suspect, Gamio felt more than a little affinity with the experiences and attitudes of his research subjects.

He regarded racial discrimination in the United States as an insult that solidified immigrant identification with Mexico. Surrounded by a sea of hostility or indifference, Mexicans generally became more aware of their national identity through their foreign residence in the United States. Unlike European emigrants, all but the whitest of Mexicans encountered racial discrimination as a barrier against mobility even in second or third generations.[46] Gamio understood that racism affected not only individual immigrants but also worked against Mexicans as a collective ethnic group. As the numbers of Mexicans crossing the border expanded in the 1920s, immigration restrictionists battled with employers over public policy. Both sides invoked the racial and cultural stereotype of the inert, servile Mexican in order to justify their position —restrictionists to state why Mexicans could not be assimilated, and employers to argue why they posed no threat to jobs beyond the unskilled agricultural, mining, and railroad tasks that nobody else allegedly wanted to perform.[47] The last half of the decade presented a constant clamor in congressional hearings and magazine articles about the so-called Mexican invasion. Even magazines for the highly educated, such as *Foreign Affairs*, raised the specter of Mexican immigrants "lowering the U.S. racial stock." In arguing against U.S. military involvement in Mexico in 1927, Frank Tannenbaum alleged that intervention would mean annexation, which in turn would "mean adding twelve million Indians to some twelve million negroes. . . . We would within the next fifty years be faced with a race problem of some fifty or more million people."[48] Gamio stood firm against this tide, arguing that the "race problem" was of U.S. rather than Mexican making: "There is . . . no scientific basis for an innate inferiority of the Mexican, nothing beyond the dark pigmentation of the Mexican to account for the racial prejudice against him and the sexual barrier between him and the American."[49]

Gamio reinforced his expansive, tolerant conception of Mexican national identity with the publication of the personal testimonies contained in *The Mexican Immigrant*. As he must have appreciated, the true value of the statements lay in their "allowing the reader the sense of hearing directly the voices of those recounting their lives."[50] *The Mexican Immigrant* offered a powerful array of personal stories about departure from home, work in the United States, national loyalty, racism, women's issues, and other threads in the fabric of immigrant everyday life. Through them, Mexican national identity spoke with a rich myriad of tones and attitudes rather than the single voice of officialdom. Recognition of this diversity within the national identity was essential for Gamio. Unlike editorialists and essay writers in Mexico City who could generalize at will about immigrants to the United States, Gamio was obliged to understand empirically a totally different social context. While his *indigenista* background often left him with a proclivity toward static systems of classification, Gamio's encounter with the life experiences of Mexican immigrants attuned him to the dynamic and subtle qualities that social relations could have in the United States. He often reflected upon the ambiguous aspects of Mexican identity north of the border, particularly the relationships between Mexican Americans and newly arrived immigrants. David Gutiérrez has observed that "both volumes [of Gamio's study] are rife with examples of the ambivalence expressed by each group as Mexican Americans and Mexican immigrants grappled with the complex issues of national and cultural identity brought to the surface by the rapid growth of the ethnic Mexican population in the United States."[51]

Ultimately, for Gamio, Mexicans belonged in Mexico. He considered racism an insurmountable obstacle for Mexicans living in the United States; it worked against the likelihood of assimilation and permanent residence. Admiration for the "economic advantages" north of the border remained balanced against "the hostility or lack of racial or social appreciation which [the immigrant] frequently receives." He looked forward to the day when "emigration to the United States will diminish progressively" due to the "visible result" of Mexico's efforts at economic development.[52] Unlike temporary migration, which Gamio believed advantageous to both countries, permanent migration was harmful. He argued that the benefits of migration would quickly "pale before the alarming outlook which the growing depopulation of the country presents and which is directly produced by the exaggerated development of permanent emigration." As a means of matching labor supply to demand and preventing "the abuses of every sort of which the immigrants are victims," Gamio recommended that both the Mexican and U.S. governments take individual actions to manage the flow, among them temporary labor visas, quota systems, and taxes. He also advocated a bi-national system of temporary labor contracts that foreshadowed the Bracero Program, created jointly by both governments in 1942 to establish a managed migration to satisfy wartime labor demand in the United States. Mexico hoped to prevent the uncontrolled movement, severe exploitation, and potential for abrupt deportation that had typified earlier immigrant flows. Gamio played a significant role in advising the Mexican government in the negotiations that established the program.[53]

Gamio recognized that the economy of the United States encouraged Mexican immigration and crucially depended upon it. He explained the root of Mexican migration in terms of the wage differential between the two countries, an explanation derived from classical economics, and hoped that Mexican development would close the gap between the two. At the

same time, he appreciated the influence of the vast U.S. demand for unskilled workers and the significance of employers' labor recruitment patterns, both factors emphasized by today's international migration theory.[54]
However, contrary to Gamio's expectations, permanent immigration to
the United States became a fundamental feature of U.S. and Mexican life
in the generations after the Depression. From his early vantage point,
Gamio could not predict that industrialization would actually increase
migration from Mexico to the United States rather than deter it.

Like many public intellectuals of the Porfiriato and the Revolution,
Gamio found himself caught between the nationalist wish to forge the
patria (fatherland) through paternalistic scientific administration, on the
one hand, and the denationalizing implications of economic modernization, on the other. The same post-revolutionary order that could not gen-
erate the means to fund his nation-building social research would fail to
incorporate the subjects of his study—indigenous peoples and international migrants. For decades following the Mexican Revolution, *indigenismo* and economic development served as powerful hegemonic symbols
for Mexico's national identity, for the image of a homeland that would
provide for all Mexicans. The passage of time has brought the collapse
rather than the fulfillment of this national project. The oppression of indigenous peoples and the international movement of migrants constitute
structural features of a dependent modernization that has no room for all
Mexicans. The marginalization of these two social groups that so strongly
concerned Gamio continues as a central issue in Mexico's enduring crisis
of self-definition.

Notes

1. Ignacio Bernal, *A History of Mexican Archaeology: The Vanished Civiliza-
tions of Middle America* (London: Thames and Hudson, 1980), 164; Salomón
Nahmad Sittón and Thomas Weaver, "Manuel Gamio, el primer antropólogo apli-
cado y su relación con la antropología norteamericana," *América Indígena* 50,
no. 4 (1990): 291–312; and Guillermo Bonfil Batalla, *México Profundo: Reclaim-
ing a Civilization*, trans. Philip A. Dennis (Austin: University of Texas Press,
1996), 115.

2. Cynthia Hewitt de Alcántara, *Anthropological Perspectives on Rural Mexico*
(London: Routledge and Keegan Paul, 1984), 9.

3. Manuel Gamio, *Forjando patria*, 2d ed. (México: Editorial Porrúa, 1960), 183.

4. Bonfil Batalla, *México Profundo*, 115.

5. David G. Gutiérrez, *Walls and Mirrors: Mexican Americans, Mexican Immi-
grants, and the Politics of Ethnicity* (Berkeley: University of California Press,
1995), 61. The book-length study by Gamio, *Mexican Immigration to the United
States: A Study of Human Migration and Adjustment* (Chicago: University of
Chicago Press, 1930; reprint ed., New York: Dover Publications, 1971), was ac-
companied by a companion volume of interviews: *The Mexican Immigrant: His
Life-Story* (Chicago: University of Chicago Press, 1931; reprint ed., New York:
Dover Publications, 1971).

6. Lawrence A. Cardoso, *Mexican Emigration to the United States, 1897–1931: Socio-economic Patterns* (Tucson: University of Arizona Press, 1980), 104; Abraham Hoffman, *Unwanted Mexican Americans in the Great Depression: Repatriation Pressures, 1929–1939* (Tucson: University of Arizona Press, 1974), 33–35, 174–75. Nearly 80 percent of the repatriations of Mexicans between 1929 and 1937 took place in the years 1929–1932.

7. Francisco E. Balderrama and Raymond Rodríguez, *Decade of Betrayal: Mexican Repatriation in the 1930s* (Albuquerque: University of New Mexico Press, 1995), 132. The Centro de Investigaciones y Estudios Superiores en Antropología Social (CIESAS) and the University of California Institute for Mexico and the United States (UC MEXUS) have recently decided to collaborate on Spanish-language editions of Gamio's work in the United States including a complete set of his original interviews. "Manuel Gamio: Mexican Migration and Repatriation," *UC Mexus News* (Winter 1998): 13.

8. Angeles González Gamio, *Manuel Gamio, una lucha sin final* (México: Universidad Nacional Autónoma de México, 1987), 84–93; David A. Brading, "Manuel Gamio and Official Indigenismo in Mexico," *Bulletin of Latin American Research* 7.1 (1988): 75–89; Alan Knight, "Racism, Revolution, and *Indigenismo*: Mexico, 1910–1940," in *The Idea of Race in Latin America, 1870–1940*, ed. Richard Graham (Austin: University of Texas Press, 1990), 71–113.

9. Gamio envisioned his work as comprehensive research on the social, cultural, and economic lives of indigenous people and migrants, including the geographical and climatological influences to which they were subject. For the posts that Gamio held between 1922 and 1942, see González Gamio, *Manuel Gamio*, 62–130; and Juan Comas, "La vida y la obra de Manuel Gamio (1883–1960)," *América Indígena* 20.4 (October 1960): 253, 261.

10. Comas, "La vida y la obra de Manuel Gamio," 252; Nahmad Sittón and Weaver, "Manuel Gamio," 302.

11. A Jewish German immigrant regarded by many as "one of the most influential figures in the history of social science," Boas played a central role in the establishment of anthropology as a discipline in the United States. His well-known students include: Ruth Benedict, Fay-Cooper Cole, Melville Herskovits, Alfred Kroeber, Margaret Mead, and Edward Sapir. Boas dissented from racist anthropological theories, arguing instead for a form of pluralism in which cultural influences, rather than genetics, determined human behavior. See Marvin Harris, *The Rise of Anthropological Theory* (New York: Thomas Crowell, 1968), 250ff; Comas, "La vida y la obra de Manuel Gamio," 246; González Gamio, *Manuel Gamio*, 17–38; Helen Delpar, *The Enormous Vogue of Things Mexican: Cultural Relations between the United States and Mexico, 1920–1935* (Tuscaloosa: University of Alabama Press, 1992), 97.

12. Located approximately thirty miles northeast of present-day Mexico City, the ruins of Teotihuacán constitute a magnificent archaeological find, possibly "the most important site in the whole of Mexico." At its apogee in the sixth century A.D., Teotihuacán may have possessed a population of 125–200,000 people, making it one of the largest urban centers at that time in the entire world. Michael Coe, *Mexico from the Olmecs to the Aztecs*, 4th ed. (New York: Thames and Hudson, 1994), 89–106; Manuel Gamio, ed., *La población del Valle de Teotihuacán*, 2 vols. (México: Dirección de Talleres Gráficos de la Secretaría de Educación, 1922; reprint ed., México, 1979).

13. Boas to Manuel Gamio, December 31, 1924; Gamio to Boas, December 23, 1924, and January 9, 1925, Franz Boas Papers, American Philosophical Society, Philadelphia, Pennsylvania.

14. Comas, "La vida y la obra de Manuel Gamio," 252–53. Ernest Gruening, *Mexico and Its Heritage* (New York: Appleton-Century, 1928), 661, offers an account of this episode, calling it "the first serious error of the Calles administration." Despite publishing in the newspapers his correspondence with Calles leading up to his departure from the Secretaría de Educación, Gamio had apparently not burned all his bridges with the regime. In the same letter in which he informed Boas of his plans to go to the United States, he wrote that the president would eventually punish those responsible for the corruption once the furor of the incident had died down. See Gamio to Boas, July 6, 1925, Franz Boas Papers.

15. Delpar, *Enormous Vogue*, chap. 3; John A. Britton, *Revolution and Ideology: Images of the Mexican Revolution in the United States* (Lexington: University of Kentucky Press, 1995), 57–62, 93–96.

16. González Gamio, *Manuel Gamio*, 86–89.

17. José Vasconcelos and Manuel Gamio, *Aspects of Mexican Civilization: Lectures on the Harris Foundation, 1926* (Chicago: University of Chicago Press, 1926). Somewhat inexplicably, both González Gamio, *Manuel Gamio*, 92, and Comas, "La vida y la obra de Manuel Gamio," 261, both refer to the Foundation as "Harry's Institute."

18. On the creation of the SSRC, see Barry D. Karl, *Charles E. Merriam and the Study of Politics* (Chicago: University of Chicago Press, 1974), chap. 7, especially 130–31; and Dorothy Ross, *The Origins of American Social Science* (Cambridge: Cambridge University Press, 1991), 401–3. Ross, 402, notes that "between 1922 and 1929, the Laura Spelman Rockefeller Memorial . . . and the SSRC dispensed about forty-one million dollars to American social science, social work, and their institutions."

19. Gutiérrez, *Walls and Mirrors*, 40.

20. Accession One, Series 1, Committee Projects, Subseries 19, Miscellaneous Projects Box 191, Folder 1134, Committee on Population Minutes, December 27, 1925, 48, 50, 56, Social Science Research Council Papers, Rockefeller Archive Center, North Tarrytown, New York (hereafter cited as SSRC Papers). Redfield's study eventually emerged as *Tepoztlán: A Mexican Village* (Chicago: University of Chicago Press, 1930).

21. SSRC Papers, December 27, 1925, and August–September 1930, 57, 333. Even the Council was not sure of the precise figure of its expenditures on Gamio's project, reporting in 1930 an "apparent total" of $20,250.

22. Vasconcelos and Gamio, *Aspects*, 169; Knight, "Racism, Revolution, and Indigenismo," 85–88.

23. Miguel León-Portilla calls *investigación integral* one of Gamio's four most important fundamental ideas: Miguel León Portilla, "Ideas fundamentales de Gamio," *América Indígena* 20.4 (October 1960): 298–99.

24. SSRC Papers, August 29, 1927, 137.

25. Gamio, *Mexican Immigration*, 187–89.

26. SSRC Papers, December 27, 1925, 57.

27. See Gamio's memo, "Why the Social Science Research Council Favored the Study of Mexican Immigration into the United States and Commended It to Dr. Manuel Gamio," Box 2, Folder 63, Series X, Ambassador to Mexico, Dwight W. Morrow Papers, Amherst College Library, Amherst, Massachusetts. Gamio strongly praised U.S. foundations that supported academic research: Vasconcelos and Gamio, *Aspects*, 185–86. In 1929 the John Simon Guggenheim Memorial Foundation began a program of Latin American Exchange Fellowships, but none of the recipients in its early years carried out projects as complex as that of Gamio. See Delpar, *Enormous Vogue*, 76–77.

28. SSRC Papers, August 29, 1927, 140–41; "Preliminary Report on Mexican Migration in [*sic*] United States," Box 3, Manuel Gamio Papers, Bancroft Library, University of California, Berkeley, California.

29. Roland B. Dixon to Manuel Gamio, October 25, 1928, Dwight W. Morrow Papers; Gamio, "Why the Social Science Research Council," Dwight W. Morrow Papers; Gamio to Boas, July 27, 1928, Franz Boas Papers.

30. Dwight W. Morrow to Manuel Gamio, November 19, 1928, Dwight W. Morrow Papers; SSRC Papers, August 29, 1927, April 4–5, 1930, and August–September 1930, 133–36, 285, 333.

31. Gamio, *Mexican Immigration*, xvi.

32. Manuel Gamio, "Los repatriados y la educación de las masas incultas" and "La investigación de los grupos indígenas mexicanos," in *Hacia un México nuevo: Problemas sociales* (México, 1935; reprint ed. Instituto Nacional Indigenista, 1987), 71–83 and 157–71.

33. Comas, "La vida y la obra de Manuel Gamio," 253.

34. Ibid., x–xi. Interviews were conducted by assistants whom Gamio hired for the project, some of whom are named in his introduction to *Mexican Immigration*. Many of the descriptions of those they interviewed were highly subjective (e.g., "The wife's way of dressing is terribly ridiculous") and were left out of *The Mexican Immigrant*. Yet even Gamio may not have known just how subjective an interview could become. One of the original transcripts has several lines struck out and is accompanied by a loose note stating that "one of Dr. Gamio's scientific colleagues has sexual intercourse with a Mexican semi-prostitute in order to get 'datos sobre mi vida.' Not worth printing." In fact, the interviewer did report "dos o tres cópulas" in the course of his information gathering. Interview of Luis Felipe Recinos with Elisa Morales, Los Angeles, April 16, 1927, Gamio Papers, Box 2, Folder 11.

35. Bonfil Batalla, *México Profundo*, 117.

36. Vasconcelos and Gamio, *Aspects*, 122.

37. Gamio, *Mexican Immigration*, 49, 67–68.

38. Ibid., 173, 63–64.

39. Ibid., 5–8, 178–79.

40. For such an analysis with regard to *indigenismo*, see Arturo Warman, "Indigenist Thought," in *Indigenous Anthropology in Non-Western Countries*, ed. Hussein Fahim (Durham: Carolina Academic Press, 1982), 75–96.

41. Ibid., 57, 74.

42. Gamio, *Mexican Immigration*, 50, 183–84, 235–41; "Los repatriados," passim.

43. Gamio, *Mexican Immigration*, chap. 8.

44. During the 1920s, Loyo had argued that emigration endangered Mexico's need to expand its population, weakened the country in the face of U.S. imperial power, and exposed Mexican nationals to labor exploitation that benefited only the United States. Gilberto Loyo, "Prológo" to Manuel Gamio, *El inmigrante mexicano: La historia de su vida* (México: Universidad Nacional Autónoma de México, 1969), 13, 15, 19; Cardoso, *Mexican Emigration*, 105.

45. Gamio, *Mexican Immigration*, 128.

46. Ibid., 52–54, 128, 155–57.

47. See Gutiérrez, *Walls and Mirrors*, chap. 2.

48. Glen E. Hoover, "Our Mexican Immigrants," *Foreign Affairs* 8 (October 1929): 104; Frank Tannenbaum, "Mexico's Internal Politics and American Diplomacy," *The Annals* 132 (July 1927): 175.

49. Gamio, *Mexican Immigration*, 172.

50. Kathleen Logan, "Personal Testimony: Latin American Women Telling Their Lives," *Latin American Research Review* 32.1 (1996): 200.

51. Gutiérrez, *Walls and Mirrors*, 62. See Gamio, *Mexican Immigration*, 53–56, 64, 154–55.

52. Gamio, *Mexican Immigration*, 176–77.

53. Ibid., 179, 182–83. The Bracero Program survived until 1964. See Manuel García y Griego, "The Importation of Mexican Contract Laborers to the United States, 1942–1964," in *The Border That Joins: Mexican Migrants and U.S. Responsibility*, ed. Peter G. Brown and Henry Shue (Totowa, NJ: Rowman and Littlefield, 1983), 49–98.

54. Gamio, *Mexican Immigration*, 30–33, 171–72, 180. For a knowledgeable discussion of migration theories, see Douglas Massey et al., "Theories of International Migration: A Review and Appraisal," *Population and Development Review* 19.3 (September 1993): 431–66.

13

Guilt by Association: Jorge Eliécer Gaitán and the Legacy of His Studies in "Fascist" Italy

W. John Green

During the first half of the twentieth century, many nations witnessed mass political mobilization on a new and vastly expanded scale. Typically, these movements boasted a lone charismatic leader who addressed an immense multitude of listeners and won a devoted following among the laboring classes. As with Hitler and Mussolini, an awareness of this dramatic public style is fundamental to any understanding of the life and work of Jorge Eliécer Gaitán (1898–1948), the leader of a populist movement in Colombia that extended from the late 1920s until his assassination on April 9, 1948. Gaitán is easily the most famous Colombian political orator of the twentieth century and often has been branded a fascist because of his unprecedented style and conscious appeal to all social classes. Furthermore, Gaitán's studies for an advanced law degree at Rome's Royal University in 1926–27 placed him in the heart of the emerging Italian fascist movement, giving all the proof that his enemies needed to link him with European fascism. For these reasons, Gaitán's political reputation has always suffered from guilt by association, although he remained outspoken in his opposition to the uncritical application of European models to Colombian reality.

Historian John Green argues that Gaitán's residence in Italy may have introduced the politician to a more modern style of mass mobilization and public oratory, but in the end, Gaitán just adapted lessons learned while abroad to a political style that he already had begun to develop while he was a student in Colombia. After Gaitán's assassination, his memory assumed mythic proportions; interpretations of his personality and goals remain a hotly contested topic in Colombia to this day. He also is linked to the next generation of Latin American revolutionaries. A young Fidel Castro was present in the Colombian capital and witnessed the Bogotazo, or massive rioting, that took place there in the days after Gaitán's death. This incident, with partisans differentiated by their attitudes toward Gaitán and his populist legacy, sparked decades of intermittent civil

warfare and ideological wrangling between the liberals and conserva-
tives in Colombia, aptly known as la violencia.

Until recently, many scholars looked upon Latin American populism
as a close cousin to European fascism. Investigations were based on
the assumption that populist leaders served primarily as the vehicles
through which elites (or portions of them) maintained their power rather
than genuinely seeking to integrate previously excluded social sectors;
Machiavellian strongmen merely spouted progressive rhetoric while actually subverting the interests of their multiclass followers. In many Latin
American cases, as with Colombia's Jorge Eliécer Gaitán, the desire to
link populists to European fascists is made all the more tempting by a
direct personal connection to fascist Italy, Nazi Germany, or Franco's
Spain. Noted historian Eric Hobsbawm pointed out in a recent book that
"it was in Latin America that European fascist influence was to be open
and acknowledged, both on individual politicians . . . and on regimes";
and he named as examples Jorge Eliécer Gaitán along with the other usual
suspects, Argentina's Juan Perón and Brazil's Getulio Vargas.[1]

A growing number of Latin American case studies, however, have
demonstrated that there were actually two opposing tendencies within the
generalized phenomenon of populism: it could be either a form of elite
social domination from above through controlled mobilization of the popular classes, or a mode of popular mobilization and resistance to the existing relations of power from below. In this way, populism could be either
revolutionary or counter-revolutionary, and occasionally both at the same
time. For Colombians at least, Gaitanismo represented a momentous surge
of popular participation in the nation's political life and proved to be an
expression of, rather than a brake on, the popular will.

Standard Communist practice throughout Latin America in the 1930s
and 1940s was to label their populist rivals "fascists" in order to gain
political advantage. In addition to time spent in Mussolini's Italy, Gaitán's
lively speaking style showcased his dramatic flare for gesticulation, emotion, rhetorical flourishes, and allusions to Colombia's national spirit, all
hallmarks of European fascist leaders' speeches as well. Furthermore, his
multiclass movement flourished in an atmosphere of tense interclass alliance and conflict. For these superficial reasons, many members of
Colombia's left-leaning intelligentsia continue to charge that Gaitán was
a fascist despite his consistent and public assertions to the contrary.[2] Their
case is based largely on circumstantial evidence and ignores direct proof
that Gaitán himself was personally hostile to fascism. After all, Gaitán
was a prime example of the left-Liberal tradition in Colombia that spawned
both the radical elements of the Liberal Party and the Communist Party
itself.

Humble Origins

Jorge Eliécer Gaitán Ayala was born in 1898 in a Bogotá neighborhood already past its prime. Soon thereafter financial problems obliged his family to move to a working-class barrio.[3] His father, Eliécer Gaitán, a political activist, founded two short-lived Liberal newspapers in 1903 and 1905, both of which quickly succumbed to financial exigencies. During his aspiring journalistic career, Don Eliécer had amassed a large collection of books to write a history of Colombia that turned out to be his only liquid asset, and, to support his family, he regretfully opened a used book shop. Although he proved to be a rather hapless provider for his family, Don Eliécer instilled in his young son a love of books, ideas, and the activist Liberal tradition. Gaitán's mother, Doña Manuela Ayala de Gaitán, had greater influence on the boy's intellectual development. A graduate of the Escuela Normal, Colombia's teacher-training institute, she gained a reputation in Bogotá and the surrounding towns of Cundinamarca as a teacher of progressive and moderately feminist views. Jorge Eliécer, the eldest of six children, was Manuela's favorite, and she spared nothing in providing for his initial education. Her highest aspiration was for him to obtain a university degree, perhaps even from a foreign institution.

An intelligent and strong-willed boy who suffered numerous insults because of his dark coloring, Jorge Eliécer fought with his teachers and his lighter-skinned, more affluent classmates. He was expelled from several schools before his parents' political connections helped him to obtain a scholarship to the Colegio Araújo in 1913. The school's founder, renowned Liberal educator Simón Araújo, made a strong impression on the young Gaitán. Since Araújo's school remained unaccredited by the Conservative educational establishment, the ambitious Jorge Eliécer transferred during his last year to the Colegio de Martín Restrepo Mejía. He graduated with high grades in 1919 and in February 1920 entered the National University to study law.

Self-reliant and pugnacious, Gaitán had begun his political career and demonstrated a gift for oratory while still a teenager attending the Colegio Araújo. In 1917 he carried out an independent speaking campaign in the towns around Bogotá in favor of candidate Guillermo Valencia, a Conservative poet who led a coalition of moderate Conservatives and Liberals against the ruling party. Though ignored at first by the uneasy coalition's leadership, Liberal caudillo Benjamín Herrera eventually dispatched Gaitán on an even more far-reaching proselytizing mission through Cundinamarca and Tolima that brought him important political recognition. Though still a university student, Gaitán became one of Herrera's closest aides and a key youth organizer in his unsuccessful 1922 presidential campaign. Herrera sent Gaitán on a speaking tour of Conservative bastions in Cundinamarca and Boyacá where the fiery student-orator stirred up considerable excitement. In this way, Gaitán developed enough of a personal following to be elected to the Cundinamarca departmental assembly in 1923.

As a law student, Gaitán read extensively in history and social theory. He was greatly influenced by legal positivism, and gave expression to this ideological perspective for the first time in his law thesis, "Las ideas socialistas en Colombia."[4] Focusing on ideas of justice and the nature of the law, Gaitán rejected classical concepts that grounded ethics in universal principles; instead, he argued that the justification for all individual rights originated in human society, and therefore denied that men were born with "natural" rights. When the rights of an individual came into conflict with the rights of society, the former had to yield. Long before he visited Mussolini's Italy, Gaitán envisioned an interventionist state that would provide equal justice and guarantee just distribution of the material wealth of society among its members.[5] For Gaitán the state not only had the right but also the obligation to change the legal, political, and economic structures that regulated society in order to correct injustices.[6]

José Antonio Osorio Lizarazo, a left-Liberal intellectual, novelist, and ardent Gaitanista, argues that Gaitán chose penal law, not for the order it could bring society but rather because of his "obsession with justice." Civil law, he believed, did not embody the same "clamor for the weak" and "dignity" that penal law exhibited in its defense of criminals who were nothing more than the products of "ignorance and misery." Civil law protected the interests of propertied classes while penal law sought the "restoration of justice."[7] Clearly, Gaitán's "obsession" with ideas of justice persisted throughout his life. Overcoming financial hardship and the demands of his burgeoning political career, the always-determined Gaitán graduated from Colombia's National University in 1924.

The outline of Gaitán's experience in Italy is well known.[8] In 1926 he enrolled in the Royal University at Rome and graduated a year later at the top of his class. After a tour of Europe, Gaitán returned to Colombia in 1928, just in time to participate in one of the most important labor crises in Colombian history. Though Gaitán's year of residence and study in Italy was most important to him personally for the doors it opened to his professional development, the experience itself had a less tangible, although equally significant, affect on his public style and political persona. While abroad, he had time to observe European politicians—their propaganda methods and the crowds' reactions to them—and to allow his own style of communication to mature. Coming from South America, where participatory politics and the incorporation of the laboring classes into the political process were still works in progress greeted with hostility and distrust by elites, Gaitán's time abroad allowed him to witness styles of political leadership and mobilization different from those in which he was raised.

A joint business venture with his brother Manuel José provided Gaitán only a meager income with which to pursue his studies in Europe, but he boldly refused the offer of a position at the Colombian Legation in Italy that his mother had cajoled from the Conservative government. Ever proud, Gaitán was intent upon owing nothing to anyone. His choice of Italy as a destination was significant. He aspired to study under Enrico Ferri, perhaps the foremost scholar of penal law in his day. Not only had Gaitán become a champion of Ferri's ideas in Colombia, but also Ferri represented a personal role model for the younger man. Ferri, too, came from a modest lower-middle-class background and went on to became an extremely successful trial lawyer and one of Italy's most famous orators. He was a member of parliament and edited the socialist paper *Avanti*, although he became a fascist sympathizer in his later years. Ferri's ultimate goal was to enact the penal codes that he believed would improve society and the well-being of all its members, especially the less fortunate. Gaitán admired him greatly and was only the second Colombian lawyer, after his fellow left-Liberal and political collaborator Carlos Arango Vélez, to study with Ferri.

It is true that Gaitán also wanted the prestige that came with a degree from a European university. Such a distinction could elevate the young, lower-middle-class mestizo lawyer to the higher echelons of Colombian society. Academic success abroad allowed ambitious youths like Gaitán to gain positions unavailable to them had they remained in the traditional domestic sphere. Travel was an important part of upper-class culture; members of the Colombian elite were often more familiar with Europe than with large areas of their own country and traveled abroad as a matter of course. In fact, domestic travel was so hindered by Colombia's mountainous terrain, thick jungles, and lack of rail and paved road, that it took less time to sail across the Atlantic to Europe than to journey between many local cities. Yet Gaitán's European experience was not the typical grand tour made by a scion of the Latin American upper classes. For him, professional and political opportunities proved a much more powerful motivation than did any desire for improved social status. Soon after his return home, Gaitán disdainfully pointed out in an interview that many Colombians abroad only experienced "the vain and superficial life of the cabaret," the implication being that he, Gaitán, was continuing to work for Colombia, just in a different environment.[9] Gaitán took his extended residence in Italy seriously as a fundamental preparation for subsequent national service; travel and foreign residence were for him a patriotic act.

In July 1926, Gaitán enrolled in the Royal University in Rome. Limited resources made his life as a student very difficult, but he was accustomed to financial adversity. He stayed in the most humble of *pensiones* (small, family-run boardinghouses), moving frequently in an attempt to stay one step ahead of his creditors. He lived beyond his means and imperfectly emulated the life-style of his upper-class associates, who viewed Gaitán as an exotic novelty and welcomed him into their exalted social circles because of his intelligence and their fascination with his dark skin. Ironically, later in his career the Colombian elite denigrated him as "*el negro* Gaitán" because of these same attributes. In fact, right-wing political cartoons of the 1940s emphasized his dark complexion and fixated on the size of his teeth. Remembering this earlier, more welcoming reception in Europe probably helped him weather the insults of his white-skinned countrymen. In Rome, Gaitán became the protégé of Ferri, and the two men rapidly formed a deep personal friendship and professional bond that validated Gaitán's accomplishments in the eyes of Colombians at home.

While in Italy, Gaitán witnessed Mussolini's dramatic style of leadership and attended Fascist rallies where he heard Il Duce speak on various occasions. Gaitán, a true student of politics, was intrigued by these spectacles. Despite being a seasoned public speaker long before his stay in Italy, he nevertheless was influenced by the techniques that the Italian caudillo employed. After his year in Italy, Gaitán's oratorical style utilized dramatic gestures and alternating vocal patterns like Mussolini's, and he also adopted the rhetorical device of a dialogue between himself and his listeners in his public speeches. After his return from Italy, Gaitán acknowledged that he had been impressed also by Mussolini's vigor and power to steer a political rally. In this way, Gaitán used the form, if not necessarily the substance, of the political experiments that he had witnessed in Italy to aid his own rise to the forefront of Colombian politics.

Though Gaitán was always a gregarious fellow and certainly cut a memorable figure in Rome, he never lost sight of the reason for his stay abroad. After just one intense year of purposeful study, Gaitán graduated magna cum laude and first in his class. His technically focused thesis, "Criterio positivo de la premeditación," was awarded the Ferri Prize for criminal law from the hand of the professor himself. Gaitán proudly remembered the emotional ceremony during which he presented his thesis orally and received his degree in the presence of King Victor Emmanuel, Mussolini, and various Italian government ministers. Indeed, he recounted the story numerous times over the years and undoubtedly embellished it for each new audience. Ferri declared Gaitán to be one of the best students he had ever instructed. As a result, Gaitán became the first Latin American member of the International Society of Penal Law's Italian section. Back in Colombia, Gaitán's winning of the Ferri Prize was front-page news.[10] His success abroad had earned him fame at home, and a national political career beckoned.

After graduation, Gaitán used the cash portion of the Ferri Prize to travel through Europe, ending up in Paris where he lingered a few months. He visited the great monuments of European culture and thereby entered the ranks of an exclusive cosmopolitan club in which relatively few Colombians could claim membership. In Paris, as he had in Rome, Gaitán made a lasting impression upon the other Latin Americans he met there. He was a mestizo from a humble background whose unexpectedly elegant charm, sophistication, and unparalleled professional success seemed peculiar and out of place at home, but received validation, even kudos, abroad. He would cherish that experience until the end of his days.

Upon his return to Colombia in 1928 it was clear that his European accomplishments had brought Gaitán across a significant threshold, and he now had to be taken seriously as both an intellectual and a jurist in his own country. He had already received a university degree and some fame as a rising young Liberal politician before he left for Italy, yet Gaitán returned as the prize pupil of a famous Old World scholar with an undeniable stamp of European approval. For upper-class Colombians this last accomplishment was especially important. As the Liberal intellectuals at a leading Bogotá paper noted, the triumphantly returning Gaitán was "an impetuous professional" and "a pleasant case of detropicalization" whose American habits had been polished to a more becoming sheen through his extended stay in a European capital.[11]

Gaitán's career spanned two crucial decades in Colombia's political development, from 1928 to 1948. During this period of escalating social conflict, Gaitán wrenched control of the Liberal Party from a traditional leadership hostile to his desire to invite broader political participation. As these serious struggles intensified, Colombian Communist Party leaders and their allies in the Liberal establishment repeatedly attempted to smear Gaitán with the stigma of fascism, drawing premature and self-serving conclusions from Gaitán's residence in Italy. His time abroad provided not only the impetus for his own rise to power but also easy ammunition for his enemies to use against him.

After Gaitán's return to Colombia, he immediately stepped into a role of public prominence. He returned to his high-profile practice in penal and labor law, and soon was elected to the lower house of Congress where he played a key part in one of the turning points in recent Colombian history: the 1928 banana workers' strike. The events of the strike and its subsequent suppression were closely followed throughout the country, a situation in large part due to Gaitán, who had learned the value of positive public opinion during his stay in Europe. The strike was the product of years of long-simmering tension between the foreign-owned United Fruit Company and its Colombian workers in the department of Magdalena known as the "banana zone." Also important was a determined organizing drive by anarcho-syndicalists and the soon-to-be Communist Party, the Revolutionary Socialist Party (Partido Socialista Revolucionario, or PSR). The Conservative government responded by deploying troops, declaring a state of siege, and carrying out the infamous "massacre" at Ciénaga in the early hours of December 6, 1928.[12]

The public attack on the Conservative government's violent handling of the affair came from the left-Liberals in Congress and most vehemently from Gaitán, who was emerging as their foremost representative. He personally traveled to Ciénaga in July 1929 for a theatrical "investigation" of local conditions. During his return to Bogotá he stopped in numerous cities and towns to tell of his findings, everywhere drawing large crowds. Back in Congress, Gaitán launched his so-called debate on September 3, 1929, before packed galleries and an attentive press, which enthusiastically pelted the government with invective and scorn for the next fifteen days. Gaitán's exploits were followed not only in Bogotá, where adoring crowds accompanied him home each evening, but also throughout the country. Gaitán's dramatic performance, coinciding with the beginning of the Great Depression, high unemployment, and a crisis in leadership, contributed to the end of the "Conservative Hegemony" and the birth of the "Liberal Republic" in 1930.

Gaitán's meteoric rise came at the expense of the Communists who had organized and led the strike. This pattern of cooperation and cooptation would be repeated more than once as the members of the Liberal Party's left wing sparred with the Communist Party (in its various guises) for popular support. Sometimes moving with parallel mobilizations, sometimes in uneasy alliance, and ultimately in open competition, Gaitán and the Communists both aspired to the leadership of the Left. Their tenuous relationship matured under conditions of flux, in which the allegiance of the urban working classes could not be held definitively by any single group.

Scholars have overlooked the kinship shared by the left Liberals and the Colombian Communist Party by investigating them in virtual isolation. However, their relationship explains much about the relative weakness of doctrinaire communism in Colombia.[13] This relationship between Communists and left Liberals is not only apparent in retrospect. U.S. State Department analysts at the time recognized that the "development of the Communist party" coincided with "the period of Liberal government," and that the Communists' grasp of leftist ideology was less than complete.[14] From the beginning there were areas of Communist strength that were also left-Liberal areas. One U.S. State Department official went so far as to claim that some of Colombia's "alleged Communism is in reality nothing more than a pronounced Liberalism which, as elsewhere in Latin America, is denounced by the Conservative element."[15]

Gaitán's organizational foray outside the Liberal Party, the Unión Nacional Izquierdista Revolucionaria (UNIR, or National Leftist Revolutionary Union), represented just one of many competing currents of popular mobilization to appear among the Colombian left in the early 1930s. Some features of his organization seemed to be inspired by European fascism: a focus on discipline, mass mobilization, and a hierarchical organizational structure that utilized local "teams," "legions," a "Central Committee," and the "Directing Commission" made up of Gaitán and his intimates. UNIR also had organizations for internal control, defense of members against employers and political violence, strike organization, public relations, and education. Gaitán "encouraged the use of hymns, uniforms, insignias, and decorations," while UNIR's program came to be known as the "Revolution of Soap" because of his stress on hygiene.[16] This hierarchical program was one of the principal reasons UNIR's mobilization has been perceived as a controlled, paternalistic affair and therefore linked to European fascist movements.

Any such similarities between the UNIR and European facism should not be taken without qualification. UNIR's founding charter proclaimed the "struggle for socialism, because the country cannot be developed on the basis of individualist criteria." The organization was dedicated to building cooperation, solidarity, and raising consciousness. Gaitán asserted that UNIR was "an autonomous, independent force of preparation and struggle, guarding the firm principles of the Left," and chief among these were land reform, social justice, and democracy.[17] Most likely, Gaitán took the inspiration for his organizational structure from the same place that Mussolini did: ancient Rome. Gaitán was an enthusiastic student of history and Spanish American political tradition and had always emulated the speeches of Greek and Roman orators. Yet while Il Duce looked to the personalist example of Julius Caesar, Gaitán instead drew upon the popular heritage of the Roman Tribunes and their most famous representatives, Gaius and Tiberius Gracchus.[18] Having spent time in the legendary home of republicanism, Gaitán could feel a direct personal link to the classical heritage of Latin American thought.

In the end, the various attempts at radical mobilization during the early 1930s were displaced by the official Liberal Party. Liberals delivered their most devastating blow to such popular movements by usurping much of their program. In his first administration of 1934–1938, President Alfonso López Pumarejo instituted the Revolución en Marcha, which focused upon state intervention and constitutional reform. Through state welfare, expanded male suffrage, benevolent dealings with workers, and education and agrarian reform, López effectively won the support of large portions of the "popular classes," including the leaders of organized labor and of the Communist Party.

Given the lack of clear distinction between the platforms of the Communists and the Gaitanista left-Liberals and both groups' intense competition for popular followings, one side, the Gaitanistas, finally played the trump card of nationalism. Labor leader Juan Manuel Valdelamar, one of Gaitanismo's most astute organizers, argued that Gaitanismo's "national character" was one of the principal reasons for which both the Communist PSR and the established oligarchy feared it.[19] While the Communist Party fixated on the international defeat of fascism, the Gaitanistas effectively used nationalism as a mobilizing agent, turning the Communists' inconsistent and abstract internationalism into a handicap.[20]

Nationalism is important to all populist movements, and in the case of Colombia, which is isolated and given to entrenched party loyalty, its appeal was especially pronounced. Colombians identified more with local Liberal and Conservative struggles than with any abstract ideological battles between communism and fascism.[21] In the 1930s the Communists' assertion that the idea of *patria* (fatherland) was only a bourgeois construct intended to confuse "citizens of the world" offended the national pride of many Colombians who might otherwise have sympathized with their cause.[22] The idea that "the worker has no fatherland" seemed absurd to many intellectuals and politicians on the Colombian left, and undoubtedly to the undereducated workers as well.[23] Liberals and Gaitanistas claimed that Communist activity, perpetrated by "agents of Moscow," was "outside the law."[24] Augusto Durán, Secretary General of the Colombian Communist Party (Partido Socialista Democratico, or PSR) in the 1940s, supposedly attacked anyone who did not pay homage to Soviet doctrines.[25] And Gaitán was hardly above inciting fear against Communist activity by declaring it a dangerous intervention into the life of the *patria* by a "foreign organization."[26] Increasingly, a history of foreign residence could be beneficial to one's career, but also could risk tainting one in the eyes of one's enemies.

The Gaitanistas' successful appeals to nationalism led the Communists to retaliate with claims that Gaitanismo was really just another form of fascism. Citing the case of Juan Perón in Argentina, they argued that Gaitanismo attracted only the *masas atrasadas* (backward masses) and was led by a demagogue who had spent his formative years in Italy.[27] The PSD pointed to a seeming alliance between Gaitán and the rabid leader of the most reactionary sect of the Conservative Party, Laureano Gómez, who gave Gaitán coverage in his paper *El Siglo* in a successful maneuver to divide the Liberal Party.

Throughout late 1945 and into 1946, the Communists pounded away at Gaitán in speeches, memoranda, and their party paper *Diario Popular* as a demagogue and a threat to the Colombian working class. Augusto Durán declared that those masses who did follow Gaitán did so because he had "a powerful throat."[28] Resurrecting the title of a 1936 anti-Gaitán polemic, they called him the "naked apostle," a representative of the most reactionary forces of Colombia. Gaitán, they argued, disoriented the working class by camouflaging his hatred of the people in phrases appealing to the interests of the people.[29] Gaitanismo was nothing more than "demagoguery and lies."[30] As Durán said in a speech in Barranquilla in September 1945, "Hitler and Mussolini also deceived the people with the demagoguery of moral restoration." Gaitán was simply Gómez's frontman, "the screen" behind which hid anti-democratic reaction.[31]

In the end, however, PSD (and elite Liberal) efforts to brand Gaitán a fascist proved a spectacular failure. Most Colombian workers recognized Gaitanismo as a radical leftist mobilization and registered their opinion in the May 5, 1946, presidential election. The results shocked Colombia's Liberal elites and their allies within the PSD's leadership as Conservative candidate Mariano Ospina Pérez easily won the election with 565,260 votes, while the official candidate, Liberal Gabriel Turbay, came in a distant second with only 440,591. Gaitán trailed relatively close behind with 358,957 votes. Significantly, Gaitán decisively carried the urban middle and working classes. While the old party machines held the countryside, Gaitán won most urban centers and departmental capitals. With this vote of popular confidence, his enemies within the party realized that even with Liberalism's entire political machine turned against him, they could not crush Gaitanismo.

To label Gaitán a fascist would be to ignore his own words on the subject. In one of his first public statements upon his return from Europe, Gaitan explicitly denounced fascism and its Italian leader. In February 1928 he characterized Mussolini as a "sad exhibitionist," yet he could not deny that Mussolini's speeches were "picturesque" and that he showed considerable energy. Yet Gaitán also called him "ridiculous" and remarked that Mussolini was fortunate that Italians simply had no concept of the ridiculous. Furthermore, Gaitán was aware of the stage-managed spontaneity of the masses at Mussolini's rallies by pointing out that in his speeches Il Duce asked questions and Italians were expected to respond in a choreographed way.[32] Gaitán also made it clear that he was not seduced by fascist thought. In fact, he argued that fascism had no discernible ideology and that it was born in the original sin of violence and ultimately had served to negate fundamental human liberties.[33] He noted that "Mussolini, taking advantage of the masses in the disarray following World War I, could jump from one doctrine to another without losing authority because he held power through fear and intimidation. He had betrayed his own ideas and his followers once in power, with disastrous results for Italy." Gaitán never publicly changed his mind regarding fascism and, when he spoke of it in later years, his judgements remained critical. Even when his beloved mentor Ferri, perhaps for political reasons, became a fascist sympathizer, there is no real evidence that Gaitán followed suit.[34]

Gaitán's experience in both Europe and America begs two fundamental questions: what is fascism, and what are its connections to Latin

American populism? Both political phenomena generally manifested a personalistic and charismatic leader making highly emotional appeals based upon notions of the "national spirit" to a mass or multiclass following. Both populism and fascism arose during the world economic crises resulting from World War I and the Great Depression, and both frequently receive the contradictory labels of "revolutionary" and "counterrevolutionary." Finally, these similarities have been reinforced by the common tendency of the organized left in Latin America to characterize their populist rivals as fascists for propaganda purposes.

This essay has been as much about Gaitán's alleged association with fascism as it has been about his time in Italy. Indeed, these questions cannot be separated. Gaitán's term of study in Mussolini's Rome occasioned the "fascist" analogy that plagued him throughout his political career and which has endured to the present day. It is true that there were elements of his speaking style and early mobilization methods that seemed to have been influenced by the Italian fascist dictator. Although the temptation to draw a definitive connection is seductive, Gaitán was attracted to "Roman" discipline rather than to "fascism" per se. In fact, the intellectual heritage of ancient Rome is itself ambivalent given the related yet mutually hostile traditions of the Republic and the Empire. Gaitán himself preferred to be known in Colombia as "the Tribune of the People," recalling the best tradition of Tiberius and Gaius Gracchus, and always tried to distance himself from the guilt by association with which his opponents continually tried to brand him a fascist.

Notes

1. Yet Hobsbawm, unlike many scholars, senses that there was a difference. "In Colombia the great people's tribune Jorge Eliécer Gaitán, so far from choosing the political Right, captured the leadership of the Liberal Party and would certainly as president have led it in a radical direction, had he not been assassinated." See Eric Hobsbawm, *The Age of Extremes: A History of the World, 1914–1991* (New York: Pantheon, 1994), 133–34.

2. For example, while doing research in the Biblioteca Nacional in Bogotá for this essay, a Colombian scholar saw the newspaper article on Gaitán from the early 1930s that I was reading and said, "You know, he was a fascist." Yet, as I will argue, this characterization of Gaitán did not spread far beyond Communist and Liberal leadership circles.

3. Information for the following section is taken from: Richard Sharpless, *Gaitán of Colombia: A Political Biography* (Pittsburgh: University of Pittsburgh Press, 1978), 29–41; Herbert Braun, *The Assassination of Gaitán: Public Life and Urban Violence in Colombia* (Madison: University of Wisconsin Press, 1985), 39–45; J. Cordell Robinson, *El movimiento gaitanista en Colombia* (Bogotá: Ediciones Tercer Mundo, 1976), 47–66. These works provide detailed biographical sketches of Gaitán. Earlier works include: Horacio Gómez Aristizábal, *Gaitán: Enfoque histórico* (Bogotá: Editorial Cosmos, 1975); Mauro Torres, *Gaitán: Grandeza y limitaciones psicológicas* (Bogotá: Ediciones Tercer Mundo, 1976). Also of cru-

cial importance are works by those who knew Gaitán: José Antonio Osorio Lizarazo, *Gaitán: Vida, muerte y permanente presencia* (Bogotá: Carlos Valencia Editores, 1982 [1952]); Luis David Peña, *Gaitán íntimo* (Bogotá: Editorial Iqueima, 1949); José María Córdoba, *Jorge Eliécer Gaitán: Tribuno popular de Colombia* (Bogotá: n.p., 1952).

4. Jorge Eliécer Gaitán, "Las ideas socialistas en Colombia," in Luis Emiro Valencia, ed., *Gaitán: Antología de su pensamiento económico y social* (Bogotá: Ediciones Suramérica, 1968), 49–213.

5. Gaitán, "Ideas socialistas," 68–69. Gaitán believed that "social convulsions and change" needed to be addressed through reform. The stress should be shifted from "punishment to prevention . . . from individual rights to defense of society." Braun, *Assassination of Gaitán*, 47.

6. Gaitán, "Ideas socialistas," 75.

7. Osorio Lizarazo, *Gaitán*, 68–69

8. This section is based on descriptions of Gaitán's time in Italy found in Osorio Lizarazo, *Gaitán*; Sharpless, *Gaitán of Colombia*; Braun, *Assassination of Gaitán*; and Robinson, *Movimiento gaitanista*.

9. *El Espectador* of Bogotá, 14 February 1928, p. 1, "Un rato de charla con Jorge Eliécer Gaitán."

10. See *El Tiempo* of Bogotá, 7 March 1928, p. 1, "Le fue concedido el Premio Enrico Ferri al Dr. J.E.G.," accompanied by a picture of a rather dapper-looking Gaitán.

11. *El Espectador* of Bogotá, 14 February 1928, p. 1, "Un rato de charla con Jorge Eliécer Gaitán."

12. Estimates of the number of strikers killed still vary widely, from 80 to over 2,000.

13. Charles Bergquist offers a different interpretation in *Labor in Latin America: Comparative Essays on Chile, Argentina, Venezuela, and Colombia* (Stanford: Stanford University Press, 1986), 279. See also Bergquist, Ricardo Peñaranda, and Gonzalo Sánchez, eds., *Violence in Colombia: The Contemporary Crisis in Historical Perspective* (Wilmington, DE: Scholarly Resources, 1992).

14. "Communist Activities in Colombia," 16 June 1943, U.S. State Department (hereafter SD), 821.00B/92.

15. Memorandum, 1 February 1938, attached to Despatch no. 1991, 8 January 1938, SD 821.00B/67. Gaitán's campaign biographer argues that he was an advocate of "leftist Liberalism" of a "socialist tendency," under which economic relations could be regulated, Milton Puentes, *Gaitán* (Bogotá: Editorial ABC, 1945), 37.

16. Braun, *Assassination of Gaitán*, 64.

17. Sharpless, *Gaitán of Colombia*, 75.

18. Jointly known as the Gracchi, the brothers held the office of "Tribune of the People," advocated land distribution, and were both murdered in the Roman Senate. Their deaths are widely recognized as one of the major contributing factors to the fall of the ancient Roman Republic.

19. Letter from Juan Manuel Valdelamar to JEG, Cartagena, 17 April 1945; Archive of the Instituto Colombiano de Participación JEG (hereafter AICPG), v.0053 "Cartas Bolívar."

20. Just as Gaitán was gearing up for his run at the presidency, the PSR seemed preoccupied with foreign policy, as U.S. State Department observers noted, "Communist Activities in Colombia," 16 June 1943, SD 821.00B/92.

21. For a good example of this phenomenon, see Ramón Manrique, *Bajo el signo de la hoz: La conjuntura del comunismo en Colombia* (Bogotá: Editorial ABC, 1937), 66–68.

22. Ibid., pp. 16–17. Manrique called himself a friend of many Communists, a Liberal "of the blood," and a "child of the Revolución en Marcha," 141–43.

23. *La Tribuna* of Barranquilla, 7 March 1938, p. 1, "La propaganda comunista."

24. *El Mitín* of Cartagena, 28 January 1936.

25. *El Estado* of Santa Marta, 1 February 1943. The *comunistas criollos* were called "unconditional instruments of Moscow," who agitated against religion. Letter from Santiago Pozo to the editor of *El Estado*, 10 January 1946. Gaitanistas in Ciénaga called the Communist Party a "sickness" rising from the "putrid corpses of Marx and Lenin." Letter from seven "fervientes admiradores y compatriotas" to JEG, Ciénaga, 21 June 1945; AICPG v.0011 "Cartas Magdalena."

26. *El Estado* of Santa Marta, 26 April 1946, p. 3.

27. Though the Colombian Communists have long since publicly declared mea culpa concerning their injudicious opposition to Gaitanismo, some Communists have remained unrepentant. In the 1960s, Communist elder Ignacio Torres Giraldo still maintained that Gaitán could not have been anything other than a "candidate of Conservative manipulation," Ignacio Torres Giraldo, *Los inconformes: Historia de la rebeldía de las masas en Colombia* (Bogotá: Editorial Latina, 1967), vol. 5, 1396 and 1401. In the same vein, a one-time director of Fedenal (the river workers' labor federation and Communist stronghold) argued that Gaitán was simply a fascist. Interview by Mauricio Archila with Roberto Insignares, 14 June 1986.

28. From the FBI report, "Summary of Communist Activities in Colombia, January 1947," 5 February 1947, SD 821.00B/3-1047.

29. *Diario Popular*, 28 August 1945, p. 2, "El Apostol Desnudo." See Fermín López Giraldo, *El apostol desnudo, o dos años al lado de un mito* (Manizales: Editorial Arturo Zapata, 1936).

30. *Diario Popular*, 23 January 1946, p. 3, "Contra los obreros y el progreso de Pereira se unen godos y gaitanistas."

31. *Diario Popular*, 5 September 1945, p. 2, "Gaitán, mampara de la reacción." *Diario Popular*, 28 September 1945; *El Nacional* of Barranquilla, 28 September 1945.

32. *El Espectador* of Bogotá, 14 February 1928, p. 1, "Un rato de charla con Jorge Eliécer Gaitán."

33. Interview with Gaitán by *El Tiempo* of Bogotá from early 1928, paraphrased by Sharpless, *Gaitán of Colombia*, 52.

34. In contrast to Gaitán, Juan Perón's personal admiration for the fascist state was never in doubt. He served between 1939 and 1941 as a military observer in one of Italy's Alpine Divisions near the French border and for a short time with the Argentine embassy in Rome. He was impressed by the "pageantry" and machine-like nature of the Italian state. This "master impression" would "inspire, and in part, reinforce the distinctly pro-Axis coloration of Perón's views concerning the war and Argentina's relationship to it. Yet even in Perón's case, it is difficult to label him an outright fascist." Robert Crassweller, *Perón and the Enigmas of Argentina* (New York: W. W. Norton and Company, 1987), 85–89.

14

Between Crusade and Revolution: Two Argentines in Civil War Spain[1]

Silvina Montenegro

The struggle for independence soured many Latin Americans' relations with Spain, but late nineteenth-century modernization and its attendant social changes often pressed elites of the region to reconsider their Hispanic heritage as a source for national identity creation. In Argentina, the nation most altered by European immigration in all of the Americas, interest in Spanish culture and political values was quite strong in the early twentieth century. Argentines across a wide political spectrum committed themselves to preserving and revitalizing the influence of Hispanic culture in their homeland. They did so from the conviction that maintaining relations with the long-spurned mother country was essential for the very survival of Argentine culture, which they viewed as being under attack by other European influences.

Argentine historian Silvina Montenegro focuses upon the dramatic impact that the Spanish Civil War (1936–1939) had upon the Argentine population, which had finally begun to embrace its Spanish heritage. The Civil War began when conservative political groups led by Francisco Franco rose up against the Popular Front government that had been elected to power in 1936. Although ostensibly a national conflict, it resonated throughout the world for many people who considered it to represent a showdown between liberal republicanism and fascism, which was then gaining strength in Hitler's Germany and Mussolini's Italy. Montenegro asserts that Argentines felt connected to the Spanish war on an intellectual and political level and that they divided their support among the Republicans and the Conservatives led by Franco. On an emotional, almost psychic plane, they saw in Spain a conflict that echoed tensions within their own nation. Both Monsignor Franceschi and Dr. Gregorio Bermann, the two Argentine travelers here discussed, were engaged with Spain on these two levels.

From "Entre la cruzada y la revolución: Dos argentinos en la España de la Guerra Civil," unpublished paper. Translated by Ingrid E. Fey

Montenegro's description of the trips to Civil War Spain by two Argentines of radically different political views reiterates a number of themes evident in earlier selections. Above all, Montenegro's chapter highlights the importance of Europe as a mirror in which Latin Americans considered their own image. Her chapter also recounts another instance of Latin Americans traveling to the "source" of inspiring political, social, and economic experiments in order to experience them firsthand. Finally, Montenegro's article underscores yet again just how actively Latin Americans, although seemingly "peripheral" to the "center" of global politics and economics, participated in events taking place in that center.

> The audacity of Catholicism's enemies grows day by day. Just because we have not yet reached the extremes now found in Spain, even though seeming providential, does not mean that we will never reach such a state, if things continue as they have been.
>
> —Monsignor Franceschi[2]

> The image of Spain held in Latin America was more than that it was poor; it was an image of a nation in clear decadence, in irredeemable backwardness. . . . Now, what a difference! . . . The America of Hispanic origin always had a hunger and thirst for Spain. . . . Yes, we Latin Americans today have the revelation of Spain, which we are recently discovering. Today we are true brothers!
>
> —Dr. Gregorio Bermann[3]

In 1936 the world prepared itself to shatter into a thousand pieces, and Spain was the scene of the first act of this drama.[4] Men and women from all over the globe gathered there to take part in this decisive battle. Some of those who arrived in Spain enlisted in one or the other army; others participated in support work behind the lines; still others observed the turmoil close up and recorded their impressions. For all, the future of humanity seemed to hover in the pitched battles between rebel fascist forces led by General Francisco Franco and those of the struggling Spanish Republican government.

Much has been said and written about the role of the governments and citizens of Italy, Germany, the Soviet Union, France, England, and the United States in the Spanish Civil War. Curiously, in spite of the close and ancestral ties between Spain and Spanish America, the impact of the war on Latin American societies has been much less studied.[5] In the case of Argentina, the Spanish conflict gradually began to correspond to a number of internal problems that transformed the conflict into a struggle in which not only the future of Europe or Spain was at stake. Indeed, for many Argentines, Spain became the land in which the destiny of Argentina would be determined.

This chapter analyzes the trips to Spain of Monsignor Gustavo Franceschi and Dr. Gregorio Bermann, two Argentine men with different personal histories and professions, and with diametrically opposed ideologies. Their observations of Civil War Spain were not intended to be mere travel accounts of the countryside or traditional customs. For both men, their impressions were infused with active political purpose. Both undertook their voyages to search for possible answers to the problems of their homeland and of the world that most preoccupied them. Following their trips to Spain, both men acted and thought with newly acquired perspectives that only their travel experiences could have produced.

Prelude to a Rediscovery

By the end of the nineteenth century, signs were evident of a change in Argentines' attitudes toward Spain, their nation's former mother country. Maligned during the decades following Independence as being the symbol of backwardness, barbarism, and traditionalism, now Argentina looked to the Spanish peninsula in its search for political and cultural models. Paradoxically, Spanish models aided in the construction of both a conservative and Catholic tradition and a liberal and progressive one. During the period between the First and Second World Wars, a process continued to unfold that reached its climax during the years of the Spanish Civil War (1936–1939). During these years, Spain moved to occupy center stage, for it was believed that from Spain's troubles could be extracted lessons that were applicable to Argentina's reality.

During the first decades of the twentieth century, Argentine society reconciled itself with its Spanish roots, which for several decades had been forgotten, hidden, or denied. This renewed interest had begun in the last years of the previous century, when the former mother country, no longer appearing as a potential threat to the independence of the new Latin American republics, completed a process of withdrawal from the imperialistic scene with the loss of its last colonies in a continent that in other times had been its own.

Various factors accelerated this change in attitude toward Spain. On one hand, the increasingly zealous advances of the United States on the region had produced a growing antagonism between "Anglo-Saxons" and "Latins." In this context, Spain stopped being seen as an enemy or retrograde nation in order to promote solidarity among the victims of the new U.S. imperialism. During this same time, Argentina was undergoing rapid transformations as it received hundreds of thousands of European immigrants. In the space of just a few years, a good part of the traditional

Creole population began to view the recent arrivals as threatening to both social order and the nation. For traditional sectors, of which Monsignor Franceschi was a member, the only way to define *argentinidad*, or the essence of Argentine-ness, was to look for their roots in the colonial, Catholic, and Hispanic past, which predated the era of massive immigration.[6] At the same time, liberal and left-wing groups in which Bermann was involved rescued a different Spanish past, which emphasized the traces of an enlightened, progressive, and revolutionary tradition.[7]

Gustavo Franceschi: The Crusade for Devastated Churches in Spain

At the end of April 1937, Monsignor Gustavo Franceschi arrived in the Spanish port city of Cádiz accompanied by thirty-seven boxes of sacred ornaments and vessels, which was the fruit of a collection drive organized by the hierarchy of the Argentine Catholic Church.[8] Planned by Franceschi and ecclesiastical authorities following an invitation from General Franco, his trip was viewed as being both an evangelical mission and a journalistic tour.

Monsignor Gustavo Franceschi (1881–1952) was one of the most brilliant intellectuals in the Argentine Catholic Church and played an active role in the social and cultural controversies of his time. In the 1920s the Church had chosen him to promote the work of the Catholic Popular Union in Argentina, an organization that joined lay activities under the authority of the bishops.[9] Later, he played an important role in the creation of the Acción Católica Argentina—inspired by the Action Française—for which he was an untiring speaker in its courses of indoctrination.[10] From 1932 until his death, he edited the nationalist Catholic journal *Criterio*. As an admirer of the dictatorships of Engelbert Dollfus in Austria and Oliveira de Salazar in Portugal, Franceschi found Franco to be the model Catholic leader. Indeed, Franco appeared to be the only man capable of regaining the preferential role that the Church had enjoyed for centuries. His trip to the Spanish peninsula reaffirmed and consolidated his admiration for the caudillo Franco.

The archbishop of Buenos Aires and first cardinal of Argentina, Monsignor Copello, had headed a fundraising drive aimed at collecting donations of jewels and other valuable objects from local elite families. The Crusade for Devastated Churches in Spain, which was the name of the undertaking, succeeded in collecting considerable sums that were then turned over to their beneficiaries by Monsignor Franceschi (Figure 6).

Under the pretext of extending aid from Argentine Catholics to their Spanish counterparts, the priest could not hide the eminently political character of his voyage, which he viewed as being intimately connected to the evangelical: "the duty of every good Catholic is to assist Spain in its struggle against communism."[11] With his acid pen he responded to

During the Spanish Civil War, the Argentine Catholic Church exhorted wealthy women to donate their jewels for the benefit of churches, which fell under the purview of Franco's cause. From *Falange Española*, 1936.

attacks by those who observed with disapproval the more political than evangelical nature of his trip. For the priest it was clear that "to expose and attack enemies of the Faith" was an eminently priestly duty: "[Perhaps] a priest who ventures to Spain in order to take religious objects . . . is obligated to turn over these objects and return, without learning anything; he should forget that he is a journalist and abstain from publicizing what he sees; . . . he should stifle his Christian vocation, abandoning [his duty] to reveal the path of truth and justice."[12] The links between the traveler and Spanish nationalist authorities were evident. General Franco received him personally in a special audience, and during Franceschi's brief stay he succeeded in interviewing almost all of the military chiefs who headed the uprising against the Spanish Republic.

During the months in which the ecclesiastical dignitary stayed in Spanish territory, he toured the zones then under nationalist control, observing firsthand the wounded cities of war: Málaga, Seville, Córdoba, Toledo, Avila, Salamanca, and the Basque region, which had been only recently brought under rebel control. From his profoundly disturbing pilgrimage, Franceschi continued to send weekly editorials for *Criterio*. The Spanish drama, which until then had occupied an important place in the journal, now became its axis and epicenter; the reality of both Argentina and the world could now be explained starting from Spain. His experience in the land of struggle was gradually carrying him to an exaltation of Franco's government that Franceschi could not and would not hide and that was absolute and without nuance. For example, in a commentary on a biography about Franco, Franceschi wrote: "In order to be won, the war needs a chief, and for the chief to be the best leader, it is necessary that he can count upon the love and admiration of those who toil under his orders and sympathize with his cause, which is the cause of a heroic and missionizing Spain of yesterday and tomorrow. . . . And even though Franco's soldiers are not unaware of who he is and what their chief has done, it is certain that the life of this extraordinary military man contains lessons that will never be sufficiently learned."[13] In general, uniformity rather than disunity was his primary impression of Franquista Spain. Franceschi

spoke with the inhabitants of the towns and cities that he visited. He could
not hide his satisfaction with the unanimity of their loyalty to the new
regime: "[there was] no one who doubted, no one who was not perfectly
in line with the spirit of the movement led by General Franco."[14]

Meanwhile, Franceschi's trip provoked indignation and ridicule in the
Argentine republican press, with which he had carried on bitter arguments
in the past few years[15]: "Monsignor Franceschi's trip to the rebel zone has
done him much harm. His stay of a few months with Moroccans, German
heretics, and generals without honor, has taught him many ugly and un-
Christian things. In the first place, he learned to lie, an ugly thing in a
minister of God, since he returned from there with a pack of lies and with
his blood poisoned by hatred and falsity. In the second place, he also
learned to defend causes of little decency. . . . Decidedly, Monsignor
Franceschi is bursting out of his cassock."[16] In nationalist Spain, Franceschi
found both a model and a warning. Spain had become the terrible lesson
of what could happen in Argentina if a stop was not put on the "anti-
Catholic and anti-Argentine campaign" that was emerging in the presence of general tolerance. The indivisibility of Catholicism and nationality
was clear in Franceschi's mind. Catholicism had shaped Hispanic culture,
the basic essence of Spanish nationality, and also of Argentine nationality. Consequently, "to reject the Church is necessarily . . . to reject the
fatherland."[17]

Not only did Franceschi believe that Argentines should take from Spain
their morality, spirituality, and Catholicism, but he also was convinced of
the necessity of liquidating democratic institutions and installing a strong
leadership that could contain social protests and halt the advance of communism.[18] Shortly after abandoning Spanish territory, news broke of the
death of pro-Franco General Mola in an airplane accident. Franceschi,
who had had occasion to speak with him during his visit to the Basque
front, dedicated a panegyrical editorial to him entitled "The Chief": "Serene, methodical, energetic without arrogance, broad in his vision, leader
of the masses, persistent in his undertakings without shrinking in the face
of adversity, General Mola was truly a *chief* in the most exact sense of the
word. And alongside of him one could place . . . the generalísimo, kind,
. . . obsessed with social justice, desiring to create a *New State*."[19] In this
same article, he highlighted—one more time—a parallel between Spain
and Argentina, comparing the dictatorship of Primo de Rivera with that
of General José F. Uriburu.[20]

Franceschi felt that it was his duty as a priest and intellectual to re-
count his experience in Spain: "Upon my return to Argentina, I will make
known with spoken word and pen what I was able to see in Spain. I bless
the time permitted me to contemplate this heroic and noble Spain which
in America is called, with all justice, the Motherland."[21] The notes that he
wrote during and after his trip soon veered away from Spain to discuss

Argentina. The Argentine reading public, as much the pro-republican as the pro-Franco, followed events in Spain with interest and passion. Franceschi directed himself toward readers who included powerful and notable figures, intellectuals, and Catholics. His articles sought to transport those who read them to the heart of Spain, through images that were simultaneously vivid and simple: "Imagine any of my readers in Buenos Aires, stripped of his legitimate authority and turned over without controls or restraints to groups of individuals who are totally ignorant, dominated by unrestrained passions, drunk with the combined alcohol of hate and power."[22] Given his hair-raising accounts in which he offered detailed narration of the profanation of temples, assassinations of Catholics, violation of proprieties—not to mention torture and even cannibalism—it is not difficult to imagine the profound commotion that these tales must have provoked in the journal's readers. In their writings, the clergy called out to "those who have eyes to see, intelligence to think," for they were "the only ones capable of saving our Argentine collective."[23]

When his trip to Spain was completed, Franceschi spent a few days in France before undertaking his return to Buenos Aires. Once home, he threw himself into a narration of the war in Spain. One year from the start of the rebellion, he published a pamphlet entitled *El movimiento católico español y el criterio católico*, in order to counteract the effect that the declarations of a group of French Catholic intellectuals on the Spanish situation had had on Argentine public opinion. These intellectuals—principally Jacques Maritain—had sought to distance themselves from the pro-Franco position upheld by the Church. Writing with pedagogical and propagandistic intentions, Franceschi proposed to demonstrate that "the seditious ones are the men of the (republican) government" and that "justice is with the revolutionaries (the Franquistas)."[24] But, fundamentally, he aimed to define the conflict as a new crusade, as a "holy war." The similarities were clear in the mind of this Catholic priest: "Is the Bolshevik war against Christian civilization any less harsh than that waged seven centuries ago by the followers of the Koran?"[25] For Franceschi, the answer was a definitive and defiant "no."

Gregorio Bermann: An Argentine Doctor in Republican Spain

Only a few weeks had passed from the outset of the Spanish conflict when Gregorio Bermann decided to offer his services as a psychiatrist to the Spanish Republican government. The expenses for his travel and stay would be paid entirely from his own resources, since he was a man of some economic means. Even so, the bureaucratic obstacles and the suspicions that he had to allay were numerous, and his first offer to the Spanish Republican government, made in September 1936, was politely refused.[26] This rejection did not dishearten the Argentine doctor, for he pressed his cause yet again before the Spanish ambassador in Buenos Aires, who interceded on his behalf in favor of the projected trip: "Dr. Gregorio Bermann . . . who has always made ample show of his commitment to the legitimate, popular Government of Spain, has once again offered his services, and it appears that he is willing to move at his own expense to our country. . . . This man occupies an economically comfortable position . . . and his reiterated offer is not the result of financial difficulties, but rather of his desire to collaborate."[27] In early 1937, without waiting for a positive result from Spanish authorities, Bermann embarked for Spain at the head of a medical mission composed of Argentine doctors, medical students, and nurses who were going to lend their services to hospitals in Madrid and Barcelona.

Gregorio Bermann, intellectual, philosopher, political militant, doctor, and one of the pioneers of psychoanalysis in Argentina, was born in 1896.[28] He was the youngest of eight brothers from a Jewish family that had emigrated from Poland when his older brothers faced conscription in the Czar's army. In his youth, Bermann became a student political activist; he was the president of the University Federation of Buenos Aires and one of the leaders of the Student Reform Movement of 1918.[29] He spent the 1920s in the relative calm of Córdoba, where he held the chair of legal medicine at the University.[30] The military coup of 1930 brought an end to the Radical governments and to the tranquility of the young doctor's life, when he was fired from his post at the University for political reasons. As a militant in the Socialist Party, Bermann agreed in 1932—for the first and only time—to be the candidate of the opposition group Alianza Civil for Córdoba's gubernatorial race.[31] Soon afterward, he abandoned the partisan militancy of socialism and, like many Argentine intellectuals of the epoch, moved closer to the Communist Party. Nevertheless, Bermann never became a member of the party and always maintained a certain independence that—as will become evident later—caused him more than a few difficulties.

Already preoccupied with the spread of fascism in Europe, the outbreak of the Spanish Civil War moved Bermann profoundly. He immediately threw himself into the creation of Committees to Aid the Spanish People in his home province of Córdoba, running from town to town to stimulate the formation of new groups. He also lent the use of the park adjoining his psychiatric clinic for picnics and other events designed to raise money for the Spanish republicans. Even so, all help seemed inadequate to help the Spanish Republic, which struggled heroically for the destiny of all humanity: "Often sympathetic liberals and leftists appease their consciences by giving just a few cents. But one's duty should be accomplished in another manner. In these moments, what is at stake is not only the independence of Spain now in the clutches of fascism, but also to a large extent the destiny of one or more generations."[32] Upon arriving in Spain, Bermann practiced his specialty, psychiatry, in the service of the Sanidad Militar of the Loyal Army. Beyond his specific functions as a doctor, he represented numerous Argentine institutions of which

he was a member: the Argentine University Federation, the Committee to Aid the Spanish People, and the Hispano-American Committee of the Alliance of Intellectuals for the Defense of Culture. During his stay of just over a year in Spain, his work was not limited to medicine: he participated in congresses, gave speeches, founded the Committee of Hispano-American Relations in Madrid, and mingled with many Spanish political and cultural leaders (Figure 7).

In spite of the obstacles, personal risks, and economic costs, Bermann had decided to cross the ocean because he believed that the battle for the future freedom of his own nation was being contested on Spanish soil: "because in this war in

Dr. Gregorio Bermann, Madrid (?), c. 1937.
Courtesy of Sylvia Bermann

Spain, the future of many peoples in the world, and especially of the Latin countries of America, is being decided, because the result of the conflict between fascism and liberty will have repercussions there."[33] Bermann wanted to see what was happening in Spain and to be a doctor for the wounded. He participated in the Congress of Antifascist Intellectuals in Valencia, where he presented a paper on the psychopathology of fascism and established relationships with a few of the most widely known leftist intellectuals in Europe during those years, including the French writer André Malraux and the German playwright Bertolt Brecht. Among the personalities from the realm of Hispano-American letters and politics, he established ties with left-wing Spanish republicans Luis Jiménez de Asúa, Guillermo de la Torre, Rafael Alberti and his wife María Teresa León— all of whom became exiles in Argentina at the end of the War—Antonio Machado, Chilean poet Pablo Neruda, Cuban poet Nicolás Guillén, Peruvian poet César Vallejo, and Spanish jurist Luis Companys, who was president of the Generalitat de Cataluña and with whom Bermann enjoyed a personal relationship. All of these people, who were outstanding figures in the world of culture during the interwar period, were linked by a strong commitment to democracy, personal freedoms, and progress. Politically, they were tied to the left—either to communism or socialism—which at that time regarded fascism as its principal enemy.

Bermann's stay in Spain was not without difficulties. His open, restless, and curious character made him anxious to know for himself everything that was happening in Spain. Quickly, his inquisitive personality raised the suspicions of the Spanish Communist Party, who questioned why this man meddled in all places and asked questions about everything. In fact, he was about to be imprisoned under the suspicion of being a spy, when assurances from his friends in the Argentine Communist Party saved him from an uncertain fate.[34]

Beyond a few reports and notes in the left-wing press of Argentina, his first impressions of the war appeared in the book, *Dialéctica del fascismo*, published in Madrid in 1937. With the hope of offering a useful contribution for psychiatric treatment in the Second World War, Bermann published *Las neurosis en la Guerra* at the end of 1940. The book recapped his experiences in a hospital center in Madrid, in addition to speeches and classes offered in his specialty.[35] The scientific nature of the work did not exclude a political thesis, for the doctor wanted to demonstrate that the mental health of the republican combatants suffered less harm during the war because these soldiers approached the struggle imbued with high ideals and deeply felt convictions. By contrast, nationalist soldiers fought out of obligation, with disastrous results for the psyche.

Gregorio Bermann's experience in Spain lasted slightly more than a year and, after a brief stay in France, he returned to his country at the end of 1938. Although he enjoyed prominence in the worlds of science and culture, he nevertheless found it difficult to reintegrate himself after almost two years outside of the country. His contact with the political and social realities of Spain left deep impressions on his manner of taking positions and analyzing reality because, in his mind, the struggle in Argentina also defined itself in terms of privileged minorities (landowners, military men, conservatives) against the popular majority, which was the true bearer of truth and justice. Nevertheless, the conclusion of the Spanish Civil War appeared to make evident the triumph—temporary in the long range, but unavoidable in the present—of the reactionary sectors. The defeat of the republicans in Spain also produced in him a state of depression and pessimism. Indeed, Franco's entrance into Madrid brought to an end not only his dreams of a new revolution that would emulate and improve upon the Russian Revolution but also of the democratic system. At the same time, the victory of Franquism, which came to complete the victories of Italian Fascism and German Nazism, augured ill for the destiny of Latin America. For many years, Bermann would maintain vivid recollections of Spain, for the wounds had not yet closed: "For the America of Hispanic origin, Spain continued as a thorn in the side of the Left, which is to say, in the zone of the heart."[36] With the passage of time, Gregorio Bermann would deepen his distance from the official line of the Communist Party and his internationalist commitment—including his Hispanist and Latin Americanist vein—to other revolutionary processes. Twenty years later, his militant support of the Cuban Revolution would revive the solidarity that he had put into practice in Spain.

In the Wake of Spain

Franceschi and Bermann went to Spain during wartime in search of the roots of Argentine problems and hoped to find the solutions to their own nation's problems. In spite of their different perceptions, both men helped to construct an image of Spain with notable commonalties: the bleeding Mother, a heroic people, the struggle for the destiny of humanity. Moreover, they shared a vague notion of the war as the foundation of a better future. They held dear the ideal of heroic life and the exaltation of sacrifice, whether in pursuit of eternal salvation or in working toward a better future here on Earth.

From another perspective, Spain's recent past was useful at the time for finding a reflection of Argentine problems: the coup and uprising against republican institutions, the fascist threat, the Red menace, the proletariat struggling for its liberties, and the military men defending order. For observers from the Left as much as for those of the Right, the similarities between the two situations were evident, so much so that it was possible to construct a universal explanation that would take into account Spanish circumstances as much as those in Argentina. In this sense, the Spanish Civil War comprised for Argentines a personal conflict or one that was at least susceptible to being appropriated by them.

As the stories of Franceschi and Bermann suggest, travel in Civil War Spain could play a vital role in the elaboration and propagation of both the right-wing and left-wing myths that were to have a profound impact on Argentine politics for the rest of the century. For Argentine nationalists, the Spanish conflict served as a unifying myth, behind which traditional, Catholic, and Hispanist sectors—which until then had remained quite dispersed and disunited—established linkages. For them, the Civil War enabled them to deepen their love for old Spain, whose heir-apparent they recognized in Franco in the uprising of July 18. For those who aligned themselves with the opposing side, the Spanish Civil War brought to the most urgent present the nucleus of the historic Spanish drama, and "allowed them to at last passionately identify themselves with a Spain that was no longer the problematic Motherland, but rather a nation that poured out its lifeblood for a struggle that should have been the struggle of all."[37]

Notes

1. This article is part of a larger research project entitled "Argentine Politics
and the Spanish Civil War," which is being undertaken with the support of a
scholarship from the University of Buenos Aires. The author would like to express her gratitude to the Instituto de Historia of the Centro de Humanidades
(under the Consejo Superior de Investigaciones Científicas) in Madrid for research support and assistance.

2. *Criterio*, May 13, 1937, p. 34.

3. Words spoken by Bermann in Madrid to military and civilian chiefs of that
city in May 1937. Reproduced in Gregorio Bermann, *Conciencia de nuestro tiempo*
(Buenos Aires: Editorial Hernández, 1971), 95–97.

4. In April of 1931 the Republic was proclaimed. It was born of elections in
which the overwhelming triumph of the republican parties resulted in the abdica-
tion and escape of King Alfonso XIII. The modernizing forces that gave impulse
to the new regime—especially during the two-year period of 1931–1933—aspired to yank Spain out of its ancestral backwardness. Their programs of agrarian, ecclesiastical, educational, and military reform pushed the population to divide
itself between those who supported the changes and those who felt attacked by
them. In February 1936 the elections were won by the Popular Front, a coalition
of republican and leftist parties that were united against the advance of fascism—
a group similar to the alliance formed by Léon Blum in France. The Popular
Front's primary aim was to deepen the reforms initiated five years earlier. Defeated in the elections of February, the conservative sectors understood that their
only way out was institutional rupture; in other words, a coup against the state.
Political violence between February and July of 1936 only exacerbated antagonisms. On July 18, 1938, a group of military men, who had been conspiring against
the government for several months, rose up simultaneously in different parts of
the peninsula, with slightly uneven successes. This uprising led to a Civil War
that lasted almost three years and culminated in March 1939 with the victory of
Francisco Franco, of the conservative forces. See Raymond Carr, *La tragedia
española* (Madrid: Alianza Editorial, 1986); Stanley Payne, *La primera
democracia española: La Segunda República, 1931–1936* (Barcelona: Ediciones
Paidós, 1995); Paul Preston, ed., *Revolución y Guerra en España, 1931–1939*
(Madrid: Alianza Editorial, 1984); Hugh Thomas, *La Guerra Civil Española*
(Barcelona: Ediciones Grijalbo, 1976).

5. Among those studies that most merit mention are: Mark Falcoff and Frederick
Pike, eds., *The Spanish Civil War, 1936–1939: American Hemispheric Perspec-
tives* (Lincoln and London: University of Nebraska Press, 1982); Consuelo Naranjo
Orovio, *Cuba, otro escenario de lucha: La Guerra Civil y el exilio republicano
español* (Madrid: Ediciones del CSIC, 1988); Mónica Quijada, *Aires de República,
Aires de Cruzada: La Guerra Civil Española en Argentina* (Barcelona: Ediciones
Sendai, 1991).

6. Manuel Gálvez, *El Solar de la raza* (Madrid: Editorial Saturnino Calleja,
1913); *España y algunos españoles* (Buenos Aires: Editorial Huarpes, 1945). For
a more nuanced view, see Ricardo Rojas, *Retablo Español* (Buenos Aires: Editorial Losada, 1938).

7. Julio V. González, *Filiación histórica del Gobierno Representativo Argentino*
(Buenos Aires: Editorial La Vanguardia, 1937); Aníbal Ponce, *Viento en el mundo:
Examen en la España actual* (Buenos Aires: Editorial El Ateneo, 1939); Manuel
Ugarte, *Visiones de España (Apuntes de un viajero argentino)* (Valencia: F. Sempere
y Compañía Editores, n.d.).

8. *La Nación*, May 10, 1937, p. 2.

9. The author thanks Professor María Esther Rapalo of the University of Buenos Aires for this and other facts on the life of Gustavo Franceschi.

10. Founded in 1898 and led by writer Charles Maurras, the Action Française operated on the extreme right of French politics. It was an intensely nationalistic organization that viewed as its mission the cleansing of France of such "un-French" elements as Protestants, Freemasons, and Jews. The group also advocated a renewed embrace of Catholicism and monarchism as a way of reinvigorating the French nation. Gordon Wright, *France in Modern Times*, Fourth Edition (New York, London: W. W. Norton and Company, 1987), 264–65. For a study of how the ideas of French right-wing nationalism impacted the Argentine right see David Rock, *Authoritarian Argentina: The Nationalist Movement, Its History and Its Impact* (Berkeley, Los Angeles: University of California Press, 1993) (translator's note).

11. *La Nación*, May 10, 1937, p. 2.

12. *Criterio*, July 1, 1937, p. 200.

13. Commentary on the book *Franco*, by Joaquín Arrarás, *Criterio*, July 15, 1937, p. 243.

14. *La Nación*, May 3, 1937, p. 2.

15. *España Republicana*, April 3, 1937, p. 7.

16. Ibid., March 12, 1938, p. 3.

17. *Criterio*, June 3, 1937, p. 102.

18. Even though in later years there would exist some justification for believing that General Juan Perón would be the one called upon to achieve this destiny, Franceschi viewed his rise to power with displeasure and he opposed himself to Peronism.

19. *Criterio*, June 17, 1937, p. 149. Emphasis given in the original.

20. Uriburu was one of the primary conspirators behind the 1930 military coup that overthrew the democratically elected president Hipólito Irigoyen, head of the Unión Cívica Radical. He also represented conservative Nationalists, who viewed the coup as an opportunity to install a permanent military dictatorship in Argentina. Although Uriburu would eventually lose power to the more moderate General Agustín Justo, Nationalist aspirations for political power would continue to impact Argentine politics for the next decade and beyond, resulting in the 1943 coup led by the Nationalist Grupo de Oficiales Unidos. It was this same coup that launched Juan Perón on his national political career (translator's note).

21. *La Nación*, May 3, 1937, p. 2.

22. *Criterio*, May 6, 1937, p. 5.

23. Ibid.

24. Gustavo Franceschi, *El movimiento católico español y el criterio católico* (Buenos Aires: Ediciones "Criterio," July 1937), 12.

25. Franceschi, *El movimiento católico*, 26.

26. "Seeing as how there are neuro-psychiatric centers in various Spanish towns that serve present needs, the help of foreign doctors is not currently needed." Telegram from the Ministry of War to the Ministry of State, Madrid, September 1936, Archive of the Ministry of Foreign Affairs (Madrid), Legajo R 527, Carpeta 7. "[The] Government is effusively grateful for Dr. Bermann's offer, but its acceptance is not currently necessary." Telegram from the Ministry of State to the Ambassador of Spain in Argentina, Madrid, September 29, 1936, Archive of the Ministry of Foreign Affairs (Madrid), Caja RE 152, Carpeta 11.

27. Enrique Diez Canedo to the Ministry of State, Buenos Aires, January 21, 1937, Archive of the Ministry of Foreign Affairs (Madrid), Caja R 998.

28. Most of the biographical details on the life of Gregorio Bermann come from an interview with his daughter, Dr. Sylvia Bermann, in her home in Córdoba,

Argentina, in Februrary of 1996. The author wishes to thank her for her help and kindness.

29. The Student Reform Movement that began in Córdoba in 1918 and spread to universities throughout Argentina and South America aimed to increase student control of university administration (calling for *cogobierno*, or co-government) and to modernize university curricula (translator's note).

30. "Legal medicine" was a new field that became increasingly institutionalized in Latin America during the 1920s. In legal medicine, racial issues and the field of eugenics greatly influenced how the problems of crime and responsibility were studied and considered. Nancy Leys Stepan, *"The Hour of Eugenics": Race, Gender, and Nation in Latin America* (Ithaca and London: Cornell University Press, 1991), 53 (translator's note).

31. The Alianza Civil was a political coalition formed by the Partido Socialista and the Partido Democrática Progresista. In 1932, in the face of the abstention of the Unión Cívica Radical, the Alianza Civil offered itself in 1932 as an electoral alternative to the Concordancia—an official alliance that eventually won the election.

32. Reports to Gregorio Bermann, published in *La Voz del Interior* of Córdoba, reproduced in *La Nueva España* of Buenos Aires, February 11, 1937, p. 5.

33. *España Republicana*, April 17, 1937, p. 5.

34. "He was there and they almost threw him in the brig because he was the kind of guy who interfered in everything in order to investigate. They thought that he was a spy. Our people who knew him saved him because all of his questioning confirmed the personality of a psychiatrist." Interview with a leader of the Federación de Organismos de Ayuda a la República Española and member of the Argentine Communist Party, Buenos Aires, August 26, 1995.

35. Gregorio Bermann, *Las neurosis en la guerra. Psycología. Psiquiatría. Psicoterapia. Psico-higiene del combatiente*, Prologue by Emilio Mira (Buenos Aires: Editor Aniceto López, 1941).

36. Written by Bermann in December of 1969, in Bermann, *Conciencia de nuestro tiempo*, 107–15.

37. Tulio Halperin-Donghi, "España e Hispanoamérica: Miradas a través del Atlántico (1825–1975)," in *El espejo de la historia: Problemas argentinos y perspectivas hispanoamericanas* (Buenos Aires: Editorial Suramericana, 1987), 100.

15

Marriage by Pros and Cons: Love in a Time of European Exile

Clara Piriz

Although Latin America's political history has been far from peaceful in the two centuries since Independence, the 1970s witnessed a wave of political violence and repression unprecedented in its brutality. In one nation after another, military dictatorships replaced elected governments, in some cases overturning well-established traditions of representative democracy. Military juntas then took it upon themselves to instigate wars against subversion to cleanse their nations of any and all groups pressing for social change. Although less well known than those of Chile and Argentina, Uruguay's military regime had a similarly gruesome record. In its campaign to root out leftist rebels, the Uruguayan military defined all criticism as an "attack on the moral strength of the Armed Forces." By 1979 some 1 percent of all Uruguayans were political prisoners, making Uruguay the nation with the highest number of political prisoners per capita in the world. Moreover, out of a population of only four million, some 500,000 had gone into exile.*

The following letter, written by Clara Piriz, a Uruguayan exile living in the Netherlands, puts a human face to these grim statistics. She is writing to her husband after twelve years of separation caused by his imprisonment, presumably for political activity. The letter not only depicts the toll that exile and imprisonment had taken on their relationship but also describes the different kinds of reactions that Clara's compatriots in the Netherlands were having to the experience of exile in a foreign land. She describes such predictable behaviors as depression over lost social and financial standing and the obsession with aiding the homeland from afar. However, Clara's letter also suggests that the challenges of starting life again in a new land had empowered her and made her more resilient and

From Alicia Partnoy, ed., *You Can't Drown the Fire: Latin American Women Writing in Exile* (Pittsburgh, PA: Cleis Press, 1988), 242–46, trans. by Regina M. Kreger. Reprinted by permission of Cleis Press.

*E. Bradford Burns, *Latin America: A Concise Interpretive History*, 6th ed. (Englewood Cliffs, NJ: Prentice Hall, 1994), 299–300.

focused. Indeed, upon her return to Uruguay, Clara resumed political
activity by working for some time in the organization of the Uruguayan
Women's Plenary.

Abcoude, Holland
May 12, 1984

Dear Kiddo,

I'm writing this letter with no margins, without counting lines, or pages, without measuring my words a damn bit. Our first communication uncensored and uncut.

The big question is if I will manage to write without self-censorship . . . internalized censorship. Fear. My fear of causing you pain, of showing myself as I am, of confusing you in my confusion. . . . My fear of losing what I've gained and gaining what I've lost. . . .

A while ago I wrote you that it would be good for you to try to get out with a passport that would allow you to come and go. Let me explain why. At the heart of the matter it just has to do with another fear: the fear of ruining your life . . . even more.

Living in exile is a bitch. "Sure," you say, "it can't be worse than prison." True, prison is much worse. But, there is one fundamental difference: In prison you have to use all your energy to survive in a situation that doesn't depend on you and that you can't change. To survive in exile you have to use all your energy to change a situation of terrible inertia and, if it changes, it will be only because of your personal effort.

You arrive here with nothing, no friends, no job, no house, no family. You don't understand the system in which you've somehow got to function. The place assigned to you is marginal socially, economically, politically, culturally, emotionally. No one gives a damn about you. You have no history. Or rather, the history you have, no one cares about. Although suddenly it occurs to some reporter to use you as material for an article. A monkey in the zoo. And you accept, of course, because it's part of the political work: call attention to Uruguay, get political pressure. But if you achieve anything, no one cares. There are too many people. Most of all there are too many foreigners. Discrimination exists, and it is rough. It sucks to feel looked down on, it sucks to have to do twice as much to get credit for half. It sucks when you say something and they look at you: "*and where did you crawl out [from]. . . .*" Not to mention worse things, like insults and violence.

But not all of it comes from outside of us; a lot we bring on ourselves. Most of the exiles resist adapting. They don't want to be here; they didn't choose to come to this country; everything is going wrong for them. The Dutch "smell bad"; "*you know how they are.*" The exiles don't want to learn this fucking language, they refuse to give two and be counted for one. *"What for, anyway, if I'm going to leave. . . ."* Result: Many of them have ended up completely screwed. Ten years of doing nothing of any worth, always running around, drinking beer and Geneva gin. Some of them read a lot, they remind me of your brother, a vagabond with books under his arm. Others have made a way for themselves, working like mules. Some have had the advantage of having studied, others of being stubborn workers with the "nasty habit of earning their living." This small group has one other problem: We are isolated because there's not enough time and energy to work, learn the language, etc. . . . and still maintain friend-ships scattered all around the country.

A while ago I was talking with two Chileans and an Argentine woman I see regularly (a recently found remedy for isolation). They said that even though they work, speak Dutch, and have Dutch friends, communi-cation with them had a limit they couldn't cross. I've heard that from other people. I must confess that is not the case with me. I have good friends who are Dutch with whom my communication is excellent.

Well, as you see I'm not painting a very pleasant picture. I can imag-ine that after twelve years in jail this seems banal, but experience shows that once you are here the twelve years of jail don't help you think, *"What a terrific time I'm having."* On the contrary, those years are one more problem.

In your case, there might be some points in your favor. Supposing our relationship works out (another subject altogether), I have made a way that can make your adjustment easier.

You might ask yourself if I am telling you this to try to discourage you. No. What it means is that I know what you'll have to face if you come here. And I don't want to have it on my conscience that I lured you with a siren song.

Our situation is not very encouraging either: two years of living to-gether in very abnormal conditions. Twelve years without seeing each other: you in jail, which has certainly changed you. Neither one of us knows what problems are going to crop up from that. Certainly, within normal limits, you've changed a great deal. But it's also logical to expect less normal changes. There is no superman who can come unscathed out of one of those places. I don't believe those people—and there are some— who come out saying, *"Prison? A great experience, it's nothing."* I also have lived through very hard experiences; I also am very much marked.

Besides, as a couple we're going to face a very strange situation. I have matured in this country, I have carried out a whole process of learning, of critical integration, of getting situated here, which you, one way or another, will have to carry out. This puts you in a position of de-pendence on me, which does not contribute to a healthy adult emotional relationship.

I'm finishing this letter today, June 24. Happy birthday! After yesterday's phone conversation I have such anxiety to see you, to talk to you, to touch you, that I can't imagine how I'm going to live from now until we see each other.

Yet there's so much we will have to discuss and go through!

And don't get all romantic on me and tell me that love, or the will to love, can overcome everything. No. It can overcome a lot, it is an essential condition, but not enough. I've seen so many who could not withstand the pressures of the change.

From a very young age, I have been bothered by rules without reasons, by *just because* or *because I said so* or *because that's the way it has to be*. It has bothered me as much in my social as in my private life. And systematically I have created a new set of rules based on my own experiences, on their analysis and synthesis and also on the reading and studies of the ideas of other (wiser) people. This attitude toward life is not new for me. Just think, if not, Carolina would not exist. Carolina was not an impulse, a mistake, a transgression. For me she was a conscious moral act which I have never regretted.

It was not always easy: For years I struggled inside myself. Because sincerity is one of my values, at times I had to choose between the risk of destroying you or lying in the gentle way, by keeping quiet. Sometimes I kept quiet, sometimes I didn't. Finally I arrived at a formula: I'd try to let you know as best as possible how I felt about a lot of things and avoid the details that could be painful for you.

But my evolution is not only in that area. Most important to me is my maturity and my independence. That's why I made that comment on the phone yesterday: "You are going to have a hard time with me." I don't like to be ordered around, or told what to do. I reaffirm my right to my own decisions, your right to your own decisions, our right to be and think differently.

When I stayed alone with the girls I had to perform all of the roles; I was their mother and their father and their pet dog too. I got used to it and from there I chose what I liked best to do, and that's not necessarily the womanly duties. Therefore (referring to a fantasy you wrote me about that frightened me): If you want homemade ravioli, make them yourself. I'll help you eat them. And I'll drink the wine. As a housekeeper I am consciously a disaster. My work is much more important to me, and my personal and professional development more than anything. For years my possibilities were limited by the urgency of moment-to-moment life, and by the girls' ages. Nevertheless, I got started with a brave effort. Now they are grown, they have their own independence, they're not attached to me, and I have found a phenomenal job. You can imagine that I'm grabbing onto that with all my strength. At my age it's my last chance, and I can't and don't want to miss it.

We don't know what each of us means by "primary relationship." You said it very blithely, as if there was a universally accepted formula. But I am certain that it's not that way. When I was twenty years old, I believed it, but not now, and that is not disillusionment, not at all, it's wisdom.

For instance, you asked me if I had a boyfriend. You didn't know how to deal with my answer. You said that could surely be the biggest stumbling block, and I answer you that the stumbling block is not that he exists . . . but the fact that *I* am capable of having a boyfriend.

I hold that I have been relentlessly faithful. Perhaps not in the way that you mean, but I'd bet if we talked about it, you'd see my way is much better.

Why do I want to see you? Because I do. Because I also allow myself the right to be (every once in a while) compulsive. I'm doing fine, I have a good job, a good social life, a serene and comforting relationship, the girls are growing up with no problems. Then why create problems for myself? Why not leave things as they are? Because I want to see you. Because I would feel terribly frustrated not to see you, because it would be a lack of respect for you, for me, for what we were, for what we are, and perhaps for what we might become. . . . Because I want a second chance. Because only you and I can decide if it'll work or not. That decision is not for time, or distance, much less for the military to take. It's ours.

On the phone I found it hard to say I love you, for fear you misunderstood what I felt. So, I'll say: In my own way I love you. We'll have to see if my way and yours will meet—and grow.

Bye,
Clara

IV

The Art of Living
and Working Abroad

16

So Far from God, So Close to Hollywood: Dolores del Río and Lupe Vélez in Hollywood, 1925–1944

Brian O'Neil

Since the earliest days of Hollywood movie production, U.S. films have found an eager audience in Latin America. In the 1920s, for instance, both popular groups and intellectuals adored Charlie Chaplin. Moreover, long before the likes of Raúl Julia or Sonia Braga hit the screen, actors and actresses from Latin America made their own pilgrimages to Hollywood to make it in the movies. As Chapters 16 and 17 show, few ever made a name for themselves, and, for the ones who did, success was often bittersweet. Typecasting, bad parts, and nagging insecurities about their ability to please both U.S. and Latin American audiences often shadowed their time in Hollywood.

Dolores del Río and Lupe Vélez were two Mexican actresses who found both fame and fortune in Hollywood primarily during the 1920s and 1930s. But, as historian Brian O'Neil explains, their successes were complicated greatly by the fact that they were living in a foreign land. Both women enjoyed many of the social and financial rewards associated with Hollywood stardom; they found U.S. society to be a relatively liberating place for women. Nevertheless, both women were hounded by critics at home who questioned their commitment to their Mexican fans. However, O'Neil posits that del Río and Vélez struggled continually to maintain a sense of national identity while partaking of new ideas, activities, and opportunities. If their continued popularity among the masses in Mexico was any indication of their ability to achieve such a balance, then they were indeed successful.

> No one ever leaves a star, that's what makes one
> a star.
> —Norma Desmond in *Sunset Boulevard* (1950)

"What artist hasn't dreamed of conquering Hollywood?" Miguel de Zárraga, Mexican film critic and dialogue writer, asked the readers of *Hoy* in May 1939. "However great the products of Paris, Mexico, or Buenos Aires may be," de Zárraga continued, "in the world of film Hollywood is the ultimate goal. To be consecrated in Hollywood is the maximum honor and all artists, whether French, Mexican, or Argentine, have their most intimate illusions fixed on Hollywood. To be able to say 'I triumphed in Hollywood!' is the ubiquitous dream that rarely becomes a reality."[1] Indeed, only a handful of Mexican actors, most notably Dolores del Río and Lupe Vélez, achieved Hollywood fame during the American film industry's "classical" period of the 1930s-early 1940s.

The creation of a Hollywood star is always dependent upon the manipulation and marketing of an actor's on-screen representations and his or her off-screen persona as constructed in gossip columns and movie magazines. In the cases of Dolores del Río and Lupe Vélez, this process was further complicated by their desire to achieve fame in the United States while at the same time maintaining a special esteem among Mexican critics and audiences, a delicate balancing act that sometimes proved untenable. With a limited selection of parts from which to choose, del Río and Vélez at times played roles that Mexican critics and officials found offensive. Moreover, as Mexico's own film industry began to establish itself in the late 1930s, many Mexican critics began to reprimand del Río and Vélez not merely for their supposedly demeaning Hollywood representations but also for a much larger offense: disloyalty. The critics contended that by continuing to work in Hollywood at a time when the fledgling national film industry needed them most, del Río and Vélez were turning their backs on Mexico and Mexican moviegoers. Despite this view, del Río and Vélez both returned to Mexico in 1943 and found that, unlike their critics, most Mexican fans had never left them.

It is no coincidence that the only two Mexicans (or Latin Americans, for that matter) to achieve lasting star status in Hollywood during the 1930s were women. Hollywood's racial politics at the time precluded the foregrounding of ethnic men in prominent roles, particularly when paired with Anglo female protagonists. Latin women, on the other hand, were viewed as less threatening. A standard narrative trope for this period demanded that any pronounced ethnicity on the part of a Latin American woman be tamed via a romantic union with a North American male. Such gendered and racialized logic provided the foundation for the rise of del Río and Vélez to Hollywood stardom. Yet, although the careers of both actresses traded to some extent on their exoticism, their respective star images were quite distinct from one another. Del Río was extolled as a cultured, artistic lady of incomparable beauty and grace while Vélez was a wild "Mexican Spitfire," a "Hot Pepper," a tempestuous "primitive soul" of uncontrollable emotion and sexuality. These public images, crafted by the studios' publicity machinery as well as by the actresses themselves, were rooted in the differing social biographies and personalities of each woman.

Dolores del Río, née Lolita Dolores Asúnsolo y López Negrete, was born in 1905 in Durango, Mexico, to an elite family.[2] Shortly before her sixteenth birthday, her father, a prominent banker and *hacendado*, arranged for her marriage to Jaime Martínez del Río, scion of one of the wealthiest families in Mexico. After a two-year honeymoon traveling in Europe, del Río settled into the comfortable life of a young society matron. In 1925 she met Edwin Carewe, an American director, in Mexico City. Instantly enraptured by her beauty, Carewe determined to bring her to Hollywood. While her parents and in-laws were against such a "low-brow" proposition, del Río's husband, who harbored screenwriting ambitions of his own, consented, and the two moved north that same year.

Del Río's rise to stardom was meteoric. Carewe groomed her with increasingly larger parts in four of his 1925–26 films. Her big break came as a French peasant in Raoul Walsh's silent classic *What Price Glory?* (1926). Following this success, Carewe further showcased del Río's talent as a dramatic actress when she played a Russian peasant in his 1927 adaptation of Tolstoy's *Resurrection*. By 1929, after having triumphed in big-budget features such as *Ramona* (1928), opposite Warner Baxter, and *Evangeline* (1929), del Río's name was regularly mentioned in the Hollywood press in the same breath with the top actresses of the period, such as Gloria Swanson and Joan Crawford.

With the coming of "talkies" in 1929, there was concern among studio production heads as to whether their top silent stars would maintain the same drawing power within the new format. Appearing in only one film in 1930–31, the mediocre *The Bad One* (1930), del Río's transition to sound pictures initially lagged due more to personal than artistic reasons. In mid-1928, Dolores filed for divorce from her husband Jaime, claiming that his incessant jealousy of her success was intolerable. Jaime died a few months after moving to Europe, and many of the Hollywood and Mexico City gossip columnists blamed Dolores for putting the interests of her career before those of her disintegrating marriage. On the heels of such bad press, Dolores felt compelled in 1930 to dissolve her five-year working relationship with Carewe when the director began to express a romantic interest in his former starlet. In that same year, Dolores met Cedric Gibbons, the renowned MGM art director, and, after a whirlwind courtship, the two wed in August. Such turbulence in her personal life took its toll. Soon after her marriage, Dolores suffered a mysterious illness (some speculated a breakdown) that kept her out of motion pictures for over a year.

By early 1932, del Río had regained her health, and her career resumed more or less where it had left off. She signed a multiyear contract with RKO Studios and quickly starred in two million-dollar productions: *The Girl of the Rio* (1932), in which she played a cantina femme fatale named Paloma, and *Bird of Paradise* (1932), in which she played the title role of a Polynesian princess.[3] While many actors from the silent era were forced to retire because their voices were not audio-friendly, either because of tone or, as in the case of many foreign players, because their accents were too strong, del Río's move to talkies was seamless. Although she took a few English and acting classes to prepare for the new medium, her voice, which had a suave "international" resonance without being markedly Latin American, proved a natural hit with producers and audiences alike.

Del Río's voice, combined with her light complexion, dignified carriage, and cosmopolitan background, was an integral part of her screen image (Figure 8). Ana Lopéz has adroitly characterized this image as "a

vague upper-class exoticism articulated within a general category of 'foreign/other' tragic sensibility."[4] Although imbued with a definite aura of foreignness, del Río's screen image was not ethnically specific— that is to say, her star appeal tended to be more sexual than ethnic. This was especially true after she struck a 1933 agreement with RKO which gave her the power to approve her own scripts. While early in her career she frequently played exotic Latinas (*The Loves of Carmen*, 1927), Indian maidens (*Ramona*), and Island princesses (*Bird of Paradise*), del Río began to demand roles steeped with a modernity and sophistication made visually obvious by her wardrobe. "I do not want to

This 1936 publicity shot reveals Hollywood's image of Dolores del Río as glamorous and cosmopolitan but not particularly ethnic. *Courtesy of the Academy of Motion Picture Arts and Sciences*

wear exotic clothes [any longer]," she told *Photoplay* magazine. "I want to be *very*, *very* fashionable. I want to show fashion through architectural lines."[5] She did just that in her next role as an aristocratic *carioca* (Rio native) in the hit musical *Flying Down to Rio* (1933), as well as in her other standout films of the 1930s: *Wonder Bar* (1934), *Madame Du Barry* (1934), *In Caliente* (1935), *Devil's Playground* (1937), and *International Settlement* (1938).

In addition to her screen portrayals, del Río's star image as a paragon of modern, cultured femininity was further bolstered by her marriage to Cedric Gibbons. A student of both modern architecture and design, Gibbons built a custom-designed residence in the hills overlooking Santa Monica Bay to celebrate his union with del Río. Fusing Modernist techniques with a Spanish mission-style framework, Gibbons created an Art Deco masterpiece, heralded up to the present day as a bold example of modern architecture in Southern California.[6] The site of regular luncheons and parties with Hollywood's elite throughout the 1930s, Gibbons's streamlined castle provided the perfect setting for del Río to play the role of "hostess in the modern manner"[7] (Figure 9).

Photographed in 1942 with Hollywood film goddess Marlene Dietrich admiring a Frida Kahlo self-portrait, Dolores del Río was ever the symbol of sophistication. *Courtesy of the Academy of Motion Picture Arts and Sciences*

While del Río relished draping herself in the modern fashions and designs of North American consumer culture, she steadfastly held on to the traditional gender conventions she had learned as a pampered girl in Durango. In one of the many fan magazine articles in which she was asked to expound on the romantic differences between the United States and Mexico, del Río extolled the "passive love" of Mexico. "Life does not hurt sheltered women," she explained to American movie fans in 1934. "There are no disillusionments, no rash disappointments for her to suffer through. She knows only the sweet beauty of love and the joy of her own calm domesticity." In choosing a career over the contentment of "calm domesticity," del Río told readers that she had "paid for her picture success a thousand times over" and often wished that she could have been "like those other convent girls I went to school with in Mexico." While she admired the way in which "American girls go after life with much gusto," she personally preferred the passive approach to love supposedly favored by her countrywomen. In summing up her views on the ways of love above and below the Rio Grande, del Río echoed the prominent stereotypes that each country held of the other: "It is all so simple here. I am always amazed at how quickly American girls get over a broken romance. In my country, girls die for love. When the adored one does not respond with lasting affection, the Latin girl has been known to pine away, in quiet solitude, until she died. It is really beautiful and very sentimental to suffer for love, no? In my country, love does not come so quickly. It is inspired by starlight and flowers and the gentle music [of the suitor's guitar]. The American girl has her freedom, true. But I think she cheats herself of so much of the chivalry which men in my country display."[8]

Despite her admonishments on the virtues of feminine passivity and domesticity, del Río herself was a committed career woman. While painfully cognizant of some of the sacrifices she had had to make in her personal life in order to achieve Hollywood stardom, she declared that "in spite of all that, I would not exchange my freedom for anything in the world." Thus, on a certain level, del Río appreciated the relatively less oppressive atmosphere toward women that she encountered in the United States. On the other hand, as the above comments indicate, she retained an affinity for the conservative customs of her elite Mexican heritage. In choosing Cedric Gibbons, an Irish-American Catholic brought up in genteel Boston, as her second husband in 1930, del Río found the ideal mate who symbolically synthesized what she valued most in both Mexican and American cultures. "Cedric is perfect," she asserted to *Photoplay*. "First, he is American, with that dash most American men seem to possess. And he is also understanding and sympathetic. He has never been to Mexico and does not know my people—but he is an artist, and in his artist's appreciation he has been endowed with the sensitivity of the Latin."

Del Río's ideal marriage, which signified her bicultural existence, began to crumble after ten years. She claimed that Gibbons had become "cold and indifferent," and the couple separated in early 1940; an official divorce was granted a year later. Concomitant with her marital problems, del Río's career began to sputter. Fewer offers came her way, and those that did usually consisted of exotic supporting roles that she summarily turned down. After becoming involved with the twenty-six-year-old "Boy Wonder" Orson Welles in 1941, her name again became regular fodder for the gossip columns. However, except for a supporting role in Welles's espionage thriller *Journey into Fear* (1942), her career continued to lag.

In 1942, Welles left her for Hollywood's reigning "Love Goddess," Rita Hayworth.

By 1943, with her professional and personal life in the doldrums, del Río decided to return to Mexico. "I want to choose my own stories, director, and cameraman," she stated. "I believe I can accomplish all this in Mexico." That same year she starred opposite Pedro Armendáriz in Emilio ("El Indio") Fernández's classics *Flor Silvestre* and *María Candelaria*. These films helped inaugurate the Golden Age of the 1940s and 1950s during which the Mexican film industry became the dominant producer of Spanish-language cinema in the world. From 1943 until her death in 1983, del Río starred in over nineteen Mexican films. She also made intermittent returns to Hollywood—most notably in John Ford's *The Fugitive* (1947), which was actually filmed in Mexico, and *Cheyenne Autumn* (1964). The legendary fame that she achieved as the "First Lady" of Mexican cinema would have been impossible had she stayed in Hollywood as an aging, semi-exotic star.

Like Dolores del Río, Lupe Vélez arrived in Hollywood toward the end of the silent film era. Yet Vélez's career in Hollywood, both on screen and off, would take a decidedly different form from that of her compatriot. Born in 1909 as María Guadalupe Vélez de Villalobos in San Luis Potosí, she came from relatively humble beginnings.[9] By all accounts, Vélez was a rambunctious child who had a natural antipathy for rules and authority. When she was thirteen years old, her father, an officer in the Mexican army, decided that she needed a more supervised environment and sent her off to Our Lady of the Lake Convent in San Antonio, Texas. In her second year at the convent, Vélez's father died defending the national government against a local insurgency, and the intrepid teenager was forced to return to Mexico City to find work in order to help support her mother and younger siblings. Having learned all the latest American dances in Texas, she swiftly secured income as a featured dancer in a local musical revue. A year later, American matinee idol Richard Bennett caught her act on stage and invited her to come to Hollywood to audition for his upcoming production of *The Dove*.

Lupe Vélez arrived practically penniless in Hollywood in 1926, but her fortunes quickly changed. Although *The Dove* did not pan out, Vélez took to the stage in Los Angeles in *Music Box Revue*, where she duly impressed film producer Hal Roach. After appearing in a few small film roles in 1926 and 1927, her big break came in 1928, when Douglas Fairbanks, Sr., cast her in a featured role as the Mountain Girl in his big budget hit *The Gaucho*. The positive reviews of Vélez's performance led United Artists to sign her to a five-year contract. Moreover, in her feature debut, Vélez exhibited the qualities that would characterize her screen image for the rest of her career: aggressive beauty, flamboyant energy, comedic timing, and an ability to unleash a barrage of pent-up emotions on her male target. Unlike del Río's vague exoticism, Vélez's film image was identified as specifically ethnic. As the industry switched to sound production in 1929, Vélez's persona of a hot-tempered, thickly accented Latin temptress solidified (Figure 10). Although she shone in the few lead dramatic roles she was given—such as Universal's *Resurrection* (1931)— she was generally confined to tempestuous supporting roles in which she played a variety of ethnicities: entertaining half-castes in *Where East Is East* (1929) and *Tiger Rose* (1929); an Asian in *East Is West* (1930); Native Americans in *The Squaw Man* (1931) and *Laughing Boy* (1934); and Latinas in *Wolf Song* (1929), *Cuban Love Song* (1931), *The Broken Wing* (1932), *Hot Pepper* (1933), *Palooka* (1934), and *Strictly Dynamite* (1934).

This still from RKO's 1930 picture *The Girl from Mexico* depicts a spunky Mexican entertainer named Carmelita (played by Lupe Vélez) clowning around with Uncle Matt (Leon Errol) while her American husband, Dennis (Donald Woods), looks on. *Courtesy of the Museum of Modern Art, Film Stills Archive*

Whereas del Río was able to demand less exotic and more modern roles for herself during the mid-1930s, Vélez's film characterizations became increasingly narrow and homogenous. In 1932, RKO became the first studio to have Vélez caricature her own public image in a film. Cast as Princess Exotica in *The Half-Naked Truth* (1932), Vélez portrayed an exotic, publicity-hungry, temperamental actress. This act of parody, which would later become the model for her Mexican Spitfire series, made it clear to both Vélez and her audience that from this point forward she would be packaged by the studios more as a novelty performer than as an actress.

For the remainder of her Hollywood career, Vélez found herself in a predicament. In order to continue working, and thus maintain her fame, she was obliged to accept roles that were simply a variation of her standard fare. While this dilemma was due in large part to the limitations that the film industry placed on all ethnic actors, it was also a result of Vélez's own making. Off screen, Vélez's life-style was wilder than that of any of the boisterous characters she played in the movies. Where del Río may have been taken aback by the relatively liberal ways of American society, Vélez revelled in them. When the fan magazines asked Vélez what she thought of the United States, her response was often ecstatic. In 1929 she told a reporter: "I love the United States. Here I'm free! I'm free! I can do whatever I want. In Mexico, a girl has to go everywhere chaperoned. If you go out alone, everyone says you're immoral. A girl in Mexico can't go out of the house after nine o'clock without her father or brother. They always keep surveillance over us, and I don't like to be watched. It forces us girls to lie. What's the point of talking to a boy if the whole time his mother is there?"[10] In the same interview, Vélez criticized what she saw as the inherent double standards in Mexican gender conventions. "Marriage in Mexico is terrible," she opined. "The husband can do whatever he wants and the wife is afraid to say anything. He can go to parties and stay out all night, but the wife must stay home with the kids and not say a word."

Thus, for Vélez, the United States was a liberating space, a place where she could flaunt social conventions to her heart's content. Summing up her rebellious spirit, she told *Photoplay*, "There are times when *you* want to scream. But you don't, because you are afraid of what people will think of you. I am not afraid. Why should I be? If I want to scream, I scream. To hell with what they think of me." Asked whether it bothered her if people viewed her as unladylike, Vélez responded, "How can they tell? To act like everyone else—is that what they call a lady? Then I am not a lady!"[11] Like del Río, Vélez enjoyed the modern material amenities that life in Hollywood afforded, and loved to be seen in the latest fashions, cars, and homes. But unlike her more genteel countrywoman, whom she publicly disliked, Vélez defined the benefits of American modernity in proto-feminist terms. Vélez's strident claim for freedom and independence from the dictates of patriarchy was a bold act for the 1930s, whether resident in the United States or Mexico (Figure 11).

It is interesting to speculate as to how much of Vélez's "Mexican Spitfire" image was a genuine reflection of her own personality, how much of it was of her own making, and how much of it was simply a product of the industry's publicity machinery. While it is impossible to know to what

"Soy Libre; ¡Libre!" --Grita Lupe Velez

"I'm free! I'm free!" Lupe Vélez appeared to glory in the relative freedoms allowed women in the United States but sparked criticism in Mexico that she had become too Americanized. From *La Opinión*, January 23, 1929

extent Vélez identified with her "wild girl" public image, her behavior off screen did little to contradict and much to reinforce it. Vélez's love life was exciting, varied, and unpredictable. She was notorious for cavorting with many of Hollywood's leading men—for a time in the early 1930s she was romantically involved in nearly simultaneous affairs with Gary Cooper, Ronald Colman, John Gilbert, and Ricardo Cortez.

Without a doubt, Vélez's most famous and tumultuous relationship was her rocky five-year marriage to Johnny Weissmuller. The match was a publicist's dream: Tarzan of the Jungle mating with a "Mexican wildcat." Married in 1933, "Johnee" and "Whoopee Lupe" and their never-ending saga of separations and reconciliations made both stars regular features in the Hollywood print media. Their public rows were infamous. "Yes, we fight a lot," Vélez explained, "but no more than the rest of Hollywood. They call each other 'dear' and 'darling' in public, and then go home and smack each other in private. When Johnee and I get sore, we get sore no matter where we are!"[12] After such spectacles, rumors would often spread that Weissmuller, who at six feet-two inches towered over Vélez's diminutive five foot-one-half-inch frame, was physically abusive toward his "darling" once they had reached home. In order to save face, Vélez would invariably deny such charges by challenging the press to find any black and blue marks on her face. It seems she viewed such reports as an implicit attack on her decision to marry Weissmuller in the first place. By early 1938, however, the sad truth emerged that Weissmuller's physical violence and mental cruelty had left her emotionally unable to earn a living in Hollywood. Vélez filed for divorce. The following year the soap opera known to movie fans as "Lupe and Johnny" was legally finalized.

To a large degree the star images of del Río and Vélez during the 1930s mirrored their relationships to their prominent husbands. While del Río and Gibbons were playing host to such internationally renowned artists and intellectuals as Diego Rivera and Frida Kahlo, Vélez and Weissmuller would be caught screaming at each other at the race track. All of this, of course, simply reinforced their respective screen images. Motion-picture presses in both Hollywood and Mexico delighted in contrasting the seemingly diametrically opposed dispositions of the two Mexican stars. Encapsulating popularly held attitudes, a Mexican critic wrote in 1934: "Women of distinct temperaments and ideologies can never be rivals. Lupe is a primitive woman, uncontrolled by social convention. Lupe is nature, all NATURE; the essence of life itself. Dolores is pure *art*, all culture and education."[13]

While their public personas contrasted greatly, both Vélez and del Río saw their careers in Hollywood sag as their marriages crumbled. With fewer and fewer offers coming her way in Hollywood during the late 1930s, Vélez looked for alternative employers. During this period she appeared in four British films, and, in 1938 she returned to Mexico to star in *La Zandunga*. Had this film been more successful, it is probable that Vélez would have moved back to Mexico permanently. Although she received strong reviews for her performance and the film did relatively well at the box office, the critics panned its formulaic plot and low production values.[14] In short, *La Zandunga* was not the international hit its producers had hoped for. Back in Hollywood in 1939, Vélez starred in *The Girl from Mexico*, a film that revived her sputtering career by kicking off what would soon be known as the Mexican Spitfire series.

RKO's eight Mexican Spitfire films, produced from 1939 to 1943, were part of the studio's strategy of jettisoning "high concept" pictures in favor of themes that would appeal to rural audiences at home and abroad.[15] By far her most successful films, the comedy series reinforced and synthesized Vélez's celluloid image. *Mexican Spitfire*, the second film in the series and the one that launched its title, epitomizes the formula. Vélez played Carmelita, a Mexican entertainer married to Dennis Lindsay (Donald Woods), a New England advertising executive. The Lindsay family is upset because Dennis has dumped blue-blooded Elizabeth (Linda Hayes) in order to marry that "Mexican wildcat." Invariably, the plot revolves around the attempts of Elizabeth and Dennis's Aunt Della (Elizabeth Risdon) to break up the marriage by showing Dennis that Carmelita lacks breeding and that Elizabeth is his true social equal. As Elizabeth declares to Aunt Della: "I still think of Dennis as engaged to me . . . of course, the little Mexican wildcat may snip a little, but we'll clip her claws." Carmelita does have one ally in her new Uncle Matt (Leon Errol), who believes that her presence brings some much-needed spunk to the staid family. When Aunt Della complains to her husband, "You know she has no more right to be his wife than I have to be yours," Uncle Matt retorts, "You know, I think you've got something there!" In the end, as in all the films of the series, Elizabeth's plots are foiled and Dennis reaffirms his love for Carmelita.

Vélez's performance in *Mexican Spitfire* received enthusiastic critical and popular response in both the United States and Mexico. Playing on her star image, Vélez, who had become a redhead, displayed her trademark characteristics: lots of eye-rolling, body movement, double entendres, and fracturing of the English language with comedic malapropisms. Complaining that she is no good for Dennis, she laments, "I am just a gallstone around his neck." Feeling that it would be in Dennis's best interest if she were to leave him, Carmelita goes to Mexico to get a quickie divorce (which, of course, much to Elizabeth's chagrin, is later deemed invalid). After signing the paperwork, she asks, "Now, am I loose?"; the smiling attorney responds, "Definitely." When Errol (playing the double role of British whiskey magnate Lord Epping) tells Carmelita, "You look very nice and fresh," she answers, "I *am* fresh, thank you."

While these examples fit into Vélez's standard repertoire, her Mexican Spitfire role did signal a departure from her previous screen image. The raw sensuality of her earlier pictures was toned down, and Carmelita was shown as the heroine committed to the institution of marriage. Moreover, Carmelita, with Uncle Matt's help, actively challenges the snobbery and bigotry of Elizabeth and Aunt Della (and by extension that of U.S. society in general) by exposing and thwarting their mean-spirited plans. In addition, in what was surely a source of pleasure for Latin American audiences, Vélez often got even with her Anglo rivals by firing insults at them in Spanish. In a bar scene in *Mexican Spitfire*, for example, Elizabeth buys Carmelita a drink and asks her to make a toast; the latter gladly salutes, "*Antipática cara de perra!*" (Dog-faced bitch!). Elizabeth repeats it, thinking she is receiving and giving a compliment.

Although the first two installments of the Mexican Spitfire series were extremely profitable, the following titles were described in the contemporary press as progressively redundant and vapid. By 1943 the series was cancelled, and, with no significant Hollywood offers on the table, Vélez returned to Mexico to star in a screen adaptation of nineteenth-century French author Emile Zola's *Nana*. Savoring the chance to play a dramatic lead, Vélez once again received positive reviews from the Mexican media. But, as had happened with *La Zandunga* five years earlier, the film itself produced a lackluster response. Disheartened, Vélez returned to Hollywood. While mulling over several potential stage and screen projects, she became involved with Harald Ramond, a little-known French actor, in an affair that turned out to be her last.

On December 13, 1944, unwed and five months pregnant, Vélez committed suicide in her Hollywood mansion by taking an overdose of sleeping pills. Explaining her decision, she left the following note to Ramond, with whom she had squabbled a few days before: "May God forgive you and forgive me too. But I prefer to take my life away and our baby's before I bring him into the world with shame or kill him. How could you, Harald, fake such great love for me and my baby when all the time you didn't want us? I see no other way out for me, so good-bye and good luck to you. Love, Lupe."[16] Vélez left another short note to Beulah Kinder, her housekeeper-confidante: "My faithful friend, you and only you know the fact for the reason I am taking my life. May God forgive me, and don't think bad of me. I love you much. . . . Say good-bye to all my friends and the American press that was always so nice to me." As a postscript she added, "Take care of Chips and Chops" (her pet dogs).[17] In the end, convention reared its ugly head. It seems that Vélez's free-spirited liberality had its limits. The woman who so greatly admired the social freedoms that her Hollywood life-style allowed had continued to maintain a conservative streak. While abortions were not uncommon in Hollywood at the time, her internalized Roman Catholic heritage forbade such a course of action. To live with the social stigma of being an unwed mother was equally unthinkable.

Prior to a nondenominational funeral service, Vélez's body lay in state at the Church of the Recessional at Forest Lawn Cemetery in Glendale, California. Over 4,000 fans and curiosity-seekers paid their respects and attempted to console her emotionally distraught mother and siblings, whom Vélez had been supporting financially since her days on the Mexican stage nearly twenty years before. In death as in life, Vélez caused sensation bordering on scandal. Among her pallbearers were former lovers Johnny Weissmuller, Gilbert Roland, and Arturo de Cordova.

Throughout their careers in Hollywood, del Río and Vélez faced the double burden of negotiating the industry's limited opportunities for Latina actresses while at the same time trying not to offend fans and critics south of the border. Given the official post-revolutionary nationalism that reigned in Mexico during the 1920s and 1930s, this latter obligation proved especially difficult. Mexican critics and governmental officials, acutely aware of the power that Hollywood films exerted in shaping international perceptions of Mexico, closely scrutinized the films of the two stars, particularly when they played Latin characters. In 1931, for example, critic Fidel Murillo applauded del Río for turning down the female lead in Paramount's proposed remake of the silent film *The Broken Wing*.[18] Not having the bargaining position nor the scruples of del Río, Vélez took the part the following year. Playing a cantina girl who dumps her Mexican bandit boyfriend (Leo Carrillo) in favor of an Anglo pilot (Melvyn Douglas), Vélez was duly chastised by the Mexican press.

Although del Río made a conscious effort to avoid such situations, she was not exempt from arousing controversy in Mexico over her screen representations. When her 1932 film *The Girl of the Rio* appeared in Mexico City, it provoked immediate resentment and threats of violence toward the theater owner. The government stepped in and promptly banned the film. In retrospect, the ban seems quite understandable. Del Río played La Paloma, a cantina singer who is in love with American Johnny Powell (Norman Foster). Enter the evil Señor Tostado (Leo Carrillo), a corrupt and debased drunkard who desires Paloma for himself. By bribing

officials, Tostado has Johnny framed for murder and tells Paloma that he
will spare the American's life only if she agrees to marry him. The commotion that the movie caused in Mexico took del Río by surprise. She
defended herself in the Mexican press: "*¡Pero hombre!* I accepted the
part under the condition that I was allowed to modify the plot and the
script development in such a manner that it would not damage our [Mexi-
can] reputation."[19] Del Río went on to argue that the critics were being
overly sensitive and that she would never do anything to hurt the image of
her beloved Mexico.

Vélez was generally less concerned than del Río about placating such
criticism of her work and life-style. In 1934, for example, much to the
dismay of Mexican elites, she was the only Mexican citizen to turn down
the government's invitation to attend the inauguration of Mexico City's
new Fine Arts Palace (del Río and Ramón Navarro both attended).[20] Still,
when the hue and cry over her behavior reached a pitch that was potentially damaging to the economic interests of her studio, Vélez felt compelled to respond. In 1929, for example, in an interview with an American
reporter, she hailed the freedom of American women and reproved the
confined state of Mexican women. When her translated remarks appeared
in the Mexican press, they provoked instant indignation, which prompted
the formation of a movement that demanded a boycott of all of Vélez's
future films. In an act of damage control, United Artists advised Vélez to
make a public rebuttal. With the help of studio publicity men, she wrote a
specially crafted letter to the Mexican government's Special Commission
on Motion Pictures, which was printed in all the major dailies. Without
specifically contradicting her previous statements, Vélez argued that the
American journalist had misunderstood and exaggerated her responses.
She ended the letter by expressing her undying love for Mexico and its
people. "I will always feel like a daughter of Mexico," she concluded,
"and deep down the esteem of the Mexican public is the dearest to me."[21]
Apparently the campaign worked, and no boycott was effected.

Given their long periods of residence in the United States and their
marriages to North American men, Vélez and del Río's romantic choices
inevitably caused Mexican commentators to question their loyalty to the
homeland. In 1932, shortly after the release of *The Girl of the Rio*, film
critic Gabriel Navarro published a long editorial entitled, "We Have Lost
Dolores del Río!" He argued that her marriage to Gibbons had "Americanized" her to such a degree that while she was perfecting her English,
her Spanish was beginning to suffer from "lamentable errors of pronun-
ciation." In short, Navarro accused the star of having values and attitudes
that were "more American than Mexican."[22] Underlying such criticisms
of del Río's Americanization was the specter of *malinchismo*, a long-
standing tradition in Mexico of tainting the reputation of women who
supposedly served foreign interests by identifying them with La Malinche,

the indigenous woman of noble descent who served as Hernán Cortéz's interpreter, guide, and lover during the Spanish Conquest. Similar accusations of *malinchismo*, or betrayal, arose after del Río appeared in *In Caliente* in 1935. Advising that the film be banned in Mexico, which it eventually was, a Mexican diplomat in Los Angeles argued that del Río's offense was not merely her displeasing screen portrayal. "She's very Mexican when she's in Mexico," he asserted, "but she doesn't feel any attraction for her country, especially now that she's married to an American and all her customs and tendencies are American. . . . What stands out is that after she and her husband enjoy such high consideration in Mexico, she turns around and denigrates our country [in this film], and not for the first time."[23]

Besides their marriages and absorption of some American values, the two Mexican stars were also criticized in the late 1930s for staying to work in Hollywood at a time when the Mexican film industry was struggling to establish itself as a viable enterprise. The Mexican government during the Lázaro Cárdenas administration (1934–1939) embarked upon a highly nationalistic economic policy known as import-substitution industrialization, a policy epitomized by Mexico's expropriation of American and British petroleum interests in 1938. By means of tariffs, subsidization, and financing, the Cárdenas government promoted the formation of an entrepreneurial capitalist class that engaged in the manufacture of goods formerly imported from Europe or the United States, such as motion pictures. Unlike the oil industry, which became a state-owned monopoly, the film industry always remained a preserve of private enterprise. Still, the Mexican government proved a significant investor. In 1935 it heavily subsidized the formation of CLASA (Cinematografía Latino Americana, S.A.) studios, the first modern production facility in Mexico. A year later, the unexpected international success of Fernando de Fuentes's *Allá en el Rancho Grande* (1936) demonstrated the potential profitability of Mexican-made motion pictures. With confidence in the nascent industry increasing, Mexican fans and cinema journalists never tired of wondering when they would have the pleasure of seeing their favorite stars perform in their native tongue.[24]

Not surprisingly, as the Mexican film industry grew in the late 1930s, so too did the offers for del Río and Vélez to return to their homeland. There is little doubt that both del Río and Vélez endeavored to remain in Hollywood as long as possible. As the quote at the beginning of this chapter from Miguel de Zárraga indicated, the "maximum honor" for cinema actors during this period was success in Hollywood. When asked by Mexican reporters if she had any plans to honor the Mexican cinema by starring in a national production, del Río typically gave a diplomatic response. "Nobody has more desire than I to do something for our cinema," she told *Cine-Mundial* in 1940. "But we can't always do what we want, when we want. We have great writers, actors, and even directors. We still lack good sound, good lighting, and good set designs. I don't doubt that in the near future we'll attain a world-class cinema, and then. . . [I will return]."[25] For del Río, this "near future" would be another three years away.

In contrast, Vélez did not have the luxury of waiting until the Mexican film industry rose to the technical level that del Río saw as a prerequisite for her services. As mentioned earlier, Vélez returned to Mexico in 1938 to star in *La Zandunga*. Directed by Fernando de Fuentes, the country's leading director at the time, and co-starring Arturo de Córdova, Chaflan, and María Luisa Zea, the film was one of the most ambitious and extravagant productions yet attempted in Mexico. A *costumbrista*, or folkloric, romantic comedy set in the rural regions of the Isthmus of Tehuantepec, the story dramatized the troubled romance between a campesina (Vélez) and a sailor (de Córdova). The press heralded the participation of Vélez as the decisive element that would signify a new era in Mexican filmmaking.

Vélez, however, showed little public concern for the fate of the Mexican film industry. She returned home primarily for the money. The producers had offered her much more than she could have earned in Hollywood: fifty thousand pesos (over fourteen thousand dollars) for four weeks of work, an unprecedented amount in the Mexican film industry. Viewing the project as just another job, Vélez was unprepared for the enthusiasm and adoration that her return ignited. Upon her arrival at the Buenavista railroad station, a human wave of over twenty thousand admirers showed up to greet her while countless others experienced the moment via a live radio broadcast. A barrage of flowers and cheers welcomed Vélez as she addressed the crowd through a loudspeaker. "During the trip here," declared Vélez, visibly touched, "I have received such expressions of kindness that I cried and laughed the whole way through. I didn't think that the Mexican people loved me so much."[26]

Vélez's frenetic reception would be echoed five years later when both she and del Río returned to work in Mexico. A sign of true stardom, the two actresses remained heroes among the general public despite years of having Mexican critics and officials decry their screen portrayals and their Americanized life-styles. No doubt, throughout their careers in *el norte*, del Río and Vélez must have frequently felt compromised by Hollywood's intransigent typecasting, which rarely permitted them to showcase their dramatic abilities. Their ultimate return to Mexico bears testimony to this frustration. At the same time, the experience of living in Hollywood proved mightily seductive for each woman. The Hollywood Dream Factory provided del Río and Vélez with a level of wealth and fame unthinkable for contemporaneous performers in Mexico. Moreover, for different reasons, del Río and Vélez liked living in the United States. Hollywood stardom allowed del Río to indulge her appetite for the most modern clothing and surroundings without sacrificing what she considered to be her core Mexican values. Vélez viewed Hollywood as a hedonistic playground where she could publicly be as loud, provocative, and audacious as she pleased. Each woman fashioned a bicultural identity, blending her respective notions of *mexicanidad* with North American values and tastes. Over the years, this cross-cultural process was repeatedly derided by nationalist Mexican critics and officials. Yet, in perhaps an indication of the gulf between the revolutionary intelligentsia and the masses, Dolores del Río and Lupe Vélez remained popular icons in Mexico throughout their Hollywood careers. During all of their personal trials and professional tribulations in Hollywood, the movie fans of Mexico stayed with them.

Notes

1. *Hoy*, May 6, 1939. Unless otherwise noted, all translations are the author's.
2. Ana M. López, "Are All Latins from Manhattan?: Hollywood, Ethnography, and Cultural Colonialism," in *Unspeakable Images: Ethnicity and the American Cinema*, ed. Lester D. Friedman (Urbana: University of Illinois Press, 1991), 404–24; and idem, "From Hollywood and Back: Dolores del Río, Trans(National) Star," *Studies in Latin American Popular Culture* 17 (Spring 1998), 5–32; Alice I. Rodríguez-Estrada, "Dolores del Río and Lupe Vélez: Images on and off the Screen, 1925–1944," in *Writing the Range: Race, Class, and Culture in the Women's West*, ed., Sue Armitage and Betsy Jameson (Norman: University of Oklahoma Press, 1997), 475–92; José Gómez Sicre, "Dolores del Río," *Américas* (December 1967), 8–17; and Allen Woll, *The Latin Image in American Film* (Los Angeles: UCLA Latin American Center, 1980).
3. For a compelling reading of how a "racialized sexuality" was played out on the body of del Río in *Bird of Paradise*, see Joanne Hershfield, "Race and Romance in *Bird of Paradise*," *Cinema Journal* 37:3 (Spring 1998), 3–15.
4. López, "Are All Latins from Manhattan?" 410.
5. Ruth Biery, "How Many Lives *Has* del Río?" *Photoplay*, October 1933, 60, 114–15; Don "Q," "Dolores del Río," *Cine-Mundial*, June 1934, 338–39.
6. For an appreciation of the Gibbons-del Río estate, see Brendan Gill, "Cedric Gibbons and Dolores del Río: The Art Director and the Star of *Flying Down to Rio* in Santa Monica," *Architectural Digest* 49:4 (April 1992), 127–33, 254.
7. "Hostess in the Modern Manner," *Photoplay*, February 1936, 75.
8. Katherine Franklin, "Dolores Extols Passive Love," *Photoplay*, April 1934, 39, 106–7.
9. The best biography to date on Vélez's life and career is Gabriel Ramírez, *Lupe Vélez: La mexicana que escupía fuego* (Mexico City: Cineteca Nacional, 1986). See also Alfonso Pinto, "Lupe Vélez," *Films* 37:9 (November 1977), 513–24; and James Robert Parish, *The RKO Gals* (New York: Arlington House, 1974), 591–641.
10. *La Opinión*, January 23, 1929.
11. Ruth Biery, "*The* Best Showman in Town," *Photoplay*, November 1931, 73, 106.
12. Quoted in Parish, *The RKO Gals*, 610.
13. M. G. Segrera, "¿Es Lupe rival de Lola?" *Cine-Mundial*, February 1934, 76.

14. The divergence of critical opinion over the merits of *La Zandunga* were evident in the reviews of Mexico City's major dailies. *Imparcial* totally panned the film while *Excélsior* hailed it as a glorious moment in Mexican cinema. See *Excélsior*, March 22, 1938.

15. The eight films were: *The Girl from Mexico* (1939), *Mexican Spitfire* (1940), *Mexican Spitfire Out West* (1940), *Mexican Spitfire's Baby* (1941), *Mexican Spitfire at Sea* (1942), *Mexican Spitfire Sees a Ghost* (1942), *Mexican Spitfire's Elephant* (1942), and *Mexican Spitfire's Blessed Event* (1943).

16. Quoted in Rodríguez-Estrada, "Dolores del Río and Lupe Vélez," 487.

17. Parish, *The RKO Gals*, 624.

18. *La Opinión*, May 24, 1931.

19. Ibid., May 15, 1932.

20. Ramírez, *Lupe Vélez*, 114.

21. *La Opinión*, January 31, 1931.

22. Ibid., May 22, 1932.

23. Quoted in Seth Fein, "El cine y las relaciones culturales entre México y Estados Unidos durante la década de 1930," *Secuencia* 34 (Spring 1996), 167–68.

24. For more on the development of the Mexican film industry, see Emilio García Riera, *Historia documental del cine mexicano*, vols. 1–4 (Mexico: Ediciones Era, 1969); and Carl J. Mora, *Mexican Cinema: Reflections of a Society, 1896–1988* (Berkeley, Los Angeles: University of California Press, 1989); Seth Fein, "Hollywood, U.S.-Mexican Relations and the Devolution of the 'Golden Age' of Mexican Cinema," *Film Historia* 4:2 (1994), 103–35.

25. *Cine-Mundial*, February 1940, 77–78.

26. Ramírez, *Lupe Vélez*, 113.

17

To Be or Not to Be Brazilian? Carmen Miranda's Quest for Fame and "Authenticity" in the United States

Darién J. Davis

Before the military dictatorship of 1964, Brazilian immigration to the United States was numerically insignificant. According to the U.S. embassy records in Rio de Janeiro, Brazilian travelers fell under three major categories: students, tourists, and artists. In this essay, cultural historian Darién Davis examines the North American career of the most famous artist of all, "the Brazilian Bombshell," also known as "the Lady in the Tutti Frutti Hat," Carmen Miranda. She came to the United States as a cultural ambassador under the auspices of the Good Neighbor Policy to improve hemispheric understanding during the World War II era, and chose to live outside of Brazil for the increased career opportunities available to her on Broadway and in Hollywood. Davis finds that Miranda's limited command of English, coupled with the film industry's tendency to portray generic Latin types, meant that her public persona was limited mainly to some version of the Bahiana, the rural woman of African descent from Northeastern Brazil. For her willingness to accept culturally indistinct, even inaccurate, roles and for her international popularization of an archetype deemed undesirable by Brazil's white elite, Carmen Miranda's success in the United States earned her much criticism back home.

Davis finds that Carmen Miranda used her music to strike back at her critics, thereby giving her a more overtly political and personal character than previously recognized. Furthermore, like Mexican film stars Dolores del Río and Lupe Vélez discussed in Chapter 16, Miranda found herself caught between two nations. All three Latin American women had to cope with ethnic and gender stereotypes held in the entertainment industry. All three also had to justify their success to critics in their home countries and used their positions to educate the American public about Latin American cultures at least in some small way. Davis's article contributes to the growing field of film history, and indicates the ambiguity

and tension that commercial success in the United States historically have
meant for Latin American artists.

Historically, American popular music has developed as a result of cross-pollination and the importation of musical forms, rhythms, and instruments brought by diverse people who are displaced from their homelands. Today, the Portuguese- and Spanish-speaking populations in the United States have attained a critical mass that allows for the importation of Latin American musicians catering to these transnational audiences in their native languages. In the 1990s, Brazilian musicians such as Gilberto Gil, Caetano Veloso, Milton Nascimento, and Jorge Bem, and younger singers such as Marisa Monte and Daniela Mercury, have performed in Portuguese to sold-out audiences in major metropolitan areas on both the east and west coasts. However, this success is still a recent phenomenon; the current popularity of Brazilian music in the United States must be seen as the third stage in a long historical tradition of Brazilian-American cross-pollination that began in the late 1930s with the arrival of Carmen Miranda, and continued in the early 1960s with the bossa nova. This chapter places Miranda within the context of the literature on exiles by examining the relationship between her musical career in the United States and the impact of her work on her sense of *brasilidade*, or Brazilian-ness, in her adopted country.[1] Because Miranda's own sense of Brazilian-ness was closely related to her relationship to her compatriot fans, it is important to explore her changing relationship to Brazil during her stay in the United States from 1940 to 1954. Miranda, like many musical performers who leave their homelands to live and perform elsewhere, was a displaced artist who occupied an ambiguous cultural space in which she attempted to affirm her own national identity while satisfying her hunger to become a popular musical performer in the United States.

President Franklin Delano Roosevelt's Good Neighbor Policy (1933–1947) encouraged the pilgrimage of Brazilian entertainers in an effort, albeit ill conceived, to sensitize American audiences to Latin American cultural traditions. Unfortunately, the arrival of Brazilians like Carmen Miranda, Aurora Miranda, Ary Barbosa, and Aloysio de Oliviera did not overcome cultural barriers as anticipated, and in fact very often led to further misperceptions and stereotypes of Latin Americans in general and especially of Brazilians. In addition, the unique experience afforded to select representatives who were creating expatriate Brazilian music in the United States engendered antagonisms between those performers here and their Brazilian critics at home who bemoaned that the music was no longer "authentic." Moreover, critics labeled many Brazilian musicians who became successful in the United States "un-Brazilian," or worse, charged that these performers had become *americanizado*. Critics constantly hurled this epithet at Miranda. Yet her own struggles as a performer, artist, and entertainer revolved around her attempt to balance her desire to achieve success and her sense of obligation to Brazilians everywhere.

While Brazilian migration to and settlement in the United States shows remarkable similarities with the "push and pull" patterns of other Latin American immigrants, Brazilians represent a most curious case for study.[2] The first Brazilians to arrive during the early decades of the twentieth century were temporary residents, predominantly from the upper class, traveling for leisure, or in some cases to study in one of the prestigious academic institutions. Foreign residence afforded them the opportunity to observe the differences between life in the United States and Brazil. For instance, the experience of renowned sociologist Gilberto Freyre as a student at Baylor College in Texas (1918–1920) and at Columbia University (1920–1922) allowed him to write comparatively about Brazilian and American culture at the time.[3] According to Freyre, his desire to write about Brazil surged when he was in New York. He remembered "with bitterness the disrespectful phrase from two Anglo-Saxon tourists that spoke of the fearful Mongrel aspect of the Brazilian population."[4] This offensive slur led Freyre to head a new wave of Brazilian scholarship that defended miscegenation, or racial mixing, as a creative force that should be celebrated.[5] Since the late 1930s, Brazilian culture has continued to make its impression on the American national consciousness thanks to the creation of icons such as Carmen Miranda and Disney's parrot Joe Carioca.[6] Of course, these representations tell perhaps more about American perceptions of Brazilians than about the people themselves, but behind them lies a trail of documents that affirms the small but growing Brazilian presence in the United States.

Carmen Miranda was not, in fact, Brazilian by birth. Born into poverty in Portugal in 1909, she moved to Brazil with her mother in 1910 to join her father, José Maria Pinto da Cunha, a barber who had already established himself in Rio de Janeiro. Although she retained a Portuguese passport for most of her adult life, Carmen grew up fully Brazilianized in the city's working-class neighborhoods, surrounded by popular music and dance. As a girl, she worked at various jobs including a stint at a millinery where she learned how to trim hats, an accessory that would later prove indispensable to her performances in the United States. As Carmen's voice gained attention from customers who heard her sing in the hat shop, she dreamed of becoming a movie star, and the opportunity for a wider audience soon presented itself.

Carmen's entrance into the epicenter of Brazilian popular culture during the populist regime of Getulio Vargas in the 1930s allowed her to showcase musical rhythms from the largely black and mulatto lower classes before a national audience. Her personal charisma and charm, combined with her ability to inject humor, satire, criticism, and laughter into her musical creations, allowed her to capture the support of the fans from the popular sectors as well as from the growing middle class in a non-confrontational, non-threatening manner. By 1935, Miranda had won several national music competitions and had already been elected by her fans as "the Queen of Carioca Broadcasting," "the Ambassadress of Samba," and "the Queen of Samba."[7] However, by the end of the 1930s, Miranda, who had already conquered the Brazilian entertainment industry and performed in several movies, was seeking new opportunities. In an era when roles for all blacks and women of any color were limited, Miranda was able to make inroads into a male-dominated industry as a white female performer of black popular rhythms and forms such as the *batucada* and the samba.[8] Her success gave her confidence and whetted her appetite for the challenges of a career in film that could reach a larger, international audience.

Although Miranda's adaptation of "the Bahiana," a typical black woman from the northeastern city of Salvador de Bahia, occurred by chance, that image played an important role in launching her movie career (Figure 12). Her professional relationship with the Bahian composer and singer Dorival Caymmi had brought her in direct contact with the musical tradition of Bahia, then considered the mecca of Brazilian music.

In 1938, Caymmi had moved to Rio de Janeiro where he met Miranda through the efforts of Almirante, an important popular musician in his own right, on the set of the film *Banana da Terra*. Caymmi allowed Miranda to perform his *samba-bahiano*, "O que é que o bahiana tem?" (What is it that the Bahian woman has?), in which she responded to the question by listing a host of ornaments including a silk turban, golden earrings, trimmed sandals, all of which adorned the singer's body and transformed her into an exaggerated version of a white Bahian woman. In *Banana da Terra*, Carmen Miranda not only became the Bahiana but also danced for the first time, making her a complete performer.[9]

Carmen Miranda's self-promotion as "La Bahiana" catapulted her to international stardom but limited her roles in Hollywood and drew criticism from Brazilians worried about their nation's image abroad. Photograph by W. Eugene Smith

Carmen's dazzling Bahiana performance at the Cassino da Urca attracted the attention of Broadway theater impresario Lee Shubert in February 1939. After seeing her show, Shubert offered Miranda a contract to perform in the United States, and she left Rio on May 3, 1939.[10] Thirteen days later, she stepped onto American soil to begin a new career in a land where people did not understand her language, and where she was far away from the popular classes that had inspired and embraced her. Luckily for Miranda, she had managed to convince Shubert and the Brazilian government to allow the Bando da Lua to travel with her so that she was not performing alone. She understood that without Brazilian musicians she might not be able to perform her tunes successfully, and therefore agreed to take a cut in her own pay in order to cover the wages of her band. Still, doubts lingered. How would she perform before this new audience? How would her music change? And how would she fare as Brazil's cultural ambassador under these trying circumstances?

The relationship between official national representation and commercial entertainment is not easily reconciled, particularly when an artist like Miranda finds herself in a context in which the aesthetic demands of the new audience are fundamentally different from those of the audiences that supported her in Brazil. Nevertheless, Miranda was ecstatic to be in the United States. She had captured the hearts of Brazilian audiences and now had the opportunity to conquer those of North Americans as well. Already, Miranda had succeeded in ways that she had never imagined, but her arrival provided her with a major challenge. How would she present herself to the American people? Almost immediately, Miranda's commercial instincts dominated her sense of national representation, and she began performing for the American press. According to Helena Soldberg, Brazilian director of the docudrama *Bananas Is My Business* (1995), "not knowing a word of English, she throws around a few words she has learned, and suddenly she sounds like a bimbo. This is not *our* Carmen. This impression would stay forever with the Americans. This is the Carmen that they will love."[11]

The undeniably white singer-dancer Miranda had evolved into the Bahiana by adopting for herself the archetype of a black woman from Bahia, thereby making the image accessible and palatable to her nation's sophisticated urban elites while inviting the rural folk into the national consciousness. In reality, an actual black Bahiana performer would never have been paid to sing or perform in any stylish club in Brazil, much less flown to New York to perform on Broadway. By expropriating popular black symbols, Carmen was simply doing what white musicians and entertainers in both Brazil and the United States had done for decades. She was, however, the first South American to take this success across international boundaries. The North American entertainment industry welcomed her outlandish image, and further modified it to entertain millions during the tumultuous World War II years. Leaving Brazil as a cultural ambassador, Carmen promised her audiences that she would not forget her roots: "In my numbers everything will be there: *canela* [cinnamon], *pimenta* [pepper], *dendê* [coconut palm oil], *cuminho* [cumin]. . . . I'm taking *vatapá* [Bahian chicken and shrimp stew], *caruru* [a dish of mustard greens, or similar leafy vegetable, cooked with fish or jerked beef], . . . *balangandas* [jewelry], *acarajé* [Bahian fritters]."[12] Indeed, American entertainment critics would agree that Miranda provided all the necessary ingredients for a memorable performance, but the extent to which it was authentically Brazilian was debatable. Many of her transplanted sambas ultimately became unrecognizable, drawing her Brazilian identity into question and allowing her critics to attack her in the area in which she was most vulnerable.

As Hollywood exported its films throughout the region, many Latin American entertainers found themselves receiving unprecedented attention. The State Department Office of the Coordinator of Inter-American Affairs under Nelson Rockefeller created a special Motion Picture section aimed at utilizing the media in promoting an ambiguous but friendly alliance between the hemisphere's northern and southern neighbors.[13] In addition to Carmen Miranda, other Latin American stars who emerged in this era included Carlos Ramírez, César Romero, Desi Arnaz, Dolores del Río, Carmen's sister Aurora Miranda, and the Disney cartoon figures of Joe Carioca and Panchito, the Mexican rooster. A whole host of Latin American stars joined their North American counterparts to produce an elaborate cornucopia of entertaining films designed to amuse and elicit laughter from the war-weary audiences, often without specific references to the national cultures from which the stars came. Indeed, one of the legitimate criticisms of the cultural practices inherent in the Good Neighbor Policy was that it contributed to the creation of a generic Latin American culture in which fun-loving people danced and sang indiscriminately to sambas, Mexican hat-dances, and rumbas. This so-called Latin music played a pivotal role in gaining Hollywood acceptance for Latin American artists, yet it also diluted their national distinctiveness. For example, in the musical comedy *Springtime of Youth*, Sigmund Romberg wrote a song called "In Brazil," with a chorus inexplicably written in Spanish even though Brazil was a Portuguese-speaking country, and instrumentation that seemed more Cuban than anything else. The great Hollywood musical therefore provided an ambiguous vehicle for the dissemination of Latin American culture among U.S. audiences. The era of internationalized Latin American styles meant that Miranda's performance of Brazilian music would become a cross-border hybrid as well.[14]

Carmen Miranda's first record in the United States was "South American Way," written by Jimmy MacHugh and Al Dublin especially for her in the musical *The Streets of Paris*. "South American Way" was part of a new genre of songs that Abel Cardoso calls *abrasileiradas*, or Brazilianized melodies. According to Abel Cardoso, Miranda and the Bando da Lua apparently adapted the original English composition to a samba rhythm, and Aloysio de Oliveira wrote the Portuguese lyrics.[15] Although the song represented a joint collaboration of a sort, the lyrics pandered to American audiences while producing a one-dimensional view of the fun-loving, laid-back, and identifiably lazy "South American way." Miranda injected humor into the performance and into the recording by pronouncing "south" as "souse," an American slang word for a state of drunkenness. Although written mainly in Portuguese to maintain a sense of authenticity, the song contained English verses to ensure that the audience received the basic message. Thus, Carmen's first Brazilian-American hybrid was born:

Ai ai ai ai
E o canto do pregoneiro
Que com sua harmonia
Traz alegria
In South American way

Ai ai ai ai
E o que faz em seu tabuleiro
Vende pra ioió
In South American way

E vende vatapá
E vende caruru
E vende mungunzá
Vende umbu

No tabuleiro tem
Oi tem tudo tem
E só não tem meu bem
Berenguedem

Ai ai ai ai
Have you ever danced in the tropics?
With that hazy, lazy like,
Kind of crazy like,
South American way

Ai ai ai ai
Have you ever kissed in the moonlight?
In the grand and glorious,
Gay notorious,
South American way

In the 1940s, "South American Way" was not only an outright propaganda piece that provided an accessible and easily digested image of South America, but it was also a show tune that created a niche for Miranda in the North American entertainment industry. The fact that Carmen dressed as the Bahiana to perform this tune in both the musical *The Streets of Paris* and in her first movie, *Down Argentine Way!* indicates the extent to which she was willing to expropriate Brazilian popular class symbols and project them as representative of the generic "South American way" that she conveniently embodied. Henceforth, her performances, compositions, and musical recordings in the United States would be limited to this model.

In *Down Argentine Way* (1940), Miranda starred with Betty Grable, Charlotte Greenwood, and Don Ameche. Director Irving Cummings gave Miranda a small role in which she performed four songs dressed in some variation of the Bahiana. Not surprisingly, the songs were indicative of Carmen's rapid transformation from "the Queen of Samba" to Hollywood performer of hybrid Latin numbers. In addition to "South American Way," Miranda sang the Brazilian compositions "Mamãe o Quero," "Bambu Bambu," and "Touradas em Madrid" in a Hollywood setting of Buenos Aires that recalled the generic Latin images. A *New York Times* review reported that the movie would certainly promote neighborliness thanks to the appearance of "the beauteous Miss (Betty) Grable and a couple of peppery songs from Carmen Miranda."[16] The film may have had a silly plot, but the reviewer predicted that it was bound to be a success because of the sensual presence of its stars. For North American directors, sensuality and exoticism were two key components central to Miranda's on-screen appeal.

After fourteen successful months in the United States during which she won over female and male audiences alike, Miranda returned home on July 7, 1940. Cannily dressed in green and yellow, the Brazilian national colors, Miranda was greeted by thousands of fans who led her in a festive parade through the southern zone of Rio de Janeiro.[17] However, not everyone was happy with her success in the United States. The São Paulo paper, *A Folha da Noite*, registered the opinion of many who objected to her particular representation of Brazil: "So that's how Brazil shines in the United States: with a Portuguese woman singing bad-tasting black sambas. It is really like that! And so that's how it should be. Because there really aren't many people in this country who are worth as much as that Carmen, that great and excellent Carmen who left to sing nonsense abroad."[18] The upper classes were particularly concerned with their image abroad and wanted Miranda to emphasize their European heritage rather than their African-ness.

To other enemies, Miranda was not Brazilian enough. Though she had grown up in Rio and had lived there all of her life, the fact that she retained a Portuguese passport, apparently out of respect for her parents, did not sit well with her nationalistic critics.[19] When journalist Damasceno de Brito asked about her nationality, Carmen replied that she considered herself Brazilian, "more *carioca*, a *sambista* from the *favela*, more *carnavalesca* than a singer of *fados*."[20] Miranda never felt Portuguese, and as Martha Gil Montero reports, she found the Portuguese immigrant community's adoration of her rather strange. She had risen to international attention performing popular music clearly associated with blacks in Brazil. Nevertheless, sensitive to pressure from her critics, Miranda did apply for a Brazilian passport before returning to Hollywood, but her request was denied; not until two years before her death did the Brazilian government finally grant her citizenship. Paradoxically, it was the harsh Brazilian criticism coupled with new opportunities to perform that drove Miranda away from her homeland and back to the United States, where she remained for almost fourteen years. Success, money, and prestige aside, the Brazilian critics' reaction was crucial to Carmen's identity transformation in the United States. Their unexpectedly severe response to her success abroad had caused Miranda to doubt her ability to fulfill the promises made to her Brazilian fans, which in turn led her to question her own commitment to her country.

Carmen's love affair with Brazil, and her own sense of *brasilidade*, depended upon her compatriots' approval. Ironically, the first song to catapult her to the status of national icon in 1930, "Tai" (I did everything for you to like me), encapsulated the relationship that Miranda had with her Brazilian fans. During her return tour of Brazil in 1940, she utilized her music to address the criticism leveled at her by the press. "Voltei pro morro" (I came back to the hills), "Diz que tem" (She says that she has it), "Disso que eu gosto" (That's what I like), "Disseram que voltei americanizada" (They say that I've become Americanized), "Ginga Ginga," "Blaque Blaque," "E um quê a gente tem" (It's one that the people have), "O dengo que a nega tem" (The umph that the black woman has) all affirm Miranda's sense of Brazilian-ness, often in exaggerated language and through a celebration of music, food, and national customs.

Most important among her recordings was "Disseram que voltei americanizada," in which she tried to convince audiences of her commitment to Brazil:

> How can I be Americanized?
> I who was born with samba
> and who lives in the open air
> dancing to the old *batucada*
> all night long!
> The *malandro* balls
> are my most preferred.
> I still say *Eu te amo*
> and never *I love you*.
> As long as there is a Brazil
> during mealtime
> I will only have shrimp
> in sauce with *chuchu*.[21]

At the same time, in an interview with *O Globo*, one of Rio's leading newspapers, Carmen staunchly declared that she was "100% Brazilian."[22] These affirmations of her identity failed to recapture her popularity among certain sectors of the Brazilian public. Nonetheless, "Disseram que voltei americanizada" would later become the unofficial hymn of many Brazilian musicians who moved abroad, and who were likewise accused of betraying their national roots for fame in the United States.

On her return to the United States in October 1940, she performed in another Schubert production, *Sons o' Fun*, in New York before moving to Los Angeles. In 1941 she embarked on a frenzied schedule that included appearances in films, on the radio, and in nightclubs and theaters. Despite the multiple media through which Carmen reached her audiences, she became best known to both Americans and Brazilians alike as a film star. Obviously, Brazilians back home could not see her live performances in theaters or nightclubs where her numbers were much more imaginative and spontaneous and where she showcased more authentic Brazilian rhythms. In these more intimate forums, she was able to perform with fewer restrictions. She delighted in playing with her Brazilian band, since, as she reported to the press: "You know very well how Brazilian music becomes Cubanized or Mexicanized when it is played by American orchestras."[23]

Between 1941 and 1947, she appeared in nine Hollywood films: *That Night in Rio* (1941), *Weekend in Havana* (1941), *Springtime in the Rockies* (1942), *The Gang's All Here* (1943), *Four Jills and a Jeep* (1944), *Greenwich Village* (1944), *Something for the Boys* (1944), *Doll Face* (1945), and *If I'm Lucky* (1946). Though her role as a sensual and exotic personality from South America emerges in all these films, Carmen also subverted U.S. stereotypes when she parodied herself in films such as *Doll Face* (in which her character refuses to become just another Carmen). Her comedic exaggeration, coupled with her use of food and outrageous fashion, gave her image a humorous and ironic edge.[24] This strategy is particularly evident in *The Gang's All Here* in which, according to Shari Roberts, Miranda "lampoons both U.S.-Latin American trade relations and notions of feminine sexuality . . . through the casting of Miranda as the overseer of countless enormous swaying phallic bananas buoyed up by lines of chorus girls who dance above other girls, who have oversized strawberries between their legs."[25] It is easy to understand why her image as the Bahiana and its various incarnations seemed especially made for the silver screen.[26]

It is likely that Miranda's decision to perform hybrid tunes that mixed English and Portuguese, or Portuguese tunes with simple and easily remembered lyrics, mirrored that of another contemporary Latin performer whose authenticity was often questioned. The expatriate Spaniard Xavier Cugat reportedly justified his flamboyant style with uncomplicated compositions for American audiences because, as he said, "Americans know nothing about Latin music. They neither understand nor feel it. So they have to be given music more for the eyes than for the ears. Eighty percent visual. The rest aural."[27] The Hollywood musical seemed based on this very assumption, and thus Latin American numbers were usually accompanied by an extravagant visual spectacle. Within this genre, Miranda excelled.

Carmen was caught up in the Hollywood game much like her American counterparts, who either played one-dimensional roles offered by the studios with which they had contracts or found no opportunity at all. Still, Miranda did choose to return to her stereotypical roles after the failure of *Copacabana*, in which she starred with Groucho Marx. North Americans seemed to love the Bahiana, and that seemed to be her only commercially viable forum of expression. A famous *Life* magazine article in July 1939 reveals that audiences enjoyed her performance because of her personal charisma and her electric body language, which interpreted the Portuguese lyrics for them.[28] Such songs as "Co, Co, Co Co, Co, Co, Ro" (1939), "I Yi, Yi, Yi, Yi, I Like You Very Much" (1941), "Chica Chica Boom, Chic" (1941), "Cae, Cae" (1941), "Chattanooga Choo Choo" (1942), "Up Upa" (1945), and "Tico Tico" (1945) were among others that contain playful uses of monosyllabic words. Their titles alone suggest that the spirit of the songs was much more important than the composition itself. Her English recordings included light upbeat fox-trots, sambas, and rumbas typical of the era, and were often sung with other popular entertainers in the United States, including the Andrews Sisters. Her recordings with American performers such as "Cuanto Le Gusta" (1947), "The Wedding Samba" (1949), and "Yipsee-I-O" (1950) all occurred after the making of *Copacabana*, when she was searching for new ways to express herself after the war.

Her final three movies, *A Date with Judy* (1948), *Nancy Goes to Rio* (1950), and *Scared Stiff* (1953), reveal that Miranda had already begun to become passé. The war had ended, and the Office of Inter-American Affairs no longer needed Hollywood to forge neighborliness. Carmen had enjoyed a remarkably long career, especially considering that her roles remained static and relatively unaltered for over a decade in an industry where movie stars come and go. By the 1950s, however, Carmen Miranda increasingly resorted to self-parody. In some cases, she settled for inferior roles, and her declining appeal at the box office was all too apparent. In *Scared Stiff*, for example, Jerry Lewis gave an exaggerated impersonation of Miranda, after an act in which Miranda herself appears in the film. It was a box-office flop.[29]

With the development of the television industry, Carmen also began to appear as a guest artist on a number of shows as some variation of the Bahiana. On the popular *NBC Texaco Star Theater* hosted by Milton Berle, she appeared as a native from a land called Texacabana. In that episode, Miranda sang "Chica Chica Bum" while Tony Martin, another guest on the show, performed "Aquerela do Brasil" in English and Spanish. Already by this time, female and male impersonations of Carmen had become common, and the show ungraciously concluded with Berle's own comical takeoff on the Bahiana. Her last public performance occurred in 1955 on the Jimmy Durante Show, as she continued to gauge her appeal to the newly emerging television audiences. Miranda died at her home in Beverly Hills the morning after taping the show, generating conflicting reports of the cause of death, which ranged from exhaustion, drinking, drug dependency, and heart problems.[30]

On August 13, 1955, the largest crowd recorded in Brazilian history to date attended the burial of Maria del Carmo Miranda da Cunha in the cemetery of St. John the Baptist in Rio de Janeiro.[31] The United States afforded Miranda the opportunity to fulfill her life-long dream of becoming an international movie star, but, as Martha Gil-Montero so aptly put it, "she knew that she had conquered Hollywood, that she would be successful, that she would earn money, but that she would never belong. She was not going to turn into an American."[32] Miranda could not have predicted that her U.S. success meant that her countrymen would consistently question her Brazilian-ness. To American audiences she was unmistakably "the Brazilian Bombshell," but for her critics back home, she had lost all authenticity and had become Americanized.

She worked in a racist film industry that accepted her in the studios but was not so relaxed off-screen, and her colleagues Harold and Fayard Nichols insinuated that racism played a role in Miranda's choice to avoid the "out-of-studio" social scene.[33] In fact, many white Brazilians have also remarked that they sensed sharper racial tensions in the United States than they had ever experienced at home. In the 1930s that harsh realization must have been particularly painful for Carmen, given her nation's officially preferred world-view that celebrated Brazilian racial democracy and downplayed racial inequalities and conflict in that country. Ironically, those same racial inequalities allowed white performers such as Miranda to expropriate black Brazilian rhythms and use them to dominate the popular music scene. At the same time, Carmen lived in a relaxed social environment where black, white, and mulatto musicians and composers surrounded her. Black and mulatto musicians and composers such as Assis Valente, Dorival Caymmi, and Synval Silva had inspired her, and she in turn had given opportunities to many rising stars such as Caymmi and Angela Maria.

Despite Miranda's wild and exotic image on screen, she lived a relatively quiet life and preferred her home to nightclubs. Indeed, it had the feeling of a Brazilian enclave. She lived with her mother and sister Aurora, and their house was open to other Brazilian residents in Los Angeles as well as to strangers who were passing through. Carmen never became a North American, nor was that ever her desire. Despite her unwritten commitment to Brazilians to celebrate and promote their music and culture,

Carmen Miranda was in the United States because her Bahiana image had become a commercially viable product that grossed millions of dollars for the entertainment industry. Investors within the industry attempted to capitalize on the "Latin craze," and Miranda willingly participated. However, she no longer exercised almost exclusive control over her "product," as she had in Brazil. In a new environment, among strangers who were driven by a different sense of aesthetics and who spoke a different language, Carmen's hybrid songs, which exposed many Americans to Latin American-like music, also contributed to the creation of Latin American stereotypes that remain present in the United States today.[34]

Like Miranda, the generation of musicians who followed her to the United States in the 1950s and 1960s were obliged to affirm that they, too, had not become Americanized, by living and working constantly in dialogue with their memory of Brazil. The opposite also holds true; Brazilians in the United States, called *brazucas*, continue to fascinate those back home. In 1994 the popular soap opera *Pátria Minha*, a Rede Globo production, depicted the problems of adjustment of two Brazilians, Pedro and Ester, who had lived in New York for eight years but ultimately went back to Rio to begin their lives anew. The return, or at least the myth of the return, remains constant in the consciousness of many immigrant groups. Like other Latin Americans, many Brazilians feel that they will go to the United States and come home with enough money to lead a better life.[35]

Intellectuals, musicians, and other entertainers were instrumental in laying the foundations of a Brazilian-American identity from the 1930s to the 1960s. Brazilian musician Caetano Veloso, who is largely responsible for resurrecting Carmen Miranda as a Brazilian icon during the 1970s, had this to say about her legacy in a recent essay for the *New York Times*: "For generations of musicians who were adolescents in the second half of the 1950s and became adults at the height of the Brazilian military dictatorship and the international wave of counterculture—my generation—Carmen Miranda was first a cause of both pride and shame, and later, a symbol that inspired the merciless gaze we began to cast upon ourselves. . . . Carmen conquered 'white' America as no other South American had done or ever would, in an era when it was enough to be 'recognizably Latin and Negroid' in style and aesthetics to attract attention."[36]

For Veloso and other musicians contemplating a career abroad, Miranda's pioneering experiences continue to loom as a point of reference. Miranda helped establish and transform the relationship between Brazilian musicians and American producers that now has created several remarkable transnational collaborations. In Veloso's words: "To think of her is to think about the complexity of this relationship: 'Olodum' on Paul Simon's album, the collection of Tom Zé's experimental sambas released by David Byrne, Nana Vasconcelos and Egberto Gismonti, Sting and Araoni; Tania Maria, Djavan, and Manhattan Transfer, Milton Nascimiento. Carmen is everywhere."

One of the winning entries in the 1995 literary competition promoted by the Brazilian-American newspaper *The Brazilians* reinforces Carmen Miranda's pioneering experience in the dialogue between Brazilian national identity and the condition of foreign residence. "Nós os brasileiros SEM BRASIL" (We, the Brazilians without Brazil) speaks of identity in a new land and the challenges to the immigrant: "Oh, sorrow that vacillates between 'who I am' and 'where I am'/ Empty my mind and transform me into a river of longing." But the poem also calls on Brazilians abroad to celebrate *brasilidade* in their new home:

> And together, we will laugh so much, oh, so much
> That we will cry from homesickness with tears, so lost and lonely,
> Tears that resemble us because we are Brazilians without Brazil.[37]

The conflicts that Miranda experienced in the United States that centered on her sense of national identity and her relationship with her homeland were magnified because of the attention of the media, particularly film. Nonetheless, her experience provides an example of the challenges of strangers in new lands everywhere.

Notes

1. George Black, *The Good Neighbor* (New York: Pantheon Books, 1988); George Hadley-García, *Hispanic Hollywood: The Latins in Motion Pictures* (New York: Carol Publishing Group, 1993); Martha Gil-Montero, *Brazilian Bombshell: The Biography of Carmen Miranda* (New York: Donald I. Fine Inc., 1989).

2. See Maxine Margolis, *Little Brazil: An Ethnography of Brazilian Immigrants in New York City* (Princeton: Princeton University Press, 1995), for a discussion of Brazilian immigration to the United States.

3. For a discussion of Freyre's racial democracy and Luso-Portuguese tropicalism see Gilberto Freyre, *Portuguese Integration in the Tropics* (Lisbon: Tipografia Silva, 1961). Of course, Freyre's myth of "racial democracy" has since been debunked.

4. Lewis Hanke, *Gilberto Freyre. Vida y obra. Bibliografía antología* (New York: Instituto de las Españas en los Estados Unidos, 1939), 8.

5. Gilberto Freyre, "O homen brasileiro: Formação étnica e cultural," *Estudo de problemas brasileiros* (Recife: Universidade Federal de Pernambuco, 1971): 167–78.

6. *Carioca* is the term which refers to people from Rio de Janeiro in Brazil.

7. Carmen Miranda Folder, Museu da Imagen e do Som, Rio de Janeiro.

8. Gil-Montero, *Brazilian Bombshell*, 31.

9. Ibid., 52–57. That same month she recorded the smash hit "O qué é qué a bahiana tem" with Dorival Caymmi.

10. Ibid., 59–70; Abel Cardoso, Jr., *Carmen Miranda: A cantora do Brasil* (São Paulo: Cardoso Junior, 1978), 129–33.

11. Helena Soldberg, *Carmen Miranda: Bananas Is My Business* (1995). Italics are mine to emphasize the Brazilian claim to Miranda.

12. Cardoso, *Carmen Miranda*, 140.

13. Black, *Good Neighbor*, 60–71.

14. For a general history see John Storm Roberts, *Latin Tinge: The Impact of Latin American Music on the United States* (New York: Oxford University Press, 1999).

15. Cardoso, *Carmen Miranda*, 474–76; "*The Streets of Paris* Moves to Broadway," *New York Times* (June 20, 1939), p. 16; "High Mark in Low Comedy," *New York Times* (June 25, 1939), section 9, pp. ix–1.

16. "*Down Argentine Way* with Betty Grable at the Roxy," *New York Times* (October 18, 1940), amusement section, p. 25.

17. "Rio Hails Carmen Miranda," *New York Times* (July 11, 1949), p. 6. See *O Globo* (July 7, 1940), p. 2. See also Cardoso, *Carmen Miranda*, 167–74.

18. Quoted in Cardoso, *Carmen Miranda*, 163. "E assim que o Brasil brilha?" *Folha da Noite*, January 30, 1940, p. 3. See also the magazine *Careta* for September 28, 1940.

19. Gil-Montero, *Brazilian Bombshell*, 215–16. Carmen reportedly held on to her Portuguese passport until 1953. She had requested a Brazilian passport in 1948, but the authorities did not grant her one until 1953 so that she could complete a European tour to showcase her music.

20. Damasceno de Brito, *O ABC de Carmen Miranda* (São Paulo: Companhia Editora Nacional, 1986), 69.

21. Unless otherwise noted, all of Carmen Miranda's recordings can be found in the archives of the Museu da Imagen e do Som, Rio de Janeiro. EMI, Brazil has also released the most comprehensive compilation of Miranda's recordings in a five-part CD entitled *Carmen Miranda* (1996).

22. See *O Globo* (July 7, 1940), p. 2.

23. Alex Viany in *O Cruzeiro* (November 13, 1948), as quoted in Cardoso, *Carmen Miranda*, 195–96.

24. Shari Roberts, "The Lady in the Tutti Frutti Hat: Carmen Miranda, A Spectacle of Ethnicity," *Cinema Journal* 13:3 (Spring 1992): 15.

25. Ibid.

26. Ibid., 12. *Copacabana* was a United Artists production directed by Richard Thorpe in 1947. Unlike the earlier shows, this film did not do well at the box office.

27. Storm Roberts, *Latin Tinge*, 87.

28. "Broadway Likes Miranda's Piquant Portuguese Songs," *Life* (July 17, 1939), 34. Also see Shari Roberts's discussion of Miranda's use and misuse of both English and Portuguese to render a comical, exotic performance in "Lady in the Tutti Frutti Hat," 10–11.

29. George Marshall, *Scared Stiff* (Paramount, 1953); Soldberg, *Bananas Is My Business* (1994); Gil-Montero, *Brazilian Bombshell*, 211–12.

30. Television recording, The Museum of Television and Sound (New York City).

31. Soldberg, *Bananas Is My Business*; Cardoso, *Carmen Miranda*, 29–30; Carmen Miranda Folder, Museu da Imagen e do Som, Rio de Janeiro.

32. "Interview with Martha Gil-Montero," *Carmen Miranda: The South American Way* (New York: A&E Television Network, 1996).

33. "Interview with Harold and Fayard Nichols," *Carmen Miranda* (A&E).

34. In the decades following Carmen's death, Brazilian musicians continued to travel to the United States, contributing to American popular music. Bossa nova—the new wave of Brazilian music—which had developed in the late 1950s around

Rio de Janeiro, made its official appearance in the United States on November 21, 1962. Antonio Carlos Jobim, one of bossa nova's major ambassadors, felt compelled to defend himself against accusations of becoming Americanized while he lived in New York.

35. "O American Dream Brasileiro," *Momento* (2:11): 5–9.

36. "Carmen Miranda," *New York Times* (October 20, 1991), section 2, p. 34.

37. Paulo Caldeira, "Nós os brasileiros SEM BRASIL," *The Brasilians* (May 1996), 7. Translations are mine.

Suggested Readings

General Histories: Latin American Exiles and Travelers

Andrien, Kenneth, and Rolena Adorno. *Transatlantic Encounters: Europeans and Andeans in the Sixteenth Century*. Berkeley: University of California Press, 1991.

Arciniégas, Germán. *America in Europe: A History of the New World in Reverse*. Trans. Gabriela Arciniégas and R. Victoria Arana. San Diego: Harcourt Brace Jovanovich, 1985.

Hahner, June. *Women Through Women's Eyes: Latin American Women in Nineteenth-Century Travel Accounts*. Wilmington, DE: Scholarly Resources, 1998.

Kirpey, Viney. *The Third World Novel of Expatriation: A Study of Emigré Fiction by Indian, West African and Caribbean Writers*. New Delhi: Sterling Publishers, 1989.

Núñez, Estuardo. *Viajeros hispanoamericanos: Temas continentales*. Caracas: Biblioteca Ayacucho, 1989.

Partnoy, Alicia. *You Can't Drown the Fire: Latin American Women Writing in Exile*. Pittsburgh: Cleis Press, 1988.

Pratt, Mary Louise. *Imperial Eyes: Studies in Travel Writing and Transculturation*. New York: Routledge, 1992.

Simpson, John, ed. *Oxford Book of Exile*. London: Oxford University Press, 1995.

Tenorio Trillo, Mauricio. *Crafting the Modern Mexico: Mexico's Presence at World's Fairs, 1880s–1920s*. Berkeley: University of California Press, 1996.

Latin Americans' Accounts of Their Own Experiences Abroad

Cortázar, Julio, et al. *Exilio: Nostalgia y creación*. Ed. Alberto Garrido. Mérida, Venezuela: Dirección Cultura de la Universidad de los Andes, 1987.

Díaz Covarrubias, Francisco. *Viaje de la Comisión Astronómica Mexicana al Japón para observar el tránsito del planeta Venus por el disco del sol el 8 de diciembre de 1874*. México: Imp. Políglota de C. Ramiro y Ponce de León, 1876.

Galarce, Carmen J. *La novela chilena del exilio (1973–1987): El caso de Isabel Allende*. New York: Ediciones Maitén, 1994.

Martí, José. *Inside the Monster: Writings on the United States and American Imperialism by José Martí*. Ed. Philip S. Foner. New York: Monthly Review Press, 1975.

————. *Martí on the U.S.A.* Ed. Luis A Baralt. Carbondale, IL: Southern Illinois University Press, 1966.

Mier, Fray Servando Teresa de. *Fray Servando: The Memoirs of Fray Servando Teresa de Mier.* New York: Oxford University Press, 1998.

Sarmiento, Domingo Faustino. *Sarmiento's Travels in the United States in 1847.* Princeton, NJ: Princeton University Press, 1970.

Torres, Olga Beatriz. *Memorias de mi viaje. Recollections of My Trip.* Albuquerque: University of New Mexico Press, 1994.

Vicuña Mackenna, Benjamín. *Páginas de mi diario durante tres años de viajes. 1853–1854–1855. California, México, Estados Unidos, Islas Británicas, Francia, Italia, Alemania, Paises Bajos, costas del Brasil, Provincias del Plata.* Santiago: Imprenta del Ferrocarril, 1856.

Secondary Sources for the Experiences of Latin Americans in the United States

Fort, Gilberto V. *The Cuban Revolution of Fidel Castro Viewed from Abroad.* Lawrence, KS: University of Kansas Press, 1969.

García, María Cristina. *Havana USA: Cuban Exiles and Cuban Americans in South Florida, 1959–1994.* Berkeley: University of California Press, 1996.

González, Manuel Pedro. *José Martí, Epic Chronicler of the United States in the Eighties.* Chapel Hill: University of North Carolina Press, 1953.

Lázaro, Felipe. *Poetas cubanos en Nueva York.* Madrid: Editorial Betania, 1988.

Lerner, Victoria. "Dos generaciones de viajeros mexicanos del siglo XIX frente a los Estados Unidos." *Relaciones* 14, no. 55 (Summer 1993): 41–72.

Needell, Jeffrey D. "Identity, Race, Gender, and Modernity in the Origins of Gilberto Freyre's *Oeuvre.*" *American Historical Review* 100, no. 1 (1995): 51–77.

Onís, José de. *The United States as Seen by Spanish American Writers, 1776–1890.* New York: Hispanic Institute, 1952.

Raat, William Dirk. *Los revoltosos: Mexico's Rebels in the United States, 1903–1923.* College Station: Texas A & M University Press, 1981.

Ronning, C. Neale. *José Martí and the Emigré Colony in the United States.* New York: Praeger, 1990.

Santovenia y Echaide, Emeterio Santiago. *Lincoln in Martí: A Cuban View of Abraham Lincoln.* Trans. Donald Fogelquist. Chapel Hill: University of North Carolina Press, 1953.

Shepherd, William R. "Bolívar and the United States." *Hispanic American Historical Review* 1 (1918): 270–98.

Simmons, Merle. "Los estados unidos en el pensamiento de Domingo F. Sarmiento antes de su primera visita a Norteamérica." *Revista de Historia de América* (México, D.F.) nos. 35–36 (January–December 1953): 59–95.

————. "Spanish and Spanish American Politician Writers in Philadelphia, 1790–1830." *Dieciocho* (Ithaca, NY) 3, no. 1 (Spring 1980): 27–39.

Wellmeier, Nancy. "Rituals of Resettlement: Identity and Resistance among Maya Refugees." *Journal of Popular Culture* 29, no. 1 (1995): 3–17.

Secondary Sources for the Experiences of Latin Americans in England

Berruezo León, María Teresa. *La lucha de hispanoamérica por su independencia en Inglaterra, 1800–1830.* Madrid: Ediciones de Cultura Hispánica, 1989.

Boulton, Alfredo. "Bolívar en Londres." *Boletín de la Academia Nacional de Historia* (Caracas) 26, no. 143 (July–September 1953): 290–95.

Dawson, Frank. *The First Latin American Debt Crisis: The City of London and the 1822–25 Loan Bubble.* New Haven: Yale University Press, 1990.

Decho, Pam, and Clare Diamond. *Latin Americans in London: A Select List of Prominent Latin Americans in London, 1800–1996.* London: University of London, Institute of Latin American Studies, 1998.

Jones, Calvin P. "Images of Simón Bolívar as Reflected in Ten Leading British Periodicals, 1816–30." *The Americas* 40 (1984): 377–97.

Lynch, John, ed. *Andrés Bello, the London Years.* [Richmond], Surrey: The Richmond Publishing Co., 1982.

Salcedo-Bastardo, José Luís. *Crucible of Americanism: Miranda's London House.* [Caracas]: Cuadernos Langoven, [1981].

Secondary Sources for the Experiences of Latin Americans in France

Cheymol, Marc. *Miguel Angel Asturias dans le Paris des Années Folles.* Grenoble, France: Presses Universitaires, 1987.

Estrade, Paul. *La colonia cubana de París, 1895–1898: El combate patriótico de Betances y la solidaridad de los revoluciones franceses.* Havana: Editorial de Ciencias Sociales, 1984.

Favela, Ramón. *Diego Rivera: The Cubist Years, 1913–1917.* Phoenix: Phoenix Art Museum, 1984.

Patout, Paulette. *Francia en Alfonso Reyes.* Monterrey, México: Universidad Autónoma de Nuevo León, 1985.

Pérez Vila, Manuel. "Bolívar y la cultura francesa." *Revista de la Sociedad Bolivariana de Venezuela* 23, no. 85 (December 1965): 773–76.

Schwartz, Marcy. "Cultural Exile and the Canon: Writing Paris into Contemporary Latin American Narrative." In *Paradise Lost or Gained? The Literature of Hispanic Exile*, ed. Fernando Alegría and Jorge Rufinelli, 192–210. Houston: Arte Público Press, 1990.

Segala, Amos, ed. *Miguel Angel Asturias: Paris, 1924–1933. Periodismo y creación literario*. Madrid, Spain: Signatarios Acuerdo Archivos Allca XXᵉ. Université de Paris X. Centre de Recherches Latino-Américaines, 1988.

Séris, Christiane. "Microcosmes dans la capitale ou l'histoire de la colonie intellectuelle hispano-américaine à Paris entre 1890 et 1914." In *Le Paris des étrangers depuis un siècle*, ed. André Kaspi and Antoine Marès, 299–312. Paris: Imprimerie Nationale, 1989.

Suggested Films

Films have gained increasing importance as historical documents used in university classrooms. They help students to see and hear history and contemporary reality in ways that the written word cannot convey. The following list includes films that can be the basis for discussing the issues of exile and foreign residency in Latin American history. All of them explore people's reasons for leaving their homeland and the difficult and varied process of integration into a host country's society. A few examine the internal workings of exile and immigrant communities, including both the ties of solidarity forged and the jealousies and rivalries that can emerge in foreign settings. While several describe the lives of famous Latin Americans, the majority look at exile and foreign residency from the perspective of fictional characters designed to represent many people who have undergone similar experiences. All of the films listed below are either in English or have been subtitled. The distributors' names have been added to assist in their purchase.

Builders of Images: Latin American Cultural Identity. 1993. (60 minutes) Part of the *Americas: Latin America and the Caribbean* film series, this documentary depicts the role of the artist in Latin American society through the lives of four individuals: Puerto Rican poet Luis Rafael Sanchez, Brazilian singer Caetano Veloso, Mexican performance artist Jesusa Rodríguez, and Argentine filmmaker Fernando Solanas. While all of the biographies are excellent, the profile of Solanas deals specifically with the problem of exile and how it has affected his filmmaking. Perhaps best used in tandem with *Tangos: The Exiles of Gardel* (see below). (Thea Annenberg/CPB Project)

Carmen Miranda: Bananas Is My Business. 1994. Director: Helena Solberg. This documentary traces the life and career of singer/actress Carmen Miranda. Of particular interest is the film's discussion of Miranda's move to the United States and how that move impacted her sense of personal and national identity. (Orion Home Video)

El Jardín del Eden (The Garden of Eden). 1994. Director: María Novaro. (104 minutes) A moving portrait of a woman's efforts to help her family adjust to and prosper in a new life on the border between Tijuana and San Diego. (IMCINE, Mexico)

El Norte. 1983. Director: Gregory Nava. (139 minutes) This film depicts the heart-wrenching story of a Guatemalan brother and sister forced to emigrate to the United States ("El Norte") by the brutal activities of their country's military. As both exiles and immigrants, the two struggle to succeed in their new land with hopeful as well as tragic results. (CBS/ Fox Video)

El Super. 1979. Director: León Ichaso. (80 minutes) The Cuban exile experience is the subject of this film about a Cuban building superintendent living in New York City. The effects of nostalgia, generational conflicts, solidarity between exiles, and Miami as the Cuban exiles' Mecca are all explored. (New Yorker Video)

La Ciudad (The City). 1998. Director: David Riker. (86 minutes) The grim social, cultural, and economic difficulties confronting new immigrants to the United States are vividly depicted in this series of haunting vignettes about new arrivals in New York City. The film's reliance upon real immigrants for most of the acting gives this depiction of life for foreigners in the United States an authenticity that eludes most films on the topic. Comparisons between this sobering vision and such Hollywood films as *My Family/Mi Familia* could inspire interesting classroom discussions. (Zeitgeist Films)

Mambo Kings. 1992. Director: Arne Glimcher. (100 minutes) Based on the excellent novel by Oscar Hijuelos, this film chronicles the personal and professional joys and disappointments encountered by two brothers who flee Cuba hoping for a better life. Set primarily in the 1950s, this film is an interesting take on Cuban life in the United States prior to Castro's Revolution. (Warner Home Video)

Mécaniques Celestes (Celestial Clockwork). 1996. Director: Fina Torres. (83 minutes) A young Venezuelan bride leaves her groom at the altar to pursue her dream of becoming a diva in Paris. She then quickly becomes a part of the exotic Latin American community in that city. While many of the logistical difficulties of exile are quickly dispensed with, the importance of Europe as a place for personal liberation and professional success is a central theme. Both the solidarity and infighting of the Latin American community are also featured. (Evergreen Entertainment)

My Family/Mi Familia. 1995. Director: Gregory Nava. (126 minutes) A sweeping, multigenerational saga of a Mexican immigrant family who settles in East Los Angeles, this film depicts the motivations for leaving Mexico, the challenges facing new arrivals, and the diverse adaptations that immigrants make to survive in an often hostile host society. This film is very popular with students, but some of the stereotyping and lack of a broader historical context should be discussed. (New Line Home Video, Turner Home Entertainment Company)

Rivera in America. 1988. Director: Rick Tejada-Flores. (60 minutes) Part of the *American Masters* series, this documentary describes Mexican muralist Diego Rivera's experiences while in the United States in the 1930s. Special emphasis is placed on the controversy that erupted after completion of his Rockefeller Center mural in New York. Rivera's life reveals not only how foreign residency impacted his art, politics, and national identity, but also how he was able to inspire a generation of U.S. artists then interested in creating art for social change. (Alturas Films)

Tangos: Los Exilios de Gardel (Tangos: The Exiles of Gardel). 1985. Director: Fernando E. Solanas. (125 minutes) Paris is the location of this dark comedy about Argentine exiles who attempt to use the tango as a mechanism for overcoming the pain of living abroad. (Cinesur, S.A.)

About the Contributors

RODERICK J. BARMAN is professor of history at the University of British Columbia. He is the author of *Brazil: The Forging of a Nation, 1798–1852* (1988), and his many articles have appeared in *The Americas* (1990), *Journal of Latin American Studies* (1981), *Hispanic American Historical Review* (1977), *Journal of Inter-American Studies and World Affairs* (1974), and *Revista do Instituto Histórico e Geográfico Brasileiro* (1973). His most recent book is *Citizen Emperor: Pedro II and the Making of Brazil, 1825–1891* (1999).

SANDRA M. BOSCHETTO-SANDOVAL is associate professor of Spanish at Michigan Technological University. She is the coeditor of both *Claribel Alegría and Central American Literature: Selected Essays* (1994) and *José María Argüedas*. Her other articles on Amanda Labarca Hubertson have appeared in *Reinterpreting the Spanish American Essay: Women Writers of the 19th and 20th Centuries* (1995) and *College Literature* (1995). She is currently at work on a book-length manuscript about Amanda Labarca Hubertson.

JOHN F. CHUCHIAK IV is assistant professor of Latin American history at Assumption College. He specializes in colonial church history of the Yucatán. His articles have appeared in *Iglesia y sociedad en América Latina* and *Saastun: Revista de Cultura Maya*, and he has co-authored *The Maya of the Yucatán: Five Centuries of Continuity and Change* (1998).

DARIÉN J. DAVIS is associate professor of history and director of Latin American studies at Middlebury College. His articles have appeared in *Ethnicity, Race, and Nationality in the Caribbean* (1999), *English-Speaking Communities in Latin America since Independence* (1999), *Latino Review of Books* (1998), and *Journal of Negro History* (1997). He is the editor of *Slavery and Beyond* (1995) and *Avoiding the Dark: Essays on Race and National Culture in Modern Brazil* (1999).

W. JOHN GREEN is visiting professor of Latin American history at Virginia Polytechnic Institute and State University. He received his Ph.D. from the University of Texas at Austin in 1994 and has recently completed a book manuscript on Jorge Eliécer Gaitán and Populism in Colombia. Green is the author of articles in *Hispanic American Historical Review*, *Anuario Colombiano de la Historia Social y de la Cultura*, and *Kolumbien Heute: Politik, Wirtschaft, Kultur*.

RICHARD V. MCGEHEE is professor of kinesiology and health studies at Concordia University at Austin. His articles on sports history have appeared in *Studies in Latin American Popular Culture* (1994), *Olympika* (1994), and *International Journal of the History of Sport* (1993, 1992).

SILVINA MONTENEGRO is completing her Ph.D. at the PEHESA-Instituto Ravignani, at the Universidad de Buenos Aires. She is currently doing research in Madrid on a scholarship and has presented papers at several international conferences.

BRIAN O'NEIL is assistant professor of history at the University of Southern Mississippi specializing in cinema history as well as U.S.-Latin American relations. He recently completed his dissertation, "The Demands of Authenticity and Wartime Unity: Hollywood's Good Neighbor Policy and U.S.-Latin Relations, 1938–1948," and received his Ph.D. from UCLA. Other articles of O'Neil's have appeared in *Classic Whiteness: Race and the Hollywood Studio System* (1999) and *Studies in Latin American Popular Culture* (1998).

ARTHUR SCHMIDT is professor of Latin American history at Temple University. He is the author of several articles including ones that have recently appeared in *El Salvador in the Eighties: Counterinsurgency and Revolution* (1996) and *Caribbean Studies* (1995), and has written the monograph *The Economic and Social Effects of Railroads in Puebla and Veracruz, Mexico, 1867–1911* (1987).

DANIELA SPENSER is a researcher at the Centro de Investigaciones y Estudios Superiores en Antropología Social (CIESAS) in Mexico City. She is the author of articles on Soviet-Mexican relations, and her work has appeared in *Secuencia* (1996). Her book *The Impossible Triangle: Mexico, Soviet Russia, and the United States in the 1920s* (*American Encounters/Global Interactions*) appeared in 1999.

ARTURO TARACENA ARRIOLA is a researcher at the Centro de Investigaciones Regionales de Mesoamérica (CIRMA) in Antigua, Guatemala. He is the author of *Invención criolla, sueño ladino, pesadillo indígena: Los Altos de Guatemala, de Región a Estado, 1740–1850* (1997) and *La expedición científica al Reino de Guatemala* (1983), and he is co-editor of *Identidades nacionales y estado moderno en Centroamérica* (1995). Taracena's many articles have appeared in *Cuadernos Marcha* (1994), *Anuario de Estudios Centroamericanos* (1989), and *Mesoamérica* (1988).

CAMILLA TOWNSEND is assistant professor of Latin American history at Colgate University. Her articles have appeared in *Colonial Latin American Review, Latin American Perspectives, Victorian Studies, Procesos: Revista ecuatoriana de historia,* and *Blake, Politics and History* (1997). She is also the author of *Tales of Two Cities: Race and Economic Culture in Early Republican North and South America* (2000).

About the Editors

INGRID E. FEY earned her Ph.D. in 1996 at the University of California-Los Angeles and has subsequently lectured there on Latin American history. Her dissertation is entitled "First Tango in Paris: Latin Americans in Turn-of-the-Century France, 1880–1920." Her articles on Latin America's presence at World's Fairs will appear in *Comparativ* (2000); and in William H. Beezley and Linda Curcio-Nagy, eds., *Latin American Popular Culture: An Introduction* (forthcoming).

KAREN RACINE is assistant professor of Latin American history at Valparaiso University. Her articles have appeared in *The Americas* (1997), *Journal of Caribbean History* (1999), and *English-Speaking Communities in Latin America Since Independence* (2000). Currently she is completing a book on London's Spanish American community in the Independence period.